The Media Relations Department of Hizbollah Wishes You a Happy Birthday

THE MEDIA RELATIONS DEPARTMENT OF HIZBOLLAH WISHES YOU A HAPPY BIRTHDAY

*Unexpected Encounters
in the Changing Middle East*

NEIL MacFARQUHAR

PublicAffairs
New York

Published in the United States by PublicAffairs™, a member
of the Perseus Books Group.

PublicAffairs books are available at special discounts for bulk purchases
in the U.S. by corporations, institutions, and other organizations.
For more information, please contact the Special Markets
Department at the Perseus Books Group, 2300 Chestnut Street,
Suite 200, Philadelphia, PA 19103, call (800) 810-4145,
ext. 5000, or e-mail special.markets@perseusbooks.com.

Designed by Linda Mark
Text set in Joanna MT 11.5

Library of Congress Cataloging-in-Publication Data
     MacFarquhar, Neil.
     The media relations department of Hizbollah wishes you a happy
birthday : unexpected encounters in the changing Middle East / Neil
MacFarquhar.—1st ed.
          p. cm.
     Includes bibliographical references and index.
     ISBN 978-1-58648-635-8 (hardcover : alk. paper)
     1. Middle East—Description and travel. 2. MacFarquhar, Neil—Travel—
Middle East. 3. Middle East—Biography—Anecdotes. 4. Middle East—
Social life and customs. 5. Social change—Middle East. 6. Political
culture—Middle East. 7. Middle East—Politics and government—1979–
I. Title.
DS49.7.M28 2009
956.04092—dc22
                                                                2009002004

10 9 8 7 6 5 4 3 2 1

For my late father, Murdo MacKenzie MacFarquhar, who started me on the journey and made certain that no matter what happened, I laughed along the way.

*Verily never will Allah change the condition of a people
until they change it themselves.*

—The Koran, The Thunder

Contents

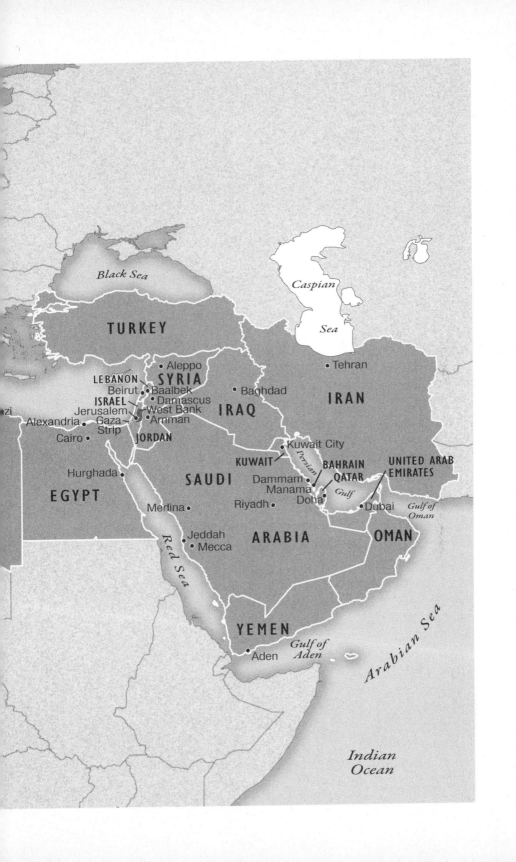

CHAPTER I

THE BEACHHEAD

"A burger and a Bebsi boolside."

WHEN I TRY TO PINPOINT the moment when the Middle East began exerting its gravitational pull on my life, I'm usually drawn back to the first diary entry I ever wrote. It was just one sentence, filling an entire page in a small spiral notebook.

"The war started with boming in Kiro," I printed in large, wobbly letters on June 5, 1967, a couple months shy of my eighth birthday. (My spelling still needs help.)

The Six-Day War, the third major conflict between the Arabs and Israel, erupted that day with Israeli squadrons bombing the Egyptian air force to smithereens on the tarmac in Cairo, roughly 700 miles and one international border east of my childhood home. My family lived along the sandy Mediterranean coast in Marsa Brega, Libya, where my father, a chemical engineer, supervised a refinery and a water desalinization plant. The town was built and operated by one of the world's major oil companies—then universally known as Esso—to process and ship the fine, light crude bubbling up from underneath the Sahara desert. Before the discovery of oil in 1959, the impoverished country's main export had been scrap iron left over from the massive battles between the Nazis' Africa Korps and the mostly British Allied forces.

We moved there in January 1965, the seventeenth family to arrive. The vast expanse of the Sahara occupied the entire southern horizon. Flat stretches of sand and rocks interrupted by periodic dunes stretched to infinity, giving us the sense that we were colonizing some distant, lifeless planet. But in the other direction the Mediterranean shoreline was a little slice of Paradise. It's a cliché, sure; yet no beach since has ever seemed as perfect to me. In those early days the coast was still all blindingly white sand and seductive turquoise water. You couldn't see the shoreline from our house because the residential part of town was built in a slight depression. After the first visit, though, it was always there in my mind's eye. It still is.

The beach became our Elysian Fields, endlessly alluring even after a decade of oil spills from tankers loading at an offshore mooring turned the sand khaki and blackened the tops of the coral reefs jutting out of the water. Once, when what was then the largest tanker in the world ran aground, my father drove home from work to take me to gape at the behemoth, a wounded dinosaur that seemed to block out the sea. During the few winter months when it was too cold to swim, we would explore the desert. A couple hours' drive due south brought us to a high, rocky desert plateau, where as a little boy I delighted in scrabbling among the pebbles to find shark teeth dating from prehistoric times when the area was under water. Later, as part of the Scorpions, my Boy Scout troop, I reveled in long camping trips to distant desert oases. We certainly imagined ourselves as Bedouins astride camels, but in fact I don't think we encountered any. The most thrilling expedition was a week spent crossing the desert to visit the wreckage of *Lady Be Good*, a B-24D United States Air Force bomber that crashed more than 400 miles inland after overshooting its airfield in a sandstorm in 1943. The bomber had been returning from a run over Italy; its nine crew members perished trekking across the desert. When the wreckage was discovered a few years before we got to Libya, the desert air had preserved the plane to the extent that the oil exploration team who stumbled across it could still fire one of the fifty-caliber machine guns and use the radio. Interesting oases, prehistoric cave paintings, and all manner of antiquities existed out there in the desert, but none of those could generate the same excitement to a boy as the American plane.

In July 1965, seven months after we arrived, some Libyan men opposed to the monarchy under King Idris sneaked into Brega's industrial area one night and blew up three oil storage tanks. A column of black smoke hung in the sky for several days. The oil company responded by enclosing eleven square miles of desert behind a heavy-duty chain-link fence, the compound roughly delineated by the sea on one side and on the other by the one-lane, potholed road that at the time constituted the Tripoli-Benghazi highway. All Libyan laborers who entered during the day had to exit after working hours ended at 5 P.M.

After the fence went up, the volatile Middle East always seemed even more distant from inside our oil company cocoon. Brega felt more Texan than Libyan. Apart from periodic family excursions to the bazaar in Benghazi—a two-hour drive down that highway—I rarely interacted with the locals. Libyans were mostly strangers viewed from afar. The few encounters were memorable because they were so rare. Some years at Christmas, for example, a Bedouin herdsman or two would materialize to tend the live sheep, donkey, and occasional camel used in the elementary school's annual pageant, the manger built from freshly cut palm fronds. If our teachers ever tried to connect us with the history of the place, it never seemed to have much to do with the Libyans. The annual school play one year focused on the life of Septimus Severus, a Roman emperor born around 145 A.D. in one of the magnificent colonies along the shoreline near Tripoli.

To amuse himself one day, my older brother Peter decided to have a Lawrence of Arabia moment by striding across the dunes to the distant golf club—three or four miles away—where the clubhouse and a salt-water swimming pool were perched on a rocky bluff overlooking the sea. He decked himself out in North African garb—a flowing headdress, long robe, and sandals. Walking across the fairways, which consisted entirely of sand with oiled "greens," he came across a Libyan in full golf mufti—a polo shirt, fancy golf pants, spiked golf shoes, golf gloves, a golf hat, golf everything. They just stared at each other in silent disbelief, mirroring worlds that never quite melded.

Nearly every day, the Libyan staff at the club's snack bar shouted out my standard order, "wahid burger wi wahid bebsi boolside"—there being no "p" in the Arabic language and "wahid" meaning "one." I didn't learn much Arabic back then. Every year the oil company would appoint some promising young Libyan engineer with weak English as the Arabic teacher. The idea was to improve his language skills so he could study abroad. But his pupils conspired together and, shaking our little blond heads in unison, avowed that, no, the previous guy had been kind of slow and we had not even mastered the alphabet. Then we all got really good grades by learning to recite "Aleph, bah, tah," and so on, as if it were the first time. We avoided grammar entirely. Now, of course, it seems a terrible waste.

In its first years Brega consisted of just three residential streets, each a block long, housing about twenty families in nearly identical, single-story homes. They were square structures built of cinder blocks with flat roofs and sandy yards that proved hostile to most vegetation. Only once did our stunted, anorexic orange tree produce a solitary piece of fruit. It looked fake, a luscious orange bauble dangling from little more than a stick. That orange became a major event, worthy of inviting over the entire street to admire. At times the howling winds raging out of the Sahara were so fierce, with the sand biting any exposed skin, that we stayed inside for a day or two.

The winds rapidly built a dune up against our back wall, our very own link to the surrounding desert. I was "camping" in the yard one night with my best friend, the two of us sleeping on cots under the dazzling battery of stars that are visible in the desert; the array makes eternity seem tangible. At first light, my friend and I went into the kitchen to raid the refrigerator. The back door was ajar and our massive freezer sat at an odd angle, as if someone had failed to maneuver it outside. We crept into the living room and discovered a Libyan man snoring on one of our couches.

"Daddy! Daddy! There's a Libyan asleep on the couch!" I yelled, running into my parents' darkened bedroom, my friend trailing me.

My father cracked one eye, put on his glasses, and glanced toward the alarm clock. "You kids knock it off. It's much too early for jokes. Go back to bed."

I grabbed his arm and tugged. "No really, Daddy, come look. There's a Libyan asleep on the couch." The hapless man, still slightly drunk when my father shook him awake, staggered to his feet and fled the house. We looked around outside and found the tracks where he had stumbled up the dune against the back wall and fallen into the yard. It emerged later that he was a customs inspector.

⌷   ⌷   ⌷

On that first day of the 1967 war, concerned that the Israeli air force might fly farther west to obliterate Libya's oil installations, Esso decided to evacuate all women and children. The government also declared a national curfew. Since there was no telling when everyone might came back, the adults threw massive parties to consume the champagne and other delicacies they had hoarded for special occasions. In the darkness, our staggering parents negotiated their way home along the tops of the thick walls so they would not be on the streets after curfew.

For the actual evacuation, every person could bring one suitcase and the company gave each family a $20 bill. All the evacuees fit aboard two U.S. Air Force C-130 Hercules transport planes, flown down the coast from Wheelus, the American air base outside the Libyan capital of Tripoli. In retrospect, it almost seems like something out of "Ripley's Believe It or Not" that there was an American base in Libya, of all places, complete with a PX that sold rare elixirs of the gods that I coveted, such as root beer and Tootsie Rolls.

The Air Force pilots evidently had trouble finding the flyspeck air strip at Brega, located near the lowest point of the Gulf of Sirte, because they arrived hours late, the powerful back-thrust of their engines tearing up great chunks of asphalt as they roared to a halt. It was a broiling day, I remember—so hot that one woman twisted her ankle when the sharp spike of her high heel sank down into the soft tar of the parking lot and snapped off. Many evacuees were crying, uncertain about what danger they faced and reluctant to leave their pets behind. Women and children slopped tearful kisses on German shepherds and poodles straining at their leashes. We had no pets; I wasn't crying. I don't even recall saying good-bye to my father. To this day I remember being utterly focused on the fact that I would get to ride on a real American Air Force plane, my rapture complete when we got onboard and the uniformed airmen handed out authentic military C-rations in small cardboard boxes.

The war ended within days, but my mother, brother, two sisters, and I spent several weeks waiting in various Swiss resorts before Esso gave the green light for all the families to come home.

Of course, nobody knew then how profoundly that abbreviated war would affect the region—in ways, it turned out, that shaped the course of much of my professional life. In every Arab nation, Israel's stunning 1967 victory triggered a religious revival. Fundamentalists avowed that the Arabs would regain their past glory only by returning to a strict observance of the faith, preaching a utopian vision of dominance that fueled much of the violence still plaguing the Middle East. The whole process of change is rooted in the legacy of that war. When I returned to the region as a correspondent, I often felt that the violence had become a barrier to understanding the region as impenetrable as the fence surrounding the oil compound of my childhood.

Our tranquil Club Med existence resumed, at least for a couple years—with barely any sense of the volcano slowly rumbling to life beneath our feet. My brother and my two older sisters, Nina and Gail, were gone most of the time in various European boarding schools because Brega lacked a high school.

In summer we basically camped at the beach. Summer vacations always started with the same ritual: My father would glimpse whatever skimpy bits of fabric my oldest sister Nina had bought as a bathing suit and declare, "You're not going to the beach in that!" Occasionally, some hapless Libyan herdsman—a few found their way into the compound to graze their flocks—spotted my blonde sister or one of her half-naked friends. He would come interrupt the teenage boys skim-boarding along the shoreline to ask how many camels or sheep he might exchange for one of the girls. A friend of my brother even managed to convince one unfortunately gullible local to show up with a camel herd.

Our days at the beach began with us all tumbling out of our 1960 green Ford Falcon station wagon, with little saddles and long-horns embossed on some manner of fake leather seating. It was the family car for my entire childhood. I would avoid my mother's attempts to douse me in sunscreen, which meant that my nose was invariably bloody and peeling from overexposure, and gun for the water. I usually swam to a raft anchored about 100 yards offshore, constructed using four oil barrels covered with boards. Just beyond the raft a long coral reef acted as a breakwater—so the inside of the bay remained relatively tranquil even in furious storms.

My brother and one or two of his friends would hunt with spear guns the brilliant parrot fish that darted about the reef, their efforts markedly diminishing the population over the years. Occasionally someone snorkeling would find treasure, like a Roman amphora or an Italian patrol boat sunk during World War II. Exporting antiquities was illegal, so one family, determined to spirit away their prized Roman pot, built an elaborate papier-mâché animal around it before giving it to the movers. On the beach, my sisters would either rig our small Sunfish sailboat or lie on their towels, sunbathing, while my father lit the coals in a small black metal hibachi. In the early years my mother devised incredibly complicated picnics with multiple courses. But after a sudden sandstorm picked the pea soup right out of the bowls and flung it across our laps on one desert excursion, the standard fare became barbecued hotdogs, hamburgers, and drumsticks. Every once in a while we grilled camel burgers, the meat slightly sweeter and tougher than beef. Fresh fruits and vegetables tended to arrive with a haggard look, acquired through days spent on docks and trucks. I'm not sure my mother improved matters by soaking them all in diluted Clorox to kill any germs. When she sent me to the grocery store for lettuce and I came back with a cabbage, she wondered aloud, not for the first or last time, whether it might not be better to live someplace where I would be exposed to more nature than just sand.

To get fresh bread, we drove to the bustling crossroads that had sprouted right outside the main gates of the compound. Amidst the confusion of garages and tire repair joints, a small bakery churned out short crusty loaves—Libya's delicious bread being one legacy of the Italian occupation. It was the perfect companion for my staple lunch—peanut butter and jelly sandwiches. I never imagined wanting to eat anything else. I honestly don't remember eating a single Libyan meal the whole time I lived there.

☖ ☖ ☖

When we first got to Brega, movies were shown at night on a tiny screen on the beach. After that, we graduated to a slightly larger screen against the wall at basketball court, with intermission every time the reel needed changing. The reels often played in the wrong order, but nobody complained much. We brought our own chairs, bundling up in winter months against the desert chill and wearing goggles during sandstorms. Eventually the company built a bowling alley and an indoor movie theater that offered a steady diet of Westerns.

One day King Idris came to pay a visit. The aging monarch had ruled Libya since 1951, when it became the first country to gain independence under the imprimatur of the newly formed United Nations. All the schoolchildren were given little paper Libyan flags—a green, a red, and a black strip with a crescent and star in the middle—to wave as he drove past the main road outside the school. There was a reception for him at the golf clubhouse. It was feared that walking up the eight steps from the front entrance to the reception floor might prove too much for the king, around 77 years old at the time, so Esso paved an entirely new parking lot and built a side entrance at the same level as the dining hall. By then the area inside the compound was fairly tamed. In our first years, packs of wild dogs roamed the dunes and as we drove to the distant clubhouse they would chase our cars with abandon. We always rode with the tailgate down, my brother wielding a Louisville slugger in case any tried to leap aboard.

The air conditioning ran most of the year in our boxy, comfortable house with its deep American sofas and stately New England antiques. During the school year the morning ritual never varied— I gulped down a bowl of corn flakes at the kitchen table while my father snapped on the BBC World Service to hear the news. After it ended, I darted across the street to Esso Elementary School. But on the morning of September 1, 1969, when I was 10, after the chimes of Big Ben heralding the news ended, the first headline was a shocker. It reported a military coup d'état in Libya. Really?! We stared at the radio in stunned disbelief, waiting for more details. In our sheltered little enclave there had been no peep, not a single sign that our world would shift irrevocably. A 27-year-old army major, Muammar al-Qadhafi, leading a group of officers called the Revolutionary Command Council, had overthrown the king.

Qadhafi modeled himself on President Gamal Abdel Nasser of Egypt, preaching socialism and Arab unity. King Idris was the patriarch of a distinguished clan of Muslim leaders. The upstart military officer, to gain credibility among the Libyans who had revered their king on religious grounds, implemented his own brand of Islamic law.

For my parents, disaster struck instantly with the implementation of a ban on alcohol, with all liquor removed from the grocery-store shelves three days after the coup. The talented chemical engineers were soon competing over who could produce the smoothest "flash," as the moonshine was called. Each house had been built with a small room for a maid behind the garage, but no one hired servants because there were none to be had. The shower stalls with their running water, however, proved excellent locations for small stills. Drunken parties, the adults crawling around on the floor by the end of the evening, a Brega trademark since the town was founded, continued almost uninterrupted.

Sometimes distilling experiments went badly wrong. My father tried to make ginger beer, filling several dozen dark-green bottles too full before stacking them in one corner of our wide kitchen counters. As the beer fermented and expanded, the bottles began to explode erratically, showering the kitchen with glass shards. For a day or two the kitchen was like a combat zone. Anyone needing something from the refrigerator cowered behind a garbage-can lid held like a shield. "Cover me!" one of us would yell as we dashed in to retrieve butter or orange juice or milk. Some experiments had far more tragic consequences. A few young Libyan trainees at the refinery went blind from distilling bad moonshine. After that, the government stopped ignoring infractions. An American engineer was deported for supplying bootleg to black marketers and a number of Britons were flogged after being convicted of public drunkenness.

For the kids, though, not much intruded on our idyll. Qadhafi's revolution imposed some cosmetic changes. All English signs in town were painted out, their script replaced by Arabic cursive. The worst imposition came after Colonel Qadhafi—he promoted himself—booted out all 20,000 Italian expatriates whose forebears had colonized the place starting in 1911. One wily Italian business-man managed to convert all his savings into gold jewelry and snuck away by sailing a small boat out to a larger yacht, in which his Italian friends had cruised over to rescue him. After that, our Sunfish sailboats were impounded for six months. The entire seventh and eighth grades unanimously agreed that the glorious Libyan people's revolution sucked because after class we could no longer run the ten minutes to the beach to sail every afternoon. It was my first but hardly last exposure to the region's bureaucratic overkill.

⬚　⬚　⬚

By then, Brega had grown to over 300 expatriate families, well beyond its original three streets. There were other changes. Qadhafi used some of Libya's oil revenue to expand the road to Benghazi to a full-blown highway, cutting an hour off the trip. The ban on Libyans living in the compound was lifted and the movie theater began showing Egyptian movies a couple nights a week. My parents ventured out once to see an early Omar Sharif epic, something about boatmen along the Nile with the requisite fight and belly-dance scenes. The compound kids never went to the Arabic movies; it was uncool.

Libyan families trickled in slowly at first because it took the company a while to build a separate school for their children. By that time I was gone most of the year to a Massachusetts boarding school. I chose one in the States because I had been there only twice during the entire decade we lived in Libya. My mother told me that the Libyans moving in complained bitterly that they'd been assigned inferior housing, stables unfit for animals, apparently imagining all those years that the foreigners were living in absolute luxury. The accusation smacked of the very kind of lingering colonialism that Qadhafi had vowed to uproot, so he swept into town to conduct the inspection personally. He went tromping through the Libyan and expatriate houses surrounded by soldiers armed with machine guns—he hadn't formed his female bodyguard contingent yet—before declaring all the houses alike. On the days before major Muslim feasts, however, you could tell where the Libyans lived because the bleating sheep bought for slaughter would batter their heads against the inside of the wooden garage doors.

We left Libya in 1975. One of my last memories was watching a large Libyan family proudly drive away in our station wagon, which sometimes had sat unused in the garage for a year at a time because Qadhafi banned Ford. Spare parts like a new carburetor or a replacement muffler became part of the hand luggage we invariably carted back from our annual vacation. It was only later, when I was at Stanford University in the early 1980s, that I began wondering what that family was like, what the entire country was like, and started asking myself the questions that had not really occurred to a kid delighting in the adventure of it all. I launched a retroactive search for what I had missed on the other side of that fence. I spent a couple summers in gruelingly intensive language courses; I read Middle Eastern history in spare moments; I attempted to make hummus in a blender; and, leaving no cliché unscathed, of course I watched the movie *Lawrence of Arabia* endlessly to hear Auda Abu Tayi, the Bedouin tribal leader played by Anthony Quinn, speak one of my favorite movie lines of all time, "I am a river to my people!" (No shortage of Arab leaders still make the same unlikely claim.)

At times I decided it was irrational to be drawn back to such a seemingly hostile, alien part of the world, and I would sign up for economics or Chinese art history and try to forget all about the Middle East. But the gravitational pull proved impossible to counteract. Some deep sense of curiosity, mingling with atonement, needed to be placated.

CHAPTER **2**

THE RETURN

"Every night a party."

I FOUND MYSELF ABOARD a flight to Tripoli, Libya, in January 2001, filled with all the anticipation and dread of a new assignment that I had been dreaming about for decades. At that point, I had been the Cairo bureau chief for the *New York Times* for all of two weeks. One pillar of my dream was making a pilgrimage to my childhood home, so I was determined to seize the earliest opportunity. I had wanted to visit Marsa Brega much earlier, when I was a correspondent in the region for The Associated Press from 1988 to 1994. But exasperatingly important events kept getting in the way, like the first Gulf War and, just as I moved to Jerusalem, the signing of the Israeli-Palestinian Oslo peace accords.

This time I made it a priority. I figured the surest route was to request an interview with Qadhafi himself, so I had asked the Libyan ambassador to the United Nations out to lunch at a fine Italian restaurant in midtown Manhattan before I left and begged for a visa. He jumped at the idea—since Qadhafi was embarking on one of his periodic attempts at image enhancement, my timing was fortuitous.

The United Nations imposed sanctions on Libya in 1992 after the country balked at extraditing the two suspects in the 1988 bombing of the Pan Am jumbo jet over Lockerbie, Scotland, that killed 270 people. Qadhafi had been defiant initially, but by 2001 he hoped to put Lockerbie behind him because the sanctions were impeding two important developments: first, his latest fantasy of being declared leader of the would-be "United States of Africa" and, second, the revitalization of Libya's oil industry, wholly American-built. Just as I was set to leave for what I hoped would be an exclusive interview, the Ministry of Information—a bureaucracy in every Arab nation that controls press visas and generally makes anything George Orwell imagined seem benign—threw open the doors to all comers. The Lockerbie trial had ended and Qadhafi wanted to declare the conviction of one of the two suspects, a Libyan intelligence agent, a sham.

I landed at a more modern Tripoli airport than the one I had left. I didn't recognize a thing. Still, I choked up, thinking of all the times that I'd landed in Libya as a boarding school student eager to get home to see my parents out in the desert. The terminal was decorated with all manner of opaque slogans from Qadhafi's Green Book, the rambling, not-to-say incoherent treatise on good government that he issued in the late 1970s. He proclaimed his Third Universal Theory the blueprint for rescuing the rotting capitalist and socialist systems of the world. It was written in such confusing language that when I first read it in English I thought perhaps something had been lost in translation. But Libyans found much of it just as baffling.

"Partners, Not Wage Earners" shouted one panel over passport control. The airport was an exception to the universal ban against signs in English, apparently to help visitors achieve a revolutionary frame of mind. I read another banner strung across the main wall in the arrivals hall: "Ignorance Ends When Everything Is Sincere." We spent a couple hours waiting for our visas to be processed. All the while the American and British TV and radio correspondents were busy filing via cell phone about the "Libyan reaction" to the verdict, although we weren't technically in the country yet and the only Libyan any of us had seen was the guy who disappeared with all our passports.

When the minibus carrying us from the airport rounded a curve and emerged onto the highway hugging the shoreline, an electric zap of recognition jolted my DNA. My father had died soon after we left Libya and I had pictured him so often on that coastline. I was home, or almost home. Coming back, I felt his loss more keenly than I had in years. He would have been excited at my being there as a correspondent. The desire to go stand on the beach in Brega had become a deep, almost physical longing. But first I had to file about Lockerbie. I vowed to complete my reporting as fast as possible and hightail it down the coast, to dive into that wide aquamarine bay where I had first learned to swim, to body-surf and to sail where so many fantastic moments of family lore unrolled.

My father imbued us with love for the sea, and did everything possible to keep us entertained there. We had always sailed, but one year he decided it was time to take up water skiing in a country where we had never seen a motor boat. He scoured Libya for one and finally found a passable, forgotten craft parked on a trailer in some hidden corner. He ordered water skis, which took months and months to arrive in the mail. Finally the exciting launch day was at hand and almost every family in town turned out to watch the christening of its first motor boat. The craft made it roughly 300 yards before unceremoniously diving for the bottom, its electronics newly refurbished but its fiberglass hull a maze of invisible, fatal cracks. We teased my father relentlessly about that boat's rapid demise.

A few days after being acquitted, one of the suspects, al-Amin Khalifa Fhimah, was flown back to Libya by the Dutch air force. The plane turned out to be a C-130 Hercules transport plane, the very type of aircraft once used to evacuate me from the country, and it landed at the Tripoli airfield that had once been Wheelus, the U.S. air force base. I took all of these parallels as a sign that the stars were aligning to close some manner of circle, that the fates would soon carry me back to Brega.

The heaving, pushing scrum of reporters, security agents, and Fhimah relatives right outside the airplane's low door was so dense that he emerged with real difficulty after first sticking his head out and flashing a victory sign. His gold-rimmed glasses were knocked off as he sank out of view in a knot of family members, some weeping and all trying to kiss him at once.

"To hell with America, such an ugly and dirty country!" I heard someone in the crowd shout in Arabic.

In typical fashion, senior Ministry of Information officials made no attempt to organize the arrival ceremony in a manner that would diminish the pandemonium. Soon after, however, they started yelling in English "To the Leadership! To the Leadership!" in panicked tones and quickly corralled the press back onto a bus.

Their agitated state indicated that we were barreling our way toward a rendezvous with Qadhafi, but I didn't quite believe it until the bus zipped through the first of a series of gray steel gates at a sprawling military compound on the outskirts of Tripoli called Al-Aziziya Barracks. Just past the third set of similarly daunting gates the bus ground to a halt and I rushed off with the rest of the press corps to find the colonel himself, then 58, standing right in front of us.

An austere Qadhafi was holding himself rigidly upright in front of the carefully preserved wreckage of his own two-story concrete house. He was wearing a traditional black wool skullcap and a dark-brown woolen cloak thrown over one shoulder, as well as a rather less traditional shirt of bright gold, red, and black paisleys. I remembered the rail-thin, handsome man with close-cropped black curly hair who first took power. Some three decades later he had taken on the wrinkled appearance of a rock star whose loud wardrobe substituted for his lost youth. Mick Jagger came to mind.

The U.S. air force had bombed Qadhafi's house in 1986. It was a none-too-subtle attempt by the Reagan administration to assassinate a foreign head of state whom the president had called the "mad dog of the Middle East." A banner draped over the gutted house read, in Arabic, "Libya—The victim of official American terrorism." Facing the house stood a twenty-foot sculpture depicting a green aluminum fist crushing a small warplane marked "USA." Green was the revolution's official color, representing both Islam and Qadhafi's aspirations for a reborn, verdant Libya. Qadhafi received Condoleezza Rice in the same spot in late 2008 when she became the first U.S. secretary of state to visit Libya in fifty-five years. The wrecked house, the sculpture, even the banner were all still in place.

The day I went, the thirty or so Western and Arab correspondents immediately mobbed Qadhafi. One short, wiry British television reporter planted himself directly in front of the Libyan leader like a Jack Russell terrier, barking over and over again, "Are you going to pay compensation? I know you speak English! Are you going to pay compensation?" Seeing the annoyed look on their leader's face, his bodyguards realized they had let the press get too close. They began muscling their way through the dense knot of reporters to insert themselves in the middle. The TV reporter gave no ground, still snarling the compensation question, and an agitated Qadhafi tried to back away, sending the scrum tumbling first right, then left.

The colonel did indeed speak English, the result of a military training course he had attended in England in the 1960s, and was soon shouting at us in two languages that the relatives of the hundreds killed and wounded in the American bombing attacks—who included an infant girl he had adopted, some said posthumously—deserved compensation as much as the families of the Lockerbie victims.

"What about us?" the colonel said, slapping the wall of the shattered dwelling, his voice rising. "Why don't we talk about our victims? Why don't we talk about the victims of 1986? They too have families. Who is going to pay the compensation for them? What does the United Nations think of that? What is America going to tell us about that? What is the court going to say about these victims? Where is compensation for these innocent souls?"

He pulled Fhimah, also dressed in traditional Libyan clothes, away from the house toward a new pickup truck where a camel lay dead, its throat slashed and its blood spattered about underfoot. That sacrifice was a traditional welcome for an honored guest, but as I tried to keep up with the colonel, my feet got stuck in the blood congealing on the asphalt on what was an unseasonably warm January day.

Still agitated, Qadhafi kept darting in one direction and then the other, maintaining his outburst for about thirty minutes. The mercurial colonel then left, but not before ordering us to return in three days when he would reveal the truth about the Lockerbie verdict: "I will speak on Monday, and when I speak the judges will have only three choices: either to commit suicide, to resign, or to admit the truth."

I spent the next day, a Friday and the Muslim Sabbath, wandering around various outdoor markets as well as through Tripoli's charming if dilapidated old city. It is a warren of whitewashed two-story houses fronting narrow streets, many barely wide enough for a fully laden camel from the caravans of yesteryear, not to mention a car. The streets, perhaps more accurately described as passageways, curve away mysteriously, and a quick turn occasionally produces a dead end. Arches span the narrow spaces overhead. Palm matting stretched over these buttresses in summer blocks out the blistering sun.

Residents complained that the government had allowed old Tripoli to become a slum with open sewers and a plague of collapsed buildings, rather than restoring a storied port that over the past 3,000 years was occupied variously by Phoenicians, Romans, Vandals, the Byzantine Empire, Islamic armies, Spaniards, Maltese knights, Turks, and Italians. But one woman, on discovering that I was an American, started to laugh at the idea that I was asking why the houses were crumbling. "American?! Once we build you will destroy it again, come with your planes to bomb, so I prefer living in a tent anyway."

Libya has something of a history of clashes with the United States. In 1801, the young American nation blockaded Tripoli harbor because its Barbary pirate masters increased the protection money demanded from U.S. ships sailing the Mediterranean. ("Terrorists again!" I heard an Islamic scholar joke once at a conference.) When the frigate *Philadelphia* ran aground there in 1804, its sailors were imprisoned and eventually ransomed. American raiders burned the crippled ship to prevent the capture of its cannons. The "Marine Hymn" immortalizes the exploit in its opening lines: "From the halls of Montezuma, to the shores of Tripoli."

Aside from the streets, I wandered through the small but engaging museum housed in the fort anchoring the city walls nearest the harbor. It sits on one corner of the vast square that links the ancient city to the more modern one, its colonnaded streets lined with pretty, low, white Italian colonial buildings built around large courtyards. Farther out, they give way to modern, monolithic apartment blocks. That central square is now called "Green Square" after Qadhafi's revolution. The government even slaps green paint across the asphalt before important holidays.

I started in the museum's basement looking at the cave paintings—circa 12,000 B.C.—found deep in the Sahara desert. The exhibits rise in a timeline, retracing the history of the three once-thriving Roman port cities that gave Tripoli its name. The modern capital now sits on one of them, but the exquisite ruins of the other two flank it. The museum's top floor was a socialistic exaltation of all the progress made in the era of Colonel Qadhafi. The museum inspired me to hire a car and driver to revisit Leptis Magna, one of the grandest, most spectacular ruins I have seen anywhere in the former distant reaches of the Roman Empire—far more complete than other impressive sites like Palmyra in Syria, Baalbek in the Bekaa

Valley of Lebanon, or Jordan's Jerash. Along the massive flagstones marking the main thoroughfare in Leptis, venues like the fish market were readily apparent. I could almost hear sellers hawking the day's catch from behind long flat marble tables, their legs carved with dolphins. The place was practically deserted, although another visitor tested the excellent acoustics in the amphitheater by belting out "New York, New York." Entire neighborhoods remain buried beneath the surrounding dunes.

Earlier travelers described a certain magic emanating from old Tripoli, which for centuries had linked the Mediterranean to caravan routes criss-crossing the Sahara. I leafed through a memoir by Mabel Loomis Todd, an American traveler, who described sitting on the roof of the British consulate after nightfall in the early 1900s, watching the moon illuminate the minarets, the domes, and the palm trees. "It might have been a fairy city, beautiful beyond imagining," she wrote.

But even in history, escaping politics proves hard in Libya. Mrs. Todd had stayed in the British consulate, and I jotted down the words off the marble plaque on the restored building, now a library, where I found her book. "The so-called European Geographical and Explorative Scientific Expeditions to Africa, which were in essence and a matter of fact intended to be colonial ones to occupy and colonize vital and strategic parts of Africa, embarked from this same building," the plaque read. A Libyan official seeing me write it down helpfully volunteered that all foreign embassies serve the same function today as dens of spies.

As I walked around, I tried to harvest public opinion on the Lockerbie verdict and on life in Libya in general. To break the ice—Arabs are often wary about criticizing their country to a Western reporter, not least because of their concern about who might be listening—I told people that I had grown up there.

"So you haven't been here for twenty-five years, that doesn't matter; this country hasn't changed in at least twenty years," said one of the first men I asked in an outdoor market where everything from oranges to live sheep were for sale. "The reason? You want to know the reason? Everyone knows the reason. . . . "

He meant Qadhafi, of course, but two plainclothes security agents interrupted our conversation. Security agents in the worst Arab police states get particularly queasy when a Western reporter starts interviewing the general public. In some countries such as Saddam Hussein's Iraq, talking to foreigners was actually illegal. Libyan security agents had long since perfected a method of sending journalists scurrying back to Al-Kabir Hotel, or the "Grand Hotel" in English, where we were all invariably housed. One agent sidled up next to me. "The Leader will speak soon," he said in a stage whisper in English, meaning Qadhafi. "Press conference. You must go to hotel."

Normally it was an effective technique. Qadhafi's erratic, often adolescent theatrics embodied the system of controlled chaos that marked both Libya's politics and its economy and, more important, ensured his long reign. He called it a state of permanent revolution, with his own role as clairvoyant and guide. Or as his official website called him, "The Guide to the Era of the Masses." Eventually he even started rebuking any journalist who addressed him as Colonel, declaring all Arab armed forces an embarrassment.

To maintain the conceit that he did not really run Libya, Qadhafi had been known to arrive late for events like state dinners honoring some visiting African leader. He would sit at a far table, diplomats who attended such functions told me, stare at the ceiling between bites, and then depart abruptly after thirty minutes without uttering a word to anybody. He never acted that way with Arab leaders, who I knew would have considered such behavior a rankling insult, but the generally impoverished Africans accepted it as part of the welcome wagon that usually included a check for at least one or two million dollars.

I found the otherwise pallid government-run newspapers overflowing with songs, poems, and other paeans to Qadhafi penned by Africans. My favorite was a lengthy ode to his smile, which occupied half a newspaper page. A typical stanza read: "His teeth are immune to stain, so that when he releases a full-blown smile, the naturally white teeth discharge radiation pregnant with sweet joy and real happiness for those lucky ones who are fortunate to be around him."

At the farmers' market that Friday, I released a full-blown smile of sweet joy, knowing I could gleefully ignore the fake Qadhafi-alert being conveyed by the agitated, less-than-undercover security agents.

"He can't possibly be speaking," I said, trying not to smirk. "He spoke to us yesterday, and told us to come back Monday." Qadhafi had announced his press conference only the previous afternoon, and I knew many of the world's major television networks had yet to arrive. The deflated cops slunk away.

Of course, the three days spent waiting for the press conference were jammed with political events tied to the Lockerbie verdict. All university and high school students had been given a five-day holiday for what had been dubbed the "Week of Uprisings" against the court's ruling. One of the most popular chants during their various demonstrations was "Intihar! Intihar!" which is Arabic for "Suicide!" The chant was inspired by the Qadhafi teaching that it is preferable to kill oneself than to accept humiliation or dishonor. Insulting the dignity of Arabs is a crowning insult, dignity being one essential value, and trying to placate this culture of shame has been the bane of many a Western official.

Qadhafi's slogan, I confess, instantly became my rallying cry throughout the region in the face of recalcitrant bureaucrats determined to thwart my reporting forays during the five years I was stationed in the Middle East for the Times. I would be sitting in some government ministry in, say, Saudi Arabia or Syria, facing yet another bumbling official with some meaningless, grandiose title who had kept me waiting for hour upon hour before adamantly refusing to issue some simple permit. "Intihar! Intihar!" I would yell out suddenly in frustration, reducing Abeer Allam, the intrepid Egyptian reporter who worked with me, to helpless giggling. My outburst invariably prompted a look from the bureaucrat as if I had taken leave of my senses, which, incidentally, was usually the very look Arabs reserved for Libyans, particularly Libyan officials pushing some bizarre Qadhafi initiative.

At one anti-Lockerbie demonstration in Tripoli, four students pretended to commit suicide by stabbing themselves in the abdomen in front of the United Nations offices. The cameramen for an Arab satellite channel showed up late, just as the doors were slammed shut on the ambulance collecting the last student. When he complained, I watched the obliging emergency medical technicians, despite the serious condition of their patient, unload him, expose his wounds, and then make a great show of shoving him back in again.

▣   ▣   ▣

Qadhafi is nothing if not a showman, his obsession with the smallest details amply on display for his infamous, post–Lockerbie verdict press conference. The now far larger press corps was again dispatched to his personal compound inside Aziziya Barracks. This time we were subjected to two security searches rather than roaring unimpeded into the colonel's presence.

A low stage had been erected in front of his pockmarked house. A herd of camels and goats wandered across the lawn that covered much of his enclosure, also dotted with several green canvas tents—all meant to preserve the conceit that he remained a simple Bedouin. After several hours, I finally saw Qadhafi step out of one tent and into the back of a red BMW convertible, waving to the reporters sitting in rows as the car made a sweeping turn to cover the roughly forty yards to the stage. He was resplendent, wearing indigo African robes, heavily embroidered, and a matching beanie on his unkempt black curls. But when he alighted from the vehicle, he suddenly halted, shaking his head before uttering inaudible orders to his aides.

It turned out he didn't like the dais. Officials quickly seized a small table from behind the dais where two lawyers were supposed to sit. Dozens of television technicians rushed forward to reposition their microphones, strapping them with duct tape to the small table. The officials looked at Qadhafi quizzically. I saw him shake his head. They brought out a bigger table from someplace and the entire dance was repeated. Again he shook his head, then swiveled angrily on one heel and disappeared into a small guesthouse. Sometime later I heard groans and a shuffling noise, so I turned around to see eight men staggering under the weight of a huge white slab of a table they were lugging across the compound. Qadhafi came out of the little house, glanced at the stage, and again shook his head.

This time the groan came from the entire press corps. We had already been on deck for seven hours with nothing to report and a fine, sunny day was becoming a chilly winter evening. Few people had brought enough clothes or anything to drink. Even the distribution hours earlier of some cans of Coca-Cola, a surprise given constant diatribes against all things American, did nothing to lighten our mood. The white table was almost as big as the stage itself! What could possibly be wrong, I wondered. Well, the color of the chair. Qadhafi waited until the brown leather office chair was replaced by an equally large white chair that matched the table. Only then, an hour after he had emerged from his tent, did he sit down.

Then commenced a marathon news conference, the longest I have ever attended as a journalist, bar none, and the only one I remember leaving because the need to urinate overwhelmed my interest in the information being dispensed. The eccentric dictator lectured us for nearly three hours, through sunset and two calls to prayer. At times I thought he sounded like a seasoned defense lawyer poking holes in flimsy prosecution arguments and circumstantial evidence. He repeatedly thumbed through what looked like a well-read trial transcript dotted with yellow Post-it notes. At other times Qadhafi might have been some late-night talkshow host discussing conspiracy theories and pounding on the table as he lashed out at unseen enemies.

"We thought that after America got rid of the wicked and crazy Reagan, it started to improve and to understand the world and to bridge the gaps between America and the world," the Libyan leader roared at us.

In the years following this particular press conference, I noticed Qadhafi improved rather markedly at sweet-talking the Americans. After December 2003, when he publicly abandoned his varied arsenal of unconventional weapons in the wake of Saddam Hussein's overthrow, he even managed to garner praise from President Bush as an example to others. The fact that Libya had agreed to pay $10 million to the relatives of each Lockerbie victim undoubtedly helped.

Once the immediate Lockerbie business was out of the way, I thought I could finally fly to Brega. Calling around for a flight, I discovered that my "hometown" was now wholly owned by the Libyan national oil company, so I needed its permission to board any plane going there. But as was all too common in the Socialist People's Great Arab Jamahiriya—Qadhafi's official name for his utopia—the unexpected intervened. The Popular Committees were called into session.

"Jamahiriya" lacks an exact translation but roughly means "the state of the masses," ostensibly because the country was ruled through Popular Committees. Even the embassies abroad had been renamed "People's Bureaus." Libya has no parliament, no military institutions, no political parties, no unions, no nongovernmental organizations, and fewer ministries all the time. This is what Qadhafi describes in the Green Book as the permanent revolution: "In the era of the masses, power is in the hands of people themselves and leaders disappear forever." Libyans note wryly that their leader has hung around since 1969, yet shows no sign of disappearing anytime soon. Every night the official Libyan television news ended with invariably dated clips of riots or demonstrations enveloping one European or American city or another, the announcer intoning that it was only a matter of time before the decaying West came around to the wisdom of governing through Popular Committees. Libyans told me this had been standard fare for years.

In theory, the people ran everything. In practice, nothing ran. But the entire country shut down for the Popular Committees, which unrolled as if a Vermont town-hall meeting had been crossbred with a Soviet block association. The Brother Leader, Qadhafi's preferred title inside Libya, would abruptly "suggest" an agenda for sessions called at random at least twice a year. They usually involved strictly domestic matters, but occasionally foreign affairs were included when he needed to make some face-saving gesture. Every office—schools, government ministries, airlines, shops—closed for days, sometimes weeks, while the committees met. Truly important decisions, of course, notably anything affecting the oil industry, were left in the hands of accomplished technocrats and never mentioned on any Popular Committee agenda.

I resigned myself to the inevitable since there was absolutely no chance of getting permission to fly to Brega while the Popular Committees were in session and clearly there would be nothing else to do. So I wandered down Revolution Street from the hotel to the neighborhood session taking place in the Rose movie theater. The lurid posters for a karate action flick were still plastered out front despite the many banners hailing the enduring importance of the committees.

The session provided a far better window on the feelings of an average Libyan than I could have imagined, proving the accuracy of the advice given to reporters everywhere: "Go to everything."

It was my first exposure to a phenomenon I subsequently experienced again and again, one that proved the hardest to convey to newspaper readers fed a steady diet of appalling violence from the region. The Libyan meetings indicated that ordinary Arabs are well aware that their nations are out of step with the rest of the world, that they are fed up with both the incompetence of their rulers and the unpredictable quality of their lives. They crave normalcy, but despair at not knowing how to attain it in the face of oppression that brings at least jail terms and even death to anyone trying to organize dissenters. One of the great failures of American diplomacy in the Middle East has been Washington's inability deftly to harness that frustration.

The Popular Committee meetings indicated just how discouraged Libyans were with their lot. Life in Libya was so unpredictable that people weren't even sure what year it was. The year of my visit was officially 1369. But just two years earlier Libyans had been living through 1429. No one could quite name for me the day when the count changed, especially since both remained in play. A newspaper headline when I arrived, for example, heralded changes in a legal bulletin, No. 4 for 1431, while the paper itself was dated with the current year, 1369. Confused? So was I.

The date is but one example of the Brother Leader's fickle decisions—switching suddenly from the standard Muslim calendar to one marking the years since the Prophet Mohamed's birth and then shifting to one counting from his death. The rest of the 1.3 billion or so Muslims around the world happily use a calendar that starts from the date that Mohamed migrated from Mecca to Medina to found the faith. Qadhafi had also decided some years earlier that he disliked the names of both the Western and the Eastern months, so he invented his own names. February is Lights. August is Hannibal.

Event organizers threw up their hands and put the Western year in parentheses somewhere on their announcements. Other Libyans just threw up their hands. "Why do we keep using different dates?" bellowed a woman at the Popular Committee meeting. I was standing in the upstairs balcony of the cavernous movie theater but had no trouble hearing her down below. "Why can't we be like every single other Muslim country and count from the time of the Prophet's migration, not from his death? What is this?" The unspoken answer was that Libya's leader liked it that way. His quixotic decisions kept the lives of ordinary Libyans endlessly veering toward bedlam. Being the only one knowing what was going on seemed to reassure Qadhafi, aside from the usual Arab internal security forces spying on everyone, that he would be difficult to replace.

It seemed to me that two Libyas existed and rarely intersected.

There was Qadhafi's Libya, a rich oil state that craved recognition on the world stage. That Libya used to attract attention by underwriting a host of violent groups deemed criminal by the West until it tired of its status as international pariah. That Libya had been seeking redemption lately by trying to play the village elder who will unify Africa. The other Libya is the country where the rest of the roughly 5 million Libyans actually lived. (I couldn't find anyone who seemed to know quite how many there are.) Their roads are potholed, their telephones unreliable, and the young lack meaningful jobs.

Arab oil states with equal oil resources ooze wealth. Despite being sacked by the Iraqis in 1990, Kuwait City is gridlocked with the latest, most expensive BMWs and Mercedes, while huge mansions line its main thoroughfares. To me it felt vaguely like Beverly Hills, if I overlooked the occasional woman driving in a full face veil. Tripoli has none of that. It looks and feels drab—its limited number of hotels so small that adventurous tourists are regularly evicted to make way for some visiting African delegation. Qadhafi once declared that anything over approximately $3,000 dollars in private bank accounts was excessive and should revert to the state. The huge number of Libyans on the public payroll—about 800,000—went through the 1980s and 1990s without a wage increase. Sometimes they didn't get paid at all for months on end.

Undoubtedly many problems stemmed from the UN sanctions. But the Libyans I talked to were incensed that they touched so few benefits from their oil revenue, which was already running to about $10 billion annually before prices catapulted into the stratosphere, reaching record-highs close to $150 per barrel. The grumbling occasionally reached Qadhafi, who then delivered a hectoring speech to his compatriots that they better get off their backsides and start working because the oil would not last forever. The rant had little effect.

"The roads here might as well have been through the war in Chechnya," said Selma Iswid, 54, a housewife addressing that Popular Committee meeting. "We are an oil-rich country, we should have better roads. They should put whoever built them on trial before the masses! All the facilities are in very bad shape: services, transportation, health care. We are not satisfied with any of this."

A proclamation I read on Qadhafi's official website stated that, "[t]he Revolution is for Libyans like the air they breathe and light by which they see." But from my experience they saw little good in it and in fact found it stifling. To me, being a Libyan is like being forced to attend a rather gothic circus that one didn't particularly want tickets for in the first place. As the Popular Committee meeting dragged on, shopkeepers bemoaned their losses. But any stores found open for business faced a stiff fine and a license suspension. Libyans told me that they had to show their stamped attendance record at odd moments—when leaving the country, for example. No stamp could mean no exit.

At this particular session, after roughly three hours of meandering discussions, I watched a large group of women suddenly break for the exit. The guards out front pushed them back inside, rolling down a heavy green metal gate to contain them. One of the stout, matronly officials running the meeting emerged and screamed at the women to take their seats. "We will record the name of anyone who leaves and say she didn't attend!" she yelled.

Occasionally the committees did manage to overturn one of the Brother Leader's more oddball suggestions. Once, for example, he announced that elementary schools should be shuttered and all children schooled at home. The outcry from the committee meetings killed the plan.

"Thanks to the Revolution, the Libyan people, who formerly lived in a state of ignorance and barbarity, have become an organized and civilized people," proclaimed Qadhafi's website in bald contradiction to all evidence—at least on the organizational front. "The achievements of the Revolution are so apparent that they have put an end to idle debate and all vain sophistry."

This does not exactly reflect the experience of the thousands of foreign businessmen who flock to Libya, only to find themselves stranded by the fact that they can't figure out who makes the decisions. But the potential windfall involved always keeps more coming. I met an Italian who manufactures pumps in Padua who had received an unexpected fax from a Libyan company asking him to come to Tripoli two months later to pitch his goods. He was sent no agenda, but sat ready in the lobby of the Grand Hotel at 10 A.M. on the appointed February day. One Libyan showed up and bought him a glass of tea, saying he would make a quick call and return after five minutes to take the Italian to the National Oil Company. He never reappeared. Two and a half hours later, a second Libyan materialized. He knew nothing about the oil company, but he took the Italian to a branch of the Ministry of Agriculture. The official they were due to meet never showed up. "In Libya you always wait for hours and you never know why you wait or who you are waiting for," sighed the Italian when I struck up a conversation with him on Day 2 in the lobby, where he was again awaiting his long overdue Libyan interlocutors.

Average Libyans grumbled to me that all their wealth was being siphoned off into Africa. Billboards around the capital showed Qadhafi's image imposed over a map of the continent. "The Pulse of the Millions!" one slogan proclaimed, but the Brother Leader seemed to be the only one feeling that pulse. He opened the country to laborers from elsewhere in Africa, who do most manual jobs such as street sweeping. The general public accuses them of bringing scourges like AIDS and petty crime, with occasional riots leaving scores dead. "What could we possibly benefit from the Africans?" Khalid, a bazaar trader, told me, speaking furtively. He was one of the few willing to even entertain a question about the leader's pet cause, but still so uneasy that he withheld his full name. "Nothing! We don't feel we are part of Africa."

Qadhafi himself is not above rather surprising pronouncements on this issue, proclaiming in the Green Book that blacks tend to have more children than other races because they are less preoccupied with work and "are sluggish in a climate that is always hot." At the same time, he hectored his fellow Arab leaders that Arab unity is an abject failure, that they would make something of themselves as a weight in the world only if they joined a new bloc of African nations.

Despite consistently wacky outpourings, Qadhafi generated a certain populist appeal in the Arab world, not least because he was often far less aloof than all other Arab leaders. At their annual summits, when most heads of state remain closeted behind layers of security in their hotel rooms, Qadhafi would drop into a local ice cream shop, buy a cone, and sit down to talk to the patrons. If nothing else, he always provided a note of entertainment for the press corps desperately scratching about for news from the habitually dull summits. The tempo seemed to pick up with his very entrance, striding ahead surrounded by his flock of female bodyguards. The bevy of glamorous Amazons decked out in blue camouflage fatigues, high-heeled sandals, and red nail polish was meant to show that Qadhafi's revolution had brought equal opportunities for women; but practice lagged.

Qadhafi, angry that the Arab rulers were not being more confrontational with Washington over the invasion of Iraq, had to be coaxed into attending the 2004 summit in Tunisia. I watched the Libyan leader, who never smoked, light a cigarette during the opening ceremony. In front of a slew of photographers, he turned to President Hosni Mubarak of Egypt and said, "It's an American cigarette!" It was his mocking way of making the point that the Arab leaders were acquiescing to all kinds of ills foisted on the region by the United States. Then Qadhafi showed his knack for publicly highlighting the problems weighing on the minds of most Arabs, problems that other leaders left unsaid. He stormed out of the Tunis gathering, eclipsing the entire summit by holding a rambling press conference in which he declared it scandalous that Arab leaders were conducting business as usual when Iraq was awash in blood under an American occupation. "If Saddam lived for another ten years, would he have been able to kill as many Iraqis and destroy as much of Iraq as the Americans have done in one year?" he asked, although later in the same tirade he compared the American revolution favorably to the one he carried out in Libya.

He also attacked the Arabs for doing nothing to alleviate the suffering of the Palestinians. He had a solution for the latter, of course. He has been pushing for Israel and Palestine to be combined into one country, "Isratine," with equal rights for all, saying the place had basically been one country since the 1967 war anyway. The proposal made other Arab leaders giggle openly. Whenever a Libyan minister stood up at one gathering or another to question why no action was being taken toward implementing the plan, I saw other ministers smirking. Yet typical of Qadhafi, the idea was not utterly outlandish. Some of the more liberal thinkers among both the Palestinians and Israelis have reached a similar conclusion, that giving everyone a stake in the success of just one country might be the ultimate solution to ending the struggle over the same piece of land.

⬚ ⬚ ⬚

Inside Libya, despite its myriad problems, most opposition atrophied. One line of graffiti I read in a downtown park—"The ruler is a dictator and the people are hungry"—was about as vociferous as the criticism got. There are hundreds of political prisoners, and dissidents abroad occasionally disappear—apparently kidnapped and shipped home to lifetime jail sentences or execution. Armed attacks by Islamic militants are also reported periodically, but overall they appear contained by the security forces. The overseas opposition has largely disbanded. I met a few young Libyans at Internet cafés who made furtive efforts to call up opposition websites, but they had to be computer savvy to reach around the filters. As in all Arab states, I found that people believe that their fate is basically in the hands of the security services.

For that reason I rarely felt threatened when I told people that I was an American. Your average Libyan or other Arab did not hold me responsible for whatever Washington was doing. They figured that I, like them, was just a pawn in the hands of the U.S. government. This tacit understanding began to break down after the Iraqi invasion in 2003, however, when the nightly news was full of gory pictures of Iraqis killed by American soldiers. But while I was in Libya that was still some years away.

Succession is almost never mentioned in Libya and Qadhafi, now in his mid-60s and the longest-ruling leader in the Arab world, is reportedly in good health. Libyans despair that he might be immortal. His eldest son from his first marriage, Mohamed, a businessman whose holdings include a chunk of the country's most significant Internet provider, keeps a low profile. Qadhafi's two oldest sons from his second marriage, both in their early 30s, are sometimes seen as possible successors although both deny any interest.

His second son, Seif el-Islam, booted out of various European universities due to Libya's pariah status, ultimately founded the Qadhafi International Association for Charitable Organizations to try to burnish his country's image. He used it to mediate various international crises involving Libya or extremist Muslim groups in Asia. He also spoke out during interviews on Al-Jazeera satellite network and elsewhere about the importance of introducing greater democracy to the region. But he had no official role and the extent of his influence was unclear, particularly since his father was still giving speeches as late as 2006 suggesting it was best to kill all enemies seeking to change Libya's ideal political system.

Another son, al-Saadi, reintroduced a soccer league in Libya, rescuing the sport from the bizarre political strictures imposed by his father. The Green Book rebuked those who watch sports rather than participate. Saadi played for the Tripoli soccer team Al-Ahli, sometimes exerting his influence to sway decisions in his club's favor. After rivals in Benghazi paraded a donkey through the streets wearing his No. 10 jersey, their stadium was bulldozed. He was ultimately drafted by an Italian team, a move dismissed as a publicity stunt by its rivals. Plagued by injuries, he played little.

Other offspring, albeit more reclusive, seemed to follow the pattern of oddball behavior associated with what might be termed Qadhafi family values. Aisha, Qadhafi's only daughter and a lawyer, gained some notoriety for volunteering to join the huge legal team assembled to defend Saddam Hussein, but it was unclear that she ever had any real role. Qadhafi's fourth son, Hannibal, generated tabloid headlines after reportedly battering a woman in a luxury Paris hotel and brandishing a nine-millimeter pistol when police were summoned. Libya organized a mass protest demonstration outside the Swiss Embassy in Tripoli after a similar incident in Switzerland in 2008, when Hannibal was arrested on suspicion of beating his servants. The last son, Moatassim, reportedly tried to buy tanks and short-range missiles for his own army brigade until his father halted the move.

▣   ▣   ▣

After the Popular Committee meetings I was again marooned, unable to get on an airplane to Brega. Juma Bilkheir, the skinny, bald, cur-mudgeonly Ministry of Information official in charge of the foreign press and the man who had promised to issue the needed permit, left the country abruptly. As in most such bureaucracies, his underlings were paralyzed with fear about making a decision in his absence, so they just put me off. For the few days while my ill-fated optimism endured, I discovered that Tripoli boasted few distractions other than satellite television and the Internet. The capital had just one nightclub, Abu Nuwas, named after a classical if drunken Arab bard who cele-brated various forms of revelry including drinking wine. I could eas-ily have mistaken the place for any other building. The outside was plastered with slogans and the foyer displayed the mandatory picture of the leader. At least the owners had found the hippest image available—a young Qadhafi, wearing cool shades and navy whites, zipping across the azure Mediterranean in a speedboat. It was very Tripoli Vice. Inside, the thick air was sticky sweet from all the water pipes, which the men and the mostly foreign women—Moroccans, Algerians, Bulgarians—smoked while watching the dancers.

If the Libyan men thought a particular dancer was sexy, they raced out and stuffed bank notes into her shirt. "Libyan women don't come here—maybe one or two, but not many," one young Libyan told me after engaging in the exercise. "It's hard for them because our traditions won't allow it. But these women from Morocco, you can fuck them, do what you like, it doesn't matter."

The music was strictly Middle Eastern. The colonel barred all Western music in public in the 1980s, and of course the alcohol ban had been around for decades, although some men seemed to be surreptitiously nipping from soda cans. When I asked the manager about his apparent monopoly on the capital's night life, he shrugged and said the Brother Leader approved: "He wrote in the Green Book, 'On every street a theater and every night a party.'"

I tried not to laugh. That was hardly the image that the colonel had achieved abroad after accumulating so many years in power. For much of the '80s he had been in the American sweepstakes for Public Enemy Number One, accused of financing terrorists from Asia to Ireland and dispatching "assassination squads" to the U.S. among other places. His treatment of political opponents was proof enough that he was capable of nefarious deeds, but it was hard to reconcile the rambling figure I saw in Libya, and the shambolic country he created, with all the menacing headlines about him. Libya came across less "Axis of Evil" than "Axis of Wackiness," although Qadhafi was clearly more wily than nuts. Once when I was working the overnight shift at the AP in New York, the first edition of the *New York Post* landed on my desk emblazoned with a headline using something like the word "Kha-Daffy" over an article about how he liked to cross-dress. The paper had even doctored a picture to show what he would look like in a wig and big loop earrings. The sourcing was dubious, but the *Post* was onto something with the daffiness reference. Rather than turning such despots into threatening figures, I wondered, wouldn't it be better to find a way to mock their many foibles and the failure of their regimes to deliver at home? The development of nuclear weaponry or the financing of terrorism cannot be ignored. But from the utter muddle of the place, it seemed the U.S. might garner more sympathy with the population and at the same time weaken the harsh ways of so many Mideast despots by making a show of their incompetence. That was definitely one characteristic common to them all. Iran, Saudi Arabia, Libya, and certainly Egypt were not run very well, not least because there was no real political opposition in any of them to hold the government accountable. Couldn't outsiders play that role, or at least boost those insiders who were attempting to challenge the competence of their rulers, thereby helping change such bankrupt systems?

It was a question I chased throughout my years in the region, but my pursuit was interrupted—sometimes for years at a time— by endlessly violent breaking news. Back in my childhood, I was cut off from Libya both by an actual, physical fence and by a mental gap rooted in lack of exposure to the people. I worked hard to erase that gap, but as a correspondent I came to see all the violent news from the region as a different kind of fence. The constant, bloody upheaval that captures most attention has become the barrier limiting our perspective on the Middle East.

Having experienced so many battlefields firsthand, I know just how exhilarating and addictive conflict can be. I skimmed over the Saudi desert in a Blackhawk helicopter watching U.S. troops surge north into Iraq during the first Gulf War, and escaped the West Bank late one inky night after some young Palestinians hurled a boulder with such force at the door of my car that they almost tore it off its hinges. I had passed day after day writing about nothing but gore. I will never forget the hours spent late one night negotiating around the bodies lining the corridors of a Najaf hospital, the floors awash in blood, after a car bomb assassinated the most prominent Iraqi ayatollah allied with the United States, along with nearly 100 other people. I was the first to find one of his drivers among the wounded wrapped in dirty wool blankets, the man describing the minutes just before a wall of fire obliterated the street outside Shiite Islam's holiest shrine. My exposure to violence was not limited to the Middle East. In Sarajevo, I vividly recall driving out to the airport where the French army outpost sold good red wine. Buildings sheltered me from the snipers in the foothills for most of the route, but I had to walk maybe thirty yards or so through an exposed area to get from my Volkswagen to the quartermaster. I could hear bullets whining past as I crouched into a slow jog with the case of Bordeaux jiggling awkwardly at my hip. Winston Churchill famously said that the most exhilarating thing in life was being shot at with no effect. But there was more to life. I didn't want to write only about Iraq or the West Bank or the latest terrorist bombing. Much as the cataclysms of violence had the potential to change the region, there was so much more there and after a while those stories felt endlessly repetitive.

The process of trying to understand the gap between the outside image and the internal reality proved more engaging, even exhilarating in its own way. The Middle East is a difficult region to grapple with. It has been on the wrong side of history for about the past 100 years. A deep cultural chasm separates it from the West; it is mired in suffocating bureaucracy, unhealthy nationalism, and a sense on some days that progress is unattainable. But despite its deadening inheritance of repression, I encountered people with real humanity, likable people whose work I admired and whose goals were uplifting. Some were political reformers, some were struggling for change through other fields. They were all inspiring.

▦   ▦   ▦

In Libya in early 2001, my two-week visa eventually expired and I had to leave, never to be allowed to return. Bilkheir, the Information Ministry bureaucrat, took exception to my descriptions of the Popular Committee meetings, declaring that I had "mocked Libyan democracy." Being completely banned from Libya was a disheartening fallout, no doubt, but I would not have written the article any other way. Since Bilkheir was the gatekeeper for all foreign journalists and had Qadhafi's ear, there was no going around him. He made a show of being polite whenever I ran into him at Arab summits in the ensuing years, but he never relented on the visa front. I hoped at some point he would change his mind so I could return to Brega, but so far he never has.

Perhaps it is best to leave the original Brega intact, preserved in my memory as if under glass—the perfect little beach town where our small front yard was crammed with sailboats on trailers and my father came home and ate lunch with me every day, a little Texas oil town inadvertently planted along the Mediterranean coast. In any case, the Brega of my childhood was long gone, as we always knew it would be one day—and there was no going back. I had always been a transient in my hometown. But in being thwarted from visiting Brega, I realized how my permanent sense that I was not from anywhere could be traced back to having grown up in a town not rooted in time or place. I was an expatriate no matter where I lived. Going back would not have changed that.

CHAPTER 3

THE GOOD LIFE

"Nothing compares to hashish."

HIZBOLLAH USED TO SEND ME birthday cards; or actually something more high tech—birthday emails, to be exact. The "Party of God," as the name translates in English, boasts a well-oiled public relations department, particularly if compared to virtually every drowsy government or semi-official organization in the Arab world. The first time I requested permission to report in prime Hizbollah country—i.e., Beirut's southern suburbs and the entire southern swath of Lebanon abutting Israel—the organization's press office handed me a form to complete that included various personal details ranging from my university degree to my birth date.

Then every year on my birthday a message popped up in my email from hizbollah@hizbollah.org. (Or at least the messages arrived until August 2006, at which point the Israelis were busy obliterating block after block of Beirut's southern suburbs in an

ill-starred war that they had inexplicably convinced themselves
would turn the Lebanese against the party.)

Here is the birthday message Hizbollah sent me in August 2003:

Dear Neil

On your birth day
I wish all the Joy your heart can hold
All the smiles a day can bring
All the blessings life unfold
May you have God's best in every thing

Happy birth day
Haidar Dikmak
Media Relations

When I first started reporting from the Middle East for the New York
Times, the only story that drew me to Beirut with any regularity was
Hizbollah. There was a certain irony in this, for the very same
bearded militants or their ilk had kept me away for so many years.

After graduating from Stanford with a degree in International
Relations, I decided that my next stop had to be an Arab capital to
finally learn to speak the language. In the summer of 1982, with
the civilian heart of Beirut under an Israeli military siege, the city
lacked a certain allure as the right place for a newcomer to sit
around studying verb conjugations. I headed for Cairo, not without
certain qualms about bypassing a major news story. I had other re-
grets, too. One favorite picture of my parents captured them out in
the town in Beirut, all dolled up and grinning widely. My father,
completely out of character, sports a tux, while my mother is wearing a dark, short-sleeved cocktail dress and a wig that I had never
seen before or since. They are sitting at a dinner table, waiting for
the floor show to begin at the Casino du Liban, a low white building still perched on a cliff just north of Beirut. The glamorous me-
mento had been snapped roughly a year before the Lebanese civil

war erupted in April 1975. They had gone on that trip alone to mark twenty-five years of marriage, my father replacing my mother's thin gold wedding band with a ring of diamonds from the Beirut bazaar. I had never been to Lebanon, but that picture had long given me a sense of missing something. Seeing it always reignited my desire to test the country's much ballyhooed mantra that on the same day you could both swim in the Mediterranean and ski the soaring, snow-capped peaks of the Lebanon range. The war had abruptly ended Beirut's reign as the capital of the good life. Still, I was always looking for signs of the resurrection of the cosmopolitan ideal that was Beirut, a Levantine city where for a brief time sect and tribe had been submerged, where being a Muslim or a Christian or a Jew was buried beneath the all-consuming task of minting money by serving as the crossroads where Western businessmen and newly oil-rich Arabs could interact comfortably.

I spent a couple years in Cairo and then returned to the States, working for a newspaper in upstate New York briefly before joining The Associated Press in New York City as an intern, counting the days until I was sent back to the Middle East. I knew a Beirut assignment was out of the question since Terry Anderson, the AP correspondent kidnapped there in 1985, was still being held hostage by Hizbollah's forebears. The AP barred its correspondents from even thinking about going to Lebanon. Most wire services and a smattering of other major newspapers and magazines had shuttered their Beirut news bureaus and transferred them to Nicosia, Cyprus. Just over 100 miles from the Lebanese coast, the island nation was close enough to monitor the war bulletins on the Beirut radio stations, which after so many years sounded like weather reports: "Significant shelling squalls near Aley, avoid the unsecured main roads."

My heart sank in the early spring of 1988, though, when the AP's foreign editor called me at home in New York to offer Nicosia. I had counted on some Arab city with a clamorous bazaar, a city where the call to prayer boomed out of the minarets five times a day and where important events happened, not some sleepy eastern Mediterranean outpost where the most momentous decision each night was whether to have octopus or squid as a dinner appetizer. I ended up writing or mostly editing stories about Lebanon from afar, slowly absorbing details about its politics, its food, the music of its most famous diva, Fayrouz, and its Arabic dialect.

The singer Fayrouz basically embodies Lebanon's history as it developed in the decades following World War II, the desire to be a cosmopolitan meeting ground where East and West melded together into something unique and widely admired. Hizbollah represents the newer reality of a region that has soured on the West. It's a militant organization rooted in local religious traditions and determined to supplant what it considers a repressive colonial hangover with muscular native power. The tension created by the fight between those two competing visions for the future has engulfed the Middle East for my entire adult life and remains unresolved.

During much of my time in Cyprus, Hassan Mroue, a charming, jovial colleague and a Fayrouz fanatic, despaired of ever convincing me that her singing was anything but caterwauling that grated on the nerves. Lebanon's civil war actually cemented Fayrouz's reputation as a beloved cultural symbol who remained above the brutish fighting between sects and parties. When shellfire ripped through Beirut and its residents cowered in their basements, radio stations of all political and religious persuasions tried to sooth jangled nerves by broadcasting her plaintive ode called "To Beirut." ("To Beirut, from my heart, salutations to Beirut . . . with its face like an old fisherman.") Throughout the war she stayed in the divided city, but refused to perform since people were not free to travel between the factional cantons. Any group that controlled the territory where she sang might try to claim her as their own. A Christian woman, she refused to take sides, registering her own protest that Beirut and indeed the region should practice tolerance. Naturally this endeared her even more to her legions of Muslim fans.

In Cyprus, I worked out a rough compromise with Hassan over Fayrouz's music. On lengthy weekend drives to the most distant beaches, he or one of my other Lebanese colleagues could play Fayrouz on the stereo as long as it served as a vocabulary lesson. I learned the words from each song as we explored the far reaches of the island. Gradually my Egyptian Arabic surrendered to the softer Lebanese. Egyptian Arabic overflows with much harder, sharper consonants and a far more staccato rhythm—Egyptians say "agnabi" for foreigner, with a hard "g," for example, while the Levantines say "ajnabi." The sensual quality of the Lebanese dialect alone seemed to confirm the country's reputation for being at the heart of all things dissolute. I eventually grew to love the music. That's how I found myself flying to Cairo to cover a live Fayrouz concert at the Pyramids, under the very nose of the Sphinx.

Fayrouz, a paragon of the highest forms of Arab music and poetry, had boycotted Egypt for a decade in line with the Arab decision to ostracize the country for signing a peace treaty with Israel. So the July 1989 Cairo concert was the first chance for Israeli Arabs to hear live a beloved diva whose songs were the unofficial anthems of Palestinian suffering. Some twenty-seven buses carrying 1,000 devotees rolled across the border from Israel for the event. When the Egyptian tax authorities noticed the hoards arriving, they doubled the tax bill for the three-night extravaganza. To pay it, the Syrian-Saudi producer from the wily Khashoggi clan just printed and sold thousands of new tickets, all stamped "Front Section." Naturally the rich Egyptians who paid about $95 per ticket, a princely sum, figured they could swan into their front-row seats at the very last second, so their chauffeured Mercedeses all pulled up at once at 11 P.M., when the concert was scheduled to start.

The crowd soon overflowed the limited seating. I was sitting near the front when two Egyptian matrons, swathed in silk and dripping gold, were bluntly informed that reserved seats had gone out with the Pharaohs and they should grab whatever chairs they could find. The two planted themselves right behind me and began to complain in vociferous tones about the uncouth peasants undoubtedly occupying their rightful and far better seats.

"Mish ma'oul! (It cannot be!)" one groused, "We paid 250 pounds to attend this concert and what do we find when we arrive? Animals in our seats!"

"You're wrong, my dear," her friend retorted. "Those aren't mere animals, those are beasts!"

The bedlam continued for hours, with all possible exits and any open space eventually crammed with chairs. A fire would have left a gruesome toll, but I thought a riot seemed the more imminent danger. Around 1 A.M., with patrons still pouring in and no seats available, the concert promoter emerged on stage and announced that he could reveal the source of all the confusion. There was a Zionist conspiracy afoot to undermine the concert! I laughed at this canard used to blame practically any unfortunate occurrence, including the weather. Members of the audience jumped from their precious seats to hurl insults, screaming at him to get his ugly, unwelcome face off the stage. "I should have donated my ticket money to a mosque!" one veiled woman yelled.

Fayrouz finally started singing three hours late, around 2 A.M., and by the time she finished just before dawn, members of the audience were in rapture. Having completely forgotten the earlier pandemonium, they pronounced the concert a resounding success.

Fayrouz's emergence as a singer paralleled Lebanon's transformation from a backwater of the Ottoman Empire to the vibrant financial and cultural heart of the Arab world, a rare oasis of tolerance that soon went up in flames. Born Nouhad Haddad in 1935, she was the daughter of a poor Greek Orthodox Christian typesetter. She was discovered at age 14 by the founder of Lebanon's music conservatory. He heard her sing at a public school, where he was scouting for a chorus for the new national radio station. An early mentor who considered her a rare gem dubbed her "Fayrouz," which means "turquoise" in Arabic. She met Assi Rahbani, a composer who became her husband, and his brother Mansour, a lyricist, at the radio station.

It was a time when Arab cities from Casablanca to Baghdad were filling with former villagers who wanted to shed their rural past and become more modern, more westernized. By combining Arab and European instruments with shorter compositions and Fayrouz's clear soprano, the trio revolutionized the region's music. "She made this wonderful mix of folkloric art and songs with European instruments and styles that was very appealing," Virginia Danielson, a music librarian and expert on the Middle East at Harvard University, told me. "The whole thing managed to be international, rural, and cosmopolitan at the same time."

It was also rendered in a voice unlike any other, because Fayrouz eliminated the nasal tones favored by most Arab singers. To me, her moody voice is reminiscent of Ella Fitzgerald or Billie Holiday, but using Oriental quarter tones.

A decade after her appearance at the Pyramids, I interviewed her again in 1999 in Las Vegas, where she performed at the MGM Grand Hotel before a roaring, weeping, clapping crowd of nearly 10,000 mostly Syrian and Lebanese expatriates. She told me both times that for many of her fans, her songs conjured up an idyllic Lebanon of simple villages and fertile vineyards that was gone, if it had ever existed. "When you look at Lebanon now, you see that it bears no resemblance to the Lebanon I sing about, so when we miss it, we look for it through the songs," she told me. "It's as if the songs have become their country."

Fayrouz maintained that her songs were not meant to carry any overt political messages. But the themes lent many of them a political shading. The song "We Will Return" ("We shall return to our village one day and drown in the warmth of hope") used to be the hymn of Palestinian refugees, but after Lebanon splintered, its émigrés adopted it as their own. In Syria in the 1960s, when rival military cliques staged repeated coups, each new junta signaled the change by broadcasting her song "Ask Me, Oh Damascus" as soon as it seized the official radio station. President Hafez al-Assad banned the song for a while after overthrowing the government in 1970 because broadcasting it was enough to spark rumors that he had been toppled. When she agreed to perform in Damascus for an Arab cultural festival in early 2008, her first concert there in more than two decades, a fierce national debate erupted in Lebanon. Opponents argued that it represented treason by endorsing the repressive Syrian regime that had done so much to undermine Lebanese autonomy, while supporters thought culture should remain above all that.

As a performer, Fayrouz presented a melancholic, rigid figure onstage. About five feet tall, dressed in a series of ball gowns that swept to the floor and covered her arms, she stood stock-still at the microphone. During a particularly stirring passage she might lift a hand slightly or twitch her shoulders. She rarely smiled. Talking to me, she laughed at the idea that even committed fans found her too serious. She told me that she has always been a shy performer, still wracked by stage fright, and tended to concentrate on singing more than on moving any part of her body. "If you look at my face while I am singing, you will see that I am not there, I am not in the place," she said. "I feel art is like prayer. I am not in church but I feel like I am, and in that atmosphere you can't laugh. And dance? If they saw me dancing they would kill themselves!"

I felt like I truly was making progress in appreciating the vibrant culture in the Middle East when I found myself playing Fayrouz as I made coffee in the morning, something of a ritual in myriad Arab households. I was getting far beyond that Brega fence, and certainly beyond the bloody headlines that so often consumed my attention. For Arabs at home and especially for the diaspora, no other vocalist evoked both the bygone rhythms of rural life and the halcyon, prosperous years before wars traumatized their region, sending many into exile.

"For us she is a legend," one Fayrouz fan in Las Vegas told me. He had left Lebanon for Canada as a student in 1971 and never returned. "It's like Americans talking about Frank Sinatra, who represents a certain era, a certain country, a certain vision of the world."

In Lebanon, many strove to resurrect that era, but it was gone, with a few reminders like the defunct St. George Hotel haunting the Beirut waterfront. The skeleton of the gutted hotel has remained largely untouched since 1975, when its last patrons fled in their limousines as the civil war erupted around them. The hotel had epitomized all that was fabulous about the Beirut of yore, the place where Elizabeth Taylor and Richard Burton rubbed elbows with spies, oil tycoons, Arab princes, and undoubtedly more than a few upscale prostitutes. The hotel's terrace had been the very soul of the city, the veritable crossroads where West met East, and the best place in Beirut to admire the view of both the mountains and the sea.

If Fayrouz was the greatest living epitome of that earlier era, it took me a couple trips to Lebanon before I understood that she had been replaced. The new icon was Hizbollah.

⬓　⬓　⬓

During my first stint as a correspondent in the region, I worked on stories about Lebanon week in and week out from my base in Cyprus with no hope of actually going there. The general ban for Americans and the specific one for AP employees held firm; anyone who went without permission risked being fired. Finally by the end of 1989, after some eighteen months, my hankering knew no bounds, and with a couple friends I plotted a sub-rosa visit. I went to the consulate with a Lebanese colleague from Reuters, Samia Nakhoul, and announced that we were engaged, but before the wedding could proceed we had to travel to one of Beirut's northern suburbs so her aged, sickly grandmother could give us her blessing. Visa in hand, I would jump on the overnight ferry from Cyprus and an AP colleague, Donna Abu-Nasr, would meet the boat to supervise the grand tour.

The first hurdle materialized in the office of the Lebanese consul. I was asked to fill out a bunch of forms specifying whom I was going to visit. The problem was that I couldn't remember Samia's surname. Frankly I barely knew her, and she was sitting five feet away filling out forms of her own. "What's your name?" I hissed as quietly as I could while smiling brightly at the consul and bemoaning the fact that we could not get married in Lebanon itself. I don't think I fooled her for an instant, but she was tickled enough by the idea of an American actually wanting to go to Lebanon while several of my fellow citizens were still hostages that I got the visa.

I was enthralled from the moment I arrived in late January 1990 in the harbor at Jounieh, the northern suburb that served as the gateway for Christians for much of the war because Beirut airport was on the Muslim side. As we docked, towering plumes of white smoke erupted in the hills as stray shells crashed down. To me they seemed more like an exuberant welcome than anything remotely dangerous.

Beirut is a stunning city—blessed at least geographically. Its downtown hugs the azure Mediterranean coastline and the residential neighborhoods crawl up into the pine-covered hills, which eventually rise sharply toward the soaring Lebanon range. Snow crowns the mountain tops much of the year. The slopes are an hour's drive north from Beirut's palm-lined thoroughfares.

I wandered from ancient ruins to ski slopes to night clubs. I started with a fine fish lunch at the small Phoenician port of Byblos, the walls covered with pictures of movie stars and singers from the go-go 1960s. Donna took souvenir snapshots of me standing in front of the "NO TANKS" sign on the freeway overpasses—the outline of a tank with a red slash through it. On the ski slopes the three ticket lines were divided into: "Adults, Children, Militias." From the slopes the stunning view reversed itself; you could see all the way down to the purplish Mediterranean from some of the lifts. That night at a disco in the Christian canton, revelers sang along with a new hit song written to the tune of Little Richard's "Tutti Frutti." This version mocked the warlords by name, with one stanza saying that Druze leader Walid Jumblatt's voice sounded like a "drat al-balaat" or "a fart on a floor tile." (Lyrics still proved a superb source for Arabic vocabulary.) It was frustrating that I couldn't write a word to reveal where I was, but at least I got a brief glimpse of how some Lebanese were trying to ignore the war.

Lulled by a sense of well-being, I dropped the initial idea of remaining in the Christian enclave and started trying to figure out how to get over to West Beirut, the heart of the city where all sects had intermingled. Beirut at that point was divided, in the endlessly repeated shorthand of the wire services, between "mainly Muslim west and Christian east." The western side was home to all the former news bureaus and the legendary Commodore Hotel. Famous institutions like AUB, the American University of Beirut, were all in the West, as were the kidnappers still holding Western hostages. A long artery of shattered, empty buildings and random earthworks contaminated with gunmen had severed the city for so long that trees sprouted along much of its length. It was called the Green Line. I longed to cross it, but the odds of a tall blond man making it through unmolested were considered poor. Every journalist I met snapped my picture. "Just in case you get kidnapped," they all said brightly.

I went as close as I could, walking a few paces into the major crossing near the shuttered National Museum, its interior Roman artifacts all encased in protective concrete. At the crossing, a Lebanese soldiers asked in English whether I was an American and when I said yes he responded "Airi bi Bush" in Arabic, or "Fuck Bush." (Literally "My dick in Bush," meaning Bush Sr. at the time.) This being the supposedly friendly, Christian side of the line, it was not a particularly auspicious omen about the possible welcome across the way.

Finally the father of another colleague, a monsignor in the Syrian Orthodox Church, heard of my wish and offered to drive me around the western side of the city, saying I would be safe since the militiamen left clerics alone. I headed over to his apartment, eagerly anticipating an excellent adventure. The monsignor caught his first sight of me from down the hallway of his apartment and his voice boomed out his instant verdict. "Too white!" he yelled.

I didn't make it into West Beirut until landing at the gleaming new airport eleven years later, in 2001. I went anticipating some version of the enchanted crossroads, of old Beirut. I kept looking for it, wandering down side streets and stumbling across the bullet-pocked signs of once famous nightclubs. The façades were still there, but inside many were just rubble and overgrown weeds. The city did not even have a bazaar, that most Oriental of symbols. The old ones were blown to bits and not yet replaced. It was oddly difficult to overcome the nostalgia for something I had never experienced, for an idea of a city that was clearly no longer there. My first clue about the different reality should have been that my editors were interested in Hizbollah and not much else.

I was introduced to Ghassan Salame, an erudite, amusing political science professor and then the Lebanese minister of culture, at the back of a movie theater where a new film by an Israeli-Palestinian director was about to premiere. Years later Salame became a United Nations political advisor in Baghdad after the invasion, a lone voice of reason among a sea of Americans and others who knew nothing about Iraq. "Here to write about the Party?" he asked me when we first met in Beirut, arching his eyebrows, his knowing smirk saying in sum, "Can't you American reporters find anything original to write about other than Hizbollah?"

I did, at times, but Hizbollah was hard to avoid. My often entertaining driver in Beirut, Hussein Alameh, naturally inspired the first story. (To my knowledge, there has never been a scientific study about how many feature stories from the Arab world originate with a stray remark from a driver, not to mention political analyses, but the percentage would be staggeringly high.)

"There was another sick American cow on Al-Manar news last night," Alameh told me one day, chuckling. "They said that the Americans are dumping inferior cows in Lebanon."

Al-Manar, or "The Lighthouse" in English, is Hizbollah's satellite television station. Its news reports were somewhat straightforward—a question of emphasis that lent the news a more subtle shading of the distinct anti-Israeli, anti-American tone that colored much of its regular programming. If an Israeli newspaper published a story about how the Palestinian uprising in the occupied territories was damaging Israel's economy, for example, Al-Manar would highlight the story. Since the government-controlled television stations in every Arab country would previously never have quoted an Israeli newspaper, Al-Manar's news took on a kind of "inside Israel" flavor that others lacked.

Given Hizbollah's flair for self-promotion—professional directors choreographed every major demonstration to create a piece of street theater—television was a natural extension of the organization's propaganda efforts. Recapturing Jerusalem was a key theme. The odds of Hizbollah being able to do it are nonexistent. But that was beside the point. The issue of Jerusalem—a city whose Arabic name, Al-Quds or Beit Al-Maqdis, literally means "holy"—touches ordinary Arabs emotionally. Sacred Muslim traditions hold just three cities worthy of pilgrimage—Mecca, Medina, and Jerusalem. Al-Aqsa mosque in Jerusalem's old city, a low-slung, plain structure overshadowed by the more famous and architecturally splendid Dome of the Rock, is considered the third most holy in the faith. Most Arabs cannot visit as long as the conflict endures.

Hizbollah has kept itself in the public eye and gained popularity by tying itself to the fate of Jerusalem and, by extension, the Palestinians. Nothing quite captured the prevailing popular sentiment like its television quiz show called The Mission, where the prize for the winner was a virtual trip to Jerusalem. I first heard about it from an American ambassador, who groused that Hizbollah had just started a game show called Name Your Favorite Terrorist.

Quick. What is the name of the Palestinian village near what is now the Israeli city of Ramla that was destroyed in 1949 and replaced by a town called Yavne?

Too difficult? It's Yibna. Try another.

What gray sandstone structure built in 1792 became the source of all oppressive decisions the world over? Need another hint? Its name is exactly the opposite of the black decisions made within its walls.

It should be easy now: the White House.

Contestants from around the Arab world and beyond competed each Saturday night for cash and the chance to win the Jerusalem trip by answering questions like these. To heighten the drama, points won translated directly into steps toward the holy city that were flashed onto a map of the region.

Some questions on *The Mission* did indeed focus on the Hizbollah men who carried out suicide operations, as the U.S. ambassador had complained. "The martyr Amar Hamoud was nicknamed 'The Sword of All Martyrs.' True or false?" True. The host, who never failed to weave the subject of recapturing Jerusalem through his patter, went on to describe the man's exploits.

"Any program at this television station must present the idea that the occupation of Palestine must end," said Ihab Abi Nassif, the high school physics teacher then in his late 20s who hosted the show. A handsome man, he was dressed in what passed for Tehran chic among Shiite Muslims—a dark blazer and plain, open-collared shirt with no tie, his beard a day or two of carefully trimmed black stubble. "That is the core issue, which is why we work day and night to keep it vivid in people's minds."

The game show was a tad more subtle than the channel's usual offerings. The program *Terrorists*, for example, played endless film loops showing Israeli attacks that killed Arab civilians. And *Sincere Men*, which drew its name from a Koranic verse about the strength of the faithful when facing battle, used a kind of breathless, you-are-there tone to profile either Hizbollah fighters who undertook suicide missions or those in waiting.

The Mission followed a standard game show format, with contestants quizzed about history, literature, geography, science, and the arts. But at least half the questions revolved around Palestinian or Islamic history, and usually at least one contestant was a Palestinian. "We wanted to put it into a form that would appeal to a wider segment of the population," Ibrahim Musawi, the director of the English news on Hizbollah, told me. "It is not in an ideological or a direct way, but in an entertaining way."

Mr. Abi Nassif, the host, attributed the show's success to Arabs identifying with the daily suffering of the Palestinians under occupation. He summed it up by quoting the famous Lebanese poet

Jibran Khalil Jibran: "'You might be able to forget the people you laugh with, but you will never be able to forget the people you cry with.' The history of the whole region is a history of suffering."

The theme of Palestinian suffering dovetailed neatly with a main pillar of the Shiite creed, that theirs is a long, sad history of oppression and anguish at the hands of greater powers. It was traditionally Sunni oppression, but the Jews worked just fine too. Some critics labeled Al-Manar unadulterated propaganda in this vein. They also believed that Hizbollah's backers, Iran and Syria, used the relatively free speech of Lebanon to promote hatreds they would not dare pronounce at home. I think that Manar at times brought out the worst in Arab propaganda—that all Jews are bad, all Americans bad, all Europeans bad. What made it interesting, though, was the slick packaging created to push the message.

The problem, said Waddah Sharara, a sociology professor at Lebanese University and the son of a prominent Shiite cleric from south Lebanon, was a certain penchant among many Arabs to follow demagogues rather than seek out truly independent sources of information. He decried the ability of such demagogues to enthrall the public with promises of restoring lost glory, rather than leaders who realistically assessed the Arab predicament and suggested manageable solutions to halt the region's drift. On *The Mission*, by dredging up questions that were not really much more than trivial pursuit in terms of the history of Israel, the West, and capitalism, the Party of God wanted to show that it was informed about areas outside Islam and thus could overcome them. "In this kind of society, those who make the greatest impression are the demagogues, the people who are the least subtle, who do not demand that people change," Sharara told me. "It's oversimplified."

It is worth remembering that the Shiites in southern Lebanon, thoroughly fed up with the violence fomented by the Palestine Liberation Organization and its despotic ways, welcomed the Israeli invasion in 1982. It was only when the Israeli army stuck around as an occupying force that the mood shifted 180 degrees. It is hard now to gauge just how much Hizbollah's constant barrage of anti-Israel, anti-Western propaganda resonates among Lebanese Shiites, who might be too intimidated to speak out against the organization. Sometimes when I was in small, private gatherings residents would disparage the group's hard-line stance. I'm sure some Lebanese Shiites would approve reaching a settlement to end the entire mess. To me, however, *The Mission* underscored why Hizbollah's propaganda efforts were so much more successful than those of Washington. Hizbollah tugged at heartstrings on the street. Washington tended to leave most of the discourse at the official level—a parade of secretaries of state or ambassadors sitting down with government ministers and then appearing briefly before the press microphones to issue platitudes about doing what was best for the Lebanese or Egyptian or Jordanian people. American attempts to do anything related to the people fell flat because they failed to present anything in a way that moved ordinary Arabs. Washington labeled Hizbollah a terrorist organization and Hizbollah responded by denigrating anything the United States tried to do in the region. The dairy cow program was a typical example.

⌸   ⌸   ⌸

I went to visit Hussein Jaafar, a former hashish farmer turned reluctant dairyman, thanks to U.S. anti-drug, pro-dairy intervention. Jaafar lived in Lebanon's central Bekaa valley, where he struggled to eke out a living from a half-dozen Pennsylvania milking cows while fervently wishing day and night for just one thing.

He longed to grow hashish again.

"Let them come and take their cows back wherever they came from," Jaafar, a thin man whose furrowed brow and receding black hair made him look older than his 32 years, told me with a plaintive look. "I will even forgive them my down payment. I swear if the government would let me grow just 500 square meters of hashish, I would sell them." Spring, the season when farmers once seeded their fields with cannabis and opium poppies, now banned, finds the Bekaa farmers facing their annual dilemma. Given their deep economic problems, farmers throughout the region itch to resurrect their outlaw traditions. Jaafar and many others described to me how the illicit crops literally made money grow on trees. The season went something like this: The farmers tossed out some seeds, periodically sprinkled a little water around if needed, and, without ever bothering to apply fertilizer or pesticides, sat back and watched the plants with their spiky leaves grow seven and eight feet tall. The drug crop was even pretty. During opium season the valley filled with poppies, mostly white, but scattered with red, purple, and gray. After the harvest, the farmers walked as far as the edge of their fields to collect wads of dollars from the brokers.

Jaafar lived just north of Baalbek, the capital of the Bekaa valley, a roughly two-hour drive over the mountains from Beirut. From above, just over the 5,100-foot Lebanon range, the Bekaa looks like a patchwork of rich green felt. After you descend and drive north, the valley grows more arid, the vegetation sparse. Rich red dirt stretches between the two mountain ranges that frame the valley. One reason the land was noticeably dry at the time was that Syria barred the Lebanese from lifting any water from the Orontes River that flowed northward into their territory.

Before the civil war, the city of Baalbek was known mainly for its annual summer music festival, held within the spectacular Roman ruins, the temple of Baal, which dominates the center of town. Louis Armstrong performed there, as did Joan Baez and the Bolshoi ballet. A charming little hotel, The Palmyra, sits right opposite the ruins. A few long, sun-dappled lunches I ate under the lofty pine trees shading its garden were among the best I ever experienced in the region. Jean Cocteau, visiting in the late 1950s, filled the walls of the now sagging establishment with dozens of exuberant drawings, and if I squinted my eyes a little bit I could feel like I was back in the pre-war era, when a musical starring Fayrouz was often the festival's annual highlight. Her debut there in 1957 had launched her career.

During the civil war the Bekaa had gained notoriety for other things—namely, Hizbollah, hostages, and hashish. Immediately before I arrived back in the region as a correspondent for the *Times*, Hizbollah had started trying to transform itself from just another guerrilla movement into a multifaceted political party. Its charismatic leader, Sayyid Hassan Nasrallah, a Shiite cleric, began running the party in the early 1990s at the young age of 32. He gained huge credibility throughout the region when his oldest son, Hadi, 18, was killed in a 1997 skirmish with Israeli forces along the edge of the strip of southern Lebanon they occupied. Most of Lebanon's feudal families sent their sons off to Europe and the United States for schooling and certainly never deployed them on the front lines.

A small picture of Hadi and another of the ubiquitous Dome of the Rock were among the few decorations in the reception area where I sat before I first interviewed Nasrallah toward the end of 2002. Photographer James Hill and I had been made to wait elsewhere in Beirut's southern suburbs and then driven in the dark in a van whose windows were covered with black curtains so we could not tell how we got to the barricaded apartment complex housing his offices.

I should point out that "suburbs" is something of a misnomer, at least in the American sense of the word. They do lie outside the Beirut city limits, along the road south to the airport, but are not exactly bucolic. Well-built apartment houses crowd closely together in an area alternatively described as slums, which I also consider an overly grim description when compared to the Dickensian conditions that the poor endure in mega-cities like Cairo. The most visible difference between Beirut's southern suburbs and its downtown was that every street was a mad jumble of electrical wires overhead, like a web woven by a spider who had lost its ability to spin a coherent pattern. Residents stole electricity from the main grid and since it was Hizbollah turf, there was nothing the Lebanese government could do. Israeli bombers obliterated entire blocks in 2006, but Hizbollah soon replaced them.

As a journalist, I needed Hizbollah's express permission to work anywhere in the neighborhood. Many journalists discovered just how closely monitored those seemingly ordinary streets were when they tried to photograph anything without permission from Hizbollah's media relations department. Bearded, black-clad militiamen materialized instantly from nowhere and confiscated their film. When I went to interview Nasrallah, security agents examined everything I would take into the room more thoroughly than in any other place I'd ever been, including each of my pens.

Nasrallah's slight lisp softens his somewhat severe look and inflammatory rhetoric. When I asked him about Hizbollah being designated a terrorist organization, he lashed out at the United States. "The United States, claiming possible threats to its own security, is making it legitimate to attack any potential threat anywhere in the world, yet they don't accept from the Palestinians or the Lebanese—whose land is being occupied and aggressively targeted, whose homes and fields are being confiscated—they don't accept that these people, the Lebanese and the Palestinians, take up arms to defend their own land.

"These are unacceptable double standards and illegitimate. You don't have to look very far for the reason why the hatred for the United States is spreading in the Arab and Islamic world." Repeated car-bombings and other Hizbollah assaults had forced the Israelis to withdraw from southern Lebanon in 2000, gaining the party and its leader unique credibility across a region where soaring promises were rarely matched by actual deeds.

Domestically, Hizbollah's newer successes came by championing the impoverished, including Lebanon's long-neglected farmers, often via its public works arm, the Jihad for Construction. "Jihad" is frequently translated as "holy war" in the West, but broadly interpreted it actually means any effort that might shine in the eyes of God. Jihad for Construction was on the case of the American dairy cows.

"We hear a lot of complaints from the farmers," Mohamed al-Khansa, the director of an experimental Bekaa farm set up by the

Jihad, told me. "Mainly that the American cows are not acclimatizing and not producing milk at the promised level. Many people say that the Americans would obviously not send their best cows to Lebanon." Those on the American side were quick to dismiss the Jihad farm outreach program. Marwan Sidani, the earnest agriculture engineer who directed the dairy improvement program, served as the liaison between the Ministry of Agriculture and the U.S. Agency for International Development. He told me that Hizbollah basically helped a limited number of its political supporters, while using the television station to broadly attack the U.S. "All they really want to do is to show that the U.S. cows are no good," he groused.

The dairy program was competing with the Bekaa region's dope-growing tradition, which stretched back at least 100 years, when Lebanon's Ottoman overlords, hardly immune to the allure of hashish, encouraged its cultivation. Farmers' eyes glistened with nostalgia as they described stacking their dollars in piles, and more than one recounted to me the story of some Americans who built a temporary runway in the valley, landing single-engine planes crammed with Smith & Wesson revolvers to trade for hashish. Now that was real American aid!

The civil war naturally proved something of a golden age for illicit crops. Hashish and the newly introduced opium poppy melded well with other dubious activities such as training militias, smuggling low-cost electronics into neighboring Syria, and occasionally hiding kidnapped Westerners. By the end of the war in 1990, an estimated 75,000 acres, or one-third of the valley's arable land, was devoted to hashish or opium, according to United Nations estimates. The two crops earned the Bekaa farmers roughly $80 million a year, or some $1,500 per capita.

By 1994, it was all gone. The Lebanese and Syrian governments decided after the war that if they could get off one American blacklist, it was the drug production list. But frustration set in quickly among the farmers because none of the promised replacements proved viable. Either the crops had trouble growing in the valley's fertile yet dry soil, or the government failed to help in marketing, or the price was too low. "The farmers could sell a kilo of hashish for $300 cash, how can you compare it to a kilo of potatoes for 20 cents?" Sidani told me. "Nothing compares to hashish."

Enter the American dairy cow. Starting in 1997, Lebanon paid $6 million for 3,000 American dairy cows delivered over four years to 1,000 farmers, one-third of them in the Bekaa. The program was extended for a further three years, with 5,000 cows coming for $10 million. The American government, unbelievably miserly in some of its aid programs, had chipped in a meager $1 million in aid for basic stuff like teaching farmers how to feed and milk the animals. The rest had to be paid back. Problems were manifold. Feed, for example, was largely imported and expensive, so some farmers gave their cows straw. This lowered milk production, yet the farmers blamed the cows.

Jaafar, the erstwhile hash farmer, told me that he spent almost no time on his five acres during the halcyon days of hashish and still earned around $30,000 a year, enough to build a sturdy, two-bedroom house, buy a car, and smoke real Marlboros. By the time I met him, he had taken to driving a school bus in the morning to help make ends meet and spent the rest of the time with his cows, who needed to be fed, nurtured, birthed, and, most important, milked each day. He had forsaken Marlboros and couldn't afford the $400 he needed to install tiles over his home's raw cement floors.

"When I got the first cow, I wasn't terribly happy with the idea of having a cow, but I thought at least I could live off it," he told me.

Jaafar's neighbor, Moheeb Lakis, moaned that in the hashish era the farmers had never heard of second-hand clothes. "Now everybody is buying second-hand clothes, no more Armani and Versace," he told me. Nothing wounds Lebanese pride quite like being too poor to afford Italian designers. They may go hungry, they may not have a stick of furniture in their houses, but many find no sacrifice too great to have the right car and the right clothes.

The woes of Lebanon's farmers reached Tehran, which stepped in with a more generous offer. An Iranian delegation showed up in Beirut offering $50 million in farm aid, including a farm credit program and food processing factories, as well as technicians to train the Lebanese in fish farming, bee-keeping, and improved mechanization. Plus cows, of course. Their cows cost $1,000 a head, $900 less than the American bovines. Officials on the American side muttered darkly that Iranian cows carried rift valley fever and produced far less milk.

Part of Hizbollah's appeal is that it preaches self-sufficiency, rejecting any form of colonialism, even indirect. It's a good line, if not exactly accurate. Iran kept the organization afloat, although businesses like a chain of gas stations helped Hizbollah grow less dependent on Iranian largesse. Hizbollah officials tried to justify the subsidies by telling me that Iranian aid money was not tainted because it came from fellow Muslims.

The cow vs. cow competition was a telling example of how the political rivalry between competing visions of the future played out on the ground, removed from the standard rhetorical jousting between Tehran and Washington. American aid might sound generous, but usually came with multiple strings attached and seemed basically designed to recycle the money back to American businesses. The dairy cow saga is typical in that way because it helped U.S. dairy farmers sell surplus cows. I found that American aid often engenders just as much resentment as goodwill—it rarely comes across as even remotely driven by the spirit of generosity. Back in the 1960s the U.S. government might have had a reputation for bounty through programs like one that delivered free milk to Moroccan schoolchildren, but now Americans are considered cheap.

That U.S. image problem in the Middle East is compounded by the fact that Israel is such a notable exception to otherwise tight-fisted government aid. Israel should receive about $2.6 billion in military aid in 2009 from U.S. taxpayers—even though United Nations statistics rank it among the top twenty-five richest nations on earth with a per capita income larger than some European nations like Portugal. In addition, it gets wide discretion to spend nearly $700 million of the money on purchases from its own defense industry and almost unfettered leeway in what U.S. weapons systems it can obtain. Egypt comes in second in terms of receiving U.S. aid at around $1.3 billion in military aid for 2009 and another $200 million in economic aid, with the latter gradually sinking. The aid started as a reward for signing a peace treaty with Israel in 1979. But Egypt complains endlessly that Israel gets a much freer hand in terms of the weapons systems it buys, plus the Egyptians must use a rigid system of contracts that basically funnels the money back through American companies. Officials and press reports often highlight this difference, so the money does little to improve relations at the public level.

I ran into variations of this issue all the time while wandering around the Middle East, concluding that the United States could definitely enhance its image by being more charitable. But instead of focusing on expanding tangible benefits, Washington tended to dream up stuff like ill-starred advertising campaigns or a U.S.-funded Arabic-language satellite television news channel that failed to draw much of an audience. It seemed to think slogans could change its image, not substance.

In Lebanon, dire poverty was driving many farmers back to cultivating drugs. Some confessed to me that they were limiting it to garden plots, swearing to the police that they merely wanted the seeds as bird food because it prompted such sweet warbling from their pet canaries. "In the days of hashish we were so happy," one farmer told me, adding with wry humor, "I once owned a car, but now, thanks be to God, I have a cow!"

The skirmishing over the cows was just one narrow slice of a much larger battle for influence in Lebanon and the wider region. The struggle over Lebanon after Hariri's 2005 assassination brought to the surface the long fight over how the Lebanese see themselves. Massive street demonstration pitted his supporters, who supported resurrecting the old idea of the Middle East, against Hizbollah and its allies.

Hariri was a Sunni Muslim who believed in Arab causes, but many Lebanese, particularly Christians, who consider themselves misplaced Europeans, identified with him. He was a self-made billionaire real-estate tycoon. He wore good suits, smoked expensive cigars, spoke three languages fluently, and lunched with the president of France regularly. He was almost single-handedly trying to resurrect Beirut to become the financial and tourism Mecca it had been before the civil war. He ran up some $35 billion in public debt doing it—but the Lebanese habitually live far beyond their means.

After his death, the street demonstrations by Lebanese blaming Syria for the killing gave the country's Western allies the leverage they needed to force a withdrawal of the Syrian troops there for almost thirty years. Participants called it the Cedar Revolution, after the tree that is the country's national symbol and adorns its flag. It was a name dreamed up in Washington, and one I could never bring myself to write in any story. The political protests did not seem to be anything remotely resembling a revolution. Nobody was demanding a fundamental reordering of the outdated division of spoils that allotted political power to various sects according to circa 1940 population numbers. Nobody expected an end to the dominance of feudal families who divided up political power and patronage among themselves. The system was not changing in the least. The only group bent on change seemed to be Hizbollah, who were countering the long-standing marginalization of the Shiites by winning more and more seats in parliament.

My unease about writing the words "Cedar Revolution" was confirmed in an odd way a couple months later, after the massive street demonstrations. I was back in Beirut around May 2005 and spent an evening with some friends at The Music Hall, a popular nightclub that often presented live music. The stage that night was crammed with musicians playing all the songs the Lebanese had been singing during their protests, complete with performers waving Lebanese flags and other red and white banners dreamed up for the protests by a polished advertising agency. The audience clapped along between drinking and eating. I sat there thinking that in a matter of weeks the glorious Cedar Revolution had gone from being a demand for change to a rousing cabaret floor show. I had once asked my great friend Nuha Radi, an Iraqi painter and writer with a dry wit who died of leukemia in 2004, whether Beirut really had lived up to its reputation as the center of intellectual ferment in the years before the war. "To me it seemed like one long cocktail party," she snorted dismissively. "I never understood what the fuss was about." Turning a "revolution" into a frivolous cabaret show within a matter of weeks made it seem to me that the cocktail party was still going strong.

Yet in another way things were manifestly different. The exact moment when I knew something had shifted, that the Lebanon exemplified by Fayrouz and that picture of my parents was extinct, came about in the weeks after Hariri's assassination in 2005. Both supporters and opponents of the Syrian role in Lebanon had been staging gradually larger and larger street demonstrations. Nasrallah, attempting to pull off the mother of all demonstrations, finally called all his supporters to rally in downtown Beirut in a show of solidarity with Damascus. This was unusual for him; such marches were normally staged only in Beirut neighborhoods or southern cities where Hizbollah controlled the security.

I was standing at the top of Bank Street in the very heart of downtown, watching the crowds walking slowly past the country's premier financial institutions, roughly a dozen banks that reportedly held up to $85 billion in funds from around the region. It was an area gradually being revitalized, full of outdoor restaurants I frequented after long hours of reporting and writing. I heard a sudden dull roar behind me, I thought from the direction of the restored hilltop palace that houses the offices of the prime minister. But when I spun around I saw a phalanx of Shiite clergymen emerge from one of the expensive underpasses that the Hariri government had built to speed travelers past all the poorer Shiite neighborhoods near the airport and into the city center.

Shiite clerics wear a distinctive garb that sets them apart from other Muslim religious sheikhs—a softly wrapped white or black turban as well as a long, smooth woolen cloak that snaps shut behind a stiff collar and cuts diagonally across the front of their bodies. As I watched, row after row of these clerics, around twenty across and all linking arms, marched silently out of the tunnel in one unbroken wave. They arrived with so little warning that I felt they had sprung whole from the earth. I just stood there gaping as two distinct worlds—the moneyed quiet of the downtown and the clamor of the impoverished Shiite neighborhoods—suddenly merged. Behind the clerics flowed a sea of chanting Shiites, many waving Lebanese flags. They had left at home that day their infamous Hizbollah flags—a green fist grasping a Kalashnikov rifle against a yellow background. Their waving the national flag was designed to signal that they were just as Lebanese as everyone else and had a right to be on Bank Street. It was as if the old Beirut, the Beirut of banks and the Casino du Liban floor show, was fading into the past with one giant whoosh right before my very eyes. It made me distinctly uneasy, in the way that watching an earthquake made my nerves jangle momentarily because it broke the pattern of the way the earth was supposed to act.

Hizbollah's emergence during the civil war, along with another now weakened Shiite party, Amal, gave the Shiite underclass its first substantial voice, and the mass presence downtown signaled that the clock could not be set back. The once downtrodden and ignored Shiites were not going to cede turf to the more secular, more westernized coalition of Christians, Sunni Muslims, and Druze. The strength of numbers shocked the other communities. From the gilded youth who usually frequented downtown, I harvested numerous quotes of the "Who are these people?" variety, invariably accompanied by a crinkling of the nose as if they had smelled something bad. The Hizbollah march left some Lebanese markedly uneasy that an alien state peopled by fundamentalists had somehow blossomed in their midst. It showed how little sects intermingled in Beirut after the war because the one great melting pot, the bazaars and the immediate neighborhood around them, was gone. "There is a whole generation who had a sort of curtain in front of their eyes, who did not realize that this country was not only theirs," said Ghassan Tueni, the retired publisher of *An-Nahar* newspaper, whose son and heir Gibran was later assassinated in the underground war that erupted after the Syrian expulsion.

Top Hizbollah clerics, including Nasrallah himself, had told me repeatedly that the party harbored no illusions about trying to impose Shiite Islamic law on Lebanon—the population of the country was just too diverse for all women to be veiled, for example. Sure, they might slap thick white sheets of paper over half-exposed breasts on the billboards advertising bras that could be seen from their neighborhoods, but forcing the country to follow suit was a different matter. "We don't think in a sectarian manner," Nasrallah had told me when I interviewed him. I didn't quite believe him— protecting Shiite interests inspired everything Hizbollah undertook. But there was no evidence that a fanatical core could impose its beliefs on all the rest.

During the mass demonstration, the final flourish naturally came from Nasrallah, wearing the black turban that denoted him a descendant of the same clan as the Prophet Mohamed, speaking from a balcony right above the terribly trendy Buddha Bar. Nasrallah mocked the idea of a sweeping revolution, and he vowed that the country would not descend back into anarchy. "Let us hold dialogue, an interior and international dialogue," he said. "Lebanon is an exceptional case. Lebanon is not Somalia nor Ukraine nor Georgia. If some people believe that they can topple Lebanon's government, security, stability and strategic choices through some demonstrations, slogans and media, they are wrong." He went on: "Lebanon cannot be built but with the cooperation of its citizens and dialogue between all its factions, as no one can impose on us his choices through words or even weapons. The country will be lost if it loses dialogue and accord; and if the country is lost, all of us will be lost."

Some analysts took heart at that. In previous years the Lebanese had tried to settle their differences with arms, each sect fielding a militia in order to stake its claim to turf and to segments of the economy. Nasrallah's words promised that if change was going to come, it would not be through militias or the armies of Western allies who had interfered in Lebanon in so many ways in the past. It was a scary prospect to many, of course, because the man arguing it was an ally of Syria and Iran, two countries with rather less-than-stellar democratic credentials. More important, it was easy for him to say because Hizbollah was the only militia that had refused to give up its arms, claiming they were needed to defend Lebanon from Israel. In fact, its gunmen later deployed on Beirut's streets in May 2008, handily winning a face-off with other domestic forces and confirming some people's fears of how Nasrallah really meant to conduct "dialogue."

Nasrallah's stance left open the question that remains unanswered across the region. Are Hizbollah and its ilk religious organizations using politics to spread the faith, or are they political parties operating under the cover of religion? If they are political parties, they could go the democratic route and accept pluralism. But if they are religious, they might well impose their own form of despotism, claiming a divine mandate. The tension from that murky struggle spills across every arena, like a slowly billowing cloud of dust that gradually envelops all in its path. Neither politics nor culture nor even mundane matters like food or clothing are immune from the debate over whether a line should divide religion from any aspect of life. One of the most vociferous, visible battlegrounds to which I paid keen attention on that score was television.

CHAPTER 4

SATELLITE TV

"If it starts with a kiss, where will it end?"

I FLEW OUT OF BAGHDAD just days before the 2003 invasion, terribly disappointed to be leaving the historic city on the eve of an epic story. Yet I had resigned myself to the fact that I no longer belonged on any battlefield. My time reporting from dodgy places like Iraq or Kabul or Sarajevo or Gaza was over. The most dangerous spot on earth for me turned out to be Fifth Avenue, a few blocks south of the Empire State Building, where a runaway bus knocked me off my bicycle on October 2, 1997. After I emerged from a coma, doctors at Bellevue Hospital's renowned emergency room told me that of all their myriad trauma cases, no one had flirted so closely with death, then cheated it. I'm certain that was due to their heroic efforts. But it took me three years to be able to walk unassisted, and too many body parts were either missing or damaged for me to do combat reporting with ease.

At the Ministry of Information in Baghdad, the Iraqis who chaperoned the foreign press had expressed some utterly uncharacteristic regret about my departure. Given the horrific carnage that has since enveloped Baghdad, the daily headache of dealing with minders seems almost charming now. But at the time they were the bane of my existence. My last transgression had been writing an unflattering piece about the naïve, ill-informed American and other anti-war activists showing up in Baghdad to serve as "peace shields" stationed at key strategic targets like power plants. Some of the peaceniks took a dim view of the article and produced an inflammatory tract accusing me of unfair coverage endorsing an invasion. "The *New York Times* has written 'People in Iraq want *WAR!*'" screamed one headline on the flier.

They plastered about fifty such screeds all over the exterior and interior walls of the warren of offices on the first floor of the Ministry of Information high-rise. The Iraqi government forced the entire foreign press corps to work there. Yet I had somehow managed to avoid the place for much of that particular day. Toward dusk, as my driver eased his white Toyota to a stop outside the main entrance and I got out, several other journalists shot me sympathetic looks, asking darkly whether my visa had been revoked. I had absolutely no idea what they were talking about. After reading the first poster, I felt my stomach lurch. Everyone reporting from Iraq was always a little on edge. Permission to stay was a constant battle, so having any article brought to the attention of officialdom was rarely helpful. Just the day before, I had watched the director of the foreign press office, Uday al-Ta'i, order a reporter who had referred to the Iraqi president in print as "Saddam" be thrown out. Reading aloud from a stack of the man's work, every time he reached the word "Saddam" the director bellowed, "Is he his friend?"

So I walked around and started tearing all the fliers down, even the ones on the glass doors of the director's office. One of his minions told me to stop, saying I had no right. "Don't you believe in free speech?" he shouted at me. It was laughable, admittedly, but I told him that the posters weren't true and kept tearing them down.

After that, the Iraqis pushed me to leave every single day, until my *Times* colleague John Burns finagled his way to Baghdad for the war with a visa of rather dubious provenance, as he put it. If they disliked my coverage, they really disliked his. None of us mustered quite the proper reverence for the Baath system, but with his arrival their disposition became downright sunny toward me. I was pulled aside and told that I would no longer have visa problems; in fact, all my troubles gaining access to Iraqi officials would evaporate entirely. All I had to do was agree to stay so they had a handy excuse to expel him—newspapers were limited to one correspondent at a time. They swore I wouldn't even have to bribe them! They would be so happy to do it that they would waive their usual laundry list of rapacious fees. I demurred.

I decided to spend the war in Damascus, writing about how the invasion was playing across the Arab world. Syria's capital seemed the most logical choice. First, it billed itself as "the beating heart of the Arabs," plus its Baathist regime was a somewhat less ghoulish version of the one toppling in Baghdad. Once there, I scored the first interviews with the mostly young, Koran-thumping zealots from other Arab countries heading across the border to fight the Americans. The buses taking them proved amazingly easy to find. At first they left from the Iraqi Embassy, which was handily located right across the street from the American Embassy. The Syrian government soon decided to move them downtown, not least due to outraged protests from U.S. Ambassador Ted Khattouf.

It was a tricky story to write because the Syrians did not want the volunteers covered, and hence the Syrian correspondents for Arab satellite channels or international wire services avoided the topic. I knew that if I broke the story first the government might well boot me out, but I had to have official comment. So I called Buthaina al-Shaaban, who was then the Foreign Ministry's spokesperson. To her credit and much unlike most so-called spokespeople around the region, Shaaban handed out her cell number and would take any question. But the morning I called, her only response was "There are no such buses."

My dilemma was that if I went ahead and published all the interviews and pictures I had, I would not only be exposing the tide of foreign fighters Syria was aiding, but I would also make the government spokeswoman look like either a liar or a fool. Any visa extension would definitely be doomed and I felt that staying in Damascus would keep me as close to any action as I could be. In those early days, there was talk of Syria being the next target. After debating what to do for the rest of the day, I finally called Shaaban back at home late that night and, telling a small white lie, informed her that I had seen a short wire story about foreign fighters transiting Syria, that the State Department was grumbling about the buses and my bosses were demanding that I file something for the next day's paper. I held my breath. At first she told me that she was unwilling to discuss the topic any further, but I knew my stay in Damascus depended on getting a response so I kept pressing. Finally she said something brief about how it was beyond the government's control if volunteers wanted to go to Iraq, and given the killing being visited on Iraqis by U.S. forces, the surprising thing was that Syria was not overwhelmed with volunteers. I had my response!

When it appeared on the front page the next day, the Ministry of Information expelled the freelance photographer working for the *Times*—to my knowledge he never got another visa—and the secret police hauled in my driver for hours of interrogation, leaving him so shaken that he refused to work for me again for five years. But I was allowed to stay.

Shaaban went on to become a Cabinet minister. When I asked Shaaban's successor at the foreign ministry for her cell number, she refused, saying, "If I have anything to say, I will call you." Needless to say, I never heard from her.

Syria and other Arab governments constantly accuse the Western press of presenting everything from Israel's point of view, while ignoring the Arabs. Yet the Syrian foreign minister, Farouq al-Sharaa, rejected every single interview request I submitted for the *Times* over the five years that I was the *Times* correspondent in the region. When I pointed out to senior Syrian or other Arab officials that they might actually talk to the press if they wanted their viewpoint covered, they claimed that they shouldn't have to sell their side because Arab lands were occupied and therefore morality should guide the reporters to making their arguments for them.

As American tanks rumbled across Iraq at speed, I spent day after day analyzing Arab coverage of the invasion on television. Given its reach, television is evidently a key arena in the process of change across the Middle East. I tried to watch as much as possible as I went from country to country. I always found it an important barometer in so many of the fights stirring Arab society—modernity vs. tradition, free speech vs. censorship, intolerance vs. pluralism, reality vs. propaganda. News stations were ground-zero of this tension, but the battle lines extended all across the television dial.

Sitting in my room at the Cham Palace Hotel in Damascus, I would intersperse bouts of channel surfing with endless phone calls to university professors, newspaper columnists, various analysts, and friends around the Arab world. One night I reached Khalid M. Batarfi, the managing editor of *Al-Madina* newspaper in Jidda, Saudi Arabia. He had been sitting around with a group of twenty or so other Saudi men, flipping through television channels to soak up every war report available. I had always found Batarfi—a slight man with an easy smile—extremely open-minded on any topic. As an analyst he offered the added advantage of salting his remarks with references to American popular culture, having obtained a doctorate in journalism and political science from the University of Oregon.

He and his friends had been sitting in a "majlis," a kind of male clubhouse included in practically every Saudi home, where the basic furnishings always consist of couches or cushions lining the walls, thick carpeting, and as big a television as the owner can afford. It's a room set apart from the rest of the house where any Saudi man can have his friends over to talk politics, eat dinner, play cards, watch the news or sports, etc., without risk of them mingling with the women of the household. Batarfi caught me off guard with the scene he described in Jidda on this particular evening in late March, about ten days into the invasion.

He and his Saudi friends were pulling for Saddam. "Whenever he appeared on television before, everyone said they couldn't wait for the day when he'd be dead," Batarfi told me. "Now when he appears we say, 'Oh God, please grant him a few more weeks.' We want Saddam Hussein to go and we expect him to go eventually, but we want him to hold on a little longer because we want to teach the Americans a lesson. Arab pride is at stake here. American propaganda said it was going to be so quick and easy, meaning we Arabs are weak and unable to fight. It's like a Mike Tyson fight against some weak guy. They don't want the weak guy to be knocked out in the first forty seconds."

That conversation proved to be a startling window into the common regional perception, particularly since it was coming from a man who both was educated in the United States and professed a genuine respect for its values. When the U.S. is seen as acting like a schoolyard bully, even its friends harbor a certain admiration for anyone willing to stand up to it. One reason the invasion of Iraq was never viewed in any favorable light, even among those fully aware of Saddam's record, is that no one believed Washington's rationale that it was done to help the Iraqi people. The idea that Americans stand up for the little guy or for principles is dead; the U.S. is always seen as promoting its self-interests. In this case the most popular perception was that Washington wanted to undermine Iraq because it was considered the strongest military threat to Israel and an alternative oil source to Saudi Arabia.

Virtually everyone I reached that night and on many subsequent nights was glued to the TV news. Most were watching Al-Jazeera, whose audience of some 40 million viewers across the region and beyond made it by far the most popular Arab satellite channel. Sawsan al-Shaer—a smart, trenchant Bahraini columnist—made me laugh by explaining she could stand only so much of the nationalistic, pan-Arab, and often religious rhetoric on Al-Jazeera, particularly from its talk-show hosts and their guests. When she felt her blood pressure going off the charts, she switched to the Kuwaiti satellite channel, where she found the commentary the television equivalent of Valium. Kuwait TV always described the invasion as going swimmingly and the Americans being welcomed with open arms, much as they had been in Kuwait in 1991.

Shaer predicted more or less what unrolled over the coming years, that the invasion would blast open the long-buried Pandora's box of sectarian differences, bringing both a heavy domestic toll and the rise of the mullahs. It was a perspective sorely lacking from the American networks all trying to outdo each other in cheerleading about the U.S. forces steamrolling toward Baghdad. The need to pull back and provide a larger perspective proved to be the main casualty of embedding so many correspondents with the military.

▣ ▣ ▣

Al-Jazeera's coverage of the Arab world, not just during the invasion of Iraq, unquestionably altered the news landscape for the better. The range of criticism against repressive governments, the sheer number of opposition voices never heard before, and the wide focus on socially taboo subjects such as police torture or spousal abuse started with Al-Jazeera. It was like seeing a city rise where there had been only desert before. Al-Jazeera cracked the obsessive monopoly Arab governments maintained on deciding what their people needed to know and when they needed to know it, plus the station opened the airwaves to a whole class of analysts and dissidents who had previously labored in obscurity. When Iraq invaded Kuwait in 1990, to take just one infamous example, the media in Saudi Arabia did not report the event for some three days. Iraq had not only invaded a neighboring country and deposed its ruling family, but Saddam's battalions were now camped at the Saudi border. Yet the heavy government hand controlling the Saudi television, radio, and newspapers ensured that nothing was said. Only Saudis who listened to foreign radio broadcasts like BBC World Service from London or had an illegal satellite dish to watch CNN and other foreign stations knew about it.

⊡   ⊡   ⊡

Al-Jazeera, founded in 1996 by the emir who ruled Qatar, Hamad bin Khalifa al-Thani, fomented an earthquake. The station came into being because the ruling prince, having just tossed out his father in an extraordinary palace coup, was determined to put his tiny, fabulously wealthy emirate on the international map. "Al-Jazeera" is Arabic for the peninsula—the Arabian peninsula—where Qatar is a Lilliputian thumb sticking into the Persian Gulf off the far greater mass of Saudi Arabia. The al-Saud dynasty mutes most criticism about its rule by buying up all media. Major pan-Arab newspapers like *Al-Hayat* and *Al-Sharq Al-Awsat*, edited in London for years, are Saudi owned. Arab reporters jokingly lament the fact that they used to bribe individual reporters—until they discovered the economy of scale that comes from owning the entire newspaper! The papers avoid even gentle criticism of the royal family, much less any discussion of its grasping ways. In 2007, for example, British press reports said that a British company that produces jet fighters might have paid as much as $2 billion in bribes to Prince Bandar bin Sultan, the former Saudi ambassador to Washington and the son of Prince Sultan, the kingdom's defense minister for four decades. The main Arab newspapers based in London ignored the accusations until Prince Bandar eventually issued a denial through the government-run Saudi Press Agency (SPA). The Saudi papers printed the denial while still glossing over the original accusation. Saudi journalists derisively dismissed the role of the official news agency by calling it the Sleeping People's Association, a label that could be applied to every official news agency in the region.

In the mid-1990s, a joint venture with the BBC to establish an Arabic television news channel quickly collapsed because the Saudis tried to censor content. So the Qataris hired a core of highly competitive veterans from the BBC's Arabic service to run their new station. Those journalists blasted away the cobwebs hobbling news in the region—reporting events in real time, interviewing Israeli officials about developments in the Palestinian territories, lending opposition figures in exile a platform to voice their views about the situation under despotic rulers at home. The station horrified and angered Arab dictators used to exercising complete control over the news, and they scrambled to find the means to silence it. Many shuttered the Jazeera bureaux in their capitals or periodically tossed its employees into jail. At various times the governments in Algeria, Tunisia, Kuwait, Bahrain, Saudi Arabia, Iraq, and Jordan closed Jazeera bureaux and barred its reporters from working. Egypt arrested a correspondent working on a documentary about police torture. At one time the closures were so extensive that an Iraqi reporter joked that it might end up being the only Arab satellite station with no bureaux operating in the Arab world.

Probably nothing accentuated the station's effectiveness more than the Arab League effort at the beginning of 2008 to find a collective means to muzzle Al-Jazeera. The Arab ministers of information—a band of dinosaurs from Soviet-inspired days, if ever there was one—got together in Cairo to agree on a "Charter of Principles" for satellite broadcasts. Although the charter was ostensibly designed to regulate something like 400 satellite channels, that claim was evidently a fig leaf to cover their attempt to silence the unfettered speech on Al-Jazeera. The charter declared satellite stations should adhere to objectivity, sincerity, and respect the dignity of all countries. The whole thing was maddeningly vague, as practically anything could be considered an insult to dignity, for example. One clause said that freedom of expression "is to be exercised with awareness and responsibility to protect the supreme interests of the Arab states and the Arab nation."

The hostility of the Saudi royal family alone was enough to keep most advertising off the station. Business owners feared the consequences of alienating the gatekeepers of the region's most lucrative market. Mohamed Jasem al-Ali, the charismatic general manager who built the station, once told me a revealing story about welcoming an important Saudi manufacturer to the Doha headquarters early in the station's existence. The man so loved the station's bold format that he wanted to buy significant blocks of advertising, signing a contract worth millions of dollars. When he got back to Riyadh and told his associates, they reacted as if he had lost his mind, pointing out that the royal family would exact revenge by obstructing all his business ventures. The panicked man called Ali and begged him to tear up the contract.

"I told him to come back to Doha and we would write a new contract for how many millions he would pay us not to run the advertisements," Ali told me over dinner at an open-air, rooftop Beirut nightclub years after the incident, laughing at the memory. Ali was a swashbuckling figure, with dark handsome looks that made women's heads swivel as he walked across a hotel lobby. He left the station after the Iraqi invasion to pursue business interests, his detractors accusing Al-Jazeera of developing overly close relations with Saddam Hussein's government in the lead-up to the war. Its reporters got extraordinary access to every major Iraqi city during the invasion, sometimes fielding four different reporters from separate places all on live at the same time.

Over the years, Al-Jazeera's coverage prompted diplomatic spats between Doha and almost every Arab capital. Egypt, Bahrain, and various others all accused it of being underwritten by Zionist bogeymen, while a Saudi delegation once refused to attend a meeting of the Gulf Cooperation Council in Qatar to mark the royal family's displeasure. On a visit to Doha, President Mubarak of Egypt asked to see the station and could not believe its unassuming, one-story studios, blurting out, "All this noise is coming from this matchbox!" The one country that Al-Jazeera never touched was its patron, Qatar. The massive American military presence, the Israeli trade office, and other sensitive issues that Al-Jazeera would have focused on like a laser beam in other Arab states were virtually ignored.

One reason I preferred Al-Jazeera to other stations was that its reporters and commentators could be refreshingly irreverent in a way that just never happened on state-run channels, particularly on unmentionable subjects like the fact that Arab leaders tend to cling to power until the grave. For example, one stock Arabic phrase used after referring to any of the ruling princes of the Gulf is "Allah yitawwal umru," meaning "May God prolong his life." Once when all the Arab heads of state were gathered in Tunisia, I watched an Al-Jazeera talk-show host make a joke out of senile, ailing princes endlessly holding on to power. "May God prolong their lives," the host started, before interjecting, "and since God prolongs their lives more than necessary, they can't attend and therefore the summit might not succeed."

But Al-Jazeera's most important accomplishment by far was creating a competitive news industry where none existed. In the quest to win viewers, government-controlled satellite stations in countries like Egypt became much more open. That initiated a spillover effect in prompting newspapers and other publications to cover a far wider range of topics and issues like corruption and labor strife. Of course some news reports remained mired in a different age. My personal favorite in terms of laughably absurd coverage was the official Saudi channel, especially when the king did something completely ordinary like fly from Riyadh to Jidda. It would lead the news, the footage showing the king working his way down a row of all the senior princes and government ministers lined up according to obscure protocol matters of royal status, age, and seniority. Then the entire process would be repeated when he landed in Jidda. Since the commentator invariably ran out of things to say while the interminable kissing of noses and shoulders went on, some manner of music would start playing in the background, most often the Blue Danube waltz.

Given that standard, naturally the American government at first welcomed Al-Jazeera as a needed breath of free speech. But the U.S. attitude quickly soured after the September 11 terrorist strikes against New York and Washington. Osama bin Laden delivered a steady stream of recorded statements to Al-Jazeera. Officials in Washington, livid that bin Laden had obtained a global platform via the station, dubbed it "All Osama, all the time." The station also infuriated much of the American public by showing bloody videotape of

U.S. soldiers killed during the invasion of Iraq and several quaking, obviously terrified American prisoners of war being interrogated there. Washington protested that the station was violating the Geneva Conventions, but Al-Jazeera noted that the U.S. had less than a stellar record on that score, citing the treatment of captives in Afghanistan and elsewhere.

Washington pressured the Qatari ruler to tone it down, and he tried to deflect the criticism by periodically announcing that the station would be privatized. The U.S. military also appeared to take measures of its own. The Jazeera bureaux in both Kabul and Baghdad were bombed during the conflicts there, with a correspondent killed on the roof of the Baghdad bureau. The American government called both incidents accidents.

Gradually more and more of the station's reporting reflected the widespread Arab disapproval toward U.S. Mideast policy. Al-Jazeera's viewpoint became even less subtle after Arab governments financed competing stations. Satellite networks like Al-Arabiya adopted a more pro-Western approach. Abdul Rahman al-Rashed, the Saudi journalist who ran Al-Arabiya, joked with me that the stations were beginning to resemble two political parties with no crossover in their membership. Since Arabiya was financed by the brother-in-law of the Saudi king, viewers basically looked at it as the Saudi counterweight to all the criticism on Al-Jazeera.

U.S. commanders in Iraq complained that Al-Jazeera correspondents sensationalized the news, showing footage of mosques being bombed or minarets toppled, for example, but did not report that snipers had been using the religious structures for cover or sniper positions. The station also had a habit of broadcasting the most gory footage of bombing victims available, far bloodier than ever shown in the West, arguing that it wanted its viewers to appreciate the full horror of war.

On another front, Al-Jazeera provided far more extensive coverage of the Israeli-Palestinian conflict than ever seen in the Arab world before, with a team of smart, well-informed correspondents constantly breaking news. Area governments had previously downplayed the conflict whenever possible to avoid antagonizing the public about the fact that even though Arab dictators were close to Washington, they had absolutely no influence over its policy favoring Israel. Al-Jazeera shattered all precedents by interviewing Israeli officials, who were generally eager to speak directly to a vast Arab audience. But the station made no secret of where its sympathies lay, condoning suicide bombers by calling them "martyrs," for example. Sheikh Yusuf al-Qaradawi, an Islamic cleric, hosted a popular Jazeera talk show on religious topics called *Islamic Law and Life*. He endorsed suicide bombings as a military tactic against Israel for refusing to withdraw from Arab lands it grabbed in 1967. Some Westerners accused Al-Jazeera of promoting terrorism, yet Qaradawi's stance was not controversial among Arab viewers.

▣   ▣   ▣

Al-Jazeera scored points by emphasizing what its many viewers considered American double standards. Commentators pointed out that Palestinians were roundly criticized for any Israeli death, even soldiers, while Israel was rarely condemned even when its attacks killed Palestinian civilians. American governments, both Republican and Democrat, adopted an emblematic formula. Whenever an Arab group carried out a suicide bombing on a bus, for example, Washington condemned the loss of life as terrorism. But when an Israeli attack leveled a Palestinian home, killing the family inside, Washington called for "restraint on all sides." Al-Jazeera invariably highlighted the difference, and thus negative views of Americans inched up another notch.

Al-Jazeera editors had a knack for picking just a few seconds of particularly inflammatory videotape to use as promotional spots for its magazine or talk shows, scenes certain to set viewers on edge. In early 2006, for example, the U.S. was trying to diminish the visibility of its soldiers in Iraq, arguing that security should be a local affair. One cameraman managed to capture on videotape a small group of American soldiers roughly pushing their way into an Iraqi house. As they entered, an elderly woman, her hair covered in a black scarf in a mark of Islamic piety, rushed forward and bent down to grab the lead soldier's hand, kissing it repeatedly. "Mercy," she begged. "Mercy!"

It was only a few seconds, but the footage neatly encapsulated all the fear and disgust among Arabs, many of whom believed that the U.S. invasion was designed to reestablish the Western, colonial dominance of their lands. Any Arab watching would be filled with both anger and revulsion at the sight of a weak, elderly, devout Arab woman begging for mercy from a stocky American in body armor and combat fatigues. Al-Jazeera played the footage over and over and over again around the clock as a promotion for a news magazine show about the American presence. The station didn't invent the scene, it was a matter of emphasis. Did its broadcasts amount to incitement toward violence, a common accusation against Al-Jazeera? If by "incitement" critics meant that the station proselytized or preached that people attack Americans or Jews or innocent civilians, I don't think so. It was never that direct. But if someone was looking for a reason to hate Americans, they didn't have to look very hard. Taken another way, the difference between Al-Jazeera versus Al-Arabiya was a little like the split between Fox News and MSNBC on cable. Neither likely win any converts to their point of view, they just confirm the prejudices of the audience already tuned in.

The station's talk shows in particular veered toward anti-American diatribes. Hosts invited some fringe figure like Lyndon LaRouche, introducing him as "an American presidential candidate" without explaining that basically any U.S.-born citizen can run for president any number of times. Then LaRouche would spew whatever venom he wanted about the United States, which to an average Arab viewer might appear to be the learned opinion of a respectable candidate for president. Documentaries could also be awful—I remember a couple detailing all the outlandish conspiracy theories about who carried out the September 11 attacks with no weight given to voices questioning the conclusions of the lunatic fringe.

Unfortunately, American diplomats did not come across that well. Most of them had to speak through translators—only two or three had sufficient command of Arabic to be interviewed in the native language. Many senior diplomats in the region from Britain, Russia, and China, in marked contrast, spoke formal Arabic fluently. This American deficiency is a damning weakness amongst a people for whom language is an art form.

I got my first big lesson in the power of language in the region when Jordanians went on the rampage against government institutions in 1989, attacking any symbol they could find, including police stations, public buses, and even village schoolhouses. It took just one nationally televised speech from King Hussein to still the riots, such was his command of Arabic. "Arab audiences can be stirred by poetry only vaguely comprehended and by delivery of orations in the classical tongue," Phillip Hitti explained in his seminal book History of the Arabs, adding that the combination of rhythm, rhyme, and music produce in them an effect called "sihr halal" in Arabic, meaning lawful magic.

It's a stretch to imagine an American diplomat casting any such spell. But I think the U.S. government's blanket condemnation of all things Al-Jazeera was misguided, particularly when it came to the station's news reporting. Al-Jazeera maintains a C-SPAN-like commitment toward covering the American government, or at least it did during the height of the war in Iraq. On that score it is something of a news junkie's dream. Whenever the American president, vice president, or other senior administration official connected with foreign policy is giving a speech or a news conference, Al-Jazeera almost invariably carries it live. In the first years of the invasion of Iraq, all press briefings by U.S. military or civilian officials in Baghdad went out uninterrupted.

While working in the Cairo bureau or any hotel room, I kept the station on as long as I was awake because it was always first with breaking news. Any time I glanced up and saw a press conference or a speech broadcast live, I would switch over to CNN or the BBC, wanting to hear the remarks directly rather than the Arabic translation.

More often than not, the English-language satellite stations either were not covering the event or broke away much sooner. On that score Al-Jazeera provided unfiltered news reporting at its best.

If American officials were a little more savvy, they would have realized from the beginning that Al-Jazeera offered them a highly effective platform to address a massive swath of the Arabic public directly. Yet they rarely exploited it, instead brusquely writing the station off as a tool of its enemies. The U.S. made various stabs at countering the Al-Jazeera effect, trying to improve Washington's overwhelmingly negative image. Most such efforts were utterly naïve. Charlotte Beers, a Madison Avenue advertising executive brought into the State Department for that very purpose, commissioned a series of television advertisements called "Shared Values" that were meant to show that Muslims in America had complete freedom to practice their religion. The spots showed various ordinary American Muslims—a baker in Ohio, a fire department paramedic in New York City—extolling religious tolerance in the United States. Most state-run television stations in the Muslim world refused to air the advertisements, condemning them, with a straight face, as "government propaganda."

The general reaction from the Arab public was that the issue of disliking America had nothing to do with the way Islam was practiced in the United States. Whenever I asked the question, I was told over and over again that it was American policy in the Middle East that they minded, plus there was a widespread sense that Washington had put Islam in its crosshairs. Soon after September 11, President Bush called the fight against terrorism a "crusade." For most Westerners, the Crusades are a distant, medieval event, but among Arabs they are still vividly alive as a time when marauding religious zealots came to sack and occupy their cities. Events narrated by Arab historians might have happened yesterday.

"I was about to begin the prayer when a Franj [foreigner] threw himself upon me, seized me and turned my face to the East, telling me, 'That's how you pray!'" wrote Osama ibn Munqidh, a twelfth-century chronicler quoted in Amin Maalouf's *The Crusades Through Arab Eyes*, which I have always found an excellent work to help understand the roots of current Arab attitudes toward the West. The American soldier shown crashing into an Iraqi home echoed that image, and the "crusader" label stuck to the "war on terrorism."

The U.S. government ultimately tried to compete with Al-Jazeera by starting its own satellite television station called Al-Hurra, or "The Free One," headquartered in suburban Washington, D.C. From the moment the broadcasts began in February 2004, the name was an instant source of sly jokes intimating that it was less than balanced. "I've neither watched The Free One nor The Slave," quipped one Yemeni man when asked his opinion of the channel. Some differences with other channels were readily apparent, like their calling American soldiers in Iraq part of the "coalition forces" rather than the "occupation forces." Instead of referring to Palestinians trying to free themselves from the Israeli occupation, as any Arab station would, one anchor asked an analyst whether the Palestinians were ready to abandon their "historical dispute" for the economic prosperity sure to follow. The station trumpeted its audience as growing ever larger, but I often had trouble finding people who had actually watched even one program.

Al-Hurra's main problem was that instead of becoming an independent news source, its choice of programs was clouded by disputes between American critics, particularly conservative critics, over what they thought Arabs should be watching. They had the paternalistic attitude that the station should be like castor oil: good for the viewers rather than what people in the region actually wanted to watch. One veteran news producer brought in to help bolster Al-Hurra's flagging audience, for example, was pilloried for airing a speech by Hizbollah's leader. This struck me as patently ridiculous for a news channel. If you don't show the newsmaking figures whom Arab audiences want to hear, then you are not going to attract an audience. As the Arab state broadcasts show, politicians make lousy editors.

From the start Al-Hurra was not good enough to overcome being too closely identified with Washington. "The people they have hired look modern, hip, and the beat is fast, but it won't have an impact on the perception of the United States," predicted Mustafa B. Hamarneh, a gregarious, bear-like Jordanian who at the time was director of the Center for Strategic Studies at the University of Jordan. "I think the Americans are mistaken if they assume they can change their image in the region. People became anti-American because they don't like American policies."

A 2006 report by the Government Accounting Office, noting that the U.S. spent $78 million annually to support Al-Hurra and its radio arm, Radio Sawa, criticized management for lacking any strategic plan and said that its claim that it attracted a combined audience size of 21.6 million in 2005 was based on unreliable assessment techniques. The management responded by saying that customer surveys were difficult in the Middle East.

Washington's tin ear for virtually all things Arab also shadowed the station's image. To overcome the Babel of dialects from Morocco to Iraq, most satellite stations use a formal version of Arabic called "fusha" (pronounced FOOS-ha) in their broadcasts. Egypt and Saudi Arabia are close geographically, but if I recorded someone speaking in the Saudi dialect, the Egyptian reporters who worked for the *Times* sometimes had to listen to it several times before they got it. (On the other hand, Egypt's long domination of movies and television series has made its dialect almost universally understood throughout the Arab world, but not spoken.)

Anyone with some education can understand minimal fusha, however, which newspapers also use, and more and more people became attuned to the form as satellite stations grew more popular. In fact, one mark of the popularity of Al-Jazeera and its rivals was the influence they began to exert on the entire structure of formal Arabic.

The difference between formal Arabic and the spoken variety is often compared to the vast difference between Shakespearean English and the various dialects now used in English-speaking nations around the world. When I first arrived in Cairo in 1982, fresh from studying Arabic for a couple years at Stanford and U.C. Berkeley, I stepped into a cab in the controlled bedlam outside the arrivals hall at Cairo International Airport and tried to use my formal Arabic to give the driver directions. "Ureedu an ath-habu ila al-funduki," I said. That was more or less the equivalent of grabbing a cab at JFK and saying, "Prithee good man, wouldst thou convey me to yonder hostelry." Naturally the cab driver turned around with a blank look on his face and said in the Egyptian accent that I would later come to learn, "What are you speaking, my brother?"

Language was another Achilles' heel of Al-Hurra. The newscasters on stations like Al-Jazeera and Al-Arabiya spoke formal Arabic particularly well, to the degree that it was usually impossible to identify their country of origin. Dialects are readily identifiable, but fusha does not come in national or even regional accents, with the notable exception of Al-Hurra's heavily Lebanese staff. The Lebanese are notoriously bad at speaking formal Arabic, prone to toss in an English or French word when groping for the right one in their own language. The broadcast team on Al-Hurra was plainly marked by either their names or their poor Arabic as Lebanese Christians, a group long suspected in the region as a fifth column for all things Western. So rather than coming across as a U.S. technical marvel, the programs and the personnel gave the station the aura of being some shoddy, second-rate Lebanese network. The combination of financing from Washington and its employees instantly stigmatized the station.

Its programming choices also struck me as downright bizarre. To pick just one story, I turned on Al-Jazeera in my Beirut hotel room in late July 2004 to find it broadcasting from the Democratic National Convention in Boston. During a break, I picked up the remote to look for Al-Hurra. After all, given that part of its announced mandate was spreading democratic values and the nuts-and-bolts process of democracy, I figured its coverage would be even more extensive. It took me a while to figure out which station was Al-Hurra because it was broadcasting a documentary about dolphins—in English with Arabic subtitles.

In contrast, after the headlines Jazeera devoted the bulk of the next thirty minutes of news to the convention—likely far more than most American network newscasts. A Jazeera correspondent had tagged along all day with a veiled Arab-American delegate from Dearborn, Michigan, explaining what she did at the convention. There was a live interview with the Reverend Jesse Jackson, with the reporter asking pertinent questions for an Arab audience, like why a commitment to Israel's security was always a campaign issue. Jackson went on at length giving viewers a basic rundown about the role of a party convention in presidential elections, all of it faithfully translated. In the summer of 2008, I found Jazeera doing it again when I switched on my TV in the Nile Hilton. Barack Obama had visited the Wailing Wall that day, and Jazeera spent a chunk of time analyzing why U.S. presidential candidates feel compelled to talk about Israel's security while the Arabs failed to muster similar support for the plight of the Palestinians. I was listening with one ear while making phone calls, but it struck me as a deft analysis of how the Israeli lobby deploys in Washington rather than any Jews-control-the-world diatribe.

In survey after survey the station ranks as the first source that Arabs turned to for their news. I think the U.S. would have a better shot at improving its image in the region if it made more of an effort to be heard via Al-Jazeera. The station may highlight the negative in America's Middle East policies, but it did have a basic commitment to giving all sides a voice.

⬚   ⬚   ⬚

As an American spending a lot of time on the streets of Arab cities, I was struck by the tangible effect of television coverage of the war. Being over six foot, three inches with blondish hair, I don't exactly blend in, but the only time I experienced overt hostility was during the year following the March 2003 invasion of Iraq. Pictures of

U.S. soldiers firing on Iraq filled television screens day and night. It was unquestionably the most hostile period toward Americans in the region that I had ever experienced. My colleagues in Iraq obviously bore the brunt of it, facing possible kidnapping and execution whenever they sallied forth from their compounds that gradually grew to resemble bunkers. But the general mood soured everywhere.

My nationality was not something I had ever really thought about during my years reporting for The Associated Press, with the noted exception of avoiding Lebanon. On my first trip to Yemen in 1992, I traveled to the northern town of Saada to write about the dwindling community of Jewish silversmiths, for example. As I handed over my passport to the clerk behind the dusty front desk of a somewhat dubious hotel, the guy called the owner to exclaim, "An American just checked in!" It was Ramadan, about fifteen minutes before sundown, and the hotel's owner told the clerk I was invited to break the daily fast with him. A small Toyota pickup truck soon materialized and I found myself hurtling along dry desert gullies until a little mud-brick fort appeared on a rise. The heavy wooden gates swung open and then slammed shut as soon as the pickup skidded to a halt. A tribal leader dressed in a shirt and dark pants, Sheikh Hussein Fayid Mujallah, emerged to greet me and then led me up some mud stairs painted dark green to the room where we would eat. The floor was covered with tightly woven baskets brimming with lamb, rice, grape leaves, and various Yemeni dishes I had never seen before, but it was the walls that held my attention.

Every single inch was covered with pictures of Saddam Hussein. What have I done, I thought to myself, realizing that even if I tried to escape I would never be able to retrace the desert route back to Saada. The man's 13-year-old son began bringing in fresh bread and other food, and on each trip my host would goad the lad to tell me his name. The boy blushed and refused each time until the father finally blurted it out: "Saddam Hussein Mujallah!" He delighted at the surprised look on my face, and I winced again inwardly.

Ultimately, despite the fact that he was an ardent fan of Saddam, whom the United States had just defeated in the first Gulf War, Sheikh Mujallah turned out to be a typically generous host and we had a lengthy discussion about what would happen in the region given the renewed effort to build a lasting peace. Nowadays, of course, I wouldn't dare jump into a car alone and roar off to an unknown destination. In fact, if a desk clerk yelled into the phone "An American just checked in!" I would likely check right back out.

While more cautious in the post–September 11 world, I usually avoided lying about my nationality—just to gauge people's reaction. For the months following the invasion of Iraq, watching their faces was like watching a garage door come slamming down. Their banter would freeze and they would hasten to conclude whatever transaction was at hand. In Yemen, the days of wandering around at will were definitely over. When I wanted to report outside the capital, for my protection the government made me move around accompanied by nine guards wearing camouflage uniforms and toting Kalashnikovs, all riding on the flatbed of a Toyota truck mounted with a fifty-caliber machine gun. My driver was thrilled. "Talk to the crew," he would bark, grinning and jerking his thumb backwards whenever we were stopped at a military checkpoint along the main north-south highway. I was rather less enthusiastic. Try interviewing people on the street when you are being shadowed by your own small army, especially after the soldiers spent the lunch money I gave them to buy qat, a semi-narcotic leaf wadded in their mouths like chewing tobacco.

In Jidda, Saudi Arabia, when I broke a tooth and had to get it fixed quickly, I found myself in the chair of a Syrian dentist. "Where are you from?" he asked, making small talk as he fiddled with equipment on a side table. When I told him, he exclaimed, "American! That's not a very popular thing to be!" then started the drill whirring and said "Open wide!" (He did an excellent job.) Sometimes the anti-American hostility was overt even when people didn't speak to me, but just saw me, since I fit the stereotype of what many Arabs think an American is supposed to look like. Again in Jidda, I was walking around the electronics bazaar one night when a full can of Pepsi sailed past my head and thudded into a billboard behind me. It was not terribly threatening, but working in the region was demoralizing while the mood endured.

On extremely rare occasions, I must admit, I got completely the opposite reaction. "I have a question about the war," a Palestinian cab driver in Amman said to me as soon as I had wedged myself into his cramped back seat. It was dusk at the end of a long day, and I groaned inwardly and braced myself for the standard diatribe about the Washington/Tel Aviv axis determined to neuter Iraq at the behest of Zionism and big oil. But he surprised me. "Why just Saddam, why not all of them?" he demanded, reeling off the decades in power accumulated by Hosni Mubarak, Qadhafi, and a string of others including some who have since died, like King Fahd and Yasir Arafat. His was, though, a minority opinion.

⊡   ⊡   ⊡

Other American invasions, however, of the cultural variety, were often welcomed by the Arabs, depending on the audience. For example, I was sitting in Cairo International Airport one evening, drinking the too-sweet tea on offer while awaiting a Saudia Airlines flight to Riyadh, when an *Oprah* show came on the television set in the departure lounge. It was a segment called something like "Hunks Who Build Homes" with shot after shot of shirtless, buff American carpenters hammering nails. Saudi women sitting on couches across the lounge were lifting their face veils to get a better look until one Saudi man got so annoyed that he stood up and yelled at the Egyptian waiters to change the channel.

Given the generally dreary aspect of the local fare, it is little wonder that shows like *Oprah*—available on illegal but tolerated satellite dishes—are so wildly popular. Women are a particularly hungry audience since so many are marooned at home. I sometimes wondered why the U.S. government, ham-handed in its own attempts to create propaganda, didn't do something simpler like making *Oprah* more widely accessible. Of course American talk shows would not be a complete panacea for Washington's public relations problems in the Middle East—if you watch enough of them you might conclude that the religious maniacs have a point that the West is an idiotic, debauched society with no redeeming qualities.

Besides, even an empathetic woman like Oprah Winfrey alienated her huge Saudi fan base occasionally. Once she aired a segment called "Women Across the Globe." Oprah interviewed Rania al-Baz, a famous Saudi TV presenter whose husband nearly beat her to death. Baz had done the unthinkable in Saudi Arabia by publishing pictures of her battered face, forcing a public discussion on the long-hidden topic of abusive husbands. Saudi women were outraged that Baz's was the only tale of abuse included in the program; women elsewhere, from Iceland to India, were all shown in a positive light. Saudi women commenting in chat rooms expressed particular indignation that Oprah had interjected a quick comment along the lines of "We are so blessed that we are born and raised in America," which was interpreted as suggesting that the problem of battered wives was uniquely awful to Saudi Arabia. Saudi women felt that they were once again being defined by an exceptional case, not to mention by a crime hardly unknown in the United States. Yet the show had its defenders, including Baz herself, who thought Saudi women were being too sensitive about their image and that anything prompting a discussion about hidden problems was good. Oprah's supporters noted that she had previously done all kinds of shows about spousal abuse in the U.S.

To me, the degree to which Saudi women actually cared about their image on Oprah was one indication of just how much of an audience the American talk-show diva commanded in Saudi Arabia. The United States is so big that sometimes we forget just how much the rest of the world looks to us to tell them what is cool. They may resent it, but they still look. I suspect that if Oprah had done a program focused on all the economic and social problems caused by the Saudi ban on women driving, or the very visible role of some Muslim-American women in public life in the United

States, it would have reached a far larger audience and had far greater impact than anything official Washington tried to promote.

☐   ☐   ☐

Television is perhaps the one venue where some Arab women manage to find a way to broach unimaginable topics, to haul the private sphere into the public, and I think that makes it a significant force for change. One of the most daring in breaking taboos was Fawzia Dorai, a brash Kuwaiti sex advice columnist, who had her own satellite television talk show, The Biography of Love, where callers from around the Arab world asked her questions. Often dressed in tight if discrete red leather, her head swathed in a matching scarf, Dorai would dispense advice on all manner of sensitive topics from a set bathed in candlelight. While ostensibly about love, many discussions touched on sex and Dorai invariably tossed in nuggets of bedroom advice. Once I heard her tell husbands that before they went to sleep after sex, they should kiss their wives on the forehead, which the women would take as a signal that they were still loved despite ardent participation in such depravity. She was also witty, ribbing one caller by asking him what his problem was exactly when he asked for advice on how to fend off the wives of all his friends who were trying to seduce him. Islamic scholarship is replete with frank, not to say raunchy, writings about sex, and Dorai always managed to find a way to skate just along the line of what was publicly acceptable by citing those traditions.

I first met her soon after the Iraqis were driven out of Kuwait in 1991, when I moved there to open a bureau for The Associated Press. Dorai had tried to publish a collection of twenty short stories called "Love Under Occupation," but the government censors rejected a couple of them as too explicit. Censorship laws banned anything that contradicted public decency, morals, or religion or otherwise might give offense. Dorai was stubbornly holding out for the publication of all or nothing—particularly brave since she was married to an Iraqi university professor, a nuclear scientist, and therefore under significant pressure to quit the country.

When I went to interview her in her office at *Al-Watan* newspaper, she started out by reading me one story in Arabic, translating the parts that I couldn't grasp. An Iraqi major named Farisdaq is supposed to be holding Zubeida, a pretty Kuwaiti nurse, as his prisoner. Farisdaq's fellow officers thought he was interrogating and torturing her in his purloined villa, but the two actually spent three days talking, laughing, and watching videos. He finally agrees to help her escape to Saudi Arabia, telling her: "For your eyes, I sacrifice my neck."

"So beautiful," Dorai sighed as she stopped reading, licking her thick coppery lipstick. She told me that all twenty stories in her collection were true—with minor details changed to disguise identities. One story included the tale of a masochistic double agent who liked to be whipped—Dorai offering to dredge up the leather whip for me as a mark of authenticity if I harbored any doubts. She had stayed in Kuwait all during the occupation, going underground once when the Iraqis tried to force her to work for their newspaper and again when an unflattering psychological profile of Saddam Hussein that she had written fell into their hands. Given the circumstances, I wondered aloud how she had managed to gather so many lurid True Romance details.

"What do you mean 'How?'! I am the most famous advice columnist in this country! Everyone calls me!" she bellowed from behind her vast desk. It seemed true enough. She had to turn off her incessantly ringing phone in order to get through the interview. As she sat there, she constantly adjusted the headscarf, which always matched the bright reds, greens, or yellows of her dress, purse, and nails.

She had earned a master's in psychology and sex education from Pacific Lutheran University in Tacoma, Washington, and devoted some of her professional life to working as a sex therapist at Kuwait's Psychiatric Hospital. She told me that she had recently discovered that the two small yellow lovebirds sharing a cage in her office were both males, "which just goes to show that I have too much sympathy with homosexuals!"

Dorai is an outspoken advocate for free speech and full equality for men and women; her frank television discussions and her columns on sex gained her a wide audience from both men and women. "A veiled woman writing about sex. Can you imagine? They love it, sweetie," she told me, laughing.

Westerners often ascribe a certain prudishness to the Arab world, not least because the fights about veiling and modest dress often make them seem so repressed. Arab students of Western Orientalism argue that there is a long tradition of ascribing to southern races, but Middle Easterners in particular, all the opposite qualities of those prized in the West. Hence during the straight-laced Victorian era, the Arab world was considered the heart of degenerate sensuality. Now that porno palaces and peep shows dot all Western capitals, however, the Arabs are criticized for being overly puritan. I found that there is certainly a bawdy undercurrent to their lives and jokes, although it tends to be segregated by sex and rarely bursts into the public sphere. Women joke among themselves about sex, and men can take any manner of sex question to the religious scholar at their local mosque. The private sphere is very tolerant. When such topics are hauled into the light of day, the problems start.

The fact that Dorai found the way to pull it off, no doubt helped by the fact that she was veiled, made her almost unique. She confessed to me that the Iraqi occupation might have saved her reputation. Right beforehand, she had finally gotten the approval of a women's organization to offer public sex education classes for Kuwaiti women, a first. Religious conservatives protested vehemently, but the class went ahead. Dorai is a rather vivid speaker, punctuating her generally clinical if explicit descriptions with delighted squeals or low moaning as the situation warranted. The religious types sent a few women to her courses to record what she was saying. They then cut up and spliced the tape, widely distributing a new version where the listener just heard Dorai saying words like "penis" or "vagina" and then issuing extended guttural moans. It sounded like a public masturbation session.

"I was finished!" Dorai admitted, laughing uproariously. The occupation erased all that and eventually she became more public than ever on television.

Sometimes, inevitably, the forces of moral outrage won, as happened in the attempt to introduce an Arabic version of the highly popular Western reality series *Big Brother*, where a bunch of unrelated young adults share a house. Similar shows had been produced without incident in Lebanon, but Arabs view the Lebanese as irredeemably decadent. LBC, a Lebanese satellite channel watched not least for the plunging décolletage of its female announcers, is nicknamed Lubnaniyat Bidun Culotte, Arabic for "Lebanese women without underwear."

It was another matter to try to broadcast a reality show from the tiny island nation of Bahrain, in the notably conservative Persian Gulf. During the first few minutes of the inaugural episode, Abdel Hakim, a broad-shouldered young Saudi, kissed Kawthar, a raven-haired Tunisian beauty, on the cheek and all hell broke loose. In Bahrain, not to mention the rest of the Arab world with the exception of Lebanon, a social kiss between a young man and a young woman meeting for the first time suggested rampant moral depravity. They might as well have made love.

"Everybody talked about that kiss," Mansour al-Jamri, editor of the leading Bahraini newspaper, *Al-Wasat*, told me when I called to ask about the show. Concerned citizens wrote to the newspaper with comments like "If it starts with a kiss, where will it end?" Parliament members damned the show as an assault on traditional values, and after the weekly Friday prayer services, clerics led 1,000 protestors chanting "No to indecency!" through the capital of Manama. The ruckus worked. After a run of less than two weeks, the show was yanked off the air by the Middle East Broadcasting Center, owned by Walid al-Ibrahim, a brother-in-law of the late King Fahd of Saudi Arabia.

Its opponents were elated. "This program showed an abnormal way of living, which is totally opposed to our thoughts, culture, everything," said Sheikh Adel al-Maawda, a middle-aged member of parliament from the salafi movement who spearheaded the protests. Salafis, their name drawn from the Arabic word for "forefathers," are roughly the Muslim world's equivalent of fundamentalist Christians who take holy scriptures as God's orders about how to live your life. "It's not reality TV at all, especially in our part of the world." He had a point.

In the Middle East, where cultural issues invariably carry a political edge, the fact that the network caved dismayed proponents of free speech. "I don't like the program, and would not want my daughter on it, but we have to respect the choice of people who want to watch it and to defend it also," said Shaer, the trenchant Bahraini columnist I always called for her opinion on important issues. "This is a step backwards."

The audience outcry had actually started somewhat earlier with two shows from Beirut, *Star Academy* and *Al Hawa Sawa* or *On Air Together*. I didn't really watch until the diatribes started. The latter put eight women together in an apartment for three months, with the votes of viewers gradually winnowing the group down to one. The winner married one of the roughly 6,000 prospective grooms who sent in videotaped proposals. The show attempted to bow to Muslim sensibilities by having the bride's mother on the set when the groom popped the question.

Star Academy featured sixteen young Arab men and women in an endless talent contest—singing, dancing, and performing music and skits, as well as cooking, eating, and sleeping. (Their quarters are sexually segregated, but there were co-ed pillow fights involving skimpily clad women.) To me, the shows looked kind of tame, not to say boring, but as far as the fundamentalist types were concerned, *Sodom and Gomorrah Live!* would have been a more fitting title. *Star Academy* was denounced as a "whorehouse" by one columnist in Saudi Arabia, where the show was also dubbed *The Devil's Academy*.

Naturally, the religious opponents went too far. Speaking on state-run radio in late 2008, a senior Saudi cleric, Sheikh Salih al-Luhaidan, a chief justice no less, labeled the owners of satellite stations "apostles of depravation" who should be executed for broadcasting indecent programs if that was the sole means to get them off the air. An enormous outcry ensued, and in his zealotry the sheikh seemed to have forgotten that some of the princes ruling Saudia Arabia owned several wildly popular channels. He soon found himself trying to explain that he meant such a death penalty might only be imposed after a fair trial.

Big Brother had its defenders, mostly business people who hoped it would fuel tourism. Bahrain was already considered the "Nightclub of the Gulf," rife with alcohol and prostitution because so many of its neighbors—including Saudi Arabia, Qatar, and Kuwait—ban liquor. I always found the nightclubs unbelievably depressing—Russian, Filipino, or Moroccan dancers gyrating to bad, ear-splitting music while much of the audience was either collapsed over their tables in a drunken stupor or jockeying to get the dancers into bed. Given the rampant vice I could find any night, though, the outraged reaction to the show seemed hypocritical, a point I raised with its leading critic.

That nightlife, Sheikh al-Maawda explained to me, generally took place behind closed doors. The decadence was not on display; or at least hidden enough that it could be denied. "When you are at your house, you can do what you like and nobody should look through the keyhole," he told me, noting that the Prophet Mohamed once declared that you could use a needle to poke out the eye of anyone who tried.

To me, that pretty much summed up the general attitude toward all manner of socially suspect behavior across the region—if you didn't flaunt it, it was fine. It was only dragging it into the public sphere that caused problems. Many attempts to challenge social customs were evidently met with resistance, and the repressive governments played up such confrontations, casting their actions as defending tradition.

Egypt, for example, had been tolerant of homosexuals for cen-turies, long attracting male tourists from the West because of its libertine ways. When I first moved to Cairo, I naïvely responded to an advertisement posted by an English teacher at the American University in Cairo for a room in an apartment with a "private student" of his, thinking it would help me learn to speak the lan-guage in a conservative society where no family was about to take in a male boarder. Some weeks after I moved in with the so-called male student, however, I was eating breakfast in the living room when he emerged from his bedroom in his underwear with an Italian tourist, the visitor taking out his wallet and paying for whatever services had been rendered. That was not the environ-ment for learning Arabic that I had anticipated.

When I moved back to Cairo as the Times correspondent, a nas-cent gay rights movement was trying to take its activity public. The government launched a widely popular crackdown that served two purposes—it helped establish its own credentials as a defender of religious values, something its Islamist opponents constantly cast doubt on, and the lurid details distracted people from widespread economic problems.

In May 2001 police raided the Queen Boat, a Nile barge whose perhaps inopportune name had been in place long before it became a floating gay discotheque. Foreigners caught in the raid were let go, but the police subjected the Egyptian patrons to hu-miliating medical examinations to prove whether they had ever engaged in anal sex and taunted suspects by telling them they obviously looked gay. Some were tortured. Ultimately, at least twenty-one of the fifty-two men arrested were sentenced to three-year jail terms for practicing "habitual debauchery." When the United States objected to the affair on human rights grounds, one semi-official Egyptian newspaper reacted with a story headlined "Be a pervert and Uncle Sam will approve." Se-cret police also trolled the Internet looking for gays searching for sex partners, then showed up and arrested anyone who answered their lures.

I would like to predict that globalization and the ready access to satellite television will close the gap between the publicly secret and the privately accepted. But while I was in the region the strength of the religious revival combined with animosity toward Western ways served to push things in the other direction, with anyone challenging conservative traditions forced to become more circumspect. The fact that the most vocal, successful political parties were inevitably religious also made breaking new ground on social issues unlikely.

Yet occasionally I found cultural material that was both topical and refreshing in its originality. For example, it actually took the holy month of Ramadan, of all times, for me to discover that the Saudis had a very public means of laughing about their own puritanical ways.

Riyadh tends to be a dreary capital, with public activity centered on endless shopping malls. Islamic strictures mean there are no movie theaters nor plays. (Of course thousands of al-Saud princes live in more or less an entirely different country, and the richer ones build movie theaters into their palaces.) The capital's museums tend to highlight objects like 40-year-old Bedouin coffee pots, and its antiseptic bazaars lack the endlessly alluring medieval architecture of, say, Damascus.

The city's main redeeming quality is that Saudis of all stripes are so hospitable. Lengthy assignments were made palatable by dinners at the homes of all kinds of people—more often than not, someone who I interviewed during the day insisted that I show up at his house for dinner that night, or old friends would invite me over for an illicit drink.

During the month of Ramadan, though, when Muslims fast from dawn to dusk, I found the city especially tedious. Saudis basically sleep all day, then break the fast at sundown with their families before many head to the mosque for a couple hours of special prayers, after which commences an endless stream of family visits and snacks until dawn. Saudis thought nothing of giving me appointments for interviews at 2 A.M. Meeting someone during the day, on the other hand, was practically impossible.

For visitors like me, trying to eat lunch proved a distracting chore because it's illegal for restaurants to open in the daytime during Ramadan. Many days I would go with the flow and fast. If I wanted lunch, the only way to eat was to return to my hotel room and order room service. A Saudi friend who hated fasting often showed up in the late afternoon for coffee and a sandwich, hanging around until the city came to life after prayers. He introduced me to one of the funniest Arab television serials I ever watched.

On screen, three Saudi women awoke to the sound of a burglar rummaging through their house. They called the police, donned their veils, and fled into the street, but when the officer arrived he refused to investigate because there was no male present. "I swear by God I would love to serve you," the officer avowed, retreating to his patrol car. "But we cannot enter if your male guardian is not here."

I laughed, as did many in the kingdom. That particular episode touched off both laughter and sustained outrage across Saudi Arabia, actually. It raised the hackles of religious conservatives for mocking the Islamic tenets and cultural traditions they believe Saudi Arabia must maintain. More liberal Saudis relished the subtle ridicule of the way the tenets conflicted with modern life.

"This show is a window that people can see us through, and we can show the world how we live," Fowziyah Abukhalid, a sociologist at King Saud University told me, summarizing the viewpoint of the educated intelligentsia. "Some of these issues used to be taboo, so to have someone talk about them and criticize them is very important."

The reaction from the Saudi puritans was rather different. One theologian rolled out a fatwa, damning not just the actors as sinners, but anyone who watched.

Its creators, Nasser al-Qasabi and Abdullah al-Sadham, who met in college while studying agricultural engineering, had grown accustomed to setting off controversy ever since the show, *Tash Ma*

Tash, was first broadcast in the early 1990s. They took the name from a children's game and it translates roughly as "You either get it or you don't." The two created just twenty episodes a year, all shown daily in prime time during Ramadan. That alone agitated the religious types, who believe Ramadan should be one extended prayer session. But even the show's creators told me that they were floored by the uproar over the episode titled "Without a Mahram," or male guardian.

The thirty-minute episode was the subject of myriad group discussions in schools and mosques. Theologians organized a protest march against the Ministry of Information, demanding the implementation of the ruling banning the show, issued by the government's very own Higher Council of Religious Scholars. At one time it would have been unthinkable for anyone to challenge such an edict. The show would have perished instantly. But Saudi Arabia, one of the most restrictive countries in the region, had become a tad more open, plus the show's widespread popularity lent it a form of insurance.

Laws in Saudi Arabia largely emerge from the tension between what the public wants and what the religious authorities want, with the royal family the ultimate arbiters. The balance tips one way or the other depending on where the leading princes sense their best interests lie. A pious king can push the religious establishment around more than an impious one. In this particular case, discussions in Internet chat rooms, which in the absence of free speech serve as an important barometer of public opinion in Saudi Arabia, raged back and forth between ardent fans versus those condemning both the show and its creators to eternal hellfire.

"If you read some of this stuff, you might get the impression that we made a sex film inside the Kaaba," Qasabi, the co-creator, with black hair, dark eyes, and cappuccino-colored skin, told me over small cups of sweet tea in his living room, referring to the holiest of holy Muslim shrines at Mecca. "It is only light social criticism, but the reaction makes it seem as if it was against God himself."

Aside from the reluctant policeman, the women in the episode encountered all kinds of typical problems when the husband of one of them was sent to work in France for six months. They couldn't rent *Cinderella* for a young daughter because women are barred from video rental shops. When the bank card of one was eaten by an ATM, she couldn't seek help inside the bank because it was a branch for men only. Ultimately, the women resort to borrowing the elementary school–aged son of a neighbor or hauling along a deaf old grandfather as their "guardian" just so they can eat in a restaurant.

"We suffer from this male guardian requirement just as much as the women," Mohamed al-Wan, a Saudi short-story writer, told me when I asked him if he liked the episode. "We are enslaved by the demands at home because a woman can't do anything without a man."

I watched the show every night, discovering that the writers found much to mock. Arabs generally have a keen sense of humor, something that often goes underappreciated amidst the endless violence. As one of my favorite Lebanese novelists, Hannan al-Shaykh, once said in an interview with *The Guardian* newspaper: "This is what the West doesn't know about us. We're used to laughing at painful things, trying to see the light side to survive."

Qasabi told me that more and more shows were focused on vital issues, the kind of political and social reforms that some Saudis eagerly await and which he thought religious conservatives wanted to block.

The show did not attempt to directly challenge the religious hierarchy, but it did poke fun at some of the more lunatic ways conservative traditions twist daily life in the twenty-first century. Yet even its most ardent fans were unsure just how much influence could be attributed to the show, whether it could be directly linked to any changes. One exception occurred in January 2008, when the kingdom quietly lifted the ban on Saudi women staying in hotels alone without a male guardian, a rule that basically harkened back to the days of camel caravans when women could not travel alone. Naturally the religious establishment grumbled that the old system was better.

One of the hardest aspects of Saudi Arabia to analyze was just how ready its people were to relax those religious rules governing everyday life. Television was an important yet unreliable barometer. Analysis of such a closed country is always imperfect—it's possible that *Tash Ma Tash* stayed on the air because it made the king laugh. Saudis basically argued along one of two lines when I was trying to evaluate social change in the kingdom. The coterie of Western-educated businessmen and academics whom I consulted for general assessments about the country invariably suggested that a silent majority of Saudis hankered to loosen the cloak of Islam—hence the popularity of the show. The religious, on the other hand, claimed that such pronouncements merely reflected wishful thinking within an isolated, overly Westernized elite.

At a minimum, the success of *Tash Ma Tash* suggested to me that a broad segment of the country found no harm in throwing open the idea for discussion. Change might be moving at a glacial pace, but there was room for debate on this and other issues, a view seconded by the crowded chat rooms on the Internet on all manner of topics. One hit show in 2008 was the biography of Asmahan, a stunning singer of the 1940s who had numerous lovers, an abortion, and spied for the British before dying in a tragic accident when her car tumbled into the Nile. The show, produced in Syria, was hugely popular, not least because it showed that Arab societies had once been far more tolerant.

The modern tragedy in Saudia Arabia and elsewhere is that the rulers keep such discussions bottled up in the private sphere—the Internet is not yet widely accessible enough in most countries—and in that restricted environment problems tend to fester rather than slouch toward resolution.

Would extremist thoughts about religion, like implementing a starry-eyed notion of a utopian Caliphate, flourish in a society where all such topics were aired and political parties were allowed to present their points of view? I doubt it. Yet jumping directly to a demand for unrestricted free speech is unlikely to succeed. In its absence, one proxy is the flourishing debates that erupt over ordinary matters like a *Tash Ma Tash* episode. If such discussions became even more public, it would help create that all-important space for civil society to exist, like pushing open the folded sides of a cardboard box from inside. That process constitutes the most important building block in releasing the region from the grip of petty despots and religious intolerance to the point where the full range of public issues can be discussed. Encouraging debates over something like the most popular TV shows might be a small step, but it is one way of enlarging the space for all manner of public discussions.

CHAPTER 5

THANKSGIVING

"We don't care if people love the beer!"

DURING MY MANY YEARS in the Middle East, I met all kinds of expatriates pursuing quixotic dreams of bridging the gap between West and East, but none were going about it with quite the same gusto as Ekkehard Zitzman. The portly, middle-aged German was, as he liked to boast, "the last brewer on the Arabian peninsula!" His Sirra Beer was most welcome in the scorching summer climate of Yemen, where the thermometer regularly hit 120 degrees Fahrenheit. Zitzman's infectious enthusiasm for his smooth, thirst-quenching pilsner was remarkable not least because he faced terrible odds and he knew it. The mullahs who ushered in Iran's Islamic revolution had shuttered his previous brewery.

The first time I went to see him in Aden—the once famous, now dilapidated port in southern Yemen—he told me that he had no need to consult a calendar to know when the holy month of

Ramadan loomed. His delivery trucks were stoned. Firebombs sailed over the brewery walls. Death threats against him and his workers rose sharply, prompting him to sleep in a different room in his house each night. After the weekly mosque sermons each Friday, hundreds of zealots aroused by fundamentalist clerics would march on the brewery, determined to torch such an obvious outpost of Satan.

Salvation arrived in the unlikely form of the army.

"The army officers here are all Soviet-trained, which means plenty of heavy drinkers," Zitzman told me. "They always bring up the big guns to protect us." A few mortar rounds fired judiciously over the heads of the demonstrators usually proved sufficient to disperse them.

Zitzman was a jolly character with a much-needed wry sense of humor, and I recognized that his was no small accomplishment since Islam forbids the consumption of alcohol and most area governments enforce prohibition. Saudi Arabia and Kuwait are both dry, while Sharjah in the United Arab Emirates, Qatar, and Oman restrict liquor consumption to expatriates. Sharjah treats alcohol kind of like a weapon—you pay a hefty fee for a police license to consume the stuff at home.

The Yemeni government inevitably got involved in the brewery battles, announcing each Ramadan that the benighted heathen establishment would have to close and this time it would definitely, certainly, absolutely stay closed for eternity. Significantly, the orders came from the capital, Sanaa, in the north, which was far more religiously inclined. Zitzman knew that the edict wounded both the palates and the pride of most southern officials. First, many drank the beer and, second, they clung to it as the last vestige of Aden's long-faded cosmopolitan past. (My visits to Zitzman predated the harbor making headlines when an Al-Qaeda suicide attack with a skiff blew a gaping hole in the side of the USS *Cole*, a Navy destroyer, killing seventeen American servicemen.)

The telephones worked intermittently and sewage from an overloaded system built by the British in flush times often flooded the streets. Socialist neglect for twenty-five years after independence in

1967 had destroyed any cachet associated with the massive natural harbor. In the heyday of the British Empire, the constant steamship traffic between England and India made Aden the second busiest port in the world after New York. Of course not everyone who visited while their ships refueled proved a fan of the low-slung city spreading out from the blackened crater of a dormant volcano. Tim Mackintosh-Smith, a witty British travel writer and long-term resident of Yemen, quoted the author Vita Sackville-West as calling the city "precisely the most repulsive corner of the world." With the collapse of colonialism and the arrival of the jet engine, Aden reverted to the boondocks. But it still boasted a brewery. Sirra Beer even reflected the glorious past, with the black outline of an old Portuguese fort overlooking the harbor gracing its distinctive red label.

The wily brewmaster always made sure to fill the storage vats before unplugging the machines at the start of the holy month. Ramadan over, he would drop into the local governor's office and casually mention that the vats were full of beer ready for bottling, wondering if perhaps he should just pour it down a drain? The top officials hemmed and hawed for a while over glasses of tea and then invariably decided it would be a terrible waste to jettison beer that was already made. Of course the carbonation in bottled beer comes from new production, Zitzman explained to me, so bottling the stored stuff meant making new brew and the entire cycle began again for another year.

Observant Muslims naturally found this exasperating, especially since the order to close the brewery remained on the books.

"We don't care if people love the beer!" Sheikh Mohamed Abdulrub Gaber, the head of the Aden branch of Islah, the largest Islamic political party, groused to me. The bearded cleric pointed out that drinking beer, along with chewing the stimulant qat, the favorite pastime of virtually all Yemeni males and no small number of women, was a drain on household budgets. A beer lover goes "to the alcohol market and spends his money, leaving his family penniless. He might even sell his wife's jewelry!"

It was true that many Yemenis drank beer to counteract the effects of qat. The beer acted as a kind of downer, akin to trying to assuage the buzz derived from drinking too many cups of espresso. Qat chewing went on day and night in Yemen. One time the elusive leader of a socialist political party, a man I had been trying to reach for days, knocked on my hotel door around 2 A.M., long after I had gone to sleep. I staggered to the door to find what appeared to be a talking tree. "Want to chew?" the politician asked from behind his bushel of qat.

For Zitzman, the struggle to keep brewing was an old story. He had arrived in Aden from Iran in 1980, a year after Ayatollah Ruhollah Khomeini's Islamic revolutionaries booted out the shah. He told me that he had managed to protect his Tehran brewery from Muslim mobs who burned down the country's four other breweries and he even continued deliveries for about six months, covering the windows of a Volkswagen van with brown paper to disguise the contents. But he knew the jig was up when a turbaned mullah materialized at the gates one day and told him that the brewing obviously had to stop.

In Yemen, the end came abruptly. Not long after I met Zitzman, the periodic tensions that followed the unification of northern and southern Yemen erupted into renewed fighting. The army, preoccupied, could not protect the brewery and the fundamentalists overran the grounds, setting the building alight. It burned down, and there was no longer any question of filling the vats before Ramadan.

I think that I, like many Westerners, use the word "change" as a synonym for "progress," a step toward increased freedom, enlightenment, and modernization. But change can also be a leap in the opposite direction. The struggle over the Sirra brewery was a telling example of how the Middle East is in flux—something perfectly ordinary at one moment would suddenly spark an uproar as a general Islamic revival exerted increased influence on how Arabs viewed the world. Anything, particularly anything deemed foreign, might get sucked into the political fray.

Through various encounters it came to me that even dietary customs could be politically charged. Food was a means to get people
to think about different cultures and alternative ways of doing
things, a lesson I learned from the most famous chef in the Arab
world.

⊡   ⊡   ⊡

One early winter evening during my first trip to Beirut as the Middle East correspondent for the *Times*, I wandered into the annual
book fair. It struck me as a sad, marginal event for a city striving to
reclaim its title as cultural capital of the Arab world. The new convention center was still under construction at that point in 2001,
so the fair was held in a series of weatherproof white tents erected
in a parking lot bordering Martyrs' Square. In the glory years, the
square had been the beating heart of downtown where Christians,
Muslims, and Jews all interacted. During the war the Green Line
dividing the capital ran smack through it, gutting it. Afterward it
was mostly a square in name, the rubble from its many destroyed
buildings carted off and the gaping open spaces paved over. The
overall effect seemed to me like an exotic jigsaw puzzle with lots
of missing pieces. The book tents looked particularly forlorn in the
cold rain, but I went inside to ask what was selling well in the off
chance it might produce a story.

I fully expected the answer to be religious books—no real story
there. I had recently written an article in Cairo about the dire straits
of the publishing trade. Numerous wars had decimated some of the
strongest middle-class markets for fiction, namely Algeria, Sudan,
and Iraq. But a more important reason was quoted to me by Abdel
Ghaffar Mekawi, a retired professor of philosophy and a German
translator in Egypt. I met him in downtown Cairo, where he had
been sitting gnome-like and withdrawn in one corner of the dark,
high-ceilinged office belonging to a new publisher trying to find
emerging writers. The professor expressed the belief, tinged with a
certain black humor, that Arabs are so overwhelmed by unending

conflicts and stagnant politics, not to mention the endless grind of daily life, that they prefer reading texts that dwell on the afterlife. "All these books talk about death, the grave, hell," Professor Mekawi explained to me. "The public doesn't want to think about their lives, but their deaths."

So I was pleasantly surprised that the best seller among Lebanese publishers was a cookbook called Chef Ramzi after its author. It was in its tenth printing, with over 160,000 copies in circulation, a runaway hit in a region where selling 5,000 copies constitutes major success. The cookbook outsold every other book for two years right after it came out, according to various publishers, and remained among the top ten a few years later when I learned about it.

Before meeting the man himself, I decided to gauge the book's appeal by accosting grocery shoppers, so my charming Lebanese fixer, Leena Saidi, suggested I canvas Monoprix, a branch of the French supermarket chain. Stopping people at random in the meat section, I encountered the Teffaha family. "Have you ever used a recipe from Chef Ramzi?" I asked. The answer was effusive. All three family members tried to tell me at once how his cooking show completely transformed their feast marking the end of Ramadan. His tutelage allowed them to boldly defy tradition by scratching stuffed lamb off the menu and penciling in an entirely different sort of meal: a roast turkey, in fact.

Prompted by a steady diet of roast turkey on imported American television shows, the family had been discussing the idea for some time, but could not fathom how to cook one. They told me how they rifled through old Lebanese cookbooks but failed to unearth a recipe. No one in their building had ever tried cooking a turkey. Then an excited neighbor called one day at noon, shouting that they should turn on the television immediately. Chef Ramzi was preparing the very thing!

"The chef sort of said this is the American turkey you see on sit-coms," remembered Ghassan Teffaha, a 24-year-old student, pausing to savor his family's holiday feast all over again. "Watching so many people eating turkey, we wanted to try it. My mom learned how to do it from his show and it turned out to be a really good one."

I harbor a special attachment to Thanksgiving and the entire bird routine. I rarely cooked at home in Cairo because I was on the road so much. (One year I spent a total of two months there in spurts of a few days.) My grand, high-ceilinged apartment overlooking the Nile, though a welcome refuge, basically served as a pit stop where I emptied my notebooks or, on a free day, fiddled with the manuscript of my novel, *The Sand Café*, before hopping on the next plane.

But from my earliest years as a foreign correspondent I always tried to do Thanksgiving. It just made me feel grounded somehow— plus I love the menu even more than hummus. Most years I worked right through Christmas and New Year's, without minding much. But missing Thanksgiving was uniquely depressing.

On my first overseas assignment for The Associated Press, in Cyprus, my alleged oven was a tight fit for a scrawny chicken, let alone the linebacker turkey that I craved. But the capital, Nicosia, still boasted a few collective ovens left over from the days when its current neighborhoods were separate villages. Poor villagers lacking an oven would trot over to the public one with bread or whatever needed baking. I could just show up with my bird, tell them what time I wanted to collect it, and the oven workers did the rest. I dropped off my turkey around 8 A.M., intending to collect it after 4 P.M. I left the stuffing in a large pottery bowl to avoid any risk of salmonella. But the oven workers didn't quite grasp the concept of stuffing the bird, explained in mime rather than in my nonexistent Greek. They ended up shoving the entire pottery bowl into the high dome of their wood-fired, clay oven. The turkey and stuffing were cooked, but the expensive pottery bowl cracked into shards as it cooled.

My next Thanksgiving near-disaster unrolled in Jerusalem. The Israelis and Palestinians had announced a peace accord reached under Norwegian auspices in early 1993, just about the time I moved to the city from Kuwait. As further negotiations over the more difficult issues dragged on, accompanied by new surges in violence, I decided some form of ecumenical Thanksgiving was in order. It seemed like a small way to endorse the optimism that peace was possible. So I invited over a few Israelis, Palestinians, and Jordanians as well as one Egyptian and a British colleague. Around noon, as I went to put the turkey in the oven, the door came off in my hands. (My very own peace process, like the larger one, was unhinged.) It was a Saturday, the one day of the week when repairmen on both the Jewish and Arab sides of town were not working. So I did what always comes first in a cooking crisis: I called my mother in Vermont.

"Ma! The oven door fell off, what should I do?" I asked, explaining that I had tried and failed to prop the door on with a chair. Duct tape melted.

"Oh!" she said. "That happened to me one year. I just turned the oven up to 700 degrees and put the turkey in anyway."

"That worked?"

"No, it came out burned on the outside and raw in the middle."

Big help! Next I called around to the foreign press corps to farm out the turkey, but no one was home. They were all gathered at a collective Thanksgiving lunch, which nobody was eager to leave. Eventually I called my guests to tell them a group effort was required—they had to surrender their ovens or starve. The problem was that nobody had an oven big enough for everything— surely there was a metaphor in there for a future peace plan, but I let it rest. Eventually the turkey went to my British neighbor, while I divided the vegetables, pumpkin pie, and other dishes between an oven on the Arab side of town and one in Jewish Jerusalem. Then I got a cab driver to work for me for the afternoon so I could tend to all three ovens—basting the turkey, then driving over to check the vegetables, then basting the turkey again before cooking the pie. I commuted between my dishes for several hours and burned only one potato dish, which is more than could be said for the peace plan.

That Thanksgiving took place during a notably optimistic moment in Arab-Israeli relations. Despite violence fomented by extremists, both sides were tentatively charitable toward the other because a brief window of hope had opened. Given the ensuing friction—due in no small part to the utter lack of attention to the issue by the Bush administration until so late in its tenure that it had no leverage—I doubt the same guests would now want to share a meal together.

⌧   ⌧   ⌧

Ramzi Shwayri, the real name of the chef who introduced turkey to Ramadan, was on a mission to transform Arab cuisine. The black-haired chef, his burly frame bursting out of his uniform, tinkered with traditional recipes and introduced foods once experienced only vicariously. He wanted Arab households to get away from standard fare like falafel or kibbeh at every meal, to sample new dishes. Part of Chef Ramzi's mass appeal was that, while cooking on television, he fielded live calls from anybody with a food question. Future Television had to add two operators to answer the phones while he was on the air. The chef, in his mid-30s, blossomed into a regional phenomenon, his satellite television broadcast considered mandatory viewing from Muscat to Marrakesh and beyond.

Watching him work felt like eavesdropping on an extended Arab living room. Once a bee plopped down into a cream dish just minutes before the show ended. Chef Ramzi told me he could not ignore it because the cameraman ("Al-humar!" he yelled in Arabic as he recounted the story—"The donkey," a crowning insult) focused right on it. So the chef scooped it out with a large spoon and proclaimed the dish unsullied.

A woman from Saudi Arabia called immediately to complain that for the sake of hygiene—and wasn't the chef always harping about hygiene in the kitchen—he should have tossed out the whole thing. The Sudanese woman who called next argued that bees were mentioned in the Koran as exceptionally clean insects with their own souls, so he should have left it. A Syrian man then phoned, wondering if they could drop the religious philosophizing and hauling the Koran into every single conversation for once already and just cook?

Occasionally food intersected with politics in a similarly amusing vein. This was especially true in Egypt, where humor acts like a force field to deflect the daily strain of living in such an overpopulated environment. After not eating all day during Ramadan, most Muslim households first break the fast by nibbling on a few dates before tucking into something far more substantial. In Cairo, the competition at the wholesale date market was fierce, so every year the sellers tried to come up with catchy nicknames for the dozen or so varieties to attract buyers.

During the buildup to the invasion of Iraq, the dates nicknamed "Saddam Hussein's Weapons of Mass Destruction" were not selling well. The moniker went to a particularly long, costly date imported from Iraq, a country once famous for producing dates so thick and chewy that I sometimes felt like I was eating chocolate. "Look at them, they look just like Scud missiles," the seller, Sayid Mahmoud, told me, scooping one out of an overflowing burlap sack. "Sales are just OK. I think people are waiting to see what happens with America. I'm sure if he uses his missiles, sales will improve."

But "Yasir Arafat" and the revived best seller from previous years, "Osama bin Laden," sold out fast. Like any good reporter, I took this as a barometer for the general mood—a reflection that the plight of the Palestinians and the general idea of sticking it to the U.S. were the preoccupations of the moment. However, perhaps the most telling sign of the prevailing mood was one of economic hardship. Lots of people ignored the politics of the derogatory name "Bush and Sharon" assigned to the absolute lowest-quality dates, more bitter than sweet. One shopper piling them into his bag shrugged as he told me, "At least they are so tough that I know they won't have any mites in them."

Chef Ramzi, which is what everyone on Beirut's streets calls him, did not set out to become a famous cook. He was the third of four children born in Beirut to a Greek Orthodox father. In 1957, the elder Shwayri started Al-Kafaat Foundation, which teaches vocational skills to troubled or handicapped youths. The son, forced by the civil war to finish his education in France, studied economics and law at the University of Lyon. Embarrassed that his father, stuck in a Beirut bomb shelter, was supporting him, he spent summers studying cooking or working in restaurants with the idea of improving the foundation's catering department. He now runs it, and once invited me there for a boisterous New Year's Eve bash with some of the hundreds of cooks and restaurant workers he trains for Lebanon's renascent hotel industry.

He told me that he wrote the cookbook because the Lebanese, emerging from the war with a craving for varied recipes with a soupçon of things foreign, could not find anything serious on the market. That and questions from his show determined the book's contents. Some of it fell into the cooking-for-idiots category. "Break the egg over the frying pan" reads roughly one-third of the recipe for a fried egg.

"I get asked," he shrugged.

But the 824 recipes detail everything from falafel to sushi to brownies. (Because he insisted on picturing every dish, the Arabic version ran to 572 pages and weighed five pounds.) It also boasted 157 pages of desserts, which helped explain the sixty-six pounds the chef gained after starting the show. The cooking program is normally broadcast three days a week but it comes on daily during Ramadan because housewives are so desperate for fresh ideas to break the fast. (Ramadan is an extended period of family meals— think Thanksgiving dinner multiplied by a month.) The cookbook mixed short cultural references along with the food—like a song women grinding wheat used to sing to men passing by. "Even if I was dead and you just shot me one glance, my bones would dance with joy," part of it went. Saudi Arabia, in a typically enlightened move, banned the work because some of the village photographs in the book showed churches.

Chef Ramzi respected the basics of all Middle Eastern dishes, but raised some hackles with innovations like using pistachio nuts frequently instead of almonds. In cooking, as in many aspects of life, Arabs can be sticklers for tradition even while expressing an interest in change. After more than 1,000 shows, the chef concluded that his most difficult task was to convince Arabs to experiment. "They know how their mother used to do it, and their grandmother, so for them this is a holy recipe, they can't change it," he told me. "I tell people not to be prisoners of your recipes, you have to let your imagination take over, and they are starting to."

Arab nations squabble about food along with everything else, so Chef Ramzi discovered that favoring a Lebanese method would prompt a flood of protest calls from, say, Egypt. So with every dish he mentioned various national alternatives. He avoided dishes containing wine or pork out of respect for Islamic dietary laws. But so many callers asked for a wine substitute for the Western dishes they were trying to emulate that he developed a recipe using vinegar.

After I had watched a few shows and written about it, the chef offered to take me on a food tour of Lebanon, revealing some of what he had discovered by wandering through remote villages and asking the older women about their specialties. An editor at the "Dining" section of the *Times* was thrilled at the idea. It was the kind of fantastic assignment that, alas, happened all too rarely in my tenure as a correspondent—driving around remote rural areas to eat all day, knowing that I would get a big splash in one of the paper's most popular sections with the lightest of editing. It was one of those days when I couldn't quite believe that I was getting paid for the work. (As opposed to many days in the Middle East, in places like Baghdad, where I was convinced they weren't paying me nearly enough.)

I confess that while driving through the Bekaa valley, the roadsides festooned with Hizbollah's martial décor, I felt it was a bit strange to be discussing the fine varieties of food found in remote villages—the very type of villages where all manner of unsavory characters might be hiding. It turned out the chef was feeling a little bit of the same, although he didn't let on until the day ended. The retired army officer ostensibly along for the ride was actually a bodyguard, with a pistol stashed underneath the seat—not that we ever needed it.

"The basic philosophy of Lebanon's cuisine is that you want a few little things to eat while enjoying the company of friends," the chef told me, expanding on the subject of mezze, Middle Eastern hors d'oeuvres traditionally served with arak, a liquor distilled with aniseed. "The original idea of mezze was to have a small glass of arak and chat for two or three hours, maybe enjoy the view. But now the mezze has become something where you sit for three hours and just eat. It has lost some of its meaning."

A large, powder-blue BMW sandwiched itself between the chef's dark-blue 1992 Range Rover and the army truck that happened to be on the road in front of us. The BMW had no license plates and the chef pointed out that the tan patches around the trunk lock indicated new bodywork. "It's stolen," he explained, noting that the northern Bekaa is particularly famous for both its creamy yoghurt and vehicle chop shops. If the cars weren't dismembered for parts, they were either ransomed back to their owners or sold cheap. The BMW sped past the army truck and disappeared.

We started talking about mezze again. "No restaurant is famous in Lebanon because of the chef," he told me, shaking his head. "Before the war, people used to go to restaurants for the chef, but now cooking is not important to them. I would like us to start over again where cooking will prevail over any other art."

One starting point, Chef Ramzi believed, might be with the traditional mezze. "Mezze" is one word Arabs use for appetizers, although it is likely Turkish in origin. The chef thinks the concept developed independently among different peoples, starting in Lebanon in the early 1920s at the small riverside restaurants in the Bekaa valley town of Zahlé. We walked beside the gurgling brook there, where travelers coming from Syria once rested before hauling over the soaring Lebanon range to Beirut. Charming restaurant terraces under pergolas now crowd both banks.

Those prototype mezzes consisted of five or six things served in small rectangular pottery plates—raw okra, olives, fried strips of eggplant, boiled eggs, broad beans cooked in olive oil and garlic mixed into labné, the thick strained yoghurt that is a Lebanese staple. (Hummus evolved later.) Eventually, however, small establishments in Beirut started competing with each other to add original dishes and salads, to the point where today it is not uncommon to find a table crowded with twenty plates including oddities for the region like smoked salmon or spring rolls. I thought mezze reflected the Lebanese themselves—gregarious, light-hearted, fun, sociable, but lacking a certain stick-to-the-ribs substance.

"Mezze should be simple and stay in small amounts, you should not worry about having enough variety to fill the whole table," Chef Ramzi told me. "I think it is something Lebanese chefs should think about, about quality. When the emphasis is on quantity it means people have lost the idea. They just eat a lot. If it is a meal, then it is too much." He thinks the best mezze consists of a balance of cold and hot dishes, but all with fresh ingredients. He recommended a few raw vegetables, tabouleh salad, perhaps tomato slices sprinkled with thyme and olive oil, then some cooked vegetables, small portions of meat, and some cheese.

It was a fine recommendation, and I also heartily agreed with arak aficionados who claimed that it is the only drink to accompany mezze. Wine or whisky shadows the myriad tangy flavors or even deadens them, while the smooth, cool, refreshing liquor, tasting of licorice with a dash of peppermint, washes the taste buds, cleansing the palate between each bite. "There are drinks to get you drunk and there are drinks to be savored with food," George Haiby, a trim 67-year-old home arak distiller, told me when I went to visit him in his village high on Mount Lebanon. Arak makers extol its holistic properties, claiming that aniseed aids digestion and relaxation. But it is, after all, liquor, and a long lunch can leave one inebriated, not least because arak is around 53-proof. Diluting it with water brings the alcohol content down to something roughly between wine and vodka.

Haiby told me that a village elder used to repeat a catchy little axiom about the native beverage. "The first glass is for medicinal purposes, the second glass makes you happy, and with the third, you eat the wind," he said, using a Lebanese expression for someone who blathers endlessly. Little wonder, then, that a Sunday lunch splashed with arak stretches easily into a five-hour affair.

Maybe all the talk about change in the Middle East is eating the wind—there were times when I grew distinctly pessimistic about actually witnessing any real progress. But after chasing Chef Ramzi around over the course of a couple years, I was convinced by his infectious enthusiasm that even food could serve as an agent for change, a raft for diplomacy and cultural understanding. In the West, the long years of civil war turned "Beirut" into a buzzword for chaotic conflict, a reputation that has lived on largely through the advent of Hizbollah. The West views the region like light refracted through a prism, choosing to see only the dark colors. It is a mistake to view the darker aspects of life in the Middle East as the entire spectrum and write off the rest. Chef Ramzi's success certainly indicated that there is a wide audience across the Arab world eager to learn more about other countries, to look beyond its traditions toward other ways of doing things. McDonald's and its ilk are not the only aspect of the West that appeals across borders. Unique national dishes like Thanksgiving dinner also have their place in opening the pathways for new ideas.

CHAPTER 6

FATWA!

I consider sport a necessity for the health of everyone's mind and body and I agree with it.

> —a fatwa from Ayatollah Ali Khamenei, Iran's supreme leader, endorsing sports

PICK A RANDOM HOTEL LOBBY in Jidda, Saudi Arabia, at almost any hour of day or night and chances are you will find clusters of men ambling through, each of them swathed in two large white bath towels. I was first exposed to this curious spectacle as a novice foreign correspondent in September 1990. I found myself unexpectedly plunked down in the middle of the Red Sea port around midnight, slightly groggy after a harrowing drive down out of the Hejaz mountains. Standing at the reception desk of the Crown Plaza Hotel, I attributed the parade of men in towels through the lobby either to an unusually popular hotel spa or perhaps to the weather—the stifling daytime humidity had not quite relinquished its grip. A giggling desk clerk set me straight—the men were all pilgrims either headed for Mecca or just returned.

For centuries, Jidda has been the coastal jumping-off point where the faithful trek inland to the holy city of Mecca, the birthplace of Islam. The annual pilgrimage, one of five sacrosanct duties for any Muslim, takes place during a specified month, but the off-season version—called "umrah" in Arabic—is popular year round. Male pilgrims all wear the same religiously prescribed garments—two pieces of unsewn white cloth, usually terry cloth. The piece wrapped around the waist drops to mid-calf or lower, and the second is thrown over one or both shoulders. A shaved head or at least very short hair is also de rigueur for those who have completed the ritual. (Women wear a white garment that shrouds them completely.)

Back in Jidda for the *Times*, I found myself in yet another hotel lobby, again watching pilgrims ebb and flow across its highly polished white marble floor. This time I was standing with Mohamed el-Dakhakhny, a garrulous Egyptian photographer who often traveled with me around the region. Most pilgrims are older and often flabby, with prominent guts jutting over their towels. So we were both struck by one fit young guy who had cinched a somewhat shorter towel tightly around his skinny waist and accessorized his newly shaved head with dark, wraparound Ray-Bans. He apparently did fine in Mecca, and would not have been out of place in Tahiti, either. I started teasing Mohamed that he might as well abandon the pilgrim business because he would never look as cool even if he shaved his thinning black hair. Mohamed laughed, but he had something else on his mind.

Both he and Abeer Allam, the Egyptian reporter who also traveled with me periodically, wanted to make umrah before we left Jidda for Cairo a few days later.

Both were practicing Muslims who knew the Koran well but wore their faith lightly—they respected the religion without being the least bit dogmatic. Wherever we traveled, though, Mohamed was constantly chatting with people we encountered about matters of religious practice, local traditions, and the like. I discovered that he was secretly pleased that he had a dilemma to resolve in this, the homeland of Islam. It gave him an excuse to call a Saudi cleric for a fatwa, a legal opinion drawn from religious law, on the matter. In theory, making any pilgrimage to Mecca wipes the slate clean in terms of accumulated sins. So what worried Mohamed was whether riding in the same car with Abeer, a colleague but certainly not his wife, would somehow negate any religious absolution. He consulted with a few Saudis and then settled on a learned sheikh to petition.

Whenever I mention the word "fatwa" to friends in the West, they usually equate it with a death sentence. This stems from the most famous fatwa of modern times, the one the late Ayatollah Ruhollah Khomeini of Iran leveled against the author Salman Rushdie in 1989, accusing him of blaspheming Islam in his novel The Satanic Verses, and sentencing him to death. In the ensuing years, the fatwas that attracted the attention of most foreign correspondents also tended to be those with some manner of grim punishment involved. But actually fatwas can be devoted to any topic, large or small, and the devout seek them out constantly like grease that smoothes all manner of daily decisions.

Religious scholars issue fatwas on questions ranging from household quandaries to major issues of public policy. Often expressed in one terse sentence, fatwas answered mundane questions like whether a Muslim woman should ride a bicycle (usually not, too publicly physical) or a man should wear soccer shorts (only if they modestly come below his knees even when he sits down). On the other hand, when the Saudi royal family needed the cover of religion to allow 500,000 infidel American soldiers to deploy in the kingdom after Saddam Hussein invaded Kuwait in August 1990, the princes twisted the arm of the grand mufti to issue a fatwa endorsing the idea. Sheikh Abdulaziz bin Baz, the chairman of The Supreme Council of Religious Scholars, declared that the need to engage all possible means to defend the nation made that permissible. He cited the Koran and other texts supporting the idea that a Muslim leader should take all necessary measures before it is too late.

But religious rulings on day-to-day issues like the one my photographer wanted to ask about—whether unmarried colleagues should share a car ride—are far more common. I figured the answer Mohamed sought was a foregone conclusion. We were, after all, in Saudi Arabia, where special religious police impose decisions crucial to law enforcement like ensuring that men and women riding in the same car are either married or otherwise related. Officially known as The Committee for the Promotion of Virtue and the Prevention of Vice, the religious police both infuriate and intimidate the nonzealous segment of the population. It doesn't take much to get a well-educated Saudi to seethe in frustration at the waste of time and invasion of privacy entailed by any encounter with the muttawa, or "volunteers," as the religious police are called in Arabic.

Take Saud, the executive director of a marketing company, who once found himself pulled over in traffic and forced to answer questions while his spouse was interrogated separately. He did not want me to use his last name lest that attract further unwanted attention.

"I'm an engineer with an MBA driving in my car with my own wife and being questioned about who she is by this idiot who probably didn't graduate from high school," he raged when the subject of the muttawa came up. "Is he God to judge me? They asked what color is our refrigerator? How many kids do we have? What is the color of our bedroom?" When Saud inquired as to why he had been stopped, the muttawa told him it was because he and his wife had been spotted laughing together in the car's front seat. "People shouldn't laugh, particularly with women," he told me. "They are for sex only. That is their attitude."

In Jidda, needless to say, when my photographer called the religious sheikh to ask about sharing a ride to Mecca with Abeer, the horrified cleric told him in the strictest terms that separate cars were an absolute, divinely ordered necessity. Mohamed, rather pleased with the idea of arranging their trip to Mecca based on an authentic religious fiat, went to Abeer to inform her that they would have to travel apart. Abeer, though steamed, told Mohamed she was fine with respecting the ruling if he insisted, but pointed out that they had already agreed to split the cost of just one car. No good Muslim could renege on a deal, she said, so he would have to pay for the cost of half of her car as well as all of his own. Mohamed was nothing if not thrifty, except for important stuff like golf clubs and sunglasses. Arguing with the wily and willful Abeer got him nowhere. The cost involved sank any lingering desire to respect the sheikh's ruling, so he hit upon a far easier solution.

"Maybe I can find another sheikh!" he exclaimed. He did, and eventually the two shared one car to Mecca and back. (The holy city is off limits to non-Muslims—made abundantly clear with highway signs that basically say "Last Exit for Infidels!"—so all I could do was chuckle about their standoff from a distance.)

Mohamed's technique is sometimes called fatwa shopping, fishing around for a religious scholar who will endorse whatever the supplicant wants. That elasticity on any topic large or small underscores both the benefit and the bane of Islam having no formal ruling structure.

On the one hand, Muslims can rely on their local mosque leader or other respected figure to help interpret complicated, 1,400-year-old religious texts in a way that they can apply to their modern lives. It makes them feel good about their own adherence to their faith. On the downside, men with the most tenuous religious training issue fatwas with impunity. The plethora in recent years has often engendered widespread confusion about which are legitimate and, more notoriously, provided rather flimsy religious justification for all manner of bloody mayhem. Although fatwas issued by official committees or senior clerical political leaders can carry the weight of law, most are nonbinding, allowing states or individuals to pick and choose as they please, which just adds to the muddle. Some prominent religious figures have suggested forming an international panel of scholars to be a kind of centralized fatwa authority, but the idea has not gained much traction. Instead, fatwa shopping has helped breed fatwa chaos.

The fatwa conundrum underscores one key problem in trying to foment any change or reform in the Middle East. There are so many competing voices, all claiming legitimacy, that it is difficult for any-one to separate fatwas rooted in a genuine desire to interpret the faith from those formulated to achieve political goals. The cacoph-ony hampers singling out any one ruling as authentic.

Who can sort out the contradictions when fatwas on exactly the same question, like whether women should run in elections, can promote opinions that are polar opposites? Critics say far more fat-was are rooted in ideology, in the desire to push a particular policy, than in weighty religious wisdom. The fact that some governments keep senior clerics on the payroll obviously casts doubt on the amount of independent thought behind their rulings. But anyone attacking fatwas risks being accused of blasphemy.

I accept the argument by secular intellectuals that the fatwa ex-plosion is another symptom of the fact that people in the Middle East feel so hopeless and powerless that they focus on the afterlife. If they had more say over their current lives, the influence of reli-gion would diminish. As it stands now, people aren't convinced that any shift in government will bring tangible benefits, which feeds apathy about pushing for change. On the other hand, many believe worship, and by extension following fatwas, will be rewarded with paradise.

One sign that civil society and the rule of law are gaining ground, that people feel as though they have the means to effect change, will be a reduced profile for religious rulings on every single aspect of life. To get to that point, people need to be treated more like citizens and less like subjects. Once people feel that their own voices matter, that they can influence what happens to them on earth, there will be less inclination to make everything conform to Islam so they can go to heaven. Or as my friend Ateyyat el-Abnoudy, an accomplished Egyptian filmmaker, would often tell me, "We say you have to make paradise on earth, not wait until death for pleasure."

Periodically when I was interviewing Prince Saud al-Faisal, Saudi Arabia's longtime foreign minister, he would find himself quoting some Arab proverb and would stop to groan, "You know we have a saying for everything." I often felt the same way about fatwas. No topic seemed too obscure, and when trying to assess the viewpoints of competing camps I found it difficult to determine just how much weight to give to the fatwa artillery they inevitably deployed.

Just to add to the confusion, all kinds of religious rulings were labeled fatwas when they were not. Technically, something should only be called a fatwa when it breaks new ground. If a supplicant asked a religious scholar if he could divorce his wife via email, for example, something that had never been done before, the ruling could be considered a fatwa because it spoke to a novel issue. But if it was a question that had been asked hundreds of times before—If you don't bathe after sex can you pray?—then the answer is just a ruling and not a fatwa. The two sides on any controversial issue would inevitably wrangle over whether it was actually a fatwa that ignited the scandal of the moment or just some ordinary opinion. Often it proved impossible to untangle. But the larger point is that people constantly sought a religious seal of approval for whatever they did.

Most fatwas or religious rulings I encountered fell into two broad categories. The first were social—the literally thousands of guidelines issued daily, designed to help people navigate life. These cover myriad matters of hygiene and sex and dress and you name it. Social rulings go largely unnoticed, frankly, although now and again one is so outrageous that the ensuing public outcry forces the religious authority to withdraw it. More often than not the embattled cleric in question will not actually rescind the fatwa, instead claiming that either his words had been "misinterpreted" or that he had merely been expressing an opinion that was mistakenly taken as a fatwa. In Egypt in May 2007, for example, a working woman asked her imam, or cleric, whether she had to veil her hair around the one male colleague whom she had worked with every day for years and years. The cleric ruled that if she suckled her colleague on her breast five times, a traditional Islamic prescription for becoming a sanctioned surrogate mother, then he could be considered family and she could remove her headscarf at work. Naturally the idea of a grown, hirsute man slurping a female colleague's bared breast so that she could discard her more modest dress, while certainly breaking new ground, defied logic and the fatwa was shouted down.

The second category can be lumped together as political fatwas, when the faithful call on religious authorities to help them decide on issues of the day, or even how to deal with a new phenomenon like elections. Average citizens often turned to religious figures for their perspective on whether the whole process of political change, and with it the democratic political tradition taken for granted in the West, was acceptable under Islam. The welter of rulings on that subject brought far more confusion than clarity.

I should point out that sheer numbers make it difficult to generalize about fatwas. Sheikh Ali Gomaa, the grand mufti and therefore Egypt's highest religious official, told me at the end of 2008 that Dar Al-Iftaa, or the House of Fatwa, the official fatwa-issuing authority under the Ministry of Justice, answered more than 3,000 queries on religious issues per day. Some twenty religious sheikhs employed full time churned them out in eight languages. The number had tripled over the previous year, which he attributed partly to religious fervor and partly to the ease of asking for them via email and the Internet. Not so many years ago it was just twenty-five fatwas per day, a number the grand mufti himself could handle. Seemingly ignoring his own pronouncements that gave the government periodic cover, he also decried the fact that the blizzard of fatwas was undermining them both as a tool to combat extremism and as a means to ensure that Islamic laws were flexible and balanced.

Those 3,000 fatwas do not include rulings from other key institutions like Al-Azhar University, the historic seat of Sunni Islamic scholarship, which maintains its own fatwa department, as does Cairo University's Center for Islamic Research and Studies. Other options have just multiplied in the digital age. Any self-respecting cleric or religious institution with a website usually has a page devoted to issuing fatwas and an archive cataloguing all previous wisdom. Media companies that offer a mixture of services to telephone customers such as a daily joke, sports scores, and horoscopes sometimes include a dial-a-sheikh service for rulings over the phone.

Fatwa programs on TV are becoming more and more popular, with sheikhs answering questions sent by email or called in live. But Sheikh Gomaa thought the fact that Egypt's House of Fatwa was attracting so many queries was a sign of success, an indication that people wanted authentic rulings rather than any old quackery from the Internet or satellite television. "It's like hospital orderlies wanting to perform open heart surgery—is that possible?!" he told me. I am not so sure. Those satellite stations seemed awfully popular, and Sheikh Gomaa admitted that opinion about them see-sawed back and forth.

To give you a flavor, one email question answered on a Saudi satellite channel was whether the faithful should clean themselves with paper or water after using the toilet. The sheikh responded, "It is forbidden to use toilet paper if water is available," then went on to suggest that some combination of the two was likely the best option. Part of the question focused on whether what you did in the bathroom was being monitored by a higher being, and the sheikh assured the viewers that toilet protocol might indeed affect your chances of entering paradise. The problem was that if you were not thoroughly clean for prayer, then your supplications wouldn't count and hellfire loomed.

The issues were taken so seriously that I often ended up collapsed with laughter, but it signaled just how central a role religion played in many people's lives. Fatwas were probably more popular among Egyptians and Saudis than elsewhere, given how devout people are in those two countries, but if you expand all the institutions as well as the services issuing religious rulings across more than two dozen countries in the Middle East, you begin to get the idea that the raft of daily life floats on a veritable sea of religious pronouncements.

During my many years reporting in the region I bumped into them constantly, even in the most unexpected places. Among the most striking, at least in terms of display, sat at the very entrance to the slopes at Dizin, an Iranian ski resort in the Alborz mountains. Skiing was an elitist sport associated with the hated shah, so when the Islamic revolution deposed him in 1979, everything was done to discourage it. Eventually the resorts were reopened in a distinctly Islamic manner—the first time I went skiing in Dizin in 1993 the slopes were segregated by gender. The split started in line for the main gondola, with women boarding for fifteen minutes and then men. The day I was there someone had evidently forgotten to brief the South Korean ambassador, who got into a shoving match with the Revolutionary Guards because they kept pulling him out of the women's line, where he was standing next to his wife.

In those days women had to wear a nylon version of the traditional chador. They billowed downhill like so many spinnakers flying loose. Men were constantly trying to sneak onto the women's slopes—some cross-dressing in the flapping nylon—so the Revolutionary Guards ran a small jail at the base used to incarcerate the ones they caught. Even I was thrown in it for a couple hours: My transgression was reporting without a government permit. After the jail's commander ripped up my notebook before my eyes and released me, I made sure to ask questions only inside the gondola.

The jail sat near a squat mosque at the bottom of the slopes that local lore said had supplanted a bar—the boom of the noon call to prayer from its powerful megaphones echoed across the mountains so loudly that I wondered if it might trigger avalanches. On Fridays, the resort operators used the megaphones to remind all the skiers where they really ought to be spending the Sabbath—the weekly mosque sermon from Tehran University thundered out live over the slopes. In those days the buildings housing the various lifts were also painted with suitably Islamic revolutionary slogans like "All Muslims Revere the Athlete."

By the time I was skiing there again in 2002, things had loosened up considerably under the government of President Mohamed Khatami. Men and women were even snuggling together—an unheard-of public infraction previously—in the restaurants on the upper slopes. But just in case anyone headed onto the lifts harbored any doubt about whether skiing corresponded with Islamic family values, the sports authority had erected a giant billboard painted with a picture of both the supreme leader, Ayatollah Ali Khamenei, and a racer shredding downhill. The lettering, in both Persian and slightly butchered English, spelled out the ayatollah's fatwa on the issue: "I consider sport a necessity for the health of everyone's mind and body and I agr [sic] with it."

Nearby, a female guard stationed right before the main gondola reminded all the women heading onto the slopes not to show any hair, a warning they ignored the second they were on the mountain. The juxtaposition between the supreme leader's fatwa and the actual behavior underscored to me the gap between the mullahs and the way people actually lived. Still, even something as mundane as skiing took place under the umbrella of a religious endorsement.

᠅ ᠅ ᠅

Perhaps my all-time favorite wrestling match between mullahs issuing repeated fatwas and Iranians openly flouting them concerned dogs. The 1979 revolution was supposed to bring forth the first pure Islamic state, so every few years the more zealous clerics would decide that pet dogs had to go. First, religious texts condemn them as unclean, plus the love Westerners shower on pets made them inherently suspect. Iran was hardly alone in this matter—the religious police in Saudi Arabia were also canine averse. In fact, dogs are not particularly popular anywhere in the Arab world because the culture of holding them in low regard affects everyone, including Christians and others. But Iranians in general are much more defiant than Arabs on such social matters.

I had learned that no self-respecting Iranian ayatollah reaches his exalted rank without producing a tome roughly the size of the Manhattan telephone directory describing in minute detail the prescriptions for leading a good Islamic life. I had also been told that some of the information on matters of hygiene comes across as entirely practical, like if while bathing you use your thumb to wash out your anus, how far you can slide it in before you move from ablution (Virtue!) to masturbation (Vice!).

Publishers in the holy city of Qom have helpfully translated the works of the grandest ayatollahs into English, so I went to a large bookstore there to research dog fatwas. The references were remarkably uniform—to the extent that they read like one had cribbed from the next—in placing dogs high on the list of unclean things that any good Muslim shuns. In addition, the Islamic Propaganda Office in Qom published an abridged compilation of fatwas called "Everything You Need to Know." Its list of things that all Muslims should avidly avoid was topped by beer, wine, infidels, and dogs.

Emerging from the bookstore, I spotted a glass storefront labeled "The Information Bank," which the Times's endlessly resourceful Iranian reporter, Nazila Fathi, informed me was a computerized reference library for religious queries. Thrilled, I went straight in to ask "What does Islam say about dogs?" The obliging staff plugged the word "dog" into their computers and all the official citations came whirring out. The Koran contains just one vague reference to a tribe that owned dogs. But the Hadith, the often disputed sayings of the prophet and his contemporaries that form the basis for much Islamic law, mentioned dogs no fewer than 430 times.

A few references noted positive characteristics such as their loyalty and herding abilities. So guard dogs and sheep dogs are condoned. But most Hadiths denigrated dogs as "najis," Arabic for unclean. "Angels do not enter a house that has either a dog or a picture in it," read one. Another said, "Whoever keeps a dog except for hunting, guarding cattle, and crops will lose one large measure of his reward every day," i.e., a pet dog is a serious impediment to entering paradise.

The religious texts warned about the perils of owning even acceptable dogs. If a guard dog licks one of your dinner plates, for example, serious scrubbing is involved to restore its cleanliness. "When the dog licks the utensil, wash it seven times, and rub it with earth the eighth time," advised one Hadith. Dog owners get around this one by claiming the Hadith is surely being taken out of context, the seventh-century dog in question probably had rabies or something. Also the arguments go on endlessly whether the Prophet Mohamed was issuing an all-encompassing edict, or just expressing an opinion befitting a very limited, one-time situation.

My initial interest in the whole doggie debate was sparked by a midranking provincial cleric whose Friday sermon fulminating against four-legged should-not-be-friends was featured on the national news. "I would like to thank the honorable police and judges and all those who worked to arrest dog lovers and to confiscate short-legged dogs in this city!" he thundered, going on to suggest that the martyrs for Islam who died in the Iran-Iraq War, which had ended a good thirteen years earlier, should consider themselves doubly blessed because they died before enduring such insults to Islamic values. "Happy are those who became martyrs and did not witness the playing with dogs!" the mullah ranted. "Now in our society women wear hats and men hold dogs!" (Some of the more daring Iranian women had tried to replace their mandatory headscarves with hats.)

Dog owners told me that a wave of fatwas condemning dogs spilled out about every two years. With the number of dogs available sharply limited since dog sellers were treated as lowly criminals, a black market thrived. I met one well-to-do woman in north Tehran who had let her tall black poodle wander a little too far, only to watch in horror as two men on a motorbike swooped past and grabbed the pooch. The woman found her pet for sale a week later in Molavi, a commercial district near the downtown bazaar and home to the main animal market—selling mostly birds but also exotic creatures like snakes, squirrels, and monkeys. Thieves trafficking in kidnapped dogs worked out of their car trunks. They deployed much like Western drug dealers, sidling up to pedestrians to whisper, "Dog, got a dog." One who approached me was more specific. "Got a German shepherd," he whispered in English right in my ear.

When I asked pet-shop owners about dogs, I always got a quick reaction. "We have all kinds of dogs, except the kind that wear turbans," laughed one. On the sidewalk I bumped into a municipal worker cruising the market looking for dogs to confiscate. He explained to me that the owner had to produce a license and a record of shots to stay any execution. He was immediately denounced by a man waving a dog license and demanding his animal back. When the city worker demurred, the man started screaming and grabbed the municipal worker around the throat, choking him and prompting police intervention.

One bystander suddenly turned to me and said quietly, "There are no laws in the way they take away dogs, just like people."

Not all fatwa fights provided such a vivid illustration of the way a country actually works. More often I was left scratching my head trying to figure out their importance. Sometimes fatwas came across as so strikingly obvious that I wanted to explore what was the point exactly, to understand why these abbreviated pronouncements were so cherished.

For answers, I went to Al-Azhar University, one of the world's oldest centers of Muslim scholarship set in the heart of Cairo's teeming medieval quarter, to speak with Sheikh Khalid el-Guindi, a young religious scholar trying to modernize the whole fatwa process.

Fatwas serve as the link between the various schools of Islam and contemporary reality, he told me, and are rooted in explaining Shariah, or Islamic law, in a way that teaches people good morals: "A fatwa is the means by which a sheikh works on repairing life through religion and closing the gap between what the religion demands and what actually occurs."

Islam can be broken down into two parts, he said, made up of
the beliefs themselves and then deeds, or the way it is lived.
Some deeds are clear-cut, like how to pray, but the bulk of life is
more ambiguous. Fatwas try to minimize that ambiguity in such
a way that society benefits. Sheikh Guindi attempted to put the
best possible spin on the fact that fatwas were all over the map,
calling the differences of opinion part of the religion's "democratic spirit" that had existed since it was founded. The Koran says
that decisions have to be made via consultation, Sheikh Guindi
told me, but given the fact that the sacred texts are all open to interpretation, there is no absolute right opinion. True religious
scholars had to approach fatwas with the spirit that "my opinion
is right, but there is the possibility that it is mistaken, and the
other opinion is wrong but there is the possibility that it might
be right." Naturally this spirit fuels fatwa shopping and more
than a little anarchy.

Sheikh Guindi was the main religious scholar behind a wildly
popular dial-a-sheikh service called The Islamic Line, and he let me
spend a few hours listening in to the hundreds of calls he got each
day. Older scholars, arguing that fatwas should be free, had criticized him because people had to pay for the service on their
phone bills. Sheikh Guindi brushed them aside as dinosaurs.
"Why are religious issues so often discussed with a frown, with
tension, with stiffness and violence?" the sheikh said to me in his
living room, where he had exchanged his clerical garb for a polo
shirt. "We reject this. As a matter of fact we—a group of religious
scholars—understand that we have to work with the new technology and to use it to serve religion."

The Islamic Line was designed to help negotiate the dense
thicket of religious tradition in minimal time. Ninety percent of the
callers were women and 30 percent of all calls were about sex,
which Sheikh Guindi believed indicated that many felt more comfortable asking deeply personal questions over the telephone than
in person. "Islam does not welcome any interference between man
and God," Sheikh Guindi told me. "But the scholars are the ones

who specialize in religious manuscripts and can transmit it to people in a way they can understand."

The irrepressible sheikh giggled at some of the calls—like one man asking how to use a condom or another demanding why, exactly, smoking hashish is forbidden or the woman wanting to know what the reward for her gender was in heaven given that men were promised a bevy of beautiful virgins. (The answer: one man, but such a good one that she would want no other.)

The sheikh could be stern when callers sounded wobbly in their practices. One woman said she owned three hotels in major tourist sites around Egypt, pulling in over $1 million in annual profit from alcohol sales alone. She wanted to confirm that giving all that money to charity would absolve her of any sin associated with selling something that Islam forbids. The sheikh warned her that the money was tainted and the only way to avoid punishment in the hereafter was to get out of the business. When a caller asked what it meant to be secular, Sheikh Guindi gave a somewhat long explanation about those who separate religion from improving the society. He said dividing the two is impossible because God created the faith in order to regulate all aspects of life.

The sheikh attributed the high volume of calls about sex to the fact that unemployed young people had plenty of free time on their hands and were more inclined to experiment. One man called asking if masturbation is a sin; the sheikh counseled prayer and lots of sports before marriage. Another man said he had a gay friend and wanted to know how Islam judged homosexuals. Sheikh Guindi said it was such a big sin that it shook the heavens and that the man's friend should repent—consulting a doctor if he is sick and getting married if he is single. The sheikh advised the caller to drop his friendship with the man lest he fall under the homosexual spell.

One woman said she was having an affair with a man who offered her a form of do-it-yourself Islamic marriage to lend their liaison legitimacy. The sheikh, who usually kept his fatwas short and snappy because the callers paid by the minute, went on at length telling her to ditch the guy before he drags her "to the bottom of a well filled with depravity." Any man worth trusting would want an officially registered marriage.

"I'm warning you seriously that this young man is fooling with you and playing with you and that he will dump you in the first garbage can when he loses interest in you and he will run away as if he did nothing," the sheikh said. "He wants to keep this sexual relationship with you while giving it the cover of a legal relationship."

To absolve herself of sin, he said, she had to regret what she had done, never repeat it, and pay money to the poor as charity if she could afford it because good deeds outweigh bad deeds and keep the whole thing secret. Sheikh Guindi told me that he wanted to emphasize the gentle side of Islam, which at least superficially appeared to be the case when, for example, two of the four-minute pre-taped sermons available over the phone on particular topics included "Why should you wear the veil?" and "Why shouldn't you wear the veil?"

The first basically told women to cover as much as possible in the most somber colors, and to avoid flashy clothes or anything called "fashion." Callers who opted for the second question were quickly admonished that they are mistaken if they thought they could be modest without veiling. "The veil is obligatory to all believing women so if you do not abide by your religion you will be punished for disobeying God's orders," the sermon said, adding that an unveiled woman will be penalized on judgment day for every man who ever looked at her.

The sheikh's answers were conservative and, to me, emphasized just how the religious establishment held sway over so many people. Pushing the idea that believers had to conform to the sheikh's every prescription in order to lead a virtuous life and thereby earn a spot in heaven kept laymen living in fear and dread of heading down the wrong path. Endless such rulings by Egypt's sheikhs ensured that the country stayed a socially conservative place, or at least forced people who wanted to flout tradition to do so surreptitiously. Ultimately, fatwas on social subjects helped put the brake on change in the Arab world. The religious scholars were not believers in opening up the windows to allow in fresh air, the old air was just fine. The government apparently agreed, giving Sheikh Guindi a prominent role on one of the most popular nightly talk shows, where his appearance helped burnish the regime's conservative religious credentials.

🔳 🔳 🔳

There were times, however, when those pushing social change managed to score a fatwa that furthered their aims. Once I stumbled across a remarkable fatwa from Ayatollah Ali Khamenei, the supreme leader in predominately Shiite Iran. It was a single letter stamped with official seals that had been pressed under a doctor's glass desktop in the vasectomy department of a birth control clinic. By the late 1990s, when the clinic opened to serve one of the poorer quarters of south Tehran, the Iranian regime had realized that it could ill afford the staggering population explosion it had initially encouraged to produce a new generation of Islamic revolutionaries. The population had roughly doubled to around 60 million since the 1979 overthrow of the shah.

Every single one of the leery men shuffling into the vasectomy department first sought reassurance that the operation would not cause their voices to rise or their beards to fall out. Then the questions invariably turned to whether Islam condoned the procedure. The doctor would just tap on the glass. The clinic's founder, Freidoun Forouhari, had wisely solicited a fatwa from Iran's supreme leader asking whether men could practice birth control. In his brief ruling, Ayatollah Khamenei listed the withdrawal method, condoms, and vasectomies as acceptable male contraception. He scrawled two lines at the end that translated roughly as "When wisdom dictates that you do not need more children, a vasectomy is permissible."

That fatwa ensured that the clinic was always mobbed. It did not guarantee full protection, however. Forouhari was one of the men stabbed to death during a campaign by rogue elements within the government to eliminate reformists. The pattern of his murder made it seem as though he was among those targeted, his grim fate underscoring how easy it was for ideologues bent on blocking change to ignore any fatwa that contradicted their own version of Islam.

Saudi Arabia served as the font of all manner of hostile fatwas, the bulk of them scolding about the evils of Western life gaining a foothold in the birthplace of Islam. Innovation, or "bidaa'" in Arabic, is a dirty word in the kingdom. Walking around upscale shopping malls in Jidda or Riyadh, I would see bearded men in short robes, the mark of a puritan because it supposedly mirrored the Prophet Mohamed's look, handing out tracts brimming with freshly minted fatwas. The pamphlets were brief, easy to read, and written in bold letters with colorful Arabic fonts.

One such pamphlet declared that having music as your cell phone ring tone was forbidden, another denounced the Western practice of bringing flowers to hospital patients. No Muslim ever did so in ancient times so it was clearly aping the infidel rather than benefiting the patient and therefore taboo. Ceremonies modeled on Western practices, like passing out awards to forty-seven exceptional teachers on something called International Teachers Day, were decried as shameful.

The variations seemed endless. I read a tract that fulminated against credit cards, saying it was a sin to use them because it meant paying interest, which Islam bars. The whole idea of how the faithful should avoid any kind of non-Muslim holiday celebration was a favorite theme. "Congratulating them on their holidays amounts to accepting non-Muslim occasions and the all-mighty Allah will not be pleased with such deeds," warned a pamphlet distributed by an organization called The Office to Propagate Spiritual Guidance in Jidda. "If non-Muslims greet you on the occasion of Christmas or the New Year, you should not reply to them," it went on, warning darkly that Muslims should also avoid attending holiday parties or even eating any kind of treat: "What you think might be courtesy in these matters is actually acquiescence in religion." In other words, scarfing a gingerbread man in December would set you on the path to hell because it is tantamount to accepting a Christian God.

Emerging from noon prayers one Friday, a friend found under his windshield wipers a forty-seven-page screed condemning the evils of the tourism industry that Saudi Arabia was trying to develop. Among its most dire warnings was that all Saudis would be forced to swim on nudist beaches—foreigners working in the kingdom had already turned charming offshore islands into "hotbeds of naked women"—and that wherever tourists gather there is sure to be alcohol and endless wanton spectacles like ballet and belly dancing. "The mere entry of these infidels into the country is itself a great vice for which we will be punished, not to mention their nakedness, their uncovered women and their depravity," the tract thundered, arguing that anyone who worked in the industry was bound to become a prostitute or a pimp. "In Egypt all tourist guides, women and men, specialize in sexual entertainment. Male guides organize sex between Egyptian women and tourists and Egyptian men with the blonde women of Europe." (In ancient Middle Eastern texts, any blond character would almost invariably do something malevolent.) The modern screed somehow failed to mention the endless stream of Saudi men who pour into Egypt for the very same thing.

The tract noted that the late Sheikh bin Baz, the grand mufti, had expressly forbidden the preservation of historic monuments and predicted that preservationists working to save any pre-Islamic monuments would go to hell while those who tore them down would be assured entrance to Paradise. This was rooted in the Wahhabi teaching that it was a sin to invest religious significance in anything related to men deemed holy (i.e., saint's tombs), that the unity of God could not be subdivided and his word alone was sacred. The pamphlet did not reserve its scorn for non-Muslims alone, reflecting just how seriously Saudi Muslims believe themselves superior to all their brethren in the faith. "Most foreign laborers create gangs," it said. "Africans specialize in armed robbery; Afghanis and Pakistanis in selling drugs; Indians in alcohol; Filipinos in gay sex; the Levant Arabs in fornication. All other Muslim workers are evil, and we Saudi Muslims are suffering from their plague." (It failed to mention that without the army of millions of foreign laborers, the country would grind to a halt since Saudis generally consider manual labor beneath them.) In the end, the pamphlet warned, Saudi youths will grow tired of rampant vice and end up cutting off people's heads in order to defend their religion.

In case avid fatwa followers did not get their fill from the daily stream of such rulings, or had a favorite religious figure who was dead and no longer issuing new ones, Saudi publishers rolled out many thick books of fatwa greatest hits. To give me the flavor, a religious scholar I was interviewing plucked off his shelf one of sixteen volumes of what he called The Wahhabi Encyclopedia, a sweeping collection of important rulings across decades. He opened it at random to a page containing two fatwas from the 1960s, attacking the idea of opening schools for girls. One said that every Muslim should avoid placing "his daughter or sister in these schools, which appear to be benign but are full of evil and sedition and will end in madness and wantonness and the loss of all morality and virtue."

Another said that any woman who had been educated automatically tore up her veil and displayed her head, bosom, thighs, and legs in public. In Arabic, it said educating girls only resulted in "tabaruj," definitely one of my all-time favorite words because it underscored the richly varied nature of the language. It literally means "to display one's charms," but in a derogatory sense as in "brazen hussy." For example, whenever the religious police caught sight of my colleague Donna Abu-Nasr, the Saudi bureau chief for The Associated Press, approaching strangers on the street to interview, even though she was always dressed in a full abaya and headscarf, they would yell at her to stop, demanding to know why she was mixing openly with men "without shame." They inevitably tried to insult her by addressing her as "Mutabaraja!" (mu-ta-BAR-raja), the noun form of the word. Or in other words, "Stop displaying your charms!"

Bookshops in the holy cities of Mecca and Medina sold one 1,265-page souvenir tome that was a kind of anthology of fatwas on modern life by some of the most popular recently deceased Islamic scholars. It was riddled with rulings admonishing the faithful to shun non-Muslims, never to smile at them, and avoid at all costs addressing them as "friend." A fatwa from one famous sheikh, Mohamed bin Othaiman, whose 2001 funeral drew hundreds of thousands of mourners, tackled the notion of Muslims living in infidel lands. The whole idea was discouraged, but anyone who found himself in that predicament should "harbor enmity and hatred for the infidels," it read in part. No one should ape Westerners in their manner of dress, another fatwa thundered. The late Sheikh bin Baz had warned his followers repeatedly to avoid even visiting the West on vacation—so forbidding summer travel "to the land of the infidels" became a favorite fatwa theme. Going to Florida, let's say, was religiously suspect because anyone who did was likely to attend a party where alcohol was served, and the idea of Saudi women unveiling in the West combined with Saudi men ogling Western women displaying all their charms was bound to lead to no good. Not that all such fatwas had much effect: Saudi Airlines used to add frequent direct flights from the kingdom to Orlando in the summer because it was such a popular vacation destination. (Saudis who flouted such pronouncements sometimes did so with a distinctive sense of humor, at least in urban legends. A group of expatriate Saudis reportedly opened a nightclub in Bangkok, Thailand called The Bin Baz Bar.)

I had an ongoing discussion with Saudi friends such as Jamal Khashoggi, a journalist who had once been sympathetic to the mujahideen fighting the Soviets in Afghanistan, about how much weight to lend such a blizzard of rulings. His viewpoint changed to the degree that he was fired from his job as editor of *Al-Watan* newspaper in 2003 after he opened its pages to a raging debate on whether Wahhabi intolerance was a root of extremist violence. (He got it back some four years later.) The cartoon that proved his undoing showed a would-be suicide bomber, but the sticks of dynamite strapped around his waist were all labeled FATWA.

Khashoggi argued that fatwas about ordinary social issues, especially those banning popular practices, only served to alienate ordinary people from the zealots and were obviously far less horrifying than any justifying suicide bombings. But he recognized that attempts at social engineering, condemning anything from the West, could have a dangerous twist once extremist religious scholars went one step further and sanctioned violence against anyone they considered to be polluting Islam.

Sometimes it seemed to me that the avalanche of fatwas trying to hold back the onslaught of Western cultural influences did indicate that Saudi Arabia and other societies were changing in innumerable small ways and that attempts to stem that tide were relatively impotent. Take Valentine's Day. For weeks beforehand the various religious organizations would paper shopping centers and other public places with fatwa pamphlets declaring that anyone who wore red on that day was an agent of the devil. Then the entire morals police would deploy to make sure that no one was selling roses or wearing the color—girls on college campuses with so much as a red hair clip would be sent home.

In her groundbreaking 2005 novel *Girls of Riyadh*, which caused a sensation among educated Saudis, author Rajaa Alsanea detailed the various ways some college-aged girls thwarted the effort. Guys also got into the act, some handing out red roses with their telephone numbers on the stem. Girls "loved it because someone gave them a red flower just like in the movies," she wrote. "All the means of celebrating love are banned in Saudi Arabia; in our country celebrating love is outlawed."

Now, an attempt by educated, well-to-do college girls to celebrate Valentine's Day did not mean that a social revolution was at hand, but such skirmishing did signify that when socially conservative values clashed with changes that people wanted, no force of fatwas or other means was likely to stop them. Exposure to other ways of living inevitably eroded the idea that people living in puritanical Muslim societies had to stick with their old traditions. That is what the religious authorities feared, that it would start with red lipstick and dogs, and end with tossing Islam aside.

The reaction to fatwas does have implications for how people in the Middle East obtain greater freedom—whether they take authority seriously, whether they deceive it, and how they might face it down. On this score, in terms of more profound matters of change, perhaps the most interesting flood of fatwas was generated by elections and other attempts at reformatting the region's ossified political systems. Never mind that the outcomes of most of these elections were designed to produce rubber-stamp bodies with little real power.

For example, both opponents and supporters of women participating as candidates in municipal council elections revived in 2002 in the Lilliputian island state of Bahrain sought religious fatwas to buttress their position.

Bahiya al-Ataawi, a kindergarten teacher in her 40s, petitioned a famous cleric who endorsed women running. That fatwa came from Sheikh Yusuf al-Qaradawi, perhaps the Arab world's most influential Sunni cleric due to his talk show on Al-Jazeera satellite network focused on applying Islamic law to daily life. His answer spoke volumes about the role of women from a religious point of view. It said as long as they were qualified, and as long as holding elected office did not interfere with being good wives and mothers, they could run. His fatwa went on to recommend that, if men and women did end up on the council together, they avoid looking at each other unless absolutely necessary. "There is a need for Muslim women candidates to enter this campaign to confront the corrupted women," Sheikh Qaradawi wrote, presumably meaning the unveiled and not the many prostitutes working in Bahrain's rather freewheeling nightlife. He also argued that it was OK because men would likely maintain a majority on any council and the Koranic injunction applied only to a woman running an entire nation.

Ataawi distributed the fatwa with all her campaign literature and it spread across the island, prompting an unidentified Bahraini man to seek an opposing ruling from a Saudi cleric. Using virtually the same sacred texts, that fatwa concluded that "men are supposed to control women and handle their affairs."

Men ordering their wives how to vote was a common problem in the Middle East, and the most creative solution I encountered was dreamt up by Nariman el-Daramali, an Egyptian woman running for parliament from heavily conservative Upper Egypt. Keep in mind that Egyptian women have had the right to run and vote since 1956, but still find male dominance a hurdle. While campaigning, Daramali carried both a Koran and a Bible, since Coptic Christians lived in many villages along the Nile in her district. Whenever a woman promised to vote for her, she would whip out the appropriate holy text and ask the voter to swear on it. Then when their husbands tried to pressure them to vote for a different candidate, they could say they had made a holy oath and refuse. Daramali won with a record turnout.

The most restrictive rules in the region, completely barring any participation by women, were promulgated by Saudi Arabia for its first nationwide municipal elections in 2005. But one religious scholar took the effort to influence the outcome a step further by issuing a fatwa about which candidates to support. The scholar, a professor of Islamic law at Imam Bin Saudi Islamic University in Riyadh, one of the country's foremost religious institutions, was asked his opinion about voting for candidates whose platforms included allowing women to drive, opening sports clubs for them, and building movie theaters—proscribed as public spaces where the sexes might mingle.

The fatwa read: "It is forbidden to vote for them, indeed it is forbidden to vote for any candidate who calls for anything that contradicts Shariah," or Islamic law. The widely publicized ruling sparked outrage among candidates not affiliated with certain religious organizations as unfair manipulation. Ultimately, religious candidates captured virtually every seat across the country.

It could be argued that the Saudi municipal elections represented a small progressive evolution because the religious establishment did not issue its habitual denunciations against elections as a heretical, imported innovation. Some scholars went so far as to dredge up examples from the life of the Prophet Mohamed that supported democracy. I've never seen Saudi men collectively as excited as they were by the municipal elections in 2005, packing campaign tents long into the night, but then again there is not a lot to do in Riyadh or other cities. Still, I suspect religious figures gauged the excitement and then their fatwas went with the general tide. My sense was that satellite television channels, exposure to the Internet, and a wider sense of the world were beginning to have their effect when it came to nascent elections. One Saudi friend told me his elderly mother was watching a story on Al-Jazeera about election returns in Peru when she suddenly piped up, wondering why there were no real elections in the Arab world. It was dawning among the general Arab public that their region was unique in its lack of such freedoms, that they were out of sync with the times, so the religious establishment figured trying to stop the trend was futile and its best shot was influencing the outcome, which it did.

Of course that influence grated on the nerves of the secular types who had been opposing various despotic rulers for years and sought to establish multiparty democratic systems. I remember one of the founders of Kuwait's most liberal political movement blurting out, "How can you be a democrat and follow a fatwa?"

The men and women pushing for change whom I sympathized with the most were those pushing for the broadest array of freedoms, including the ability to establish political parties and a flourishing civil society. They wanted to be allowed to criticize any government policy and to suggest alternatives without facing arrest. I'm certain that such freedom would have lanced much of the anger and frustration caused by the stunted horizons many people faced, anger that ultimately led some to religious extremism and violence.

The fact that fatwas were used to slow change more often than to promote it left me pessimistic at first. It was easy to bemoan the fact that the public, rather than rushing out to embrace change, was turning to religious scholars to consult medieval texts as to whether or not participating in elections was a good idea. But the mere fact that they were asking such questions, casting about for answers in the only manner they knew how, did underscore that people were interested in change; they wanted something different in their lives. If it took a fatwa to get them to explore further, well then I finally decided that a fatwa could be a stepping-stone toward still strange and uncertain progress.

CHAPTER 7

TALKING ABOUT JIHAD

So when the sacred months have passed away, then slay the idolaters wherever you find them, and take them captives and besiege them and lie in wait for them in every ambush.

—The Koran, The Sword verse from *The Repentance* (9:5)

ALTHOUGH SOCIAL AND POLITICAL ISSUES constitute the bulk of fatwa traffic, the most charged debates erupt around a third subject: jihad. Given the wars in the region, the question about what constitutes legitimate jihad is always bubbling in the background. But the general squabbling took on new urgency after attackers claiming a divine mandate struck in Arab cities. The extremists maintained that their quest for change justified any violence against oppressive systems, an assertion that their detractors rejected in light of the civilian toll. Many incidents prompted these debates, but one in particular stands out for me.

In Riyadh, the Saudi capital, I was facing the lush palm gardens outside the lobby of the Intercontinental Hotel—a low-slung structure built of rough-hewn sandstone—when a massive explosion erupted nearby. The lobby's floor-to-ceiling windows bowed inwards and the lights flickered off for a minute. A black column of smoke spiraled into the sky. I rushed toward it with my colleagues from the Times's Cairo office, Abeer Allam and Mohamed el-Dakhakhny. The target turned out to be the headquarters of the traffic police, its entire façade cracked open like a dollhouse by a suicide bomber who had detonated a Chevrolet Blazer crammed with explosives. The attack killed 5 people, including an 11-year-old-girl, and wounded nearly 150.

Abeer and I were among the first people on the scene, splitting off from the photographer because we thought he might attract too much attention. We had barely started trying to find eyewitnesses when the Saudi crowd that materialized—long fed government propaganda that any bloodshed was a foreign plot—suddenly turned on the two most visible foreigners present. They grabbed at me in near hysteria, tearing at my clothes and wrenching two fat, almost full notebooks from my hands. My lungs constricted and I found myself gasping for air at the thought of losing ten days' worth of important interviews. Hemmed in on all sides, I desperately tried to follow with my eyes the trajectory of my notebooks as they passed from hand to hand. I didn't want to yell out lest that drive the crowd to shred them on the spot. My thin wool blazer ripped up the back as I strained to dive through the slapping, kicking mob to retrieve them—to no avail. Voices in the throng yelled for the police to come check our cell phones to discover whom we called to confirm that the bombing succeeded.

A couple policemen bundled us into the back of a squad car, prompting screaming Saudis to rock the vehicle and to press themselves against the windows, yelling things in Arabic and English like "How did you know to be right here when the bomb went off?" Baffled that anyone rational could think that we planned the bombing and were hanging around afterward to take souvenir snapshots,

I maintained a ludicrous optimism that reason would prevail. I kept repeating that I heard the explosion just like everyone else. It made no impression.

After we were driven away from the mayhem we discovered that the squad car lacked a radio—the officer who controlled our fate carried only a cell phone. The network was so overloaded with people checking on each other after the bombing that for several hours he could not reach his boss to get instructions about what to do with us. We kept suggesting he just let us go and all he would respond was, "You talk a lot." After more than four hours locked in the back of the cramped car we were finally driven to a police station, where the anxiety that had been eating at me all afternoon ebbed as soon as I caught sight of my two notebooks in the hands of the desk officer. He handed them back and, after checking our passports, released us. The police shrugged off our furious complaints about being detained in the midst of a breaking story. I didn't belabor the point. I just wanted to get out of there to file. At least the officer holding us had eventually gossiped on the phone with his pals about all the gruesome things he had seen right after the explosion. So I had a few quotes.

The next day an unknown group with a typically grandiose name, The Brigade of the Two Holy Mosques—the Saudi kingdom being home to the two earliest mosques in Islam at Mecca and Medina—posted an unverifiable claim of responsibility on two websites. The group bragged that their jihad rained devastation on the "criminal, apostate" Saudi government.

Up until then, April 2004, Saudis had been generally supportive of the idea of volunteering for jihad, including fighting the Americans next door in Iraq, but that attitude swung 180 degrees when the killing arrived on their doorstep. The public outrage was fed not least by the fact that virtually every Saudi adult male in the capital had to visit the traffic police headquarters to collect a driver's license or car number plates.

"May God curse you, you vermin, you people of filth and not jihad," said a comment on one website that had posted the responsibility claim. The bombing happened to coincide with the release of the first wrenching pictures of dead U.S. soldiers being transported home from Iraq en masse—the unauthorized photographs showing a military transport plane crammed with coffins draped in American flags. In case anyone missed the point, right underneath that comment cursing the Riyadh attackers, the picture of the American dead was posted over the caption: "This is jihad."

Most Muslims will tell you that "jihad" is the Arabic word for struggle, and that the jihad demanded by their religion is actually the lifelong struggle to make yourself a better person as well as to augment Islam's place in the world. They argue that using the word interchangeably with "holy war" constitutes a Western attempt to exaggerate and sensationalize their faith by depicting it as brimming with blood lust. Semantically, they are right—jihad does indeed mean a struggle.

But those who argue that the word contains no implication of violence are glossing over the fact that for some zealots, jihad means only one thing: an armed fight against the enemies of Islam that they believe they are destined to carry out in perpetuity. Hence fatwa smack-downs over "justifiable" jihad rage back and forth relentlessly, particularly on the free-for-all format of the Internet. Evidently Al-Qaeda has captured much of the attention by actually trying to implement this vision of jihad, but it is hardly the only voice out there. These arguments within Islam generally fail to attract sufficient attention in the West.

A key challenge in trying to shape and define Islam has always been its lack of a central authority. Even when there was a caliph, or commander of the faithful, his ability to dictate religious laws was limited by the basic Islamic understanding that nothing should stand between any Muslim and the Koran, the word of God. (Never mind that the caliph was often just a figurehead co-opted by absolute rulers wielding the real power.) Hence there is no one authority to settle an argument.

The general tone and the public perception of the jihad debate is one key to change, to diminishing the level of violence so devastating to the Middle East. It was easy for Arab Muslims to support the concept of jihad when it was in distant lands like Afghanistan, Bosnia, or Chechnya. But the militants who committed repeated atrocities in the Middle East—in Amman or Riyadh or Casablanca—found a distinctly less welcoming public. The best prospect for quelling the level of violence is to ensure that people understand the cost it levies in innocent lives. Authoritative voices must demand that it stop. Thus far that message has been left ambiguous in the Islamic world.

There are Muslim thinkers who call for a complete overhaul of the way the holy texts are interpreted as the best means to eliminate any question that the faith does not condone terrorism, much of it carried out in the name of Islam. Such arguments started with the advent of modernism in the late nineteenth century, but have taken on renewed urgency now that so many Islamists are trying to manipulate the concept of jihad to fit their own political aims.

The jihad question is debated throughout the region, but perhaps nowhere as vehemently as in Saudi Arabia. The kingdom is arguably the most important country on this issue given that the Wahhabi ideology there has spawned some of the most intolerant teachings on how Muslims should view the rest of the world. Three of the four main branches of Sunni Islam reject the idea of an offensive jihad, of Muslims initiating hostilities. "You should never initiate fighting without a reason; you undertake jihad when you are 'defending' an Islamic nation, like the situation in Iraq or Palestine," Abdel Rahem al-Lahem, a Saudi lawyer and a former militant, explained to me. "All jurisprudents agree on this and there are many religious texts to prove it." Lahem is a brave, outspoken lawyer willing to take on all the hardest cases of Saudis who fall afoul of the government or the religious establishment. He defended the woman sentenced to 200 lashes in 2007 after being raped, the sentence handed down against her because the assault occurred after she got into a car with a man who was not her husband. (King Abdullah later pardoned her.)

The one Sunni school that endorses offensive jihad is the Hanbali school, of which the Wahhabi sect dominant in Saudi Arabia is the main offshoot. "For them, to defend the religion and to glorify it you have to attack your enemy first," Lahem told me. "That is why it was only when attacks started here in the kingdom that the Wahhabi religious scholars finally began to make the distinction between an offensive and a defensive jihad; they spoke against offensive jihad after those attacks." The chain of suicide bombings targeting mostly civilians that burst forth starting in May 2003 in Riyadh sparked a debate within the kingdom over the degree to which that Wahhabi intolerance inspired terrorism. The religious establishment utterly rejected the idea that any discussion was warranted and quickly moved to squelch it. The royal family, dependent on the powerful clerical network for their claim that they ruled as defenders of the faith, caved in to the pressure, smothering the discussion in the press after about three weeks. But the arguments raged on anyway.

The creaking princes running the country retreated into their favorite denial—claiming that any violence carried out in the name of Islam was foreign to the kingdom. If Saudis were implicated in any attacks, they must have been influenced by misguided Muslims abroad; Egyptians, for instance. This dubious argument became quite the stretch when Saudis were blowing up Saudis in the very heart of the capital, but the most senior royals kept it up anyway.

There had been a brief window of vague candor right after the September 11 attacks, when the ruling dynasty at least admitted that their Islamic credentials were under siege. Prince Nayef, the dyspeptic interior minister in his 70s who has run the powerful security agency since 1975, told a police conference in October 2001 that even if the extremists had emerged from Saudi society, they were a cancer that had to be chopped out of the body of Islam and people had to respect senior religious scholars.

He went on to admit that there were, in fact, Saudis who subscribed to the terrorists' view: "But unfortunately, we find in our

homeland those who sympathize with them. We tell the simpletons
and the misled: Come back to your senses, calm down and let the
duties be handled by those responsible." But it took only a matter
of months before he was diluting this, back pushing the ludicrous
"foreign influence" argument. He publicly upbraided Saudi journalists who had the temerity to ask him whether the internal atmosphere intolerant of anything other than Wahhabism might have
contributed to the emergence of extremists.

He was hardly alone. Prince Sattam bin Abdul Aziz, a spry figure
in his early 60s and the longtime deputy governor of Riyadh, is
the next-to-youngest son of King Abdul Aziz, the kingdom's
founding monarch. The sandstone governorate building in downtown Riyadh was built to echo an old Arab fort, with a rather more
grand interior. Prince Sattam holds audiences in a soaring office
half the size of a football field. The walls are of white stone and the
carpeting a sort of modern Bedouin—bands of triangles and other
geometric shapes executed in bright shades of pink and blue.
When I asked the courtly prince about the role of fatwas that condemn the West and encourage jihad, he told me, "You cannot say
those people represent Islam," and then waxed nostalgic about attending a Roman Catholic university in San Diego. On the subject
of the jihadi mindset and the September 11 attacks he said, "I am
not saying Saudi Arabia has no extremists, but not as many as people think or the press shows to people." The press was the favorite
scourge, right behind foreign religious ideology. "They say that fifteen people who have done this are from Saudi Arabia," he continued. "But those people were in Afghanistan; they took their ideas
not inside Saudi Arabia, but outside Saudi Arabia." That ignored
two important points. First, the travel pattern of fifteen Saudis
among the nineteen hijackers indicated that they had been
recruited inside the kingdom and, second, bin Laden had been
raised on Wahhabi ideology, which he used as the basis for his
violently anti-Western views.

The senior princes are reluctant to face the discussion honestly, at least in public, but fortunately other Saudis were not so reticent. I met Mansour al-Nogaidan right after the May 2003 bombings, which killed eighteen Westerners and seven Saudis, as well as nine suicide bombers. For several years he had been at the forefront of a committed group of former radicals arguing that terrorist violence springs from the intolerance if not the downright hostility with which the Wahhabi sect faces the outside world. Since the Saud dynasty rules with a kind of divine mandate issued by the Wahhabi establishment, his arguments were a brave if indirect attack on the monarchy as well.

Nogaidan is a short, stout, almost child-like man with bulging eyes and a quiet voice. He was born in 1970 in the central Saudi town of Buraydah, once a caravan stop on the route between Kuwait and Mecca. Despite its modern veneer of gas stations and strip malls, common to all Saudi towns, Buraydah has remained a kind of Disneyland theme park for all that puritanical Wahhabis hold dear. Women scuttle about the place with only their eyes showing and any infraction against Islamic traditions, like smoking tobacco, never occurs in public.

At age 16, torn by doubts about religion, Nogaidan joined a high school club called The Islamic Enlightenment. The fanatical readings and extremist discussions encouraged by the club eventually led him to believe that Saudi Arabia, perhaps the most Islamic country on the planet, was actually run by infidels due to the heavy presence of expatriate workers and foreign products in the kingdom. So he dropped out of school, opened his own mosque, and started issuing fatwas censuring as "infidel" everything the government approved, ranging from an international soccer tournament to the entire education system. Nogaidan withdrew into a subculture of salafi Muslims who seek to emulate the life of the Prophet Mohamed. "Salafi," once again, is the Arabic word for forebears, meaning the original companions of the prophet who converted to the new faith. Eventually moving to a salafi-dominated quarter in Riyadh, he inspired his followers to blow up one of the most popular video stores in the capital because it was spreading Western corruption. (Some critics argue that the natural course of all salafi thought eventually leads to violence.)

Long jail sentences eventually led Nogaidan to expand his reading into Western philosophy, which convinced him that Wahhabi ideology suffered from serious flaws if an adolescent could issue fatwas promoting violence. "There is a tradition in Wahhabism that any sheikh can write letters to describe the correct Islam, the right path," he told me. "I thought of this as being loyal because I was obeying Wahhabi ideology. I wanted to make it active and the religious sheikhs were not; they were always saying we can talk to the ruler, it can be solved by negotiation. I thought change was the priority and even if you use violence, it's legal because you are trying to build a city of God."

The number of militants willing to carry out attacks inside Saudi Arabia was small—it required really hard-core extremism to believe that infidel ideology somehow riddled a country where Islam is practiced night and day. But the possibility of anyone following in Nogaidan's footsteps has increased exponentially now that any website can crank out fatwas—a teenager doing it would not even have to identify himself as such.

In Nogaidan's case, he was first jailed for being too Wahhabi, and then eventually, after his change of heart, for not being Wahhabi enough. His newspaper columns criticized the religious establishment, calling the extremists the fruit of its efforts rather than an aberration. He was denounced as an infidel, with numerous religious scholars issuing fatwas excommunicating him and one calling for his death. Insults and death threats piled up in his email and on his cell phone. He was often blocked from publishing and monitored incessantly by security agents. Both times I spoke to him over tea in the lobby of the Riyadh Intercontinental, several men moved to the chairs near us to eavesdrop.

Excommunicating people is a favorite tool in the constant skirmishing over social issues in the Middle East. The word for infidel in Arabic is "kaafir," and the related ideology used to declare

someone an apostate is "takfir," from the same root. Takfiri ideology seemed absurd to me at first, like school yard taunts. "You're an
infidel!" "No, you're the infidel!" But it could produce deadly results. Declaring someone an apostate was a religious license to kill.

Nogaidan thought the jihad problem was rooted in the tradition
of trying to emulate Prophet Mohamed's life. Since the prophet and
his immediate disciples had been spectacularly successful in creating an Islamic empire far beyond the Arabian peninsula, hard-core
Wahhabis believed being in a state of constant warfare was the duty
of any Muslim seeking to follow the prophet's example. Or so they
claimed. Nogaidan and other former extremists suggested it was
just a convenient excuse. Since any form of political expression was
illegal, jihadis found a religious means to pursue political goals.

"Groups that want to gain power will revive the most radical
thoughts and call them something divine and force people to accept them," Nogaidan told me. "They think that the only religiously
sanctioned way to spread Islam is jihad. The main thing supporting
jihad is that it is a holy, unchanged rule. Any reinterpretation of this
is forbidden because it came from Allah. People are afraid to argue
against jihad because they think the public and the old sheikhs will
oppose them."

Indeed, during this period a guest columnist in *Al-Watan*, a newspaper owned by the descendants of King Faisal and considered the
kingdom's most progressive, wrote that the West is the natural enemy of Islam, disputing another writer who said the religion is
peaceful. "He says that Islam means peace, while I say no interpretation ever said so, and God said to fight all the infidels," wrote Mohamed al-Rameh, a government-paid official who sat on The
Supreme Institution for the Judiciary. The newspaper did publish a
dissenting response, but it was sent in from Spain.

"You cannot live with jihad all the time in order to spread
Islam," Nogaidan told me. "Jihad has to be just. You can't fight people all the time. But radical groups draw their justification from
Wahhabi thoughts." Any ruler who opposed it risked losing the
support of the religious establishment and its followers, he insisted.

"How can any ruling prince convince those who in their hearts think jihad cannot be stopped?"

It was remarkable just how callous the Saudi religious authorities could be about the violence. The first wave of suicide bombers who struck Riyadh targeted sprawling housing compounds whose mostly expatriate residents maintained something close to a Western lifestyle. Some young Saudis, though, usually those educated in the West, also enjoyed walking to the pool and the soccer field in their shorts, or the fact that their wives could drive to the internal supermarket rather than having to be chauffeured everyplace. But the religious saw the compounds as a stain on the landscape of Islam's holy land, dens of iniquity where alcohol and all manner of unspeakable vice were undoubtedly rampant. The condemnations after the compound bombings were less than universal, even though some victims were Arabs and Muslims. That pattern continued as the violence spread around the country. The ordinary Saudis I met were shocked at the gore, and the government condemned the attacks. Religious scholars in official positions eventually got around to censuring them, too, as distant from Islam and "a grave sin."

But some independent sheikhs maintained a noted silence when the victims were mostly Westerners, as did their followers. For example, websites popular with the more religious Saudis brimmed over with condemnation for the April bombing of the traffic police headquarters in Riyadh where all the victims were Saudis, while they virtually ignored two subsequent attacks that took place the next month when the victims were Americans and Europeans.

The more time I spent in Saudi Arabia, the more I got the sense that the religious establishment subtly pushed the idea that only Muslims, and Saudi Muslims in particular, were God's creatures and everyone else was somehow sub-human. It was this attitude that lent the fatwa flood its dark side. One appalling fatwa I read from a religious website neatly encapsulated the poisonous attitude. In 2003, the obsessively secretive Saudi government took the unprecedented step of printing up posters with the pictures of the twenty-six most wanted terrorists, slapping them up on pillars around big cities and offering a reward for their capture. A Saudi male asked a religious sheikh for a fatwa on whether he should report someone he knew was among them. "I am very confused," the man wrote. "I either report one of the wanted suspects to clear my conscience before the state, or I don't report him and suffer with my conscience. If I report him I will upset his parents. Help me please?" The fatwa he got in response was a study in the equivocation that gave license to target non-Muslims. "If he is a danger to Muslims, it is your duty to report because it will serve as an admonition to Muslims and help to maintain security. But if he is not a danger to Muslims and leaving him alone will give him the chance to repent, it is much better to protect his secret."

I always looked forward to talking to Saad A. Sowayan, a lively Saudi university professor who specialized in Nabatean poetry. That pre-Islamic civilization carved the spectacularly ornate cave façades in Petra and elsewhere made famous in modern times by the opening sequences of Indiana Jones and the Last Crusade. Sowayan sported a thick black beard, which he was quick to point out was not a fierce badge of fundamentalist pride but a "Berkeley beard" first cultivated during his 1960s graduate studies. He saw the fatwa phenomenon as an attempt to keep Saudi Arabia isolated from the rest of the world: "There is official encouragement to be insular because if you are exposed to other cultures and societies, you will realize there are alternatives to what you have been taught politically, religiously, or whatever."

The professor believed the entire attitude toward jihad was rooted in the harsh culture of the desert, which the advent of Islam did not dislodge. That culture condoned the idea that the faithful were innocent of any harm inflicted on those with whom they lacked a religious bond. "It harkens back to the days when any stranger was inherently suspicious," he said. "You could kill anybody if he was not a member of your group, not a member of your sect, not a member of your village, not a member of your tribe. If that was the case, nobody would hold you responsible for killing anyone."

Intellectuals thought the attitude had died out as education and modernization changed the face of the country. But its seeds were fertilized anew by the humiliating defeat at the hands of Israel in 1967, which exposed the empty promises of pan-Arab nationalism. Starting around 1979 with the Islamic revolution in Iran, the idea that righteous zealots could do no wrong resurfaced with particular vehemence. "When they feel politically wronged they resort to their religion to justify their hate," Sowayan said.

Just how widespread that Saudi-centric thinking was, even if it did not involve condoning bloodshed, hit me sometimes like an icy bucket of water. It made me question the likelihood of any real reform progressing under such a mindset, despite the fact that there were some Saudis, particularly a core group of former radicals, committed to change. One night I was visiting the comfortable walled compound of a young business executive whom I had first met in a Riyadh cassette shop around 1993. At that time, I had been discretely asking the clerk for some of the wildly popular clerical sermons attacking the royal family that I had heard were circulating via little stores selling religious tapes. The salesman feigned ignorance, but a young man with a scraggly beard pulled a yellow cassette out of the pocket of his robe and said in American-accented English, "You'll like this one." The very idea of contraband cassettes seems quaint in the Internet age, but at the time they were considered an exciting challenge to government repression. Airport security was waiting for me early the next morning and confiscated my cassette, but the young man became a successful business executive. He was one of those Saudis whose years at an American college had convinced him that the United States is a spiritual wasteland and moral sinkhole overflowing with crime and pornography, lacking any redeeming qualities. Yet he graciously invited me to dinner whenever I was in Riyadh. He ardently cultivated his lush, verdant lawn, and sometimes we would play with his young children on it while awaiting dinner. On this particular night, I was sitting on his carpeted floor drinking tea and discussing the roots of extremism and xenophobia in the kingdom when one of his friends, a university professor of Islamic law, turned to me somewhat in exasperation because I did not seem to be getting his point. "Well of course I hate you because you are Christian, but that doesn't mean I want to kill you," he said.

No matter how many times I went to Saudi Arabia, flashes of that kind of thinking never failed to startle me, doubly so in this case because it was coming from a law professor. I worried that I would never understand what thoughts might be lurking in the shadows, especially given that Saudis on the more religious end of the scale like the professor could make such declarations while expounding on the peaceful nature of their beliefs. Few Saudis acknowledged the problem, and fewer still spoke up about it publicly. One notable exception was Prince Bandar bin Sultan, who, while still ambassador to Washington, published an uncommon newspaper column in the kingdom calling the domestic Saudi effort against terrorism too feeble, lacking mass mobilization. The prince noted the long history of violent movements opposed to mainstream Islam arising on the Arabian peninsula itself, starting at the time of the Prophet Mohamed right through the 1920s. A band of zealots mutinied then against King Abdul Aziz, Bandar's grandfather, deeming him insufficiently devout. "It has nothing to do with America or Israel or the Christians or Jews," Prince Bandar wrote. "So let us stop these meaningless justifications for what those criminals are doing and let us stop blaming others while the problem comes from within us." Elsewhere in the article he noted that the kingdom's learned religious scholars "have to declare jihad against those deviants and to fully support it, as those who keep silent about the truth are mute devils."

Prince Bandar was just one prince and seen as almost American following his long tenure in Washington. But Muslims in general and Saudis in particular often referred me to the history of violent, dissident sects emerging within Islam almost since its founding, sects who advocated permanent jihad. Some argued that bin Laden and his followers are just the latest example of the phenomenon. The Saudi government played up the comparison by always referring to Al-Qaeda terrorists as a "deviant minority."

The original "deviant minority" was called the khawarij, or Kharijites in English, derived from the Arabic word for leave or withdraw. That dissident sect emerged in the late seventh-century wars of succession among the early Muslims. The Kharijites held that any pious Muslim who strictly adhered to the Koran could be elected to lead the faithful, it did not depend on family or other ties, and he could remain the leader as long as he was without sin. More important, they treated jihad as the sixth pillar of Islam, using the sword to spread their version of the truth. Their fanatical adherence to those ideas made them intolerant of most Muslims, declaring war on virtually everyone else and remaining in a permanent state of rebellion against the ruling Caliphate. Ira Lapidus, in his fat study, *A History of Islamic Societies*, described the Kharijites as forming small bands of 30 to 100 men. "Each group was at once a terrorist band and a fanatical religious sect," he wrote. The more militant were crushed in the eighth century and the remnants abandoned their attempts to change the world, seeking to lead pious personal lives instead and living, as Lapidus describes it, "in an atmosphere of mourning for lost hopes and messianic dreams."

Their twenty-first-century Muslim brethren carrying out terrorist attacks also believe that any violence used to defend or spread their righteous form of Islam is warranted. Ali al-Omeim, a Saudi journalist who specializes in radical movements, said he could hear the earlier fanatical creed echoed in the basic teaching of the movement starting in the 1990s, that "jihad was the way to Paradise and it's the best job a Muslim could get." Recruiters trying to draft young men hanging around mosques told them that they existed solely in order to undertake jihad in its most violent form. Omeim believed that it was impossible to fight such believers on theological grounds because they are utterly convinced that they alone truly understand what it means to be a Muslim. The only way to oppose them was to argue that mass slaughter is culturally abhorrent, and even that had its limits. "This kind of rebellion has happened periodically through history and there has always been a security solution, which has been to kill them all," he said. (Both the Saudi and Egyptian governments seemed to subscribe to this viewpoint.) Various people ranging from religious scholars to American diplomats suggested to me that all the problems that Westerners blamed for creating extremists—ranging from the curriculum in Saudi schools to mosque sermons to Muslim summer camp—were basically superficial manifestations of a more deeply rooted flaw. It was more like a deadly virus that emerged cyclically to invade the main body of the faith.

When Saudi Arabia got around to removing preachers inciting an armed, violent military struggle against anyone deemed a nonbeliever, many of those singled out just went underground or onto the Internet where they still attracted young followers. Momentum definitely stayed with the extremists. A fatwa posted on a popular Islamic website by a somewhat obscure religious sheikh in 2004 went into detail about when it was acceptable for a Muslim to mutilate the corpse of an infidel. It basically said it was permissible in two cases—to avenge Muslims being disfigured or when it might be a service to the Islamic nation. In that second, infinitely broad category, the reasons listed included "to terrorize the enemy" or to bring joy to the heart of a Muslim warrior. The fact that a cleric could post such a fanatical argument on an open forum without anyone objecting strongly illustrated how easily radical texts flourish in Saudi Arabia.

Saudi intellectuals told me that the government's approach was too shallow. It treated radicalism as a security problem by hunting extremists but dismissed the ideological arguments as simply misguided. It was trying to mollify the clerical establishment, who treated any criticism of their role or the way the religion was taught as an attack on Islam itself. Even the most open-minded Saudis in the religious establishment rejected anything related to religious teachings when looking for the causes of the violence. Muhsen Awaji, a prominent Islamist lawyer who had been jailed in the 1990s for his criticism of the government, was among the few accessible sources for foreign correspondents looking for an explanation of the conservative mindset. Awaji avoided the checkered red

scarves most Saudi men wore on their heads, always wearing a
sharply pressed white one. He brought a young militant to my hotel once to contribute to the discussion, but the man fidgeted
briefly and then insisted on leaving because of the canned music
and the men smoking cigars in the lobby—both smoking and
music are forbidden under puritan Islam. "Those militants are the
outcome of Guantánamo, Abu Ghraib, [Israeli prime minister Ariel]
Sharon, and the American policy in the region; they are angry
against anything foreign and want to retaliate against anything foreign," Awaji told me. He did concede that the religious establishment was not blameless, up to a point, showing me just how
flexible he was by using the word "Wahhabi." "Some of those unofficial Wahhabi object only vaguely to these armed men, they are
hesitant to fully condemn them, and some even try to justify what
they do, but it was not Wahhabism that produced them, it is the
other circumstances in the region."

To put it briefly, those opposing the religious establishment argued that the violence was rooted in narrow Wahhabi teachings
and the entire tree needed to be felled, while religious figures
maintained that just one crop of fruit had turned poisonous, mostly
because of the weather around the tree.

Saudis pushing for change argued that those who blame factors
outside the kingdom are purposely examining just half the issue.
"The problem is that the official religious establishment does not admit that there is a problem inside Wahhabism itself," said Abdullah
Bejad al-Otaibi, another young former radical turned reformer—in
his case the change occurred when he fled Saudi Arabia briefly for
more tolerant Arab countries. "They ignore it, as if these problems
landed in our society by parachute. They do not want to admit
that the problem is within them, that such a big violent phenomenon is a result of the radical, extremist religious discourse. This
is the difficulty. When they do not admit the problem, that it is
coming from this official religious institution, they close the door
on solving it or finding any way out." The sluggish response led
some Saudi intellectuals to conclude that at least the more militant

elements of the religious establishment basically supported Al-Qaeda's goal of driving foreigners out of the Arabian peninsula and establishing some kind of Taliban-like Caliphate.

Abdul Rahman al-Rashed, the Saudi head of Al-Arabiya satellite network, took the example of Nogaidan's fatwa that led to blowing up the video store. The jihadis, he told me, would blow up the store, whereas those in the sahwa "Islamic Awakening" camp would buy the building, cancel the video store owners' lease, and then find out what outstanding loans the guy had and call them all in. "Most political Islamists fall into the sahwa school, but the minority capture the attention," Rashed explained. Both schools consider jihad a duty even if there is no obvious reason for it, like an invasion, and both condemn all Arab regimes who have associated themselves with the West. "Emotionally and ideologically, they are in the same camp, but they compete for adherents," he told me. "The sahwa school has become more radical to please the market."

He thought the government's lackadaisical response reflected the idea that the extremism would fade over time, just as earlier such groups had throughout history. His solution echoed that of Nogaidan and other Saudis, mostly those outside the religious camp. "The only way to fight them is to open up the chance for dialogue within the country," he said. The kingdom needed a new religious discourse, but how it was going to achieve that was unclear.

The princes themselves are no small hurdle to hopes for change in this field, particularly the older ones who wield power. Most of the roughly two dozen surviving sons of King Abdul Aziz are in their 70s, and the window for those still in contention for eventually becoming king narrows by the day. So they are constantly trying to foster popularity and supporters not unlike the head of a political party, and each is reluctant to alienate any group that might weaken his power base by defecting to one of his brothers. Saudis would sometimes compare unfavorably the way their princes curry favor with important religious figures to rulers elsewhere on the Arabian peninsula with similar strict religious traditions, like neighboring Oman. The monarch there, Sultan Qaboos, for example, developed an affinity for classical music. Since strict Islam forbids music, Qaboos invited the senior religious scholars to join his entourage whenever he attended a concert. Refusing the sultan was unthinkable. Everyone saw both the country's ruler and the religious leaders listening to music, so it could no longer be considered a taboo. There was no room for debate.

Saudis opposed to extremism ponder how best to bring about similar change in their country. "They have to disengage from deformed Wahhabism," said Jamal Khashoggi, the *Al-Watan* newspaper editor. "But it will be difficult. How do you distinguish a good Wahhabi from a bad Wahhabi?" Lacking concrete changes in that direction, the message that armed conflict is the only way to spread the true faith will not disappear. The extremists are confident popular opinion supports them. Khashoggi told me, "One of them said to me once, 'We will drag you into jihad by your beard.'"

There is nothing quite like an actual war to provoke wrestling over the subject of jihad. When it came to Iraq, to try to let off steam about Americans killing Muslims, the Saudi monarchy allowed mosque preachers to inveigh darkly against the U.S. at the end of Friday mosque sermons, a moment for proclaiming special prayers each week. Just days before the bombing of the traffic police headquarters, I had been sitting in a car outside a suburban Riyadh mosque when such invective came booming out of the minaret's loudspeaker: "Oh God, avenge America, oh God, avenge its allies," the prayer leader shouted. "Oh God, order your soldiers to show them torture! Oh God divide them! Oh God avenge them for what they are corrupting in Iraq!"

The problem with allowing preaching like this was that once those sentiments were unbottled, the consequences could not be fully contained. More liberal Saudis found it difficult to counter the argument that the United States was hostile to Muslims, given the fact that the Americans had invaded both Iraq and Afghanistan and routinely avoided condemning Israel's occupation of Palestinian territory. The fact that the jeremiads against the West were rooted in the doctrine of jihad compounded the problem. "There are limits you can't cross, you can't cross the principles," explained Khalid Batarfi, the U.S.-educated managing editor of *Al-Madina* newspaper, saying that many Arabs are caught between sympathizing with the cause and being ashamed of the methods. "You can't say we don't need jihad, but you can say it's not the time, there is no need for it today." Indeed, in the period between 9/11 and the invasion of Iraq, at one point scores of leading intellectuals and religious scholars circulated a petition suggesting that Muslims could find common ground with the West. They were roundly pilloried for the effort.

"You give the false impression that many people condemned the war against America," read one such denunciation on a popular religious website. "But the truth is that many people are happy declaring this war, which gave Muslims a sense of relief." Another posting, by an elderly religious scholar named Sheikh Hamad Rais al-Rais, criticized the manifesto writers for showing too much sympathy for the victims of September 11, while debasing Islam by neglecting to mention that jihad is a central tenet of the faith. "You cry for what happened to the Americans in their markets and offices and ministries and the disasters they experienced," he wrote, "and you forget the oppression and injustice and aggression of those Americans against the whole Islamic world."

▧   ▧   ▧

Aside from funding schools and mosques abroad, Saudi thinking has spread far beyond its borders due to the hundreds of thousands of Arabs and other Muslim laborers migrating to the kingdom for work. Mohamed Shahrour, 65, with thinning gray hair and an avuncular manner, is one of those rare, brave voices who has written extensively about the need to revise the religion itself. When I went to visit him, sitting behind his desk in the downtown Damascus villa where he works, the first thing he told me was that urban Islam was always more civilized and pluralistic than any other strain. Surrounded by architectural drawings, the civil engineer, trained in the Soviet Union and Ireland, reeled off a list of Arab cities once famous for their cosmopolitan mix of peoples and faiths—Damascus, Aleppo, Baghdad, Cairo.

"Unfortunately with oil, Bedouin Islam has prevailed," he grimaced, using the word as a pejorative to encompass all the Gulf Arabs but the Saudis in particular. "This is our disaster." As an example, he pointed out that Gulf money funds all the satellite channels devoted to religion. "They spew hatred of civilization, they call for more veiling, more isolation of women. They even dare to call it a renaissance!" Shahrour argues that only a thorough reappraisal of sacred texts will enable Muslims to disentangle their faith from the increasingly gory violence committed in its name. Instead of plodding back fourteen centuries to define the future, he believes the religion desperately needs to find a way to uncouple some of the excess baggage it has been hauling along all this time. To start with, Shahrour fearlessly tackles the Koran. The entire ninth chapter, the sura of Repentance, he believes, chronicles a failed attempt by the Prophet Mohamed to form a state on the Arabian peninsula. Shahrour would like to quarantine that chapter to its original context. The verses used to validate extremist attacks on civilians as legitimate jihad with lines like "slay the idolaters wherever you find them" mostly come from chapter 9, basically verses 5 and 29.

"The state which he built died, but his message is still alive," Shahrour told me. The religious hierarchy cannot be relied upon to effectively curb the violence carried out in the name of the faith. In Shahrour's eyes, it's like expecting foxes to hunt foxes. First, there is not enough distance between the hierarchy and the extremists because they use exactly the same references from the Koran, as well as other sacred texts. Second, the people carrying out beheadings and the like are not exactly sitting around worried that they won't get a Good Muslim housekeeping seal of approval from establishment sheikhs.

Shahrour has written at least four books on the subject of reex-amining Islam's holy texts, and some fifteen have been written at-tacking him, he reckons. "Mohamed as a messenger is infallible; Mohamed as a prophet is not. And it was as a prophet that he built a state," Shahrour said in summarizing his thesis. "So we have to differentiate between the religion and state politics. When you take political Islam, you see only killing, assassination, poisoning, intrigue, conspiracy, and civil war, but Islam as a message is very human, sensible, and just."

Any religion holds certain contradictions, and Islam is no differ-ent. The revelations suggesting that Christians and Jews are perverse emerged while Mohamed clashed with them in the role of leader, Shahrour said, while elsewhere they are treated as worthy of re-spect. "Mohamed's goal was building a state, so sometimes he fought and sometimes he made truces," he goes on. "It all has to be reviewed to make it consistent, it is all inconsistent now. The idea is not to negate it as the Koran, but to negate it as law. Just like Moses is history, Joseph is history."

Even to my infidel ears it sounded like he was skirting blasphemy in dividing Mohamed's roles, but his hypothesis does offer a rather trim way around the common conundrum faced by agents of change that the Koran cannot be parsed in the same way as the Bible. If Jews or Christians decide certain passages in the Bible are obso-lete, those passages are eventually reinterpreted, sometimes to the extent that they are basically disregarded. Not so the Koran, which is taken as the word of God to be applied in all places and all times, hence the importance of interpretation throughout Muslim history.

Shahrour pointed out that there were precedents, however, to modern sensibilities eventually overtaking even the Muslim holy texts. The Koran allowed slavery, for example. It is admittedly a rather grudging endorsement suggesting anyone who frees slaves has a better chance of entering heaven. But the practice continued until quite recently because the holy texts said it was legitimate. In fact, it was only in 1962 that Saudi Arabia took the political deci-sion to make owning slaves illegal via royal decree.

Shahrour and another dozen or so like-minded intellectuals from across the Arab and Islamic worlds provoked bedlam when they presented their call for a reinterpretation of holy texts following a Cairo seminar entitled "Islam and Reform" in the fall of 2004. "Liars! Liars!" someone screamed at a news conference infiltrated by Islamic scholars and others who shouted and lunged at the panelists. "You are all Zionists! You are all infidels!" It had the feel of an Egyptian government rent-a-crowd, the kind President Mubarak's administration turned out with such ease when it wanted to burnish its Islamic credentials or to tarnish critics. The hecklers included a few strapping young men in short haircuts and "civilian" striped shirts who couldn't quite disguise their intelligence-academy bearing, plus a smattering of veiled women, all spouting the standard put-downs during such protests. "You are just agents for America! What kind of Islam are you talking about? Are there any Islamic scholars here? Where are they? You are Jews! You are wrecking Islam and rotting the minds of the young!"

Whether the tumult was government inspired or not, the internal debate over political violence in Islamic cultures exists, with seminars like that one and a raft of newspaper columns breaking previous taboos by suggesting that the interpretation of Islam needed revisions. On one side sit mostly secular intellectuals horrified by all the bloodshed, joined by ordinary Muslims dismayed by the ever more violent image of Islam around the world. They are determined to find a way to wrestle the faith back from extremists. The liberals seek to dilute what they criticize as the clerical monopoly on disseminating interpretations of the sacred texts, although they also realize that doing it without clerical allies will not advance their cause very far.

Arrayed against them are powerful religious institutions like the Saudi religious establishment, Cairo's Al-Azhar University, prominent clerics, and a whole different group of scholars who argue that Islam is under assault by the West. Fighting back with any means possible is the sole defense available to a weaker victim, they say. Shahrour believes that in general Muslims, despite making up some 20 percent of the world's population, are excessively isolated. Too many subscribe to the idea, one that I witnessed so vividly in Saudi Arabia, that the faithful will go to heaven while everyone else is destined for hell. "Therefore your life is not important," he said, indicating me as an outsider. "We are confining ourselves in our own culture."

The debate started on a wide scale with the September 11 attacks against the United States, but gathered momentum with each new incident such as the slaying in September 2004 of more than 300 people at a Beslan school—half of them children—or other killings in the Netherlands, Egypt, Turkey, Indonesia, or Spain labeled jihad by the perpetrators. Iraq created its own hellish category of debate fodder. Home videos produced by insurgents there showed them beheading Western victims as a Koranic verse, including the line "Smite at their necks," scrolled underneath.

The verse comes from chapter 9, The Repentance, and actually has its own name, The Sword. (Muslims learn the chapters by name, so citing the chapter numbers causes confusion.) The use and abuse of this verse provide a perfect example of all the fog surrounding the practice of applying seventh-century pronouncements some 1,400 years later. In its original context, the Prophet Mohamed was talking about pagans who still lived in Mecca who promised to rally to his side for an important battle, then failed to appear. Mohamed was naturally furious at his cowardly allies, including some Muslims who also did not show up, but the chapter goes on to suggest that God accepts all repentance even if his messenger did not. Other verses refer to respecting those with whom you have a treaty and forgiving those who sue for peace or who have done nothing to harm you. Indeed, Shahrour and others argue that the overall name of the chapter, The Repentance, suggests that forgiveness preponderates.

Abeer, the Egyptian reporter who worked with me, remembers that when she was in primary school in Cairo in the 1980s, The Sword verse was always taught strictly in reference to the Meccans. The infidels existed among the people of Mecca: They were not

Americans or anybody else from the modern world. But the militants have removed that verse from its original context in order to justify their killing of hostages and other attacks. Their actions are buttressed by the fact that the verse was historically sometimes applied in that way—for example, during the thirteenth century, when the Arabs were trying to repulse invasions by the Mongol hordes. It was the infamous jurist Ibn Taymiyya who ruled that the Mongols and their local allies should be treated just like the Prophet Mohamed treated the "mushrikeen," or pagans. Arabs opposed to the Americans often compared the U.S. occupation of Baghdad to its sacking in 1258 by the Mongols. Expanding The Sword verse to encompass all non-Muslims coincides perfectly with the extremist mindset.

Nonetheless, even if ordinary Arabs were horrified that the United States was attacking yet another Muslim country, that did not automatically generate sympathy for the Iraqi resistance—far from it. "Resistance was never like this—to kidnap someone and decapitate him in front of everyone," said Ibrahim Said, an Egyptian delivering pastry in a middle-class Cairo neighborhood. "This is haram"—forbidden or shameful—and then he pulled out his own favorite quote from the Koran. "Verily never will Allah change the condition of a people until they change it themselves."

In a similar sentiment, Abdul Rahman al-Rashed, the Saudi director of the Dubai-based Arabiya satellite network and a columnist, created a ruckus with a 2004 column in Al-Sharq Al-Awsat newspaper saying Muslims must confront the fact that Muslims perpetuate most terrorist acts. He specifically took on prominent clerics who call Islam a religion of peace while simultaneously issuing fatwas calling all foreign civilians in Iraq fair game. The mosque used to be a haven of peace and tolerance apart from all the Arab nationalists and leftists calling for violence, he wrote, but that has changed into a universal war cry. "We cannot clear our names unless we own up to the shameful fact that terrorism has become an Islamic enterprise; an almost exclusive monopoly, implemented by Muslim men and women," he wrote. "We cannot redeem our extremist youths, who commit all these heinous crimes, without confronting the sheikhs who thought it ennobling to re-invent themselves as revolutionary ideologues, sending other people's sons and daughters to certain death."

Ultimately, it is only the Muslims themselves who can resolve the issue of jihad and violence. Rashed sensed there is a movement in the Arab world, if perhaps not yet a consensus, that understands that Muslims have to start reining in their own rather than constantly complaining about injustice and unfairness. The violence has not only reduced sympathy worldwide for just causes like ending the Israeli occupation of Palestinian territory, he said, but set off resentment against Muslims wherever they live in the world.

To plumb the opposing view further, I went to visit Abdel Sabour Shahin, a linguistics professor at Cairo University and a talk-show stalwart, whose basic line was that the Muslim world must defend itself at all costs. On television appearances I had heard him say that most foreigners in Iraq are fair game since they came as unwelcome invaders to a Muslim land. In the new middle-class suburbs stretching into the desert beyond the Pyramids, Professor Shahin greeted me inside a small gated compound of high white walls that included his own mosque. He preaches there most Fridays. Bookshelves overflowing with religious texts crowded the upstairs room where he sat behind a cluttered desk. When I asked him what he thought of those who chop off heads, he, like many, switched the subject to Israel and the United States and why their actions in Palestine and Iraq were not labeled terrorism. "When a missile hits a house it decapitates thirty or forty residents and turns them to ash; isn't there a need to compare the behavior of a person under siege and angry with those who are managing the instruments of war?"

The debate on the reinterpretation of Islam remains largely confined to an intellectual elite, but even raising the topic erodes the taboo that the religion and those schooled in it are somehow infallible. In talking to people on the streets or listening to stuff like the regular program called The Pulpit on Al-Jazeera where callers can express whatever is on their minds, I got the sense that Arabs are grappling with these issues. People want to find a way to disassociate Islam from so much killing, to draw a clear line between what is resistance and what is criminal violence or terrorism. The absence of free speech in most Mideastern states limited the debate, as did the lack of a central religious authority to referee. There is no single definition of jihad that draws a clear line to distinguish resistance from terrorism. There is no independent body of "ulema," the Arabic word for religious scholars, that serves as a universally recognized, ultimate authority on such issues.

I often found myself treading on eggshells in any interview on the subject of religion. I could feel people tense as they waited for me to say something derogatory, or else they would start aggressively interrogating me on why I had failed to convert to Islam—something always expected since it was the culmination of the previous Abrahamic faiths. When Sheikh Mohamed Tantawi, the head of Egypt's storied Al-Azhar University, began to take offense at my line of questioning about why the religious hierarchy was having so little success curbing extremists, he rebuked me for my posture. I had already committed the faux pas of crossing my legs in front of him, deemed a snub. "Sit up straight!" he shouted at me, as if I was one of his slower pupils. "And uncross your legs!"

A gentler voice on matters of Islamic law, Sheikh Ali Gomaa, Egypt's grand mufti, the country's highest Muslim cleric, chuckled when I mentioned Shahrour's name, dismissing his ideas as overly influenced by his Soviet education. Shahrour's theory was rooted in the idea that the Prophet Mohamed himself wrote the Koran, Sheikh Gomaa said, dismissing the idea that the divine book could be parsed. "Shahrour believes that Mohamed composed the Koran himself, therefore he is going to take this chapter 9 and just kind of interpret it himself because it came from Mohamed," he continued. "But Muslims believe that the Koran is from God, not from Mohamed. Shahrour is free to do it, but that does not constitute knowledge." The mufti was using the word "knowledge" in this case as referring to the study and mastery of religious texts.

Sheikh Gomaa did endorse some points Shahrour had been making as valid in terms of the Koran corresponding to humanitarian law. Support for all that the Geneva conventions prescribe for the conduct of war and treatment of prisoners can be found in the holy texts, for example, Sheikh Gomaa said.

Even those who sympathize with Shahrour, while lauding his willingness to speak out, recognized that getting religious figures on board was the most significant challenge to bringing change.

Shahrour, living in secular Syria, is confident that he and an increasing number of intellectuals will not be deterred by clerical opposition. He reels off a list of what he denigrates as ridiculously archaic Hadith, or sayings, attributed to Prophet Mohamed. The Hadith were assembled in nine bulky volumes some 100 years after the prophet's death and are now the last word on how the faithful should live, although they have been pruned to around 7,000, down from 100,000. "'A female monkey was stoned for adultery.' How can someone who wrote that be trusted?! 'If a fly falls in your soup, then you should drown it because one wing carries the disease while the other holds the cure.' 'Any day you eat seven dates grown in Medina, poison won't affect you.'" At the time, these wildly exaggerated statements probably had some role as parables, but the context has been lost and in direct application they sound ridiculous, Shahrour explained. He would like to harness the same skepticism that such obviously absurd formulas inspire and apply it more widely to beliefs that he argues undermine the faith. He cited the popular saying that "the religion of Mohamed is the religion of the sword." "It is like this now because for centuries Muslims have been told that Islam was spread by the sword, that all Arab countries and even Spain were captured by the sword and we are proud of that," he said. "In the minds of ordinary people, people on the street, the religion of Islam is the religion of the sword. This is the culture, and we have to change it." He takes the argument a step further, blaming religion or at least the clergy for a mindset that he said blocks progress in any scientific field in the Muslim world.

Given the endless desire to relive the era of Mohamed, he told me, everything always gets evaluated through the filter of what is "hallal," or religiously acceptable, and what is "haram," or forbidden. "The Arab mind will always ask if something is hallal or haram before asking how it works," he said. "Because of the emphasis on emulating the era of Mohamed, Arabs find it almost impossible to produce knowledge. They are incapable of innovation. All the universities in the Arab world can produce doctors and engineers, but they don't produce knowledge. Instead they have this analogical mentality, they will take something from Germany and try to match it."

That limitation gets magnified by the fact that Arabs love to talk, he argued. "In our mentality the man who speaks well is more respectable than the man who works well. For centuries in the Arab world we have had thousands of poets and not one scientist, we don't search for facts." The saving grace, he felt, is that although Islam remained the central formative element in the Middle East, there was also a widespread feeling among Muslims that something is seriously amiss.

After hearing all this, I put his hypothesis to Sheikh Khalil al-Mais, the grand mufti of the Bekaa valley right over the Syrian border in Lebanon, who scoffed. "Heaven forbid!" he exclaimed as soon as I uttered Shahrour's name. Taking up the point that Islam should not be considered a religion of the sword, he argued that it is often ordinary Arabs who bear the brunt of violence visited on the region. "They have swords and tanks and bombs falling on them, so what do you expect? Take away the sword and then come talk to me. The only way to get rid of a sword hanging over you is with another sword."

CHAPTER 8

POLICE STATES

"Is this an interrogation?"
"No, it's just tea."

WHILE I TALKED TO VARIOUS ARABS and Iranians about the need for change in the normal course of my reporting, I could never focus exclusively on the issue due to the swirl of events. Then the American government embarked on its campaign to make democratization and political reform a key plank in its policy toward the region. With that, I began fishing around for a way to assess prospects for a different Middle East. The American argument—badly conceived by accentuating democratic elections and soon abandoned—was at least rooted in a sound idea, namely that creating open societies is the most effective long-term means to undermine extremism.

I decided the best way to proceed was to search out reformers pursuing that goal. There were plenty of political types or the usual analysts sitting around in think tanks ready to discuss it. But what about the women and men actually wrestling for a better future in one manner or another, I wondered, people like Sameer al-Qudah in this chapter? Seeking them out allowed me to figure out the key challenges, and what changes were actually being pursued to bring about some manner of reform.

I couldn't go everywhere, so I decided on six countries. I picked three of them—Jordan, Bahrain, and Morocco—because they had young leaders who were the most vocal about the need for change. The other three—Egypt, Saudi Arabia, and Syria—carried the most weight in terms of population, wealth, and adherence to pan-Arab ideology, respectively.

While Middle Eastern states are sufficiently different that they should not be lumped together as a monolith, I did find common problems facing reformers across the Arab world as well as Iran. In this chapter and those that follow, I examine those problems in turn, using one country to exemplify each. They come roughly in order of importance as reformers detailed them for me: the stifling control of the secret police; the absence of any rule of law even if the constitution seems to guarantee it; the fact that one tribe or one clique has controlled each government for so long; the inherent difficulty in working alone because organizing is mostly banned; the daunting power of the Muslim Brotherhood or other religious parties; and, finally, the keen disappointment that a new generation of rulers did not automatically introduce a new way of thinking.

The individual experiences of these reformers are emblematic of the hurdles that need to be surmounted before the Middle East can hope to overcome its history of despotic regimes. If the reform rallying cry echoes the question that the Libyan woman shouted out in the Popular Committee meeting—Why can't we be more like everybody else?—these are the reasons and what reformers hope to do about them.

Sameer al-Qudah knew that a summons from Jordan's intelligence police was inevitable after he stood up at a cultural festival to recite his poem depicting Arab leaders as a notch below pirates and highwaymen. He read the poem on a Thursday evening, the start of the weekend. His cell phone rang two days later, with the officer on the line telling him to present himself at the local governorate to discuss the work. Qudah was apprehensive but not surprised. Secret police agencies, or "mukhabarat" in Arabic, are a powerful and ubiquitous force in every Middle Eastern country. Any public declaration even hinting at criticism of the regime inevitably attracts their attention.

Qudah discovered that an undercover officer had surreptitiously videotaped him. The interrogator ran through the recording, stopping to ask him to explain what exactly he meant with lines like "beware of becoming an Arab leader." Prison loomed. Qudah had been through it before, sentenced by State Security Court to a year in jail for "slander" in 1996 after reciting a political poem called "The Manager," which mocked how Arab leaders pretend to garner public consensus before issuing their edicts.

"We are hungry for freedoms like the right to express ourselves," said Qudah, a stocky civil engineer with a shaved head whose day job is supervising construction projects. "But our country lives under the fist of the mukhabarat."

In Jordan and across the Arab world, those seeking democratic reform describe the role of the mukhabarat, with their octopus-like reach, as perhaps the most significant hindrance to bringing change. (It's pronounced mu-kha-ba-RAAT. Arabs use the word to lump together all the overlapping agencies spying on the citizenry and each other, but usually one central security apparatus carries the name "mukhabarat" officially; in Jordan it's the General Intelligence Department, or GID.)

In the decades since World War II, as military leaders or Middle East monarchs like Jordan's late King Hussein, the father of King Abdullah II, smothered democratic life, the security agencies amassed sweeping powers. Since every autocrat depends heavily on the mukhabarat to squash opponents, no leader old or young is expected to dismantle those powers anytime soon. Weak governments find it far easier to compensate for their lack of a popular mandate by strengthening the secret police rather than opening up the system.

The security agencies have become a law unto themselves, their reach pushing far beyond security into politics, the media, and business. In Jordan they have a hand in approving who gets to be a university professor, an ambassador, or an important newspaper editor. Students must obtain a good-behavior certificate from the GID if they seek admission to a public university under certain government programs. (The GID denies that anyone is obliged to obtain such a certificate, although it notes that some organizations "require" them.) The mukhabarat eavesdrops with the help of thousands of Jordanians on its payroll, similar to the informant networks in the Soviet bloc. Secret police chiefs live above the law. One recent chief, a chain smoker, used to overrule the ban on smoking when he was on board Royal Jordanian flights. No one dared challenge him, and passengers who complained to the airline were told there was nothing it could do.

The State Department's annual human rights report on Jordan released in March 2008 repeated a list of charges that has not changed much in recent years. The report was unusually critical of a staunch ally, particularly one whose security services have cooperated closely with their Washington counterparts in capturing terrorism suspects. The report noted that both the mukhabarat and the regular police are accused of acting with impunity, including frequent allegations of torture, arbitrary arrest, and prolonged detention. "The government harassed members of opposition political parties and restricted freedoms of speech, press, assembly, association, movement and some religious practices," the report stated.

Some Jordanians, while telling me that they support political reform, argued that the central role of the secret police is essential until the Middle East becomes more stable, or at least until the threat from religious extremists diminishes. But political activists deem progress impossible until such overweening influence is curbed. "The Jordanian state has failed to find a balanced formula between security and democracy," Labib Kamhawi, a businessman and longtime human rights activist, told me. "The issue of security has become a nightmare. If you give a speech against the policy of the government, this is a threat to security. If you demonstrate against this or that, it is a threat to security. It hits on all aspects of life and it is a severe hindrance to any change."

The issue is hardly unique to Jordan. It was a complaint I heard repeatedly from all Arabs and Iranians pushing reform. Foreigners are not immune to the long tentacles of the mukhabarat, either. Indeed, "mukhabarat" is likely among the first Arabic words any expatriate learns.

My Egyptian assistant and I were detained in late 2001 for loitering outside the Cairo headquarters of the secret police. (Our attention was focused on a school opposite its front door.) After several rounds of questioning and demands for identification, one false release, and a couple telephone calls to the Ministry of Information to confirm that we were legally registered journalists, we were eventually ushered into the office of a major. He politely asked us in English to sit down, and as I did I noticed the wall behind his battered desk was hung with roughly ten diplomas from the FBI, including one for sharpshooting and another for interrogation.

"Is this an interrogation?" I asked brightly.

"No, it's just tea," the major responded, grinning as an aide scuttled in with small, sugary glasses of the stuff.

We had a brief, friendly conversation about my impressions of Egypt, during which the major assured us that he was only acting in his capacity of protecting the well-being of some 5,000 Americans resident in Egypt. Then he let us go. But in the years afterward, whenever I was involved in any reporting in Egypt that state security considered dubious, the major would call. On one occasion I was out shopping for the latest underground tapes of sermons by extremist prayer leaders—and the cell phone rang. "What was on the tapes?" the major wanted to know. (Abeer, God bless her, told him, "Go buy your own!") Outside the mass trial of some young Muslim Brothers, I got into a rare heated argument with some of their relatives. I generally tried to avoid arguments, but they got me going by defending Saddam Hussein's human rights record as not all that bad. (This was before the American invasion.) The major called to ask with whom I was arguing. Sometimes he would call to suggest story lines, which we would diplomatically agree to consider in hopes it might diminish the scrutiny. I never actually took one up. I lived with the creepy feeling of being watched, though, or at least being watched around certain types of government opponents. All Egyptian employees of Western news organizations were put under even greater pressure.

I confess, however, that the vague connection with a major in the secret police periodically had its advantages. On a black, rainy night in a squalid village in the Nile delta, for example, we tracked down the family of a senior Al-Qaeda operative whom the United States had killed in Afghanistan. After some initial hostility, his brother and a few beefy friends agreed that I could interview them just as soon as we went with them to get permission from the mukhabarat headquarters in the village. We followed them in our car, wondering what might have prompted their sudden change in mood. Nervously eying the darkened building behind a chain-link fence and the line-up of thugs with biceps the size of my thigh, we stalled inside the vehicle, quietly calling the major. Fortunately this was one time that he answered immediately. He told us that the local State Security building was in no such location. We did a quick U-turn in the car and high-tailed it out of there as the thugs scrambled for their own vehicle. The goon squad remained in angry pursuit even after we skidded out onto the highway, the men leaning out the windows of the car, cursing and raising their fists at us.

Ⓢ   Ⓢ   Ⓢ

In Jordan, the "Big Brother is watching" form of implied threat, not to mention more direct pressure like arrests and trials, crops up repeatedly in the lives of all those pushing for political change. Jordan has never been a police state on the gory scale of neighbors like Iraq or Syria, where dissidents either disappeared or lived out their lives in jail. Indeed, one reason I can use Jordan as the example of an ill that plagues the entire Arab world is that so many people were willing to talk about their encounters with the mukhabarat. In most other countries people were too afraid. In addition, the GID once made the head of its domestic affairs branch available to me to discuss the agency on condition that he not be identified. Getting an interview with any senior mukhabarat official was extremely rare. "There is no freedom like that in Jordan," the official enthused to me in Arabic. On my last visit to Jordan in 2008, I was told that the mukhabarat was attempting to become more user friendly, less intimidating. I opened its website to see if I could tell. Perhaps my favorite page on that particular outreach program was the "Frequently Asked Questions" segment, of which there were just four. I would have thought that the most common query would be something along the lines of "How do I find out which dungeon my relative is in?" but apparently Jordanians were more curious about the sartorial aspects of the job. "What does the GID staff wear?" was one question. (Perhaps people wanted to recognize the secret agents in their neighborhood.) The site explained that although most officers had military ranks, they were required to wear civilian clothes.

A European friend, an academic who spent decades in the Arab world after we first met in a Cairo Arabic class in 1982, calls Jordan "an inconspicuous police state." My encounters with Jordanians echoed that description. Some people whispered "the friends" in conversations with me about the secret police just in case any were eavesdropping. Around 80 percent of the respondents surveyed in repeated annual polls taken by the Center for Strategic Studies at the University of Jordan said that they feared criticizing the government publicly lest they face trouble with the security services or elsewhere in their lives. More than three-quarters also said they feared participating in any manner of political activity ranging from demonstrations to opposition forums for the same reason. Such lingering fear regarding the secret police was one strong indicator that Jordanians doubt that King Abdullah II has an active reform program, despite how much he talks about it.

Sameer al-Qudah, the poet, summed up the general attitude for me: "We are supposed to be happy because we are not as bad off as our neighbors—the Palestinians under occupation or because we have more democracy than the Syrians or the Saudis and are more stable than Iraq. We are the best of the worst."

⊡ ⊡ ⊡

Born in 1970, Qudah was named after an uncle, a young lieutenant killed in the 1967 Arab-Israeli War. The oldest of nine children, his father an English teacher, he grew up in Ajloun, some thirty miles north of the capital, Amman. He remembers his first poem was an ode to the snow falling on the local reservoir that fed the surrounding orchards of apples, figs, and olives.

Qudah's political education started in grade school, when he was particularly struck by the history lessons surrounding the Sykes-Picot agreement, the British-French pact at the end of World War I that divided the Arab world into separate countries and laid the groundwork for a Jewish homeland. It is taught in the Arab world as the foremost of many modern betrayals that the colonial powers inflicted on the region.

His budding poetic talents were recognized by his teachers in the one-story limestone schoolhouse, chilly all winter, where he attended elementary school. On all national holidays Qudah was assigned to stand on top of the stairs and recite a few lines. That view, looking out over the cypress pines and oaks dotting the rolling red hills, still provided inspiration, he told me on the day he drove me around his hometown.

Qudah's history of encounters with the secret police started in high school, when he helped lead a 1988 demonstration protesting the death of Khalil al-Wazir, a Palestinian Liberation Organization leader assassinated by Israeli commandoes in Tunis. By the time he was an undergraduate, his fellow engineering classmates used to call him "The Poet of the University of Jordan." He remembers being summoned by the mukhabarat some twenty times while at university.

Arabs hold dear their long tradition of expressing ideas through poetry, and so topics of wide public interest like political reform invariably provide inspiration. Criticizing the lack of freedom in Jordan or the wider Arab world always brings an enthusiastic response from the crowd whenever he is invited to recite, Qudah noted. "If you can express these feelings through poetry, the reaction is even warmer because Arabs enjoy poetry a lot. It is like music; you are making a speech but in a musical way."

Many politically active Jordanians like Qudah argue that the country has regressed under King Abdullah II, particularly compared to the political reform wrought by his father during the crisis of 1989. At that time, Jordan, spurred by the International Monetary Fund, lifted the subsidies on some basic goods. A day after widespread bread riots rocked the entire country that year, I drove through the southwestern highlands and found that virtually every government building had been sacked. Even in small villages where there were no state offices, residents had burned down the schoolhouse. The unrest over the economic costs prompted King Hussein to usher in political liberalization. He allowed free parliamentary elections, loosened the tight gag on the press, and lifted martial law, which had been in place since 1956. Under King Abdullah—on a host of issues including parliamentary life, election campaigns, the right to assemble, the right of free speech, and a free press—many Jordanians decried the lack of change given the emphasis put on the reform issue by the royal palace. In many cases, that lack is blamed on the influence of the mukhabarat.

Major General Rouhi Hikmet Rasheed served in the Jordanian army for thirty-three years, retiring as the military's chief dentist. He decided to run for parliament in the 2003 elections and his stump speech suggested that the goal of reform should be a real constitutional monarchy. The head of the mukhabarat called to tell him to desist, Dr. Rasheed said when I went to visit his clinic.

"He told me that if I meant we should have a monarch like Britain's, this is not in the best interests of the country," recalled Dr. Rasheed, who retained a ramrod military bearing, adding that the warning came with a threat. "He said, 'You are a son of the regime, we trust you, but if your sons want to work in Jordan in the future, it might affect them.'"

Dr. Rasheed told me that back in his army days, he would not have believed the story if someone had described the kinds of threats he faced. "Our system is a civilian dictatorship, which is far more dangerous than an individual dictatorship," he said. "At least with an individual dictator you can point your finger at him, but with a constitutional dictatorship you can't point your finger at anybody." It is a key problem in Jordan, and common to regimes across the Middle East, that the royal court or presidential coterie carrying out most of the important policy decisions is not accountable to anybody except the monarch.

Politically active Jordanians say the constant zigzagging over reform reflected King Abdullah's own ambiguity. The way he addresses it in the United States is markedly different from the way he rules. On frequent visits to the U.S., where he is a favorite on the talk-show circuit, he stated repeatedly that the goal of reform in the Hashemite kingdom is a constitutional monarchy. He is prone to make pronouncements that political change is needed so that the "Crown can take a step back and the people can take a step forward," as he did during one visit in 2005. Statements like these encouraged many reformers to begin pushing for a return to the 1952 constitution, with its more extensive checks on royal power, which prompted the king to announce at home that any discussion of amending the constitution to conform with that older version was unacceptable.

The king spoke the language of reform in excellent English. He was, after all, sent to Deerfield Academy, the rigorous Massachusetts boarding school (as was I) and Sandhurst, the British equivalent of West Point. Some people conclude that a few democratic values must have rubbed off along the way. But Abdullah, born in 1962 of an English mother, was thrust onto the throne unexpectedly in 1999. King Hussein switched the line of succession on his deathbed, reportedly prompted by a family feud. He removed his own brother Hassan, who had been crown prince for decades, and made Abdullah, his oldest son, the heir. The young monarch was a special forces commander who had been expecting to spend his life in the military.

The carping started early about Abdullah's poorly pronounced, barracks Arabic—far too much soldier and no poetry. He lacked the deep connection that tied his father to ordinary Jordanians. He even resembled his English mother. The difference was exacerbated by the fact that Prince Hamza, the oldest son of King Hussein with his fourth wife, the American-born Queen Noor, was anointed crown prince. Still a teenager, Hamza had not only inherited his father's dark looks and gravelly voice, but Jordanians told me he and his siblings had been raised with the help of Bedouin nannies who perfected their Arabic. It did not take King Abdullah long to try to minimize the unflattering comparisons by removing his half-brother as crown prince.

People in Jordan complain that the king, relishing the chance to rule, has tried to adopt an almost Saudi style of playing the magnanimous monarch, claiming state assets as his own. Newspaper headlines in the summer of 2008, for example, trumpeted the fact that the king had "donated" forty-five ambulances to Jordanian hospitals. "We have gone from having rights to accepting royal handouts," said Kamhawi, the activist businessman. "This is absurd. The government buys forty-five ambulances and he gives them to the people." A country cannot be built on handouts, Kamhawi added; it needed a solid middle class. Jordan's was shrinking.

Many mocked Abdullah's taste for advertising slogans that allegedly captured the mood of reform, while he avoided doing anything tangible. On one of my first visits after he took the throne, billboards showing people from various walks of life loomed large. One featured a yuppie in rimless eyeglasses and a tie, the next a village woman with a gold tooth wearing a headscarf and embroidered dress. "Jordan" the advertisements proclaimed in huge, stylized Arabic letters, while smaller script flowing near the bottom quoted an obscure line of medieval poetry that translated loosely as "You reap what you sow." When I asked the supervisor at a roadside restaurant selling grilled chicken near one of the billboards what it meant, he waved his hand dismissively. "Please ask someone else because I have no idea," he told me. "People don't get jobs from what it says on such billboards." If the king wanted to raise the spirit of Jordanians, educated Jordanians outside the royal circle wondered, then why did he go outside the country to hire the London firm of Saatchi & Saatchi to create his advertising campaigns? The king seemed to have absorbed from the West the business model for selling detergent.

◙　◙　◙

The key problem for Jordanians seeking meaningful reform and not advertising slogans, Qudah told me, is finding an outlet under the baleful gaze of the mukhabarat. "You cannot form a political party by reciting poetry," he said, although it's effective for conveying a message, creating the right atmosphere. "If you want to create a reform program you have to take political action."

Political parties were not just reviled but had been banned for decades. Open membership meant jail. They are legal again, but they either are religious or promote failed ideologies like Baathism and Arab Nationalism. None really espouses a vision for a reformed Arab world, Qudah noted, questioning how something like a revived Baath Party can expect to be taken seriously as pushing reform when it declares undying admiration for a bloody despot like Saddam Hussein. The only glimmer of hope, Qudah asserted, is brave dissidents who speak out, but most of them act as individuals rather than forming organizations. "One day reformers will take the first step down the right road," he said. "Sometimes I think I am one of them and want to be part of that." He and other young Jordanians sit around in each other's homes discussing how they can do something effective, but they have yet to hit upon a solution. Hovering over all such conversations, whether it is spoken or not, is always the cost of any serious effort. "If you work in the daylight you might be imprisoned for a year or two, but you can still come back and work," he said. "But to work in the daylight you have to be very persuasive, serious, honest, and you can't quit as soon as the government offers temptations so you compromise."

The headquarters of Jordan's professional associations is the hub of the unofficial opposition, a role the government has sought to curb. "Engineers should talk about engineering," one former interior minister groused to me. But on any given night some manner of politically tinged seminar unrolls within the building's conference rooms. Once four stories, another three have been pasted atop the original building in a hodge-podge of architectural styles, and dirt streaks run down the entire façade. In a perfunctory stab at native culture, the ground-floor windows are arched and the driveway entrance planted with a row of scraggly palm trees. The exterior is often decorated with giant, grisly posters of Palestinian children or other civilian victims of the Israeli military. If architecture is destiny, the overall effect of disorder outside perfectly reflected the habitual bedlam within.

One night while I was there, the minister of political development showed up to discuss reform. Participants mocked the very name of his ministry as absurd, a prime example of the top-down attempts at reform that are doomed for lack of public participation.

The mukhabarat had sent one of their usual spies to the session— one man at the table with a dark-blue shirt and a black moustache busy scribbling down every word. Qudah, there to give a poetry reading, told me that everyone knew who worked for the secret police. To make his point, as a couple of them left he called out in a jocular manner, "Good, go home so that we can say what we want."

When it came time for the poetry, the difference between Qudah and the others was starkly evident. He was sandwiched between two melodramatic poets lamenting the bloody death of Baghdad as a storied Arab capital. Qudah's poem talked about the eagerly anticipated autumn of Jordan's current political system.

⬓   ⬓   ⬓

The mukhabarat fortified their central role after both Jordan's 1994 peace treaty with Israel and then King Hussein's 1999 death. While peace diminished the external threat, making the military less important, the mukhabarat was deployed to monitor widespread opposition to the treaty. Then when the king died, having been on the throne for forty-seven years, the mukhabarat helped provide stability and support while his young, green heir found his feet. That support naturally encouraged Abdullah to give credence to the mukhabarat viewpoint that opening up civil and political life would only provide cover for enemies of the state.

Many reformers believe one key reason that Jordan's elected parliament remains so weak is that the mukhabarat interferes not only in elections but how members vote once in office. The GID denies any such interference, but parliament members claim heavy lobbying by the mukhabarat does change votes. Not that they need to sway many opinions. During the years I was working in Jordan, numerous MPs told me that roughly one-third of their number were either former security agents or military officers.

"Some members of parliament allow the mukhabarat to intervene in how they vote because they depend on them for help in getting re-elected," Mahmoud A. al-Kharabsheh, a maverick MP who joined the mukhabarat in 1974 and retired as its head in 1991, told me. "They enter into 90 percent of the political decisions in this country." The mukhabarat can make all the difference in an electoral campaign by getting hundreds of voters to the polls, he and other MPs said, as well as providing access to government jobs for constituents, money, and other facilities. "It's a carrot and stick. They tell the MPs that whatever they want in the future, they will support them. It is well understood that they will turn against any MP who fails to do what they ask," said Kharab-sheh. Jordan's own semi-official National Center for Human Rights criticized much about the election system in its annual report issued in 2008, covering the previous year. It said that the wholesale transfer of registered voters from one district to the next undermined the concept of free and fair elections, and that the new, more restrictive law on political parties would stall their development.

Most resentment toward the mukhabarat stems from their interference in all manner of political issues. "Policy should guide the security services and the security services should not be setting policy," said Hamza Mansour, leader of the Islamic Action Front, the Jordanian branch of the Muslim Brotherhood and the country's strongest opposition party. Security police who visited the party headquarters at one point demanded that the organization hang pictures of King Abdullah on the walls. Many organizations saw the hand of the mukhabarat behind the strenuous regulations for getting permits to hold a public meeting and the rules covering public demonstrations. March organizers were told that the only flag that could be waved was the Jordanian flag. No banners were permitted. Raising pictures of King Abdullah was also obligatory and there could be no chanting. The protests would, to outsiders, look like a rally supporting the king. "If no permit was required, there would be a demonstration against the United States and Israel every day and you would not be able to navigate the streets," the GID spokesman told me, defending the list of conditions. "There has to be some sort of system." Political reformers believed that the restrictions were popular among a new class of businessmen grown rich off the war next door in Iraq. They disliked any hint of instability in Jordan.

When any demonstration was deemed problematic, the reaction from the security services was swift and harsh. During one particularly tense period, I attended a Friday prayer sermon whose hundreds of participants planned to march on the Israeli Embassy afterward. As the march formed, helmeted riot police wielding clear plastic shields moved in behind a wave of water cannons and tear gas. I sought shelter along with some participants in a nearby apartment building. Police shattered the glass front doors with their heavy wooden batons, then ran up and down the stairs, beating every man or woman in their path.

The head of the GID, the main intelligence agency, reports directly to King Abdullah, whereas the minister of the interior runs the other security agencies. The king sets broad policy guidelines, but leaves it up to the mukhabarat themselves on how they implement them. Some Jordanians find that the secret police involve themselves in even the smallest matters to a degree that leaves people seething with frustration.

Mohamed Atiyeh, a Jordanian businessman, once tried to establish an organization for single parents after his divorce. At first the Ministry of Social Affairs rebuffed the application, saying Jordan had enough private organizations (there were 700), but eventually issued a permit. Then Atiyeh was rejected as the elected president of the board in a decision eventually traced to the Minister of the Interior's secret security arm. Ultimately, approval took seven months. "It was an NGO for single parents, it had nothing to do with politics, and yet they interfered," Atiyeh told me. He thought Jordanian citizens should have the right to know what reports in their secret police files prompt such rejections. "I have never done anything against the society or the government or the regime, so I am still waiting for someone to explain why."

In another incident, Atiyeh and a few friends, in a puckish mood one weekend, decided to decorate a long empty stretch of exterior wall at his house with graffiti. One man wrote a line from the constitution stating that personal freedom is protected. Another wrote "Love is immeasurable." A third wrote "Life comes first." Atiyeh himself wrote an Arab proverb about the absence of choice. Three days later, the secret police summoned him. The officer who questioned him eventually said the graffiti should be painted over because it might be "misinterpreted" by people who don't care about Jordan's future. Atiyeh stalled for two months, arguing that it was a freedom-of-speech issue, but eventually tired of the constant harassing phone calls.

The head of a newly independent radio station was called by the mukhabarat after it aired a program discussing how a magazine editor had been blocked from taking up his post because he failed to win secret police approval. The officer calling suggested the station not mention the organization on the air again, ever. Indeed, any mention of the mukhabarat or hint at its central role typically brings a rapid slap.

Emad Hajjaj, one of the Arab world's most talented editorial cartoonists, once subtly suggested that the mukhabarat, which he represented as a ghostly disembodied hand, was behind all government appointments. He too was summoned and warned never to mention the organization in a cartoon again. I asked him if he had obeyed the order and he looked surprised, then laughed at my naïveté. "They are the mukhabarat!" said Hajjaj. "We can barely bring ourselves to express our opinions to our wives in our bedrooms and even then we are afraid."

Hajjaj displays on his website, www.mahjoob.com, all the cartoons that have been censored over the years for being politically sensitive. (He stamps each one with a little picture of a woman's slipper, a visual reference drawn from Hajjaj's work that shoes represent oppression—his main recurring character, Abu Mahjoub, uses his wife's slipper to beat her in some cartoons.) The most recent in 2008 was a classified ad suggesting that all of Jordan had been put up for sale to outsiders. (When I started asking around about other censorship examples, several people I interviewed said that a newspaper editor close to the king had called to warn them not to talk to me. The editor insisted my line of questioning was proof that "Neil is an enemy of Jordan.")

Hajjaj was often forced to barter over the wording in his cartoons. The haggling could continue for days, he said, lighting a cigarette. He was once fired from his job at a government-controlled newspaper after drawing a series of cartoons that mocked the leading cell phone company, among others. "We dream of a free newspaper that the government cannot order around," he told me in his office, decorated with bold primary colors and a life-size cardboard cutout of Abu Mahjoub—a skinny Arab man with a bold chin wearing a checkered red and white headdress.

By the time I dropped in for a coffee in 2008, Hajjaj said he was censoring himself more often, focusing less on political and social reform issues because they elicited such a negative reaction from readers. For much of the year, for example, Arab women had been transfixed by a Turkish soap opera named *Noor*. The handsome Turkish lead, a man with blue eyes and blond hair named Muhannad, was an unusually sensitive Muslim male who showered his wife Noor with attention. Arab women were completely gaga about the series, and Hajjaj drew a slightly mocking cartoon, suggesting that Muhannad, drawn in a tuxedo, could be as abusive as he wanted toward any of his Arab female fans, represented by an overweight woman with dyed blonde hair. In the bubble over her head, Hajjaj wrote: "She can't vote; she accepts beatings from her husband; she doesn't mind being the fourth wife; she only wants to give birth to sons, not daughters; she gave up her education to get married because that is what tradition demanded." His mobile did not stop ringing the day the cartoon ran, he said, with angry women telling him he was taking the wrong side in the battle between the values of the free world and those of Islam. Women told him they thought that it was in fact OK for their husbands to beat them because the Koran sanctioned it. (That stems from a widely debated interpretation of one key verse from The Women, chapter 4, verse 34.) The conservative Saudi Wahhabi clerics who dominate the increasing number of religious satellite television stations naturally sanction the beating interpretation, Hajjaj told me, and such channels were becoming more and more influential. "You cannot tackle these issues. People were calling to tell me that we had to be frank about how raising issues like human rights and freedom of speech were really about confronting Islam," he said. "Defending democracy and human rights is like saying a bad word."

⊡   ⊡   ⊡

Hajjaj is not alone in censoring himself. There are numerous topics that anger the Royal Court that journalists tend to avoid. They range from the role of the monarchy to the repercussions of the Jordanian-Palestinian split in the population to why some ordinary Jordanians express support for the likes of Osama bin Laden. "Whenever I write or speak, I feel like I am two people," Helmi al-Asmer, a noted columnist in *Al-Dustour* daily, said while describing how the extensive process of self-censorship works for almost all Jordanian journalists after decades of intimidation by the mukhabarat. "On the one hand I am addressing the readers, but part of me is addressing all the security services watching me."

The GID official told me that his organization was too busy chasing terrorists to monitor the press, but Samir Habashneh, the former interior minister, said he saw nothing wrong with the mukhabarat calling journalists to advise them on how to "explain" the need for certain government policy changes to the public. I went to see Habashneh to get the viewpoint of senior security officials. Sitting out on his balcony with its sweeping panorama of the surrounding hills, sipping small cups of sweet coffee, he said that freedoms taken for granted in democratic countries cannot be practiced in Jordan because it sits, as he put it, "in the eye of a hurricane." With the explosive American occupation of Iraq across one border and frequent violence caused by Israel's long occupation of the West Bank across the other, he felt that Jordan needed to work overtime to ensure its own stability. If the security apparatus relaxed its vigilance and civil liberties including free speech and the right to assemble, and unlicensed political parties were granted without condition, it might easily lead to similarly bloody chaos here, he argued.

It was ironic, given that the Bush administration cited the need for democratic change in the Middle East as a reason for going to war in

Iraq, that the instability there, just across the border, was cited as the reason to curb democratic freedoms in neighboring countries.

In any conversation, senior security officials invariably harkened back to 1970, when the Hashemite dynasty barely held onto its throne by facing down various armed Palestinian factions in pitched battles on Amman's streets. They fear a repeat.

Although Palestinians make up some 50 percent of the roughly 6 million population of Jordan, they have been barred from the security services since 1970. In addition, when the election laws were rewritten in 1993, the parliamentary districts were gerrymandered to prevent heavily Palestinian areas from holding significant numbers of seats. A parliament dominated by Palestinian legislators, senior security officials argued, would likely concentrate so much on Palestinian affairs that Israel would be able to argue that Jordan be designated Palestine. Hence, the argument ran, political reform in Jordan will have to await a solution to the Palestinian crisis. The landslide victory that Hamas won in the Palestinian elections in 2006 spooked Jordan. It postponed election reforms again and tightened rules governing free speech.

A pronounced split in Jordan distinguishes citizens descended from the once nomadic Bedouin tribes who have long inhabited the east side of the Jordan River and the Palestinians, many of them refugees forced there by a series of wars, particularly the 1967 war when Jordan lost the West Bank to Israel. Broadly speaking, the Jordanians fill the ranks of the armed services, while the Palestinians run much of the private sector. Both sides resent what they see as unwarranted privileges given to the other. Some of the most conservative Jordanians object to Palestinians getting passports, suggesting they be treated as they are in the Gulf states where they often formed the nucleus of the technocrat class—granted residency but rarely citizenship. Certainly none should be allowed to serve in the Cabinet or other top government posts.

During the years when all political activity was banned outright, the tension between the two sides crystallized in the fierce rivalry between two competing soccer clubs: al-Faisaly, dominated by native Jordanians, and al-Wihdat, whose players are mostly of Palestinian descent. The latter name comes from one of the largest Palestinian refugee camps. After King Abdullah took the throne, Faisaly supporters taunted their rivals in the stadium by chanting for him to divorce his wife, Queen Rania, because she is of Palestinian descent. "Hiya min wein? Hiya min wein? Tala'ha Tala'ha, Ya Abu Hussein," went the rhyming chant, which means "Where's she from? Where's she from? Divorce her, divorce her, Oh father of Hussein." (Both Abdullah's father and oldest son were named Hussein.) They also chanted for Israel to strengthen its army.

     ▣   ▣   ▣

Jordanians pushing for reform, especially the young like Qudah, dismissed the whole security argument surrounding the question of Palestine as just a pretext for those in power to hang on indefinitely. They sometimes joked darkly that the government did back one strong political party—the mukhabarat. Nothing underscored the limits on freedom more than the fact that Qudah was once imprisoned for a work of political art. The poem he recited in August 1996, which criticized the way "The Manager" ran an unidentified country, had lines like these:

> He has never taken any decision
> Without asking for the public's permission
> Or without a public referendum.
> What a public!
> Whenever something urgent comes up
> The public assembles
> Then there is a comprehensive speech, whipped up by
>   The Manager
> Followed by a ululation and a blessing
> And the auction is open for whistling, drumming and
>   for honking
> And afterwards, the audience claps

And this is the consensus in my state
And this is freedom of expression.

Qudah had been invited to recite poetry at the annual convention for Jordanian dentists, which was held that year inside the historic tower castle of Ajloun, his hometown. His ten-day interrogation, though civil, focused on his goal in reading the poem, whether he was trying to incite an anti-government rebellion and whether he belonged to any subversive organization. Qudah believed his jail sentence from the State Security Court was pre-ordained from the moment he was charged with "italat lisaan," which in Arabic literally means "elongation of the tongue," but translates as slander or defamation. He spent a year at Swaigah prison in the southern desert playing soccer with other inmates and leading discussions on the need for political and social change, he told me. "That year just deepened my sense that reform is necessary and made me want to challenge the system more."

Trouble with the security services creates a ripple effect. Qudah wrote enough poetry to publish four collections, but got permission to distribute only one book finally in 2008. The book consisted of mostly love poetry. The few poems that were political dealt with the Arab-Israeli dispute or other regional subjects. Qudah has never been invited to recite at official festivals, although Jordanian critics call his work witty and subtle. "If you were the most important writer in the world, you couldn't get published in any Jordanian newspaper without the consent of the secret police," he said. "Whereas if you become their ally, you would get a very prominent column."

By the time I caught up with him again in 2008, drinking beers during a hotel happy hour while he smoked a cigar, Qudah had developed even deeper scorn for the state-controlled radio and Jordanian television. It was being used to create a personality cult around King Abdullah, he said, with songs lauding the monarch set against videotapes showing him shaking hands with President Bush or delivering aid to poor people. "We might be the only country in the world where you turn on the radio and don't hear any songs about love or girls. We only sing about the government and the king," he said, grimacing. "It's disgusting. If you are driving in your car you can't turn the radio to a Jordanian station because that is all you will hear."

(Defamation of the king or the royal family can bring a jail sentence of up to three years. Perceived slights crop up in the oddest places. Suha Maayeh, the Jordanian reporter I worked with frequently, told me she was admonished by security officers not to wear her Victoria Beckham–designed jeans because the rear pockets were decorated with a crown.)

Qudah thought he stayed behind bars for merely twenty-four hours after reciting the poem questioning the honor of Arab leaders because an important cousin intervened. Qudah is a member of a sprawling Jordanian clan, a significant government ally, and his cousin represented their hometown of Ajloun in parliament. He took me to meet Falah al-Qudah, who argued that the fact that Sameer spent a year in jail for the first poem and just one night for the second proved that the mukhabarat was becoming progressive. "They were more sympathetic the second time because they realized that he didn't threaten the state's security," he told me, adding that he supported the idea that the security services maintain vigilance at all times. As soon as we were out in the office hallway and his cousin was out of earshot, Qudah shook his head, noting that the legislator spoke for roughly an hour about reform without really proposing anything concrete.

Qudah told me that the problems with the opposition in Jordan stem from both a lack of organization and a clearly defined demand to pursue. "If you are going to be thrown into jail anyway, you might as well make big demands," he said. He wanted to see an organized opposition party that pushed for major, specific demands, like appointing the prime minister from among the elected members of parliament. He then reeled off a long checklist of the building blocks of democracy—freedom, transparency, equal opportunity within the democratic process, social justice, strong institutions, and the rule of law. "Everyone should be subject to the constitution and the rule of law." He doubted that the current system will ever change itself, in Jordan or anywhere else in the region. Yet greater political openness should be the demand of any Arab with a brain, he argued. "To respect your own intelligence means you cannot accept the way things carry on in the Arab world," he said. "We live a big official lie that everything is fine in the Arab world, which nobody should accept." Some activists think it will come only with a stronger economy, which would embolden a presumably larger middle class to demand that the mukhabarat not interfere with their lives. Ideally a middle class would want real laws that stick, not hidden laws promulgated by the secret police.

There are times when Qudah thinks about escaping politics, just kicking back and watching European soccer on television or hanging out with his wife, but he is always sucked back in. "If you have stability but life is desperate, what does that bring you?" Qudah says. "We Arabs, all of us, are marrying, drinking, laughing, making love. So why can't we live in a free environment? Why can't our freedom just be one aspect among many in our lives? Why do we have to wait? What for? We have been waiting for more than fifty years."

Like many Arabs seeking reform, Qudah was torn by the United States pushing the issue. American economic and military aid to Jordan expanded to more than $650 million in 2008, giving Washington considerable leverage. On the one hand, he thought outside pressure helped bring change, but relying on the U.S. for such pressure was a bitter choice given that it is generally seen as hostile to Arab interests. He also found a certain hypocrisy in the brief American attempt to demand reform. "They gave the green light to all these Arab leaders to create police states, then the reaction to all these police states was religious extremism," Qudah said. "You raise someone for fifty years to go the wrong way down a one-way street and then suddenly tell them that they have to respect the law."

CHAPTER 9

Above the Law

The King's person is inviolable and sacred.

—Article 23, Moroccan constitution

As the train from Rabat to Marrakesh rocked along, the late afternoon sun burnished the deep reddish hue of the barren, undulating hills into ever more striking tones. But the stunning vista had failed to distract me for more than a few minutes from the book I was reading. Walter Harris, a British correspondent who had preceded me by roughly 100 years, wrote Morocco That Was, a memoir describing life circa 1900 amidst the royal courts in Marrakesh and Rabat. Before reporting from any country for the first time, I tried to read at least one good novel about it—fiction illuminating the people and the culture in a far more intimate manner than any guide book. But I also delighted at the works of long-dead newspaper reporters because they provided a yardstick for how much—or how little—the vagaries of the country and my own particular profession had shifted.

Harris remarked on the propensity of each potentate, from the reigning sultan to the local governor, to maintain his own unspeakably vile jail. All-powerful grand viziers, fallen from grace, ended their days imprisoned in cramped cages or worse. One was fed to a lion kept around the palace grounds. "In every governor's Kasbah, deep in damp dungeons—as often as not holes scooped in the ground for storing grain—there lay and pined those who had committed, or not committed, as the case might be, some crime, and still more often, those who were rich enough to be squeezed," Harris wrote. "In such suffering, and in darkness, receiving just sufficient nourishment to support life, men were known to have existed for years, to emerge again long after their relations had given up all hope of seeing them." Often the only reprieve came with the death or disgrace of the man in power, in which case the dungeon gates were thrown open to release "the wrecks of his prisoners."

"What horrors of prisons they were, even those above ground and reserved for the ordinary class of criminal. Chained neck to neck, with heavy shackles on their legs, they sat or lay in filth, and often the cruel iron collars were only undone to take away a corpse," Harris wrote.

The passage startled me, for in Rabat I had met a graceful man in his 60s named Ahmed Marzouki. More than anyone else I encountered during my many years as a correspondent, Marzouki had lived the horror of the capricious legal systems that plague the Arab world. He had been locked away for more than eighteen years of solitary confinement inside Tazmamart, a desert fortress built specifically to imprison junior officers who played minor roles in two attempted coups. A military court had initially sentenced him to five years in the early 1970s.

"The king was not happy with the sentences so he tossed them out," said Marzouki, a trim figure with a dwindling fringe of gray hair. "He had the idea of sending us away to die like rats in Tazmamart."

Of the fifty-eight men first incarcerated, just twenty-eight emerged alive.

The Middle East usually felt compact, almost cloistered. It was rare that I sat on an airplane for more than an hour or two. The first time I flew to Morocco from Cairo was on a whim—some friends in New York called to suggest I join them for the weekend in the charming southern fishing town of Essaouira for the annual festival of exuberant African music called Gnaoua. I jumped at the chance. En route, I finally glanced at my watch at some point, noting that three hours had passed, and asked the stewardess if we were landing soon. She told me Casablanca was still more than two hours away. Yes, Morocco faces the Mediterranean, but the country, slightly larger than California and inhabited by around 34 million people, boasts a far longer Atlantic coastline. It sits entirely on the opposite side of Africa from the heart of the Middle East.

In some ways, Morocco has opened an analogous social and political distance between itself and the rest of the Arab world. Civic organizations can be formed with relative ease, and scores of them are working on everything from improving prison conditions to lowering the country's abysmal illiteracy rate, stuck around 45 percent. A new family law means women are treated less like chattel. I found a vibrant and outspoken press in 2005. But the government has since largely succeeded in muzzling it by manipulating the less-than-independent courts. Judges have levied crippling fines against the most activist publications in a series of questionable defamation suits.

Morocco mirrors its Arab brethren in that the entire system of law rests not on a framework of checks and balances but on the whim of the king. Morocco's ruling family traces its lineage back to Ali, the nephew and son-in-law of the Prophet Mohamed. Article 19 in the constitution calls the king "emir al-mumineen" or the "prince of the faithful," and Article 23 declares that he is sacred. Other Arab constitutions do not proclaim the ruler holy, even though an official reverence cocoons all the leaders. The absolute powers claimed by both the ruler and the secret police form the twin poles of despotism in virtually every Middle East nation.

Moroccans carry their reverence a step further than most. When the current king's grandfather, Mohamed V, was exiled by the French, his subjects claimed to be able to see his face in the moon. One Moroccan editor I spoke with compared his fellow citizens to a field of sunflowers turning all day long to trace the path of the sun—following their monarch seemed genetically encoded. The effort the monarchy expended to preserve this hallowed role was striking; challenging it even tangentially involved no small peril. In an infamous recent case, a journalist was charged with the heinous crime of insulting the king by suggesting a beachfront royal palace was going to be sold as a luxury hotel. The prosecutor hauled a chunk of palace stone the size of a grapefruit into the courtroom and argued successfully that any stone in the kingdom became sacred and thus inviolable as soon as the monarch used it. As long as the system held that the king floats above the law, reformers told me, Morocco will remain just another despotic Arab state rather than a truly free country.

This raises a central question that echoes across the Middle East: What is needed to turn states run by despotic whim into genuine nations of law?

In Morocco, many reformers believed that the essential first step would come via an open reckoning with the abuses that the system spawned in the past. But an attempt through a reconciliation commission instead underscored the profound limits that hobbled real change. Ahmed Marzouki, in fact, took the extraordinary step of testifying at a public forum about the misery he endured in Tazmamart. The name became shorthand for the abuses Moroccans suffered under the thirty-eight-year rule of King Hassan II, who died in 1999. Moroccans refer to the notably dark, middle decades of his reign as "the years of lead." Marzouki chose not to testify before the official Equity and Reconciliation Commission, however, established in 2004 by King Mohamed VI, Hassan's son, ostensibly to lay bare the human rights abuses of earlier years. The commission's public hearings were without precedent in the Middle East. The royal advisors I interviewed always pointed to them as evidence of the significant accomplishments Morocco has made in its democratic transformation. Ultimately, the government paid out some $100 million to around 10,000 victims of torture and other abuse. The commission also made a series of recommendations for constitutional changes to ensure that excessive human rights violations would never be repeated. They included greater separation of powers, an independent judiciary, more oversight over the secret police and other security services, and tangible respect for individual rights by implementing international standards of law.

Yet to former prisoners like Marzouki, the commission hearings proved lopsided and inadequate from the start, and the fact that the recommendations were basically shelved only confirmed their fears. Yes, former detainees freely described the kidnapping and torture they endured or gruesome prison deaths they had witnessed—a few times even live on state television. But they were barred from mentioning the names of those responsible. "The most important thing is that Moroccans never again experience this excessive abuse of authority," Marzouki told me in French over small, robust cups of coffee in his modest apartment in Salé. The working-class neighborhood of three- and four-story apartment buildings sits across a narrow, muddy river from the crenellated walls of the capital, Rabat. "These men must come out of the shadows." Instead, he said, some of them retained their powerful positions. "Who were we supposed to reconcile with? There have to be two parties for it to be a real reconciliation."

Holding no one accountable for past misdeeds was an open invitation to repeat the same mistakes, Marzouki believed. It still only required a simple phone call to have anyone in Morocco arrested. "It is a problem throughout the Arab world. As long as there are no clear reforms, as long as those responsible do not consider themselves subject to the law, anything can happen again."

Indeed, many reformers argued that it happened all over again in the wake of gory suicide bombings in Casablanca in May 2003 as well as the widespread involvement of Moroccans in other attacks ranging from Madrid to Saudi Arabia. The most ardent reformers questioned the point in the government establishing a reconciliation commission to amend past wrongs, only to turn around to scar a whole new generation of political activists through similar human rights violations of abduction, torture, and even a few mysterious prison deaths. More than 3,000 suspected Islamists have been arrested since the Casablanca bombings that killed some thirty people, and hundreds languish in jail.

"They ask where all this terrorism comes from, yet all you have to do is stand outside parliament in Rabat on almost any day and you can see the police brutalizing the university graduates protesting because they have no work," Marzouki said. He compared the present to his own experiences more than thirty years ago. Most of the hundreds detained after the suicide bombings "had done nothing but were considered suspicious—they wore beards—and nothing prevented them from being arrested and condemned to unconscionable sentences," he said. "I don't mean to say those who kill people should not be brought to justice, but there must be one law that is above everybody."

Moroccans use an Arabic word in a slightly mocking way to describe the interlocking power of the monarchy, the security services, and the ruling elite. It's called the "Makhzan," which literally means storehouse and was an historical term for the government treasury department. Reformers blame the reluctance of the Makhzan to relinquish any power even in the face of changed laws as their main challenge. By the time I spoke to him at the end of 2008, Marzouki had grown pessimistic about the prospect for lasting change. The king had appeared on television to demand reform in the justice system, notably in the Ministry of Justice. "How can the king demand judicial reform when the order can only come from him?" Marzouki wondered aloud. "He has all the power. How can you have reform when he is the prince of the faithful, the head of the army, and the chief of the government? How can there be reform if it does not come from him?"

Marzouki was born poor, the sixth of nine children. Unable to afford university, he earned a spot in the officer training program at the Royal Military School. In 1971, he said, he was among a group of junior officers told to prepare for a live-fire exercise. They were driven to the royal palace at Skhirat and ordered to open fire on what they later learned were guests of the king playing golf. The king survived. The main coup plotters were executed by firing squad live on television, while the junior officers were sentenced to a few years in prison. Then in 1972 the military attempted another coup, this time by opening fire on the monarch's jet. King Hassan decided to make an example of the younger officers, throwing them into Tazmamart. Neither their families nor the public knew about the prison, but the military did, and the punishment served as a stark warning to other officers. Marzouki, who entered jail at 23 and emerged at age 41, chronicled the hellish deprivations he endured in a book called *Tazmamart, Cell 10*, published in French.

It described in searing detail how the men decayed, their hair and beards growing long and unkempt, their bodies shriveling from hunger. At first they divided four loaves of bread among the fifty-eight prisoners each day. More than half died—some had gone insane and flung themselves against the walls of cells they rarely left; one wasted away from a painful, paralyzing disease during eleven years without ever seeing a doctor. "It is hard to find words to describe the horror we lived—all alone, no light, no medicine, little food," Marzouki said to me. Every time I asked him to remind me how long he had been a prisoner, he always responded "eighteen years, three months," not rounding off a moment. "It was an eternal night."

By bribing sympathetic guards, the men finally got word to their families that they were still alive despite the fact that King Hassan and his senior advisors denied that Tazmamart existed. The first significant break came after one officer's daughter, a high school senior, scored among the top ten students in the entire country on the mandatory university entrance exams. During an audience with King Hassan, the king asked if there was anything they wanted and the girl bravely asked when her father was going to be released from Tazmamart. As Marzouki described it, the king calmly turned to an aide and asked, "Is anyone still alive in Tazmamart?" It took several more years before an international campaign finally pressured the monarch to release the men in September 1991. "We were ghosts, skeletons who could barely walk," Marzouki said.

Some reformers in Morocco argue that Tazmamart lies in the past, that something fundamental shifted under the new king. Assia el-Ouadie, a lawyer, was born in 1949 into a family of political activists. Her father fought the French occupation, and later the monarchy. Ouadie was 2 years old the first time she visited her father in jail. Under Hassan, he vanished into prison several times, disappearing for all of 1973. Just as he was released, two brothers, a sister, and a brother-in-law were arrested, and all four sentenced to up to twenty-two years in prison. After decades of prison visits, Ouadie said, it was still the image of her father during his last jailing that remained fixed in her mind. "He was such a strong man, and when I saw him in prison he was very skinny, a broken man," she said. Her eyes watery, she turned away and asked quietly to change the subject. When a companion wondered if she was crying, she responded: "No, I'm not crying. I don't cry anymore."

Ouadie spearheaded a now government-backed foundation that gave hundreds of young prisoners vocational training like auto repair, carpentry, and barbering. She was not so sanguine as to believe that torture and beatings had been eliminated, but she did think they diminished markedly. "Before, the idea was 'once a criminal, always a criminal,' and there was no need to rehabilitate them," she said as she took me through the bright, airy workshops of a juvenile prison in Casablanca. "When you treat the prisoners with a little respect, when you treat them like human beings, you are already 60 percent of the way toward rehabilitation. This was never done in Morocco."

I found my own presence in the prison something of a confir-
mation of the change, or at least of her clout. I had arrived in Morocco only the night before and was touring the jail the first thing
in the morning. It was virtually impossible to visit any prison in the
Arab world, much less without addressing a single formal request
to a government ministry. Before arriving, I had envisioned endless
bouts of tea and paperwork.

Early in his rule, King Mohamed himself had toured the prison
on an official visit. A few days later, he drove Ouadie back in his
own car, without an entourage. What he saw persuaded him to help
establish the prison education foundation that she now heads. As
Ouadie walked me through the vocational schools, she shooed
away the guards and then peppered scores of inmates with questions. She demanded to know whether they had been beaten and
whether they were getting good bread and the visitors they wanted.
Each addressed her as Mama Assia, and she responded to all of them
by name. Prison officials had laid out an elaborate spread of cookies
and tea for us, which she promptly handed over to the inmates. I
walked around the room, asking them about their classes and why
they were in jail. "Every one of them will tell you he did nothing,
that he is innocent but some mistake landed him here," she said
and the boys all laughed. Pictures of the last royal visit decorated
the walls—the king resplendent in a sharply tailored tan suit and
Ouadie tucked into the entourage somewhere, a short matronly figure in a sensible blouse and dark skirt with an impish smile.

The prisoners complained that the warden barred them from
playing soccer. Ouadie marched into his office later and demanded
to know why. The warden sputtered about the risk of escape and
started to tell her that none of the guards can coach. She cut him
off: "There are no security problems and if you need a coach go
find one!" She turned to me to explain that the boys wouldn't flee
because they were eager to learn a trade.

When I asked her if the jail training program meant the country
had changed permanently, she thought for a minute. Democracy
could not just tumble out of the sky one day, she told me; it was

something that had to be learned. The momentum had to come from Moroccans themselves, she noted. "We could not bring real change if only the government was responsible," she said. "We are on the route toward reform, but it is a long, rocky road." Removing the monarchy while that process was happening would only bring chaos, she said, noting that given her family's history of imprisonment she should be the first to reject the king.

Her brother Salah, younger by two years, was more optimistic. Jailed himself for a decade starting in 1974, he helped found the Equity and Reconciliation Commission. Torture used to be a systemic policy, but that has changed, he argued. Other reformers were not so sure. Lawyers defending young men arrested on terrorism charges said their clients were all tortured. Allegations of abuse also surfaced in cases far removed from terrorism or radical Islam. When Fouad Mourtada, a 26-year-old Moroccan computer engineer, was arrested in February 2008, he was accused of "villainous practices" and of usurping the identity of Moulay Rachid, the crown prince. Mourtada had created a fake profile of the prince, the king's brother, on Facebook, the Internet social networking site.

Police slapped and beat him at the station the day he was arrested, he said later, but his trial judge refused to investigate. He was sentenced to three years in prison and fined $1,310. The case inflamed the Moroccan blogosphere, which used it as a prime example of the country's deteriorating freedom of expression. Hundreds of prank profiles exist on Facebook for prominent figures like George Bush and Osama bin Laden. At least four fake Prince Rachid pages sprouted after the arrest, all apparently created from the safety of overseas.

The case provoked an international outcry, and the king pardoned Mourtada after a few weeks. If there is one thing that bothers Mohamed VI, it is preserving his hip image. "The king is very worried about being perceived as not cool," said Aboubakr Jamai, the former publisher of a Moroccan weekly who was hounded out of his job through repeated lawsuits. Jamai contrasted Mourtada's case to that of another Moroccan which unrolled at about the same time. Ahmed Nasser, a 95-year-old mentally unstable man confined to a wheelchair, got involved in a tussle with a policeman while boarding a bus to go visit his family. He had muttered something against the royal family that led to a similar charge: insulting the sacred values of the country. His case garnered scant local attention and none on the Web. The man was sentenced to three years in prison, and died there just a few months later.

Those types of incidents confirmed for many Moroccan activists that the Equity and Reconciliation Commission came and went without affecting real change. Jamai had expressed his doubts from the beginning when I first went to visit him in Casablanca in 2005, his magazine inhabiting cramped offices in a grungy building just off the city's main commercial avenue. "We are absolving the regime of its sins, without getting a commitment for democratization in return," he said.

By 2008, he himself had become the poster child for Morocco's slackening progress toward change. The press had assumed something of the role of the political opposition, particularly Jamai's *Le Journal Hebdomidaire*, or *The Weekly Newspaper*. The magazine was written in French, which limited its audience to Morocco's elite. Jamai, a youthful man with thick black hair and frameless glasses, said that in founding *Le Journal* he decided that everyone, even the king, should be held accountable for his actions in a government viewed as thoroughly corrupt by most Moroccans. The magazine and its publisher were the target of repeated lawsuits for defamation and violating various press laws. In a 2006 defamation suit, the court fined *Le Journal* the astronomical sum of more than $300,000, at the time an unprecedented court award in Morocco. The case stemmed from a story suggesting that the Moroccan government had manipulated a report about the Western Sahara to recast the guerrilla movement seeking independence there as a Muslim terrorist organization. Jamai resigned from the publication to prevent all its assets from being seized even while appealing the sentence. Another magazine, *Nichane*, was temporarily closed in 2007 and its editor given a suspended sentence after being accused of insulting Islam. The magazine had published a lengthy issue focused on jokes and cartoons in Morocco, including a few that mocked political Islam. In one, a clearly religious man was pictured calling his newborn son "my little bomb."

Outside the press, nongovernmental organizations have also been the target of official ire. In 2007, severe jail sentences of one to three years plus heavy fines were meted out to seventeen members of the Moroccan Association for Human Rights accused of "undermining the monarchy," some of whom chanted slogans critical of the king, according to reports compiled by Amnesty International. King Mohamed eventually pardoned that group.

Such cases illustrated that arbitrary arrest and detention and stiff prison sentences remained a sad reality despite the reconciliation commission. Expressing critical views of the monarchy was one of three taboo subjects in the kingdom along with questioning Islam and Rabat's domination over Western Sahara, the former Spanish colony just south of Morocco along the Atlantic coast. Morocco has repeatedly thwarted the United Nations' efforts to organize a popular referendum there to allow its people a choice of government. Rabat exploits the low-grade conflict to silence critics, claiming that disparaging the government is only serving its enemies during a time of crisis.

In cases involving accused extremists, defense lawyers told me they were stymied by judges who disregard the basic letter of the law. They reject requests to cross-examine witnesses whose sworn statements were used to sentence their clients to lengthy prison terms. Mustafa Rameed, a middle-aged Islamist politician from the Justice and Development Party, a mainstream religious party, took some of the hardest cases. "The government, in the name of fighting terrorism, has been eroding human rights," he said. "Without question there are terrorists, criminals who do threaten public safety. There might be 20 or 30 or even 60, but there are not 600 or up to 1,000."

Speaking in his Casablanca law office, the walls decorated with Koranic sayings engraved in brass, Rameed said the only opinion that really mattered was that of the king. "The political path is determined by the mood of the king and not the mood of the people," he said. "We have left the authoritarian years behind us, but we are not yet a democracy." Rameed, like many others of all political stripes, said the constitution needed restructuring to strengthen the role of parliament and the political parties, while defining the monarchy within a framework of law. That was another recommendation of the Equity and Reconciliation Commission that has languished.

Opponents viewed the late King Hassan as a dark, Machiavellian figure. He was quick to anger, and liable to pound the table with his hands when in a rage. Aides were hesitant to raise unpleasant topics with him. King Mohamed exhibited far more concern with humanitarian issues, yet not once since assuming the throne in 1999 has he ever suggested diluting his power. Various ministers and senior aides told me that the king was trying to create a democratic culture, that the country was in a fragile, transitional period not unlike a snake molting, shedding one skin for another. Democracy activists tended to agree with the snake analogy, but suggested that with the old skin gone it's still the same old snake.

Rare for any Middle Eastern country, Morocco has its own royal dissident, a charming down-to-earth prince who spends much of his time at American universities studying the issue of political reform in the Arab world. When I caught up with him at Stanford University in 2008, Moulay Hicham Benabdallah ("moulay" means prince) was sporting a scruffy salt-and-pepper beard and wearing a baggy hooded grey sweatshirt. From the way he talked about his first cousin, the king, and the enduring influence of the Makhzan, it was clear why he was no longer welcomed with open arms around the palace.

"Upon his succession to the throne, Mohamed VI had a unique opportunity!" the prince told me. "All previous monarchs had to fight to consolidate their power. He received the throne with an enormous reservoir of hope and good will. He had the constitution behind him, all the parties were behind him. Everyone was behind him, and everyone was looking for reform. I think he wanted to reform, he didn't want to crack down. And he did achieve some limited reform. But eventually the weight of the political establishment, the security apparatus, and the desire to avoid any destabilization won out. The net result is more continuity than change, and a golden opportunity has been squandered."

When asked for an example of why the king is viewed as a reformer who somehow lost his way, many Moroccans cite the issue of women's rights as an important arena of change. The family code, or Mudawwana, rewritten in 2004, was perhaps the most significant reform carried out through Mohamed's prompting. The old law, from 1958, institutionalized the idea that women were inferior and had to obey men. The basic philosophy was that a woman had to mind her husband, who maintained her in exchange. The new law replaced that with the idea of joint responsibility, significantly reducing the ability of men to treat their wives as property. Men are supposed to inform the wives before seeking a divorce, and must get a judge to sign off on marrying additional wives, with Islam permitting up to four. The legal age for marriage was raised to 18 from 15.

Far removed from the famous blood orange–colored ramparts of old Marrakesh, Al-Nakheel Association for Women and Children is housed in two cramped apartments in a low-income neighborhood. I spent a day there to witness the parade of abused women consulting the center's lawyer. One was beaten so hard that she could no longer hear. Another, infertile, found a younger wife for her husband only to be tossed onto the street without any of her jewelry or other possessions. A third sought child support for two children conceived out of wedlock.

Zakia Mrini, who helped found the center, said none of the women would have come forward before the law changed. Afterward, she got referrals from the police, the courts, and the hospital.

When women's rights advocates in Marrakesh first organized the center in 1998, she said, they could not publicly talk about poverty, the slums, or the marginalization of women. All were considered taboo. "After the king first spoke about passing a new law in October 2003, women started appearing by themselves, without a father or other male relative, because they felt they had a kind of royal protection and could come and talk about their problems," Mrini said. Before the new law, a woman who had been beaten would be told at the police station to bring witnesses, evidently a difficult prospect if she had been battered in the privacy of the family bedroom, Mrini noted. "Now the police summon the husband."

Throughout Morocco, women activists acknowledged that they lost some aspects of the battle—many would have liked to ban polygamy outright and to make inheritance laws more equitable. But changing those would require huge cultural hurdles in a traditional, patriarchal Muslim society where religious-oriented political parties command attention. Some mosque preachers continued to inveigh against the changes that were implemented, but did so quietly because the king had backed them. Key remaining hurdles include convincing conservative judges to follow the law and trying to prove widespread corruption whereby husbands pay off judges to rule in their favor. Ingrained practices threatened the spirit of reform. "Law alone won't change a society," Mrini told me. "If we don't change the mentality, make people responsive to the law, it will stay just that, a law."

▣   ▣   ▣

Overall, activists described the gradual evaporation of the climate of fear as perhaps the biggest shift. Marzouki recalled that when he was first imprisoned, his family dug up the tiles in their modest village house and hid his pictures under the floor, afraid of the consequences if the security services were to search the house and find them. That fear lasted through the 1990s, after his release. When the security services learned that he was writing a book about Tazmamart, they tossed him back into jail for forty-eight hours and gave him a stark choice: Keep writing, and you will be sent back. Stop writing, and we will give you a nice villa, find you a pretty wife, and pay for your pilgrimage to Mecca. He demurred, but postponed publishing the book until after Hassan died.

Marzouki noted with gratitude that he received some financial support from the current king, who paid for an expensive implant surgery in France after his young son lost his hearing. The government also granted lump-sum compensation to all the former prisoners, enough to buy an apartment and start a small business, but many now face health and financial problems. Support for them should be a matter of legal rights rather than periodic charity from the royal palace, he said, with the former prisoners seeking a monthly stipend and health insurance. The men were promised as much when released, but the government didn't deliver. "We suffered torture at the hands of the state, so they should be responsible for us," he told me in 2008. "It is unconscionable that former detainees like us don't have the resources needed to survive. They just tell us that our case is over." Marzouki believed that the Tazmamart revelations helped change some people's attitudes toward the country's jails, but did not provide a sufficient catalyst to reshape the entire system.

॥   ॥   ॥

Many reformers feel that the United States has a role to play, even if simply nudging the king toward wider change. Mohamed is one of the few Arab leaders who still trumpets his close ties with the White House—any praise from Washington prompts banner headlines. So gentle criticism could have some impact. It would be a stretch for the king to boast of praise from Washington and then try to ignore any disapproval. In addition, pressure via the blogosphere worked in some cases in a way that outside influence never could with his father. But supporting change from outside can prove difficult. A group of Moroccan lawyers—professionals tend to be heavily Islamist in virtually every Arab country—stormed out of a seminar on improving the country's judicial system when word spread that it was being funded by the U.S. government, for example. Zakia Mrini said her Association for Women and Children had considered announcing that it would reject all U.S. funding, a popular step taken by some other progressive NGOs, but rejected the move as too drastic and ultimately harmful to the goal of change. But she said Al-Nakheel was becoming much more discriminating about its American donors, taking money only when she developed a personal relationship and felt that the outside organization shared similar ideals.

For Prince Hicham, if Washington wants to have a real impact it needs to develop a different vocabulary. Rather than always holding up American traditions of democracy and freedom as the example, the U.S. should spend more time focused on what local traditions might be emphasized to help speed change. "You have to make the discussion indigenous, talk about justice and dignity," he said. "Democracy is discredited because it is too compromised and too identified with the West. You need something more rooted locally, so people know they have a stake in defining and constructing that."

॥ ॥ ॥

Despite Morocco's progress, every reformer knows it could all disappear in a flash. That is the reason that Marzouki pressed for changes that will bring a real parliament, a strict separation of powers, a serious fight against corruption, and the fair distribution of wealth. Marzouki told me that without such deep-seated changes, all government promises were worthless. In early 2006, he returned to Tazmamart to film a documentary, only to find the main prison building bulldozed into rubble. The government had assured the former inmates that it would preserve the cells as a museum and memorial to the men who died inside. Tombstones stood where the prisoners had once lain in anonymous graves, but Marzouki knew they could not match the impact of seeing the cramped, dark cells. "I was shocked, utterly shocked that we were betrayed anew."

It was extraordinary that Marzouki, having endured so much, emerged with little evident bitterness. He calmly asserted that trying to right all past wrongs would only lead to carnage. For him, the way forward was to ensure a different future.

"We never knew that the arbitrary could have no limits until the moment we were incarcerated," he said, looking down into his coffee cup and then up at me. "It was only there that we realized, we understood, that man's ambition is limitless, that power is a dangerous force that will crush all humanity in order to preserve itself. Ambition is good, but it must be channeled by law."

CHAPTER 10

TRIBES

"We don't think of them as a royal family, we think of them as a tribe."

RAW CINDERBLOCK HOUSES CROWDED the narrow streets of the ramshackle Shiite Muslim village where Ali Abdulemam, the most notorious webmaster in Bahrain, was spending National Day with his family. I sat down next to Abdulemam on the low cushions along the walls of his father's cramped reception room, watching him try to circumvent government censors to log onto the widely popular website that he founded. His fingers tapped frenetically on a laptop keyboard.

Batelco, the government-owned telecommunications company, held a monopoly on providing Internet access. So it blocked opposition websites with impunity. The young, darkly handsome computer engineer spent about ten minutes whipping through various servers around the world before finally pulling up Bahrainonline.org.

It was a temperate evening in mid-December. The short winter brings relief to the sweaty Persian Gulf where Bahrain, a Lilliputian island nation, sits just off Saudi Arabia's eastern shore. About five miles away from us revelers packed downtown Manama, the capital, to celebrate the holiday with fireworks and music. Giant pictures of various ruling princes had loomed over the major intersections I drove through as I left. Long strings of red and white lights—the national colors—encircled everything from office blocks to the artfully pruned palm trees lining the main thoroughfares. The night air glowed crimson.

The attempt to block Bahrain Online was evidently futile, since once Ali logged on we found a couple hundred people chatting in the "National Forum" section, the website's most popular feature. Almost all of them scorned the very idea of celebrating the day when a Sunni Muslim monarch ascended the throne to rule over a Shiite Muslim majority.

"In Bahrain, glorifying the king means glorifying the nation and opposing the king means betraying the homeland and working for foreign countries," wrote one participant, mocking the formula as the trademark of a dictatorship. "Should we be loyal to the king or to Bahrain?"

Throughout the Arab world, people are inspired by the desire to be treated as citizens rather than subjects. The privileged position accorded the monarch and the secret police agencies often extends to the entire ruling minority. The problem is particularly acute because minorities rule so many countries—either one family, one sect, or a military clique. Outside that privileged circle, to be in the wrong tribe means facing almost certain discrimination. So another key question hanging over reform in the Middle East is whether its numerous minority governments can find a peaceful formula to share the decision-making process in some meaningful way. The al-Saud tribe imposed its name on the kingdom of Saudi Arabia and is not inclined to cede any real power. Central issues like how much oil wealth the ruling family soaks up are not even broached publicly. In Syria, the ruling Assad family and its confederates from the

Alawite minority succeeded in passing the thirty-year rule of the father to his son, even altering the constitution because the heir was too young. Egypt and Libya seem to be slouching toward dynastic rule, while hereditary monarchs control the rest of the Gulf as well as Jordan and Morocco.

Of course Iraq became the biggest, messiest experiment in changing the practice of minority rule. The country's once metastasizing chaos pushed many Arabs to conclude that the systems they suffered under were just fine thank you, given the violence involved in creating an alternative. The American occupation there struggled to answer the question of whether real elections can forge a democratic government in the Arab world, or if the attempt will drown in a cauldron of sectarian bloodshed. The results were being closely watched perhaps nowhere more than Bahrain because the Shiite-Sunni split roughly mirrors that of Iraq; Shiites constitute some 70 percent of its native population of almost 530,000. In 2008 the government put the total population at just over 1 million. Expatriate workers make up the difference.

Back in the 1970s the newly independent Gulf princes, flush with sudden oil wealth, developed comfortable welfare states. They provided fat government paychecks to anyone who wanted a job along with free education, medical care, and housing. In exchange they monopolized power—ask nothing from us for we give everything to you. But during the ensuing population boom the rulers were unable to provide the same handouts to the swelling numbers of young men like Abdulemam who question authority.

As he told me over the course of numerous conversations and several years, members of the young, well-educated next generation will reformulate the relationship between rulers and ruled. "They will create a lot of change even if the royal family doesn't want it," he said. Abdulemam's grandfather may have been an indentured laborer forced to work construction for the royal family, but "the time when they were the lords and we were the slaves is gone." He and his peers are inclined to mock their leaders.

As we scrolled through the various comments posted on National Day, one effusive comment jumped off the screen: "Congratulations to Bahrain and to the King!"

"Someone in the government must have posted that," Ali said dryly.

Bahrain bills itself as a leader of political change in the Arab world, a claim echoed in repeated praise from the United States. Washington considers the flyspeck island crucial for its military ventures because Bahrain serves as the headquarters for the U.S. Navy's Fifth Fleet. The somewhat disingenuous sign at the front gate reads "U.S. Naval Support Activity," playing down the fact that a military base sits behind the intimidating cement walls. The base provides logistical support for at least one aircraft carrier battle group always deployed in or around the Persian Gulf, whose current tasks include flying bombing and other sorties over Iraq and Afghanistan. That service rendered by the royal family has shaped relations with Washington more than any other factor.

Members of the ruling Khalifa family described various new elections, including national votes for parliament in 2002 and 2006, as a vibrant process that will ultimately establish a local strain of democracy. Yet some of its most senior members and their Sunni allies repeatedly suggested that progress is threatened by the fact that Bahrain's Shiites serve exterior interests, that they are agents for the Shiite majority in Iran and Iraq. For its part, the mainly Shiite opposition calls the reform process stalled, accusing the ruling dynasty of questioning their loyalty to avoid making any hard decisions about sharing power. They say the Khalifas, Bedouins from the Arabian mainland who conquered this island from its Persian masters in the late eighteenth century, lack any intention of making more than cosmetic changes. Their main evidence is that almost nothing has been done to alleviate the entrenched discrimination faced by the poorest segments of the Shiite population.

"The problem with the royal family is that when they give us any democracy they think that it is a gift and we have to thank them for it," Abdulemam told me as we sat reading his website. He was wearing a traditional long white Arab robe for the holiday, his beard neatly trimmed to thin stubble. "We don't think of them as a royal family, we think of them as a tribe."

Undoubtedly some of those agitating for reform used the issue to camouflage their sectarian goals. But a core of committed activists, like Abdulemam and members of more secular groups, were pursuing the concept of equal rights for all, with those of any minority protected.

Bahrain's first parliament, elected in 1973, proved too boisterous in questioning the government of King Hamad's father, who dissolved it after just eighteen months. Opposition demands to restore it escalated continuously through the 1990s, marked by bombings and other sporadic violence that left forty people dead. The authoritarian government subjected political activists to widespread arrest, torture, and forced exile.

When King Hamad, born in 1950, inherited power in 1999, Bahrainis like Abdulemam anticipated significant change, not least because the monarch promised them democracy comparable to any in the West. "Areeqa" he described it in Arabic, which means deeply rooted. Even using the word "democracy" bordered on revolutionary. The press had previously been so restricted that newspapers were banned from writing it; the accepted euphemism was "public participation."

At roughly the same time, Abdulemam, born in 1978, established his groundbreaking website, determined to give Bahrainis a place to share ideas and to develop plans to deepen political reform. "It seemed like a golden time, when the country was moving from one period in its history to another," he said. "Everybody needed a place to talk so I provided it." He was part ringmaster and part blogger, distributing information not readily available in the mainstream media.

The young king swiftly implemented a series of measures that appeared to confirm that change was afoot. He released some 300 political prisoners, granted amnesty to the political exiles, and disbanded the dreaded State Security Courts whose draconian laws had allowed police to hold suspects incommunicado for years. The reform package was incorporated into a somewhat vague National Action Charter, which seemed to suggest that Bahrain would become a constitutional monarchy with an elected parliament. It passed overwhelmingly when put to a public referendum. Bahrainis were so happy that during a visit to one Shiite village, a group of men took the unprecedented step of hoisting their ruler onto their shoulders.

Convinced that Bahrain really was on the path to significant political change, Abdulemam, who had run his website anonymously, started using his own name in 2002, about the time that I first met him. But the king had other plans. Apparently spooked by the idea that Bahrainis really did expect a significant voice in running the place, he tried to stuff the genie he had unleashed back into the bottle. Without any of the promised public input, he announced a new constitution, which concentrated more power in his hands. He created an appointed upper house in the parliament, the Consultative Council, and gave it powers equal to that of the elected parliament, the Chamber of Deputies. Amending the constitution required a two-thirds majority of both houses, making it impossible without the monarch's blessing. Parliament could only propose laws, not write them. An audit bureau that had previously reported to parliament was replaced with one that would not subject the spending of the royal court or the 2,000–3,000 royal family members to any public scrutiny. Bahrainis found the process a bitter joke. In the Arab world, they said, a constitutional monarchy meant the monarch wrote the constitution.

Bahrainis suspected the king changed because hard-line relatives convinced him that sweeping changes were not in the family's interest.

"I had been full of hope that a new era was coming to Bahrain," said Abdulemam. "But what happened next threw us all in the dirt. When the king brought in the new constitution, everyone was crushed." In the old days, with its monopoly over TV and radio and the ability to shut down newspapers, the Khalifa dynasty would have controlled the debate. No longer. In fact, one reason the Internet became so popular—scores of villages have created their own websites and chat rooms—was that far more can be said about the ruling family online than elsewhere. "Freedom of expression is something you have to take, not something that will be granted to you," Abdulemam told me, but he despaired that wider latitude to speak out represented true reform. "Their policy basically comes down to 'Say what you want and we will do what we want.'"

Bahrain Online definitely became the go-to political site. Royal princes, parliament members, opposition leaders, and just about anybody with an interest in politics told me that they consulted it daily to find out what the opposition was thinking. The easiest way to ensure a wide turnout for any demonstration, the leader of the main Shiite opposition assured me, was to post it on Bahrain Online. By 2008, Abdulemam said, he was getting some 150,000 hits a day, or more than one-quarter of the native population. "If something happens anywhere in Bahrain, usually within five minutes maximum something about it is happening on my site," he said. Blogging had not really taken off on the island; forums where the discussion goes back and forth seemed more popular. Abdulemam wasn't sure why, but guessed it was because the exchanges on a forum mimicked traditional discussion sessions, the "diwaniyyas," where a leader or activist threw open his reception hall, or "diwan," for a few hours at night for a freewheeling discussion. Blogging was too solitary for most Bahrainis, he said.

After discovering that the Internet and satellite television were outside its reach, the government resorted to desperate tactics that failed, like tossing Abdulemam and two of his fellow webmasters into jail for a couple weeks in 2005. Ultimately, the opposition orchestrated repeated demonstrations and international interference to win his release. But legal charges never disappeared entirely as a continuous means of pressure, plus he was banned from traveling for a couple years.

Abdulemam and the site's other young webmasters are often criticized for creating a "tabloid," quick to spread rumors and to bad-mouth those considered enemies. Ghada Jamsheer, a women's rights activist who criticized the Shiite clergy for opposing a proposed new family law that gave more defined divorce rights to women, said her face was pasted onto a naked body. Abdulemam countered that his site gets blamed for trash posted on any site in Bahrain, and his webmasters monitoring what can run to 1,000 posts a day removed anything that promoted violence. He laughed as he recalled after his arrest how little his interrogators knew about the workings of the Internet, blaming him for the content of every single comment. By 2008, though, after years of tension between the Shiite and Sunni communities, he said he was being outflanked by websites on both sides that seemed to promote the sectarian rift, supporting violence or sometimes even the mass deportation of the Shiites.

Mansour Jamri, editor of the *Wasat* daily newspaper and the son of a famous Shiite opposition cleric, explained to me that many of those who wrote on the websites were hyperactive men in their 20s. "If you don't shout with them, you are a corrupt person, you are basically a dog used by the government," said Jamri, who has been drawn as just that. Part of the issue is that the press remained hobbled. When Abdulhadi al-Khawaja, a prominent human rights activist, was arrested after giving an infamous speech, attacking the royal prime minister openly over corruption, no paper printed what he said. For that the pubic turned to Bahrain Online. As in much of the Arab world, the newspapers, whether directly run by the government or not, depend on official advertising, so little criticism gets printed. Just the opposite, in fact. On National Day, one Bahraini newspaper, *Akhbar Al-Khaleej*, or *Gulf News* in Arabic, printed a giant picture of King Hamad seated next to a flag facing an entire page of poems lauding the monarch. "You are the shadow of God on earth," said one, while another compared him to the clouds that drop water to quench all thirst. An opposition march did not merit even one sentence.

Jamri thought Bahrain Online and its imitators were counterproductive because they basically soured those in power on addressing the opposition's problems. One Shiite Cabinet minister explained to me his frustration that the young Web commentators would howl that there were not enough Shiite Muslims in the Cabinet. Then as soon as Shiites were appointed to head ministries including both health and labor, the webmasters turned around and labeled the ministers quislings. "There are serious websites out there, but it's hard to compete with those where the royal family are labeled invaders, foreigners, thugs," Jamri, the newspaper editor, told me. "This pocket of anarchy is a by-product of half-hearted democracy."

Whenever I wanted smart, dispassionate analysis of any event in the Arab world, I often turned to Sawsan al-Shair, a vibrant Bahraini woman who worked as both a columnist and a talk-show host. I liked Shair because she was both honest and forceful, plus she wielded a lively sense of humor. Shair wrote boldly about the need for reform in Bahrain and elsewhere, but she was not afraid to criticize its advocates periodically as unrealistic. When officials at the state-run television station tried to censor a discussion about poverty on her chat show, *The Last Word*, labeling it too negative, she shut down entirely rather than bow to any limits on freedom of expression. The king interceded to restore the program and called off the censors. Her opposition critics repeatedly accused her of being a tool of the king, depicting her in a cartoon as a belly dancer in his court. I figured she must be doing something right if both sides targeted her.

"OK, if we want full democracy, we are going backwards," she confirmed. "But if you compare it to reality, it's a big step forward." She noted that in the old days, democracy pretty much consisted of the ruler throwing open the doors of his palace periodically to listen to any complaints. It was a Bedouin system still widespread in all Gulf countries, but the growth of both the population and the complexity of government makes it impractical. Sometimes I got the impression that the monarchs in the area kept thinking if they could just tweak that formula a bit then everyone would shut up about democracy already. "We want stability and you cannot have that without giving people some role in making decisions," Shair told me. Poverty had to be addressed first, she thought, because the needy were more concerned with getting food and housing than larger civil rights issues like government transparency. But she was also exasperated over how any type of reform was attacked as being an American plot against the region, an argument that became ever more widespread and popular after the invasion of Iraq.

Once, for example, Shair wrote a negative column about a speech by the young new Syrian president. "When I listened to that speech it was like his father's soul talking," she wrote. "It was his father's voice, nothing new." She expressed her disappointment that the young leader had become captive to the old guard rather than the reverse. Some readers scolded her, admonishing that she was wrong to attack Syria because it was the last country in the region that would stand up to the United States. When she wrote something negative about the U.S., on the other hand, readers were thrilled. "People are against any reform because they imagine it is an order from the U.S.A.," Shair said. Even a long-established subject like how to change the education system is now considered dubious because it is viewed as an American enterprise. "This kind of debate makes me angry because we have been asking for it for ages."

If it turned out the U.S. was funding some worthy cause like a study of child abuse, the study would be denounced as "helping the enemy." When Shair published a column endorsing the need for such a study, she was accused of being on the payroll of the American Embassy to promote its ideas. Anyone pushing reform was tarred as an American agent. The combination of the failure in Iraq and years of promising to resolve the Arab-Israeli dispute without actually forcing a solution had taken its toll: Nobody believed anymore that the United States would deliver on its promises. That mood meant that Americans had to maintain their distance from any reformers, she felt. Any help had to stay very low-profile. "As soon as the Americans encourage this party, these people or that group, they are finished," she told me. "They are traitors."

The rulers knew that was the popular mood and exploited it to their advantage. Bahrain's government booted out the local representative of the Washington-based National Democratic Institute, a nonprofit organization largely funded by the U.S. Congress and loosely affiliated with the Democratic Party, which promoted civil society in the developing world. The expulsion was widely popular with lawmakers and activists belonging to both Sunni and Shiite religious political groups, who thought that the NDI was meddling in Bahrain's internal affairs.

The monarchy and the opposition used parliamentary elections in 2002 and 2006 to buttress their arguments about change. To the royal family, allowing elections for the first time in thirty years signaled a measured, gradual move toward democracy of a Bahraini stripe. The opposition derided the vote as a Hollywood set with nothing behind the façade. In 2002, Bahrain Online led a fight to boycott the elections. It worked; the Shiites mostly stayed away. The vote ultimately exacerbated the sense among Shiites that the Khalifa tribe, and Sunnis generally, were not interested in treating them as equals. Election districts were gerrymandered so that sparsely populated Sunni districts in the south got almost as many members as the heavily Shiite villages in the north. Sunni Islamists won the largest bloc in the forty-seat parliament, but they muted any opposition to the government out of concern that they might help spread the influence of Shiite Islam.

Bahraini political observers estimated that the new parliament spent half its time bickering over issues of religious practice. It won a fight to allow fully veiled women to drive. It proposed that scantily clad window mannequins be banned as morally corrupting. It tried to separate boys and girls in all school classrooms. Government attempts to placate the devout alarmed the business community, particularly since the fight by religious parliament members to ban alcohol as well as hotel concerts by sultry Lebanese singers damaged the tourism industry. There was a hint of change when the deputies tried to exercise what limited powers they had by investigating corruption in government organizations. But what parliament did not do, at least not with sufficient vigor for most Bahrainis, was confront the government over solving the chronic housing shortage and unemployment, particularly drastic among Shiites. The gap between the largely Sunni haves and the heavily Shiite have-nots became ever more apparent and fed simmering frustration.

Abdulemam, for example, earned a decent salary working as a computer engineer at an international, American-owned technology company. Yet he was nowhere near able to afford the $130,000 price tag at the beginning of 2006 for a plot of land to build a house for his wife and newborn son and was not sure he ever would be. He is the youngest of ten siblings, four of whom still lived with their children in his father's two-story house. Fifteen people live in the house; each nuclear family is allotted one room. "I know we deserve better," he said.

Exact numbers were hard to pin down in Bahrain, but there were tens of thousands of people on the waiting list for subsidized government housing, while unemployment stuck officially around 15 percent and was estimated at around 30,000, or close to one-third of Shiite youths in their early 20s. Shiite Muslims are generally barred from joining Bahrain's security services, and Gulf youths suffer from a strong sense of entitlement, so they avoid tough jobs like construction. By 2008, the government had quieted some of the rancor over unemployment by levying a new tax that fed an unemployment fund. The unemployed received a stipend—not enough to live on, but enough to stave off complete despair. On housing, opposition members accused the royal family of exacerbating the shortage by monopolizing all available land. Occasional brazen acts supported the charge: One of the king's cousins seized the entire seafront of one village and banned fishermen from beaching their boats. The king reversed the seizure after riots erupted. The country encompasses an archipelago of some thirty small islands, and the opposition claimed that various princes appropriated them to create private resorts. They are certainly secluded enough—when the American superstar singer Michael Jackson needed a place to hide after being acquitted on charges of molesting children, he sought refuge on a prince's estate in Bahrain.

Royal family members conceded to me that public housing needs improvement, but denied hoarding land. Still, Bahrain earned a rebuke by the committee within the United Nations Commission for Human Rights that monitors racial discrimination. Its 2005 report noted that although Bahrain paid lip service in its laws to barring discrimination, actual practice lags. In response the government set up its own Human Rights Commission, which seemed better at issuing press releases saying what a great job it was doing than actually changing long-entrenched practices.

When Abdulemam was arrested in 2005, he found that his interrogator was an elderly Egyptian, one of hundreds of Sunni Muslim mercenaries from the Arab world or Pakistan recruited into the security services and given comfortable bungalows and usually citizenship. "He was asking me whether I was loyal to this country," Abdulemam said sourly. "How can an Egyptian ask me about my loyalty? There are many ways to love your country and what I do is one of them." Following the collapse of Saddam Hussein's regime in Baghdad, opposition members said they started hearing Iraqi accents among the police suppressing their demonstrations.

                                 ▧   ▧   ▧

By 2006, the main political groups decided it was better to agitate from within parliament, not least to try to block the kinds of laws that had been pushed through limiting demonstrations and other activity by government opponents. The Wifaq National Islamic Society, a mostly Shiite organization and the main opposition party, won all seventeen seats it contested. Led by a charismatic young cleric, Sheikh Ali Salman, it became the largest bloc in the Chamber of Deputies. But deputies supporting the government still dominated, and the ruling family maintained tight control over key Cabinet posts.

Sheikh Ali warned repeatedly that his followers were growing disillusioned with the idea that democracy could improve their lot, doubting that peaceful means would reverse the discrimination that Shiites had suffered for so long. The young were not seeing any results on the ground, and the sheikh predicted accurately that the overall sectarian tone of every debate combined with the lack of tangible progress was a volatile mix bound to fuel more violence. He lambasted the government for trying to paint legitimate protest as terrorism, using that as a stalling tactic and an excuse to unleash the security services. "When they say it takes time, they mean let's take no steps forward," Sheikh Ali told me in the fluent English he learned during five years of forced exile in Britain. His own credibility was also on the line. By 2008, Abdulemam felt that support for any party that had won seats in parliament was fading, but particularly for the religious parties that promised to change so much. "Most people don't believe in this parliament," he told me. "Instead they think that all the people who entered parliament have forgotten all their promises. They are liars." Liberals, he noted, were gaining ground.

Frustration ran especially high among the hundreds of political exiles who returned, expecting that their amnesty meant the changes they had been agitating for would finally occur. "Democracy has been reduced to a little bit of expression," said Abdulnabi al-Ekri, the spokesman for the returned exiles, when I asked him about Bahrain Online. "It should be a system, institutions, not just demonstrations, a little bit of talk on the Internet and limited elections." The elections were accompanied by a major gerrymandering scandal. Salah al-Bandar, a British citizen working as a government consultant in Bahrain, compiled a thick file of what he said were letters and checks that outlined the efforts to boost the number of parliamentary seats for Sunni areas and in general undermine the Shiite opposition. He was immediately deported, and the press barred from mentioning the scandal, dubbed "Bandargate." Any websites that reported on it were blocked. By the end of 2007, young Shiites were again battling the government security forces in violent clashes, and scores of human rights advocates or political protestors were being tossed back into jail. Widespread accusations of torture resurfaced.

Royal princes had long maintained that in their absence, such violence would only increase. The "après moi le deluge" sentiment was a mantra of ruling dynasties across the region. In Bahrain, royal family members kept a firm grip on power. Princes filled about half the Cabinet, including all the main security posts, as well as the top leadership in the military. Key appointed positions like senior judges or the head of the University of Bahrain were often Khalifa family members. Sheikh Mohamed al-Khalifa, the prince who heads the Economic Development Board, argued that Bahrain should not become a democracy in the Western sense: "As traditional Arabs I don't think democracy is part of our nature, I think all people want is accountability."

▣　▣　▣

To an extent the repressive regimes ruling the Arab world all grapple with the same problem. They believe they can find the magic balance required to maintain their grip on power while introducing just enough openness to ease the simmering frustration of the next generation. I doubt the formula exists in the way they imagine. The increasingly young populations are too angry about their inability to function, to find jobs, and to buy houses—the latter a crucial condition for marriage in traditional societies. Theirs is a generation watching the rest of the world advance while they stagnate. When they look just beyond their own hobbled lives, they see the war on terrorism as an assault on Islam, live daily with the inability of the Arab world to improve the lot of the Palestinians, and seethe even more. "How can you stop the fire inside people?" hissed a rail-thin 25-year-old standing in a Bahraini government unemployment office. "You have to put something in their mouths.

People have no chance to live." He gave me his name, then retracted it when he noticed several police and other officials who had suddenly materialized behind him. He'd suffered periodic arrest and beatings and didn't want to go through that again. "People are quiet because the clerics say be quiet, let's wait and see what the government does. How long are we supposed to wait? In two to three years the people will do something again because every day the fire inside becomes a little bigger than it was the day before. I will be honest. I am hungry. I want to eat."

Although Manama lacked the fantastical skyline of neighbors like Dubai, its downtown exudes a certain wealth. But behind the bank buildings sheathed in mirrored glass, behind the malls crammed with boutiques like Gucci, behind the manicured lawns and sculpted date palms, much of this capital and the arc of Shiite villages immediately to the west consists of streets so narrow that a car negotiates them with difficulty. Schools are overcrowded, sewers leak, and electricity comes haphazardly. Such impoverished warrens fuel the angry demands for change. The graffiti ranges from diatribes against the absolute rule of the Khalifas—"We want freedom"—to warnings from the religious against aping the thousands of U.S. Navy personnel stationed in Bahrain. "American-style haircuts are the start of being corrupted," reads one. I saw these slogans in impoverished villages just a few hundred yards from the main international airport where U.S. Navy planes came and went, villages where Israeli and American flags were painted on the road so everyone entering or leaving would drive over them.

In the 1980s, while its Gulf neighbors were dozing, Bahrain briefly turned itself into a regional financial hub, aided by the fact that Beirut had disintegrated into civil war. But it had been gradually losing ground to far richer, more aggressive emirates like Dubai, Abu Dhabi, and Qatar. I thought of Bahrain as sort of like the Nevada of the Gulf. When it was losing population, Nevada basically legalized everything banned in California—prostitution and gambling flourished. Bahrain played a similar role in the Gulf, with the main attraction being the alcohol flowing freely in its many seedy bars and nightclubs staffed by Russian, Asian, or Moroccan hookers. Sin succeeded in attracting a steady stream of visitors, even if conservative Bahrainis like Abdulemam deplored the idea that the country sold alcohol to Muslims. By some estimates, 50,000 Saudis roared across the twenty-five-mile causeway to the tiny country every weekend to rollick in all manner of activity banned at home. Drunks were a common sight. But they hardly monopolized all the fun. Saudi women, barred from driving in their own country, gunned up and down Manama's streets in their SUVs. Intellectuals prowled its bookstores for censured works. Saudi Shiites participated openly in religious rituals like self-flagellation deplored by the Wahhabis.

Bahrain was not remodeled much after the 1970s boom, so the capital feels small and drab now compared to the battery of gargantuan luxury hotels, wild amusement parks, and other glittering, over-the-top attractions of its neighbors.

Prince Mohamed, Bahrain's head of economic development, told me that math alone spelled out the need for reform. He had developed a simple formula—those states producing less than one barrel of oil per citizen will have to change while the rest can likely buy time. In Bahrain, there are three citizens for every barrel of oil produced—in contrast to Kuwait, which had five barrels per citizen, or Qatar, which had up to eight or nine. Bahrain's fields are likely to start running dry within fifteen years or so. "We created a welfare state that we cannot sustain," he told me. "We cannot do things like subsidize electricity for everyone forever."

Of course the rich Saudis next door have been willing to grant Bahrain large subsidies. They sought to avoid any Gulf state creating a new social or political model that restive youths elsewhere in the region might want to replicate. The Saudi rulers especially don't want their own Shiite Muslim minority of some 2 million, most of whom are concentrated in the Eastern Province just over the causeway from Bahrain, to get any ideas regarding political power from their Shiite brethren.

Both branches of Islam revere the prophet's family, but the Shiites take it a step further by considering his descendants infallible. During his lifetime, Mohamed played four significant roles in the nascent faith. He was, naturally, their spiritual leader, transmitting the tenets of the faith directly from God. He was also their political leader, chief justice, and military commander. Shiites ascribed all four roles to his descendants, including the idea that the rightful heir should never be second-guessed in his religious pronouncements. Sunnis granted the caliph the three later roles, but not the first. (Modern Turkey formally abolished the position in 1924, centuries after the Ottoman Empire sapped the post of any real power. Extremists like Osama bin Laden seek to restore the Caliphate, or rather pursue a utopian vision of the role.) For Sunnis, religious fiats can come about only through the consensus of modern learned scholars; the prophet himself was the sole infallible guide who could act alone.

Shiites believe that the imam or religious leader who is Mohamed's rightful heir disappeared and will return to declare Judgment Day is at hand. In the meantime, they too reach religious decisions by a kind of consensus, much like the Sunnis. But Iran's Islamic revolution created the post of "supreme leader," who enjoys sweeping powers that mirror the four roles of the prophet. For Shiites, the concept of martyrdom for the faith took on its holy aura after Ali, the prophet's son-in-law and cousin, was assassinated and two of his sons slaughtered in the late-seventh-century battles for succession that unrolled around what became the holy cities of Najaf and Karbala in Iraq. Many Shiite religious festivals center on recreating the suffering of the prophet's descendants, with ritual tears and self-flagellation. Such rituals have long made Sunnis uneasy, not least because it was their generals who carried out those killings.

In Bahrain during one of the marches organized by Shiite opposition groups to mark National Day, some of the marchers chanted "Margh Bar Khalifa" or "Death to Khalifa" in Persian, the language of Shiite Iran, knowing it would both irk and slightly spook the

Sunni Arab minority. (Even in a demonstration about reform, the traditional pecking order held. First came the men, followed by a couple hundred women, mostly invisible beneath their black sacking. Behind them, a knot of Asian laborers in bright-yellow uniforms brought up the rear, collecting the empty water bottles and other trash dropped by the marchers. That scene captured the dilemma of the rich Gulf nations in a microcosm. The demonstrators were protesting unemployment, but not one would be willing to take the menial jobs filled by South Asians. Women were always stuck in limbo.)

The postings on Bahrain Online included portraits of prominent Iranian ayatollahs, particularly the late Ruhollah Khomeini and his successor as supreme leader, Ali Khamenei. They put in appearances during demonstrations as well. This seemed to negate the Shiite argument that they were strictly spiritual leaders. Shiites countered that, as Bahrain's original settlers, they wanted neither to go elsewhere nor to pledge their loyalty elsewhere.

Still, Sunnis used such displays to accuse the opposition of being in thrall to the mullahs across the water, asserting that the Shiites sought to establish an Iranian-style theocracy in Bahrain. Pledging loyalty to a foreign power negated their claim of being the island's original inhabitants, Sunni government supporters contended. Iran aggravated the problem in the summer of 2007 when *Kayhan*, a Tehran newspaper that reflected the supreme leader's views, printed an inflammatory editorial claiming that Bahrain was a lost province. The Islamic Republic dispatched its foreign minister to Bahrain to deny it, but the damage was done. The incident buttressed existing suspicions that the Shiites were a fifth column awaiting orders from Tehran. Jamri, the newspaper editor, was among those who believed that Iranian influence has been exaggerated to help justify repressive measures. It got to the ludicrous point where the government was even trying to change the names of any villages it believed had a Persian ring to them, he reported. To counter the accusation that Shiite loyalties lay outside Bahrain, the ayatollah portraits disappeared from demonstrations.

Pictures of Ayatollahs Khomeini and Khamenei once hung on the wall of Abdulemam's father's living room, and the day I was there he looked around suddenly when I raised the ayatollah issue, surprised that they were gone. During one of his secret police interrogations, he was asked what outside power was paying him. "Saving my country doesn't require payment," Abdulemam said he retorted.

I certainly thought the influence of Iran was exaggerated. The younger generation were avid consumers of news, and thus fully aware of the oppression inside the Islamic republic. They didn't consider that a model. Their fight was about social issues and civil society, and while they were influenced by outside religious leaders, I think it was more as spiritual than political guides. Politically they seemed intently focused on Bahrain. There are those who argue that the Sunni-Shiite divide will come to define the Middle East in the coming generation, but I am less than convinced. There is no question that Iran is reasserting itself as a regional power, helped not least by the emergence of an Iraqi government dominated by Shiites, courtesy of the United States. But the basis of Iran's appeal is its confrontation with the United States, not as a religious or social model. Arabs and Persians are ancient enemies. If Washington manages to defuse its image of targeting Islam, the appeal of the Islamic Republic will fade in tandem. After all, Tehran never really succeeded in exporting its revolution as a model. The crux of the issue was perhaps best summarized by one of the prominent Shiite ayatollahs in Lebanon when he said to me, "Let Americans occupy the hearts of the people rather than their country."

Most Shiites do follow one senior cleric on matters of religious practice in their daily lives. Abdulemam said he used to look to the Iranians, but switched to Ayatollah Ali Sistani in Iraq. Sunnis in Bahrain are sometimes incensed when Shiites fax Sistani questions such as those asking whether they really have to obey traffic laws like stopping at red lights. (The ayatollah faxed back to say yes, they do.) A reference to Sistani as an "American general" in a pro-government newspaper sparked outrage in the Shiite community. The split seemed to widen constantly. Sheikh Ali, the head of the

Shiite opposition, told me that nobody gave money to charity any-more unless they were assured that it would be spent only in their own religious community. That didn't happen before. Hiring had also taken on a sectarian tone, he said.

Sunnis tend to blame the tension on the Shiites. "They chant Shi-ite slogans during their demonstrations that call for violence, for death to the ruling family, which creates fear," said Sheikh Maawda, a fundamentalist Sunni leader who often led the fight to implement Islamic laws in Bahrain.

Both sides tried to widen the sectarian rift. At one point large banners apparently quoting one of the most revered Shiite clerics on the island appeared in Shiite Muslim areas. Signed by an organi-zation called The Islamic Enlightenment Society, they read: "The battle of Karbala continues between the two sides at present and in the future. It is taking place within the soul, at home and in all areas of life and society. People will remain divided between either the Hussein camp or the Yazid camp. So choose your camp." Yazid was the Omayyad caliph who dispatched the army that killed Hussein, Ali's son and the prophet's grandson Hussein, at Karbala—part of the war that created the Shiite faith. Members of parliament and Shair, my favorite columnist, denounced the banners for flagrantly fanning sectarian tensions. The society that sponsored the banners issued a statement claiming that the Sunnis were deliberately dis-torting the banners to make them seem violent. On the other side, Shiites were incensed when a pamphlet was passed out at a girls' school that had been printed by a Sunni organization, claiming that Shiites worshipped their own religious figures more than the Prophet Mohamed. Abdulemam deplored the sectarian spin that began to dominate much of the discussion about change, but he also felt that continued discrimination would threaten stability. "We are always thinking this guy is a Sunni, this guy is a Shiite," he told me. "This is a dangerous way of thinking. It helps the royals to pit one against the other."

The idea that Bahrain, its society increasingly divided by a 1,400-year-old fissure and ruled by an absolute monarch, could bill itself as a leader of progressive change was a sad commentary on the state of reform throughout the region. Perhaps the problem was that the king, in first announcing his plans to introduce deeply rooted democracy, raised expectations too high for immediate change when he meant to implement something more gradually. But the government doing so little to address the sectarian divide bodes ill. The opposing sides came to blows in parliament during one heated debate over the budget for the security services, with Shiite members criticizing the government for importing foreigners rather than hiring their constituents. The young seemed particularly angry. A minority element sought to confront the government through street violence. The riots that erupted in numerous Shiite villages in late 2007 indicated just how easily the country could slip back into its chaotic problems of the 1990s.

Bahrain is in fact a model of how the process of change can stall. The biggest issue, as for much of the Middle East, is that one family has monopolized power for so long. As Khawaja, the outspoken opposition leader, told me: "The people who run these countries are tribal families. They are families, not a political party. They are one tribe against an entire people, and they hold all the political and economic power. They know that sharing power means losing power."

Young Bahrainis bent on reform want to change that formula. As Abdulemam said as he contrasted the general public tone of the National Day celebrations with the protest pouring forth on his website, "Everybody is congratulating the king, his uncle, and his son, but nobody is congratulating the people."

⊡ ⊡ ⊡

Given that the Bush administration declared that it supported democratic change across the region, and that Washington would no longer champion despots merely for backing American policy, it would seem to follow that the U.S. would speak out forcefully about the issue of minority rule. But the overriding concern that Islamists overtly hostile to Washington might take power and boot out the Navy base has muted any criticism. (Despite occasional chants against the base at demonstrations, I found that it was generally viewed in a positive light as a source of money and jobs, particularly after the U.S. Navy cracked down on drunken sailors cavorting in Manama.)

In an interview with Arab newspapers before visiting Bahrain in January 2008, for example, President Bush was asked for his assessment of the changes in Bahrain. "I have complimented His Majesty on recognizing that Bahraini-style democracy, a democracy that reflects the traditions, customs of Bahrain, is an important part of dealing with real threats that we face in the world, which is extremism based upon hopelessness," he told the reporters. He went on to say that the U.S. couldn't dictate the form that democracy took in every country in the Middle East. "I don't expect Jeffersonian democracy to break out instantly, nor do I expect the forms of government to reflect that which we have in the United States," he said. "But I do hope that people recognize that popular sovereignty, that listening to people and responding to people, is how to build a stable and peaceful world."

If that was meant to be a nudge, the president soon punted. During the arrival ceremony at the king's main palace, Bush praised the monarch for holding two national elections, not hinting at any flaw. "Your Majesty," Bush said, "I appreciate the fact that you're on the forefront of providing hope for people through democracy." Bahrain's critics felt that the U.S. is a little too effusive in its praise of the king. The monarch used the president's comments as a ringing endorsement.

I thought the fact that Bahrain was poorer than its neighbors actually gave it hope for real change, given that the price of inaction involves a real risk of going up in flames. Lacking the oil wealth to continuously buy off its population, perhaps it will be forced to come to some kind of meaningful accommodation with pressure from the young. To achieve a stable political system, the royal family is going to have to address those demands repeatedly raised by the mostly Shiite opposition—constitutional reform, unemployment, housing, and citizenship. The U.S., if it is to help, must do so with great discretion on an invitation-only basis.

CHAPTER 11

WORKING IN ISOLATION

"No women may sit in this shop."

I WAS MISSING $2,000, and I knew exactly where it had disappeared. I had stashed the lump of $100 bills inside the shoe-box-sized safe in my hotel closet in Abha, capital of Saudi Arabia's southwestern Asir province. In my rush to check out, hoping to catch the last evening flight to Riyadh, I forgot the cash. (I traveled with a money belt stuffed with cash for two reasons—drivers and others who worked for me on a day-to-day basis had to be paid, plus I sometimes needed to fly on a moment's notice to countries like Iran, where American sanctions meant my credit card was useless.) In hastily decamping from hotels a couple times in the past, I had left similar sums. The money was returned via either check or a credit on my Visa card. This time, however, when I contacted the hotel, the manager called back to tell me that he found the safe empty.

Now I faced a terrible dilemma. If I reported the loss to the police and the manager or the Asian room cleaner was convicted of stealing, either could have his right hand amputated under Saudi Arabia's draconian punishment for theft drawn from the Koran. Was my own dumb, absent-minded moment worth a man losing his hand? Worse, what if the country's dubious justice system meted out that punishment specifically to make the point to a visiting reporter that Islam condemns crime in the harshest terms? I spent a sleepless night before swallowing hard and deciding not to report the theft.

Experiences like that made working in Saudi Arabia utterly disorienting, a problem compounded by the 1,400-year gap between what the place looked like and how it functioned. American consultants planned much of Saudi Arabia's development, so the country presents a familiar façade to the world. The freeways crisscrossing the vast deserts and the major cities all look American. They are jammed with Chevrolet Suburbans and Cadillac Escalades and every other sort of gas-guzzling behemoth that Detroit produces. Along the roads, food chains like Kentucky Fried Chicken and Baskin-Robbins crowd one strip mall after the next, the English signs at least as large as those in Arabic. But the beating heart underneath that modern veneer pulses to a rhythm established in the seventh century, when the Prophet Mohamed founded Islam. It's only when you did something like step into some random Baskin-Robbins and notice a little sign on the counter that said "No Women May Sit in This Shop" that you remember, Dorothy, you are not in Arizona anymore.

In any other country on earth I would have reported something like losing a wad of cash. No matter how often I went to Saudi Arabia—and some years it was almost monthly—I always arrived feeling a certain ambivalence. Its oddities made for excellent stories, my yardstick as a journalist, and its vast oil wealth certainly made it important. But it was consistently nerve-wracking to work there.

The Saudis I spent most of my time with were the main redeeming factor. They were unfailingly gracious—well-educated, interesting, cultured, generous hosts whose endless hospitality extended to gestures like sending ten pounds of the world's most delicious dates to my hotel room. Or I would sit with friends in the family section (No Single Men Allowed!) of a chic restaurant like the Java Lounge in Jidda, watching one stunning young woman after the next sail past with her supposedly enveloping abaya not quite on, and think maybe the country was not so bad after all. Ultimately, I knew that when my tolerance for Saudi weirdness reached its limit, when I tired of the religious overtone of the place which forced so much of real life behind closed doors, I could leave. Hence I developed abiding admiration for the enlightened Saudi men and women who chafed at the joyless, repressive nature of their country, yet cared enough about its future to engage in the risky, troublesome fight over changing it, of trying to reshape how its Islamic legacy will be passed down to future generations.

Here and in virtually every Arab country, reformers attempting to alter the political landscape tended to work in isolation. The process of creating open, freer societies depended on the sum of these brave, committed dissidents chipping away at the traditional order rather than on any organized movement or national discussion. Reformists repeatedly found themselves hobbled by the utter lack of a platform to so much as discuss change. Any endeavor to create such a platform, through something as simple as a blog or as large as a political party, was often treated as a crime.

The attempt to establish any kind of progressive organization to guide the process is illegal in virtually every country in the Middle East. Both free speech and the right to assemble are sharply curbed. Merely gathering in the same place to talk about how to achieve change can provoke arrest and sometimes a harsh prison sentence. For many reformists, both in Saudi and elsewhere, the lack of such simple freedoms grates most; obtaining basic civil rights constitutes a far higher priority than elections or other formal ingredients of Western democracy.

In trying to assess the chances for reform in Saudi Arabia, I sought out a couple of people whom I thought were tackling the two biggest issues in the country: First, the utter intolerance with which it faces any other religion, including any form of Islam outside its Wahhabi brand. Second, the fact that women need the approval of a male guardian to do anything—to travel, to work, or even to report domestic abuse. Hassan al-Maleky, a controversial theologian, argued that the Wahhabi sect should not hold a monopoly on interpreting Islam in the kingdom. Fawaziah B. al-Bakr, an associate professor of education at King Saud University in Riyadh, agitated to change the inferior status of women, and was still paying a price for being among the forty-seven protesters who took part in the notorious November 1990 demonstration against the ban on women driving.

The two didn't interact, but reached remarkably similar conclusions on what needed to change. The lack of contact among reformists is a hurdle everywhere, but particularly emblematic of Saudi Arabia, which ranks among the most closed Arab countries. The right to assemble does not exist, political parties are banned along with nongovernmental organizations, and the ruling princes constantly rein in the press by telling editors what they can print. Defying such an order is impossible since royal princes or their close associates own all ten major dailies. Local television is almost all clerics, all the time. Even more important, wrestling over reform in Saudi Arabia proved exceptionally difficult because its laws are so entangled in religious traditions. Since it is the birthplace of Islam, the ruling al-Saud princes and the myriad theological institutions that help maintain their rule like to present the kingdom as a perfect society. The religious establishment determines the parameters of any public debate, evaluating everything through the prism of the Wahhabi teachings unique to the Arabian peninsula, and vehemently rejecting any alternative.

Maleky, the theologian, was imprisoned briefly and fired from his government job for repeatedly raising doubts about Wahhabi interpretations. The Wahhabi sect is one group within the larger salafi—or what in the West might be called the Islamic Fundamentalist—movement. Hard-core adherents despise the term "Wahhabi," rejecting the very idea that their Islam should somehow be set apart. For them, the Wahhabi school is Islam, all the others are wrong.

Maleky argued that the caliphs of the Omayyad dynasty, the first pan-Arab regime, which ruled from Damascus between 661 and 750, were garden-variety despots. Their methods have warped Islamic rule ever since. It was the Omayyads who introduced hereditary rule, he noted, and they also decreed that the public had no right to question any decision from a ruler guided by the true faith. "After the Omayyads, Islamic thought left everything to the ruler, absolute obedience was expected in all circumstances, and that is not right," Maleky, a studious figure in a long white robe, white headscarf, and gold aviator glasses, told me when I went to see him in his house in a poor Riyadh neighborhood, the walls of every room lined with books. On my first visit in 2005, the interior doors still bore the scars where thieves had smashed through to steal his computers. "There were many internal revolutions led against the Omayyads by people who were asking for justice for the most part," he said. "Thousands were imprisoned."

Maleky viewed Saudi Arabia's religious establishment as the spiritual descendants of the repressive Omayyads. "The salafis blindly defend the Omayyads despite their many injustices," Maleky said. The Omayyads slaughtered Prophet Mohamed's descendants because they were competitors, creating the schism that led to the birth of the Shiite sect, a group whom strict Wahhabis revile as heretics. Maleky described how during one of his arrests, he found himself in the absurd position of being questioned by Saudi security officers regarding his views about the second Omayyad caliph. "What does the Interior Ministry have to do with that?" he said mockingly, noting that each such experience deepened his conviction that religion in Saudi Arabia desperately needed revision. An article critical of the Omayyads got him expelled from Imam Mohamed Ibn Saud University, Riyadh's prestigious center of Islamic higher education, he said. At least that is what he thinks did the trick. He was never given a clear explanation. He won his lawsuit to be reinstated, but the court ruling was ignored. His books are banned and he is not allowed to travel abroad. He has never recovered his stolen computer hard drives. Years of research disappeared and he remains convinced that the unsolved robbery was carried out by one of his many government-backed critics. The loss still shocks him. But it has not dimmed his zeal to expose the Omayyads and their successors.

"The Islam that we have is the political, historical, military one, not the divine one," he told me in the summer of 2008. "The way the Koran treats many issues is really different from what we now practice. In the Koran it is up to anybody to believe in whatever he or she wants. In the Koran there is no jihad against anybody but an aggressor." His voice changed slightly, with a deeper, longer inflection, as he quoted a verse: "Fight for the sake of God those who fight you and don't be aggressive because God dislikes aggressors." He ticked off a list of differences. The Koran never mentions killing anyone who converts to another religion, it just says they will die in sin. "Political Islam says they should be killed," he said. The Koran celebrates the use of the mind to question the world, whereas political Islam condemns that. In order to embroider what they wanted into religious interpretation, Maleky argued, it was the Omayyad rulers who introduced the idea of emphasizing the Hadith, the sayings and practices of Prophet Mohamed passed down from ostensible witnesses, which form the basis for much of current Islamic law. "The Hadith were used to nullify some of the verses of the Koran, to say they were no longer applicable," he explained. "Whenever a verse called for mercy, they said it was overruled by another Hadith."

Maleky, born in 1967, grew up in a poor family of banana and coffee farmers in mountainous southwestern Saudi Arabia, where he walked five kilometers to elementary school every day. His parents were illiterate. Since the region just over the nearby border with Yemen is heavily Shiite, the Sunni religious establishment rooted in central Arabia has tried to undermine Maleky's credibility by suggesting that he is a closet Shiite.

When I visited the region, natives sometimes waxed nostalgic for the more joyous, open-minded form of Islam that prevailed even twenty-five years ago, when traditions like men performing folkloric dances at weddings were commonplace. Eventually mainstream Wahhabi clerics from the central Nejd desert region crushed such rituals by labeling them shameful. In his pivotal history, Philip Hitti referred to the Nejd as "Wahhabiland." Saudis from both coasts often told me that their country's basic problem stemmed from the conservative, religious Nejdi culture never melding with the more cosmopolitan leanings of the coasts. Open tribal warfare may be a thing of the past, but beneath the surface the tribes and regions still compete fiercely for predominance. In the 1950s, the al-Sauds moved all the government ministries from the eastern port of Jeddah, long the country's gateway, to Riyadh, anointing what had been a mud-brick village as their capital basically so their Nejdi allies would run the government. Coastal residents mock traditional Nejdis for saying, "Thank God I have returned to the land of tawheed," or the oneness of God, whenever they come home from someplace they consider debauched like Jeddah or Dammam. Nejdis return the favor. They view residents of Jeddah and the western Hijaz region as rabble blown ashore during centuries of pilgrimage to Mecca, denigrating them as "tarsh bahar," or vomit of the sea. The eastern Gulf coast was even more evil, heavily populated by Shiite Muslims, the lowest form of infidel in their eyes. A Shiite once showed me some of the derogatory literature Nejdis put out about them, including a pamphlet discussing whether they grew tails underneath their robes. The utter absurdity was amusing to a degree, but the tone of the thing was deadly serious.

Maleky was the first person in his family to reach university. When he was younger, he had anticipated a place where he could ask all kinds of questions. Instead he found it even more rigid and formulaic than his earlier schooling: "In studying religion, I thought I'd find a pursuit of justice, but it wasn't really so." By focusing on the small, inconsequential details of daily life at the time of Prophet Mohamed and the following generation, the Saudi education system ensured that students were taught to keep their minds firmly in the past. The religious establishment always called for "dawa" or proselytizing, but never for research or revision. "Where are the concerns for public interest and other big issues?" he lamented. "These things have no presence. Preaching here is not for knowledge and thought. The salafi tradition is against reason. You see, you cannot find answers here. Philosophy is forbidden and they combat questions. The salafi way is to surrender."

He got up from one of the deep, plum-colored armchairs in his living room and went to a wall of books to extract one tome from a sixteen-volume set that contains most of the important religious fatwas, or rulings, that dictate the rituals of daily life in Saudi Arabia. He read a few lines each from fatwas that talk about keeping women covered, keeping them out of school, about how policemen should not wear uniforms because pants ape Western garb, and some completely inexplicable rulings like how listening to the noise of gurgling water is excessively sensual and therefore a sin. In conducting his own research, Maleky unearthed some appalling fatwas issued by Ibn Taymiyya, a thirteenth-century theologian and a pillar of Wahhabi thought. He had suggested, for example, that Shiite Muslim children should be taken away from their parents so that they would be raised as Sunnis. Ibn Taymiyya wrote about the Omayyads as model Islamic rulers. When Maleky was first arrested, security officials searched his papers and discovered that his personal journal included writings critical of the theologian. "It was like they had found drugs!" he told me with a bitter laugh.

For Maleky, like others bent on reform, a basic problem with the education system is that it fosters the idea that Wahhabi Islam is utopian: "We have to abandon this mentality that thinks we are the only ones bound for heaven and everybody else will go to hell, we have to realize we can make mistakes just like everybody else." Wahhabi thought started as a puritan movement that tried to reform and streamline the faith, condemning rituals like worshipping at saint's tombs as unnecessary. There was also supposedly no hierarchy—the direct relationship between man and his God was paramount. But after centuries of practice it has petrified, he said. It has gone from seeking purity to making a cult out of the smallest rituals, like what length a man should wear his robe given that Prophet Mohamed wore his above the ankle. Maleky argued that such rigidity was ultimately the font of religiously sanctioned violence: "If Wahhabism doesn't revise itself, it will produce more terrorists."

Most Saudi reformists have concluded that holding up Wahhabi beliefs as unquestionable fueled the zealotry of men like Osama bin Laden and his followers. Extremists have convinced themselves that anyone implementing a divine mandate to spread the glory of Islam is above reproach, no matter how violent the means. To try to combat that idea, the Saudi monarchs rolled out clergymen rooted in exactly the same tradition to condemn extremist acts. "This is not Islam," they repeated endlessly to no apparent effect—the radicals dismissive of most clerics on the government payroll.

Instead, Maleky and others argued, Saudi Arabia should lift the ban on studying Islamic traditions outside Wahhabism. Islam consists of four different schools of thought and law, not just one. If all four schools were widely known, Saudis would have more tools to counter the extremists in their midst. "Students would know that there are some other thoughts in Islam," he said. In addition, the whole society should be allowed to participate in the discussion, not just religious sheikhs, reformists told me. But since the clerical establishment endorses the idea that the al-Sauds can reign as they see fit, the royal family traditionally confronted them only on issues that menace princely authority. Naturally the clergy, like the Christian church in medieval Europe, opposed anything that might dilute their own influence.

Maleky's groundbreaking writings on these topics were too elite to influence regular Saudis, but they did help inspire a small core group of former extremists who are increasingly vocal about criticizing Saudi Arabia's blind allegiance to Wahhabi thought. They too have faced arrest and other legal harassment from the religious establishment, not to mention fatwas sanctioning their death, but the mere fact that Saudis could raise the word "Wahhabi" in public, once banned, means that at least the terms of the debate have become more realistic. But Maleky does not think discussions about extremism and changing the education system in Saudi newspapers have had much effect. He hopes that the Internet will prove a boon to spreading competing ideology, since banning any writings other than the Wahhabi school no longer keeps them out of the kingdom. Railing against them is only going to inspire the young to go look for what they are missing.

Reform attempts like Maleky's gained new significance with the recognition, at least in some quarters, that the Arab world's stifling political and economic conditions helped spawn the extremism behind the September 11 attacks. The fact that fifteen of the nineteen hijackers were Saudis made that argument particularly vivid in the kingdom, despite the foot dragging and denial by the ruling princes. It was only after terrorists linked directly to Al-Qaeda unleashed a series of bloody domestic attacks starting in May 2003, indiscriminately murdering Saudis and non-Saudis alike, that the royal regime was forced to abandon its mantra that Islamic extremism was foreign to the kingdom.

This gained some space for reformers in Saudi Arabia, as in other Arab states, to air their grievances. Still, while Arab leaders may have adopted the word "reform" as a catchphrase, through a combination of pressure from Washington and their own people, they all inch timidly toward even the mildest changes. Anyone too vocal about it faces jail. The oldest princes who wield real power seem to consider change an unnecessary, uncalculated adventure. One of my favorite, die-hard Saudi women activists always used to make me laugh by telling me, "If you are optimistic, you think reform is a long ways away."

For change to be realistic, it has to be endorsed by a majority of the princes. But it is unclear just how much anyone among the swelling population of al-Sauds wants to alter the system—the number of adult males alone is pegged at 7,000 and the entire clan at around 30,000. After all, ever since oil was discovered in 1938, the al-Sauds have exercised complete control over the world's richest oil resources, one-quarter of all known reserves. Who would voluntarily relinquish that? Indulgence toward reformists tends to rise and fall in tandem with the price of oil—in lean times, the royals are more prone to react to grievances than when they are flush with cash and feel they can buy everyone off. There is also a long history of dissidents growing complacent as they became millionaires. The kingdom earned more than $200 billion in 2007 alone, well before the oil price hit record highs around $150 per barrel in 2008 and then dropped again—still giving them vast means to stall reform.

The ruling Saud dynasty and the Wahhabi clerics each buttress the authority of the other. Their alliance dates back to the eighteenth century, when Mohamed Ibn Saud, a tribal chieftain in the central Nejd region, joined forces with Mohamed Ibn Abdel-Wahhab, a puritan bent on purging Islam of worshipping idols or any symbols other than God himself. Ibn Saud harnessed their puritan zeal to vanquish the other tribes and the pattern was set, even as the al-Saud tribe's power waxed and waned until King Abdul Aziz unified what is today Saudi Arabia in 1932. That original covenant remains the foundation of the Saudi system. Take the division of labor in the Cabinet. Royals control security, foreign affairs, and the economy while descendants of Abdel-Wahhab form the backbone of the religious establishment, holding sway over social issues and education. The clerical hierarchy views even the idea of laws emanating from public debate with suspicion, as if that process might erode God's mandate.

Despite the sprawling size of the ruling dynasty, it remains shrouded in mystery. Crucial issues like where the finances of the family stop and those of the kingdom start, not to mention the question of succession, are closely guarded secrets kept behind high palace walls. The country will likely remain a gerontocracy for the foreseeable future, with just a few senior royals—including the king, the crown prince, and the interior minister—making all the major decisions. That system worked well enough when the kingdom consisted largely of impoverished nomads. But it hardly constitutes efficient management for some 27 million people, a quarter of them foreign workers, spread over a country slightly larger than a fifth of the continental United States. Saudi Arabia is not run terribly well, and the endless succession contest shapes family actions like none other, stirring factional rivalries that are another significant brake on change. No prince champions a process whose unanticipated consequences might damage his path to the throne. The main rivalry pits the Sudeiri brothers against the descendants of King Faisal. One of King Abdul Aziz's favorite wives, Hussa Ahmad al-Sudeiri, bore seven sons. They included the late King Fahd; Prince Sultan, the defense minister for decades and King Abdullah's crown prince; Prince Nayef, the interior minister; and Prince Salman, the governor of Riyadh. The Faisal branch included Prince Saud, the foreign minister, and his brother Prince Khalid, the governor of Mecca, as well as Prince Turki, a former head of intelligence and briefly ambassador to the United States.

The older princes, born before their legendary father united the kingdom, have also lived through an era of unprecedented changes, with billions earned during the two oil booms of the 1970s spent on the construction of airports, highways, schools, hospitals, and housing. Even though the welfare system has frayed and unemployment soared as the population nearly tripled, the ruling princes feel that the al-Sauds have brought unimaginable bounty to their people, who should be grateful. The princes were born into a mud-brick fort that still stands in downtown Riyadh, with bare bulbs hanging from the ceiling and a wooden cover over the primitive toilet.

"For years we were poorer than everybody; we had nothing," Prince Abdullah Bin Faisal, a grandson of the founding king through his Sudeiri mother, told me. "The older generation will remember that they would go out to the desert to look for bones, hoping that it would not be human bones, and actually grind them and eat them like powder, just in case there was some nutrition."

Whenever the press pack descended on Riyadh, Prince Abdullah, the affable former chairman of the Saudi Arabian General Investment Authority, which encouraged foreign investment, would host a lavish evening buffet under the stars in the courtyard of his home. He invited over all kinds of Saudi professional men and, unusually, women. "We came from well below zero, we had no schools until the '50s, we were dying of hunger just two or three decades before and with no experience at all, no education, suddenly we were able to handle the big boom," said the prince, himself born in 1951. "It is still remarkable. Of course we made mistakes, there must have been some damage, we must have got into bad habits."

While crown prince, King Abdullah had a reputation for being austere. But I always compared him to the late King Faisal to understand just how oil wealth had shifted the standard. A mark of King Faisal's austerity was that at the time of his assassination by a nephew in 1975, he was still using the same Chrysler he acquired in 1964. Abdullah was called austere because his sons didn't own private jumbo jets. Abdullah seemed to endorse reform when he curbed some of the excesses of the royal family, demanding, for example, that they start paying for quotidian stuff like their phone bills and airline tickets out of their annual government stipend. (The amount of the stipend was impossible to confirm, but Saudi businessmen estimated that it started around $120,000 annually.) The phone company, for example, announced quietly in 2001 that unpaid phone bills from 1998 through 2000 amounted to $880 million. It went without saying that the people who could run up unpaid bills of that magnitude were princes. As to Saudia, the national airline, members of the al-Saud family treated it like their private carrier. When out of the country, senior princes would commandeer planes for errands such as flying them fresh milk from their favorite camels. The airline enjoyed a monopoly on all domestic travel, and in this case the pampering of princes worked very much in my favor. I was delighted to discover that I could almost always get on a flight by buying one of what I dubbed the "prince seats." No Saudia manager would want to risk the ire of a prince by telling him the flight was full, so they always kept at least two first-class seats unsold in case a royal showed up at the last minute. I can't count the number of times I beat the competition to some news story by bargaining for one of those seats just before the airplane door closed.

For Saudi businessmen, royal land deals were a constant source of grumbling. Land grants, once modest parcels distributed by the royal court for palaces, have mushroomed into a multibillion-dollar real-estate industry that generates most of the royal wealth outside oil. Before major construction projects like airports, for example, the princes in the know will get a grant for the airport land and then sell it back to the government at a huge profit. It is all perfectly legal. But it infuriates regular Saudis and made me completely understand why so many viewed the entire royal tribe like a swarm of unrepentant leeches.

King Abdullah, born in 1924, may not have all that many years to implement reforms. Succession passes down the line of the sons of King Abdul Aziz, of whom about twenty of the original forty or so survive, with the youngest born in 1947. Not all are considered monarch material, but having doddering princes at the helm for at least another decade will prevent any sweeping change. The fact that the ruling clan has yet to figure out how to skip to the next generation remains a possible source of instability. Change could emerge from a fight within the ruling family for predominance. But since many princes ally themselves with the religious establishment to fortify their own position, any such internal battle would be unlikely to induce liberal reforms. After the last major family rift erupted in public in the early 1960s, the princes who had suggested the most radical changes were ostracized. Some Saudis consider that the best hope for reform lies in the alliance between princes in business and their commoner counterparts. They pushed through Saudi admittance to the World Trade Organization and it was pressure from them that created a more structured court system in 2007, including commercial courts. (Not that change on paper has ever guaranteed change in substance. New laws passed in 2002 specified that suspects had the right to a lawyer and that trials be held in public, but judges accustomed to ruling their courtrooms expelled lawyers with impunity and most trials still proceeded in secret.) When the proposal to join the WTO was first broached, religious conservatives protested vociferously that the organization's rules would force the kingdom to import pork and alcohol in contradiction of Islamic laws. That was nonsense, of course, and the changes needed to join were pushed through, largely because the Saudi business community wanted them. Nothing quite irritates businessmen as much as the kingdom's exasperating bureaucracy and its capricious, uncodified legal system, which helped make the Emirate of Dubai immensely rich. Rather than Jeddah, Dubai, which streamlined its commercial laws and built a state-of-the-art container port, became the commercial and banking center for the region, as well as its distribution hub, business that should be Saudi Arabia's since its wealth and its population make it the area's largest market by far.

If reform gains any momentum, I expect it might come from the frustration within the business community rather than from women or religious dissidents. Only businessmen have sufficient influence to counterbalance the religious establishment, plus princes invest in companies with increasing frequency. Years ago they avoided business, but now the royals are also hemmed in to some extent by the encumbering rules. The need to create jobs is also a key factor.

▣   ▣   ▣

To illustrate the struggle involved in pushing against tradition to effect any kind of change for women, Fawaziah B. al-Bakr, the education professor, described a workshop she taught for supervisors on new ways to evaluate teacher performance. One of the more enthusiastic teachers approached Professor Bakr at the end of the three-day workshop and handed her a slim envelope. Inside was a fatwa, a religious ruling, that the woman had commissioned from a local cleric, admonishing Bakr that plucking her eyebrows was a sin. Bakr left the hallway depressed that three days of hard work had been reduced to whether her eyebrows conformed to how God thought they should look.

"Religion has been made so superficial!" she told me, echoing a common frustration among educated Saudis. "It is about symbols that are void of meaning and an obsession with details like not plucking your eyebrows, whether you can dye your hair or not, whether women should wear white or not because men wear white, whether women should wear tennis shoes. They limit every-thing to trivial details. They keep us busy with all the little details so we don't worry about the big things."

Reformists believe the problem starts from the earliest years in school. The ministry of education, long a bastion of religious con-servatives, set the goal of the education system as promoting "the glory and proud heritage of Islamic civilization."

Conservatives consider Saudi Arabia the main bastion of that civ-ilization, and so they battle anything which they fear might dimin-ish its status. For example, when educators first proposed introducing English in first grade as one route toward improving much-needed job skills among Saudi graduates, the conservatives managed to kill the idea, arguing that it would dilute the emphasis on Arabic as the language of the faith. English is now supposed to start in the sixth grade, but even that has not been implemented across the kingdom, in part due to a lack of qualified teachers. "They can't understand that the whole world around them is changing, they think any kind of change will affect the values of Saudi Arabia, so they try to control everything," Bakr told me in 2008. "The government is struggling to get it out of their hands but it can't."

In elementary school, at least 30 percent of the time is dedicated to religious study, but that rises to about 70 percent when you con-sider the way religion enters other topics like history and Arabic, according to Bakr. Many lessons are of no use in the modern world. She reeled off a long, random list. Fourth graders are taught how to clean themselves in the Islamically acceptable manner with rocks after going to the bathroom in the desert. What Saudi family, if they go camping at all, ventured forth these days without a chemical toi-let, Bakr asked dryly. A lesson that incorporated a Hadith, one of the sayings of the Prophet Mohamed, about seeking knowledge as far away as China, showed a boy riding a camel to get there.

In Saudi schools, the entire system of rote teaching is designed so that students don't ask questions. Bakr and other reformers told me that Saudis are taught from the very beginning to avoid expressing any independent opinions, with both the curriculum content and the aura of the classroom pushing the idea that Islam contains an answer for everything. Finding those answers merely involved consulting learned religious scholars. "Why waste time on these trivial things, I don't get it," she said. "Teach the students how to think, give them a scientific project, teach them skills! If you go to the objectives of the education, the practices in the schools, all you find is religion, religion, religion."

A few years ago the blanket influence of religious fundamentalists at the university was such that she would not have dared raise such questions, particularly in her own classroom, Bakr noted. The spurt in domestic terrorist attacks gave her a little leeway, but some barriers remained. Bakr conducted the interview with me in her tastefully decorated Riyadh home with her husband or teenage son always present, so no one could later accuse her of welcoming an unrelated man into her house alone. I was perplexed at first, but later realized that would have meant she committed an act of "khulwa," or illegal segregation between an unrelated man and woman. She could have been arrested for it. Permanently suspect for taking part in the 1990 driving demonstration, she remained vigilant not to give the religious establishment any means to further undermine her reputation. When I first told her the Times would need to take her picture, she said it was absolutely no problem. By the time we got to her house, however, she had reconsidered. If she was unveiled, it might be used against her, but she didn't want to appear as if she walked around the house veiled, either. Finally, she agreed to have the picture taken walking down her street, but she brought her young son along, again so nobody could accuse her of being alone with strangers. The energetic boy barely reached her hip, but in the eyes of the clerics he could be considered her guardian. After constantly glancing over her shoulder uneasily to make sure the religious police were not roaring around the corner to ask questions, she finally called a halt to the session after about fifteen minutes. At first I thought Bakr was being overly cautious, but when I later encountered some women who had been jailed and beaten by the religious police, I recognized her bravery for what it was.

Professor Bakr enumerated some of the barriers she encountered daily that limited the role of women. Male professors barred their female colleagues from attending departmental meetings, for example, because Islam dictates that men should hear a woman's voice only when absolutely necessary lest they become aroused. Textbooks stressed that the role of women was to be wives and mothers, and then they can use any spare time left over to become teachers or doctors. "Women are usually portrayed inside the kitchen," explained the professor, a dynamic mother of four, giving a wry laugh as she cited a few examples of sentences from an elementary school reader: Hind helps her mother cook dinner. Nuha is sewing her brother's shirt. While Nuha works, her brother is playing with paper. "The boys don't have a job, a role inside the home, but the girls are always cooking and sewing and ironing," she told me.

Sadly, Bakr noted, the effects of years of this kind of education, with increasing doses of religion added over the past two decades, are all too apparent. When a group of incoming freshwomen were asked a few years ago what they wanted from the university, the most frequent requests were for a rule requiring female students to wear their black cloaks over their heads rather than on their shoulders and for a ban on women's sports. Not one mentioned any kind of activity that any normal undergraduate elsewhere in the world would consider fun. "You expect the new generation to be rebellious, but these girls just died in those schools. Fifteen years of this kind of teaching made them completely passive; all they think about is the afterlife and they see the world in a very dark way."

By the fall semester in 2008, Professor Bakr told me, reform was still difficult but King Abdullah had at least engineered a shift in tone. He appointed professionals educated at some of the world's best universities to run the Ministry of Higher Education, which was not the same as the Ministry of Education. They were putting a new emphasis on quality in college classrooms. The realization that Saudi graduates were generally unfit for any workplace forced the change. Bakr was reconsidering her view of the university as a hopeless case. Someone had suggested building sports facilities for women, and a few students, infected by a new sense of openness, were talking about trying to get scholarships abroad. "The mood is changing," she said with cautious optimism.

Bakr told me that she had wanted to rebel against certain Saudi ways of doing things from her earliest years—when men in her neighborhood yelled at her for playing in the streets while little boys could kick a soccer ball around freely, or when her teachers bellowed abuse at her or even hit her with short bamboo prods be-cause her abaya was constantly askew. As an adolescent, she was ap-palled to discover that women whose husbands took a second wife could be evicted from their homes with little recourse. She made a precocious debut as a newspaper columnist while still in high school, railing against women's lack of rights in the kingdom.

But any open rebellion outside the framework of what the ruling dynasty and its devout supporters find acceptable is well nigh im-possible, as Bakr, who was born in 1963 but looks a decade younger, learned the hard way. She had just returned with her doc-torate from the University of London and was appointed to the ed-ucation faculty at King Saud University, had been in the post all of two days, in fact, when she took part in the 1990 driving demon-stration. A group of forty-seven women, demanding that the ban on women driving be rescinded given the looming attack on neighboring Iraq, drove on Riyadh's modern freeways for all of about fifteen minutes before being stopped. I was in the kingdom at the time, and the liberal elite was abuzz with praise for the women and excited about the possibility for change. Taking any protest to the streets was unprecedented, particularly for women! Then came Friday, and virtually every prayer leader in the country stood on his pulpit and condemned the women as whores, demanding they be punished; some suggested they be jailed and forcibly divorced from their husbands. The women were branded with all manner of derogatory labels: red communists, dirty American secularists, advocates for vice. The government, typically, suggested that the women must have been raised abroad. The nameplate on Professor Bakr's door at the university was torn off and "Kafra," or infidel, scrawled in its place. Hate mail arrived in bushels, along with an occasional rose from a secret supporter. She lost her job and her passport until King Fahd reinstated the women eighteen months later.

Amazingly, the protest still resonates. Despite the passage of years, the professor has been denied promotions and only recently served on a government-run panel for the first time. The enduring price made other Saudis reluctant to take to the streets to demand change. Women activists optimistically predict annually that this is the year they will gain permission to drive, that the economic costs endured by the middle class for hiring foreign drivers will ultimately force a change. Bakr is sometimes dumbfounded that so many years later women have still not won the right. But important royals are insulated from the costs by their fat annual stipends, and the issue has become a kind of Alamo for religious conservatives. Women will get the right when either the king or one of the senior princes in line for the throne is bold enough to endorse the idea directly. Instead, the ruling family has attempted to deflect the international criticism with vague pronouncements like saying that the idea was being studied, or that Islam itself does not ban women from driving, it's, you know, a cultural thing to protect them.

Saudi rulers are masters at making gentle statements about proceeding with change while avoiding tangible steps. The al-Sauds have been particularly harsh toward those who continue to demand such steps—agitated that princely promises are considered insufficient. Activists are warned to stop being so vocal, to address any grievances to royal princes and not the general public. Occasionally the princes demand that they even halt the flow of petitions, the time-honored way of asking tribal elders for change. Anyone who defies such an order is jailed, basically for being uppity. The princes are prepared to allow limited discussion in the press, but certain events like a gathering of 100 reformists from across the country at a hotel near Riyadh airport in February 2004 provoked their wrath. The organizers were either imprisoned or barred from traveling abroad, a common fate for anyone considered too outspoken. The first prominent Saudi blogger was jailed for four months ending in April 2008 after being critical of the ruling family online. Such cases provide the litmus test for the government's real attitude toward reform.

꙰   ꙰   ꙰

The absence of elected representation grates less among Saudi reformists and their supporters than the utter lack of civil rights. Perhaps the most glaring example of that is the way the religious police run roughshod over all public behavior—Saudis are taught in schools and told in mosques that actions by state institutions like the religious police cannot be questioned because they operate under the mantle of Islam. A 31-year-old businesswoman bitterly detailed her nightmare experience of being hauled in by the religious police and accused of adultery as well as drug abuse. The religious police, formally known as The Committee for the Promotion of Virtue and the Prevention of Vice are usually referred to as the "muttawa" or volunteers, because many of them are. (Some expatriates mock them as The Promotion.) They patrol the streets and malls to ensure that everyone complies with Islamic teachings: that women are covered, the sexes are not mingling, all shops close for prayers, and men go to the mosque to pray. Oh, and they also police for anyone practicing sorcery, which would be funny if people weren't still being condemned to death occasionally, convicted of practicing the dark art.

The woman I met, who asked not to be identified out of fear of further arrest, said that one day her father was ill so she went to his office to open the safe for the manager. Soon after she arrived, the muttawa raided the place. Later she found out that an Indian worker whom she had fired had gone to them and claimed she was having an affair with the elderly Lebanese office manager who had been working there for decades.

"Don't you fear God?!" she recalls them screaming, demanding that she not address them from behind a desk because women don't belong there. "It is a sin that you are sitting in this office around men!" The woman said one policeman groped her breasts while ostensibly searching for drugs before dragging her kicking and screaming into an unmarked Toyota. She had called her husband as the raid started, but when he tried to collect her from the police station, they pretended she was elsewhere. Instead they locked her into a jail infested with cockroaches and scuttling rats for three days and forced her to endure an extended lecture from the prison's religious sheikh about the sin of adultery.

In the end, they handed her a heavy black face veil and gloves and would not let her walk out of prison until she was completely shrouded. "We don't have any laws, that is the problem. You are only OK as long as your husband protects you and your family is respected. The muttawa are political police for the government." Such traumatizing tactics succeed; the woman has never returned to the family business.

Another, older woman listening to the story said she faced exactly the same trumped-up charges a decade earlier. Her car was stopped on the street right after she walked out of a party alone— her husband was away on business. When she was hauled into the police station and tried to complain to the officer in charge, he took off his leather sandal and slapped her across the face with it. She was lashed seventy times after being falsely accused of drinking alcohol. There was no appeal despite the utter lack of evidence, she said, and she was fired from her government job. Although the muttawa are widely despised, there is a huge social stigma to being detained. A young Saudi woman could well ruin her chances for marriage if they haul her in, the assumption being that her morals are somehow suspect. "Their goal is to break you inside," said the older woman.

One significant problem in living in a society where men and women are segregated starting in elementary school is that the sexes never really learn to deal with each other in even the most rudimentary way. The gap between the two is acute enough in the West, where co-education is the norm, but it takes on monumental proportions in Saudi Arabia. "There is a phobia about women in Saudi Arabia," Professor Bakr explained to me. Most men have never spent any time around women. The conservative customs prevalent in the kingdom basically teach that women are for sex, which they crave, and hence many men limit their view of women to that level. "Men think that they will be corrupted," she said.

The mandate of the religious police to prevent any form of corruption is based on several Koranic verses, lending it an Islamic seal of approval. Still, some opponents have pushed back. The first scandal that raised serious questions came in 2002, when an overcrowded girls' school in Mecca caught fire and religious police prevented some pupils from fleeing because they had left their enveloping abayas behind. Fourteen girls under age 15 perished. Yet it was not enough to provoke some senior princes into criticizing the police publicly. Soon after the 2003 bombings in Riyadh, seen as rooted in the kind of religious intolerance espoused by the muttawa, a Saudi journalist asked Prince Nayef, the interior minister, whether the Mecca fire and the bombings meant the government would curb their mandate. Prince Nayef berated the reporter, telling him he should be ashamed of himself as a Saudi for asking such a question.

Eventually Saudis exasperated with the sweeping powers of the religious police, not to mention the arrogant, aggressive manner they deal with the public, took the unprecedented step of challenging them in the courts after a series of terrible incidents in 2007. In two separate cases, the families of men who died while in muttawa custody accused the police of beating them to death, one for allegedly being with a woman who was not his wife and the second for selling alcohol. But the conservative judiciary is a staunch ideological ally of the muttawa, and the seven or so policemen involved were initially acquitted in both cases. A higher court ordered a retrial in one of the deaths and, in a highly unusual rebuke to the judge, admonished him to at least make an effort to get at the truth by interviewing witnesses and hearing medical testimony. In another case, a Saudi businesswoman and her Syrian male associate were arrested for sharing a coffee in Starbucks after their office building lost power. The immediate uproar prompted royal intervention to get the two released.

In response to growing public outrage, the head of the muttawa felt compelled to start a public relations campaign for the first time. At a rare press conference, he denied persistent reports that many muttawa were former convicts released from prison early because they memorized the Koran. Liberal Saudis made bitter jokes that the only real purpose the morals police served was as an employment agency for tens of thousands of Saudi men who concentrated solely on religion throughout their education and were thus unfit to work anywhere else. The organization also rolled out studies showing that 99 percent of Saudis supported their role. Opponents were convinced that the organization invented the results.

▦ ▦ ▦

King Abdullah, even before taking the throne, inaugurated a formal National Dialogue to address specific issues like the problems of education or women or youth. But in typically Saudi manner such conferences were carefully scripted. Participants were hand-picked and the discussions unrolled behind closed doors. Saudis gave him credit for at least providing a platform to air their problems, but there was little follow-up. Any sign of reform large or small usually ended with dashed hopes. Saudis thought that the municipal councils elected in 2005, for example, might be a first step toward getting some say over their lives. But they were soon disabused of that notion. It took the government about eight months to seat the councils, which then had no effect. Still, there have been some changes. In 2008 the king issued a royal decree to amend an article in the labor law so that women are now allowed to work in a mixed environment, as long as it does not contradict "Islamic tradition." The move was designed to encourage the private sector to hire more women. Until the new decree, a business would have had to create a completely separate work environment for women. Women from the Chamber of Commerce in Jeddah printed copies of the royal decree to distribute widely to businesses so they could wave them in the face of any muttawa who tried to arrest either the women or the business owner for not segregating the sexes.

Saudis who consider reform far too slow believe some outside pressure can be helpful, since the ability to organize domestically is so constrained. Direct criticism from the United States or other Western capitals, however, often backfired because it was depicted locally as an attack on Islam. Right after September 11, Washington singled out the religious instruction in Saudi textbooks which, for example, taught that Muslims should be loyal to their own kind and shun everyone else. The Saudi government said the lessons were removed, but domestic activists accused the Education Ministry of just shuffling them around to other grades. The real goal should be changing the mindset of the teachers.

A high school theology teacher sat down with me to go over some of the changes in the tenth-grade religious textbooks. An earlier one had language like "One of the major requirements in hating the infidels and being hostile to them is ignoring their rituals and their festivities." In other words, saying "Merry Christmas" would set you firmly on the path to hell. That sentiment was more generalized in the new textbook, which instead emphasized that importing foreign ideas was demonic. It described any political system outside Islam as "a dark rule," even if it was labeled modernization and practiced in advanced nations. "Using human rules and regulations is outside Islam and shirq, worshipping someone else with God." Wahhabis consider shirq a sin of catastrophic pro-portions. The new textbook dropped the earlier prescription that named outsiders explicitly as the enemy, but it had hardly em-braced an enlightened liberal code. The new book described the secular as those who advocate separating religion from the state.

Conservative clerics depicted any curriculum changes as a Western-inspired plot to dismantle the country's religion. "Saying that the Jews and the Christians are infidels is part of our religious dogma," Saleh al-Wohaibi, the American-educated secretary gen-eral of the World Assembly of Muslim Youth, told me when I went to see him in the plain white office block housing the organiza-tion's headquarters in Riyadh. "It doesn't mean we try to incite ha-tred against others, but my religion has its own principles that should not be violated nor changed."

Saudi Arabia calls the Koran the only constitution it will ever need. "They say Koran, Koran, do you want something other than the Koran?" groused one retired professor, also declining to use his name because of the sensitivity of his criticism. "Of course you have to say no."

Saudi reformers believed that the American administration made a tactical error when it pushed the Saudi government to delete some of the textbook lessons seen as feeding extremist thought. Such direct pressure only inspired the conservatives to drag their feet, to decry it as scandalous that an outside force might try to dic-tate how future generations learn Islam. Rather, reformers think the conservatives who run the education system should be forced to respond to its academic shortcomings. Professor Bakr thought a far wiser approach would be to try to embarrass the Saudi government about how poorly graduates cope with the world, to ask aloud what it is about the curriculum that means that Saudi Arabia in par-ticular and the Arab world in general produce so few scientists and contribute nothing significant to the world's technological ad-vances. That approach echoed the concerns of most Saudi parents, and would be a far more effective form of pressure than criticism seen as an assault on the culture and the religion.

It is an approach across many fields that Arab reformers throughout the region recommended as a way to bolster individual efforts. Rather than the U.S. providing prescriptions for how change should proceed, Washington should listen more closely to domestic critics and try to shore up their position by echoing their ideas without undermining the activists by endorsing them directly.

Another point that Maleky, the theologian, and other reformers throughout the Muslim world made is that Western governments should root their criticism in well-established Islamic terms. There should be an emphasis on justice, for example, rather than on democracy. Democracy can be reviled as a Western notion that has no heritage in the Islamic world, because it elevates man's laws over those of God. The quest for justice cannot be so easily dismissed; the Koran endorses the concept. So stressing human rights and civil society as an argument for spreading justice is one that echoes Islamic teachings. The United States could do better at listening to other cultures for signals on how to interact with them.

◻ ◻ ◻

Among themselves, Saudi reformers sometimes argued that they were too slow and too timid about challenging the status quo, that writing and talking didn't muster enough pressure. But others believed that gradually pushing Saudis to alter their way of thinking was more important than open confrontation. In 1995, Professor Turki al-Hamad, an American-educated political science professor, sought early retirement from King Saud University at the age of 45. He wanted to write novels, considering that a far more effective means of prompting young Saudis to reconsider their worldview as opposed to his frequent political columns in various newspapers. He was also tired of being dictated to about what he could teach in his classroom.

The problem was not a lesson here or there, he said, but that the sum total taught young Saudis that the rest of the world deserved their scorn. "Of course not every Saudi is violent, not every graduate is violent," he told me, conceding the point that the government made repeatedly. "But if you give a young mind the idea of hating others, of not belonging to this world, that the world is against you, it doesn't mean he will be violent automatically, but you plant the seeds for such a thing."

Hisham al-Abir, the central character in Hamad's coming-of-age trilogy, hardly conformed to the ideal image of a Saudi youth. He drove a prostitute named Raqiyya out into the desert beyond Riyadh for drunken sex. He joined an underground political organization. He dismissed as backward some prominent religious works used to bolster what he considered overly rigid Islamic traditions. When Professor Hamad published the novels in the late 1990s, the unusually frank books shattered just about every social taboo going and the Saudi government's reaction proved typical: All three were swiftly banned. Some members of the religious establishment, interpreting the novels as autobiography, decided that the author had confessed to adultery, among other damnable sins, and rumbled out four fatwas condoning his death. They also objected to lines of dialogue like "Oh my poor God," grousing that God should never be described as poor. King Abdullah, then still crown prince, intervened to silence the uproar. Hamad was evidently grateful, but some critics found his writings about the rulers excessively fawning after that.

To Hamad, the whole point of the trilogy—entitled *Adama, Shumaisi*, and *Karadib*—was to cast light on subjects like sex, religion, and politics that Saudis discuss endlessly in private, yet rarely broach publicly. "In Saudi, sex, religion, and politics used to be the three taboos," he told me after driving me into the flat yellow desert outside the eastern city of Dammam late one afternoon. When we left his apartment, a green Toyota sedan tailed us, but eventually Hamad's driver made a few judicious twists and turns and lost it. We built a small fire in the sand and drank tea as the sun set. "Everybody has sex, but they don't say it. Everything is kept underground. Everybody, when they get together, talks about politics, about religion, but underground. Everything goes on underground. If you keep everything underground for a long, long time, it will rot. Everything should be brought up under the sunshine. We practice these things, but we say we don't, which is a kind of hypocrisy. I wasn't talking about these things just for excitement, no, I was talking about them because they are facts of life."

He paused for a while to describe how in the years he was a student in the United States, he found all that greenery oppressive, longing for the open vistas of the desert. I laughed because I had exactly the opposite reaction. When I was first back in the region, I would find the sweeping empty vistas of the deserts majestic in their solitude and understated beauty. But after years of nothing else I would start grumbling that the Middle East was a barren, arid wasteland and I longed to be surrounded by water and trees.

"Here is the problem in our society," Hamad went on. "Our society wants to present itself as complete, as a perfect society. That is not human; we are a human society, just like other societies. You have good points, you have bad points, and if you don't act naturally you will be sick at the end. The more you try to be perfect, the sicker you will get. No society is perfect."

Arab literary critics agreed that none of Hamad's books match the multilayered novels or high Arabic style of writers like the late Abdel Rahman al-Munif, a Saudi exile, who painted a damning portrait of the effect of oil on the kingdom in a series of novels starting with *Cities of Salt*. But Hamad described his aim as writing simple books that might reach the widest possible audience. Novels, he believed, even if they have to be smuggled into the kingdom, were a means to circumvent the lack of free speech.

The Winds of Paradise, a novel of Hamad's released in 2005, is a thinly disguised sketch of four September 11 hijackers. He wrote the book hoping to dent the widespread feeling among Saudis that their countrymen could not have been involved in such an atrocity, that there was a missing link somewhere, that the Israelis had probably done it. He told me that he wrote the book "just to say that the problem is not from outside, the problem is from ourselves—if we don't change ourselves, nothing will change." The next generation, exposed through the spread of the Internet and satellite television to how such freedoms work elsewhere, is more likely to push against their restraints, he said.

In working for reform, Hamad drew a parallel with soccer. Saudi Arabia played soccer according to the same rules as everybody else. So Saudis need to learn that their society, too, can afford the same kind of open debate and discussion allowed in other countries. "If you teach people that you are totally different, you are totally special, you don't belong to the world, the world has a kind a conspiracy against you, everybody is waiting for the opportunity to attack you. What does this bring you?" Hamad said. "You are making an explosive mind, a very hostile mind. So how can you have democracy in such a situation? You have hostile minds and at the same time you want democracy. You cannot combine these. The first thing is that you have to use the educational system to spread different values, human values."

🔲　🔲　🔲

I know exactly what he meant. I have deliberately avoided dwelling on violent incidents in this book because the notion of a violent Middle East tends to monopolize people's view, to the detriment of everyone. But among the many gruesome attacks I wrote about, one disturbed me more than the rest. Maybe it was because the incident unrolled in a smaller version of the compound where I grew up, planting a dark cloud over the memories of my childhood idyll. Or maybe the savagery of the gunmen going from house to house, killing every non-Muslim they could find, twenty in all, struck me as so utterly removed from anything I associate with religion. But I think the strongest reason might be the fact that I heard the story from an Iraqi-born American engineer who survived the attack.

A day after the siege of the compound ended, the rest of the press corps made the mistake of waiting for their official Saudi minders to grant them entrance to the place. They spent most of the day sweltering outside the walls in the summer heat, drinking tea. I drove to the compound and walked in—finding survivors still staggering from what they had endured. I spent a few hours in there until the FBI team helping the investigation arrived in a series of Suburbans with tinted windows. They didn't want to get out while a reporter and a photographer were walking around, so the Saudi liaison officer in charge asked me politely to go away. The engineer I interviewed had an Arab name that he had shortened to Mike in the States and that is all he wanted me to use—gunmen he could identify by sight had escaped and he was evidently still jumpy about the idea that they might return for him. After he first heard bursts of machine-gun fire, Mike, a stocky 45 and bald, with a fringe of black hair and gold-rimmed glasses, went to find security. He ran right up to two guards who turned out to be terrorists disguised in official uniforms. They demanded his Saudi residence permit, which stated clearly that he was both an American and a Muslim. A dispute erupted: One terrorist argued he should be killed because he was an American, the other that he should be spared as a Muslim. A few yards away lay the corpse of a Swedish neighbor, oozing blood.

The argument seesawed for several minutes, both men displaying a certain calm determination. Mike stood by silently, hoping, praying that the older man would prevail. "I was on the borderline," he told me. "But finally the older one said, 'We are not going to shoot you.'" Instead, they gave him a brief lecture about the merits of Islam and their cause before trying to force him to point out the houses of the infidels in the compound. "They told me: 'We are here because we want to promote Islam. We don't want non-Muslims to come to our country. We are promoting a Muslim cause,'" Mike recalled.

I covered far too many such murderous attacks in Saudi Arabia. My ambivalence about going there gradually solidified into dread, despite the fact that there were many Saudis I still seek out. The ruling al-Sauds were right that the attackers constitute a sick, violent fringe. But the ruling elite remains entirely too passive about mustering the courage to dismantle the ideological underpinning of such groups because it provides the same pillars that hold up their rule. Reformists have reached the unanimous conclusion that restructuring the education system is the key to change, that as it stands now the curriculum plants the seeds in some minds that are then twisted into believing that only Muslims deserve to live. Mike was lucky. Others were not.

CHAPTER 12

THE MUSLIM BROTHERHOOD

"Astaghfurallah!"

THE AMPLE, PASTY-WHITE BREASTS of the mostly Russian tourists lounging topless poolside glowed almost translucent under the bright September sun, and the heavily bearded Egyptian lawyers in their thick suits pretended not to look. "Astaghfurallah!"—"I ask God's forgiveness!"—many cried out when they first spotted all that unabashed, wanton nudity, slapping their hands over their eyes. Then, their hands still on their faces, they spread their fingers and ogled, slowly stumbling toward the conference room of a beach resort in Hurghada, the main town along Egypt's Red Sea coast. "Astaghfurallah, astaghfurallah, astaghfurallah," they continued muttering all along the way. I was sitting next to the open windows in the hotel lobby, trying not to laugh, but also intrigued by my own reaction. After so many years in the Middle East, I found that I had absorbed its conservative mores to a greater degree than I recognized. On my first trip out of Egypt after staying there as a student, I was boarding a KLM flight, and at the foot of the airplane stairs, I looked up to see a tall, blonde Dutch woman in a short sky-blue miniskirt smiling down at me. She was a vision from a different planet, my first glimpse of bare legs in public for about eighteen months. The startling exposure was a tonic, and I distinctly remember my brain erupting with one single focused thought: "Flesh!" In Hurghada, after a couple decades spent mostly in the Middle East, part of my brain responded to the scene like those Egyptian lawyers. Rather than delighting in all that naked pulchritude, I was somewhat shocked. Of course, I found the entire hotel tableau sad because on my first trip to Hurghada during that same student epoch, there had been only one Sheraton resort, far beyond my means. My friends and I slept on the open sand and paid a fisherman a few bucks to take us offshore to snorkel around the stunning coral reefs. Mangrove trees filled with nesting white herons dotted much of the coastline then. Now, wall-to-wall hotels stretched for hundreds of miles and were pushing farther south every year.

The Tropicana Hotel where I was staying, newly opened, had sold all the rooms in one three-story wing pointing out toward the sea to Russian and Italian tourists, who paid rock-bottom prices of a few hundred dollars for airfare plus a week of lounging in the sun under blaring disco music. The other wing was fully booked by the Egyptian Lawyers' Syndicate, a group dominated by members of the banned Muslim Brotherhood, the grandfather of all Islamist political movements. They are often simply referred to as the Ikhwan, or Brothers, in Arabic (pronounced ikh-WAN).

I had come to their 2002 annual convention to get to know a young lawyer named Mohamed—he wanted only his first name used. Mohamed intrigued me not because he was a member of the Brotherhood—he wasn't—but because he found it insufficiently radical—neutered, in fact. Most of the leftist intellectual types or Westernized journalists I made friends with populated the other end of the spectrum—distrusting the Ikhwan because they suspected the group's ultimate goal was to create a rigid theocracy, a country where the government would force women to veil their hair, ban Muslims from drinking, and legislate all manner of morality.

I overheard some Italians nearby ordering cappuccino for breakfast so I called over the waiter. I asked Mohamed if he wanted one and he asked me warily what it was. In appearance, Mohamed was typically Egyptian, with a slightly dark complexion and tightly curled black hair cut short. Poverty kept him rail thin. We settled on tea. "So what's a group of devout Muslim lawyers doing staying in a hotel full of naked women?" I asked first. He laughed and shook his head. "These Muslim Brothers are decadent, just a bunch of opportunists," Mohamed answered, going on to explain why he subscribed to the teachings of the more extreme "Gamaa Al-Islamiyya," or The Islamic Group, which advocated overthrowing the Egyptian government by force. Mohamed considered the Brothers too complacent, their goal of creating an Islamic Egypt mere pretense. "They have been saying since 1928 that they would implement an Islamic state, more than seventy years!" he told me. "Wouldn't you call that a failure?"

Yet during those many years, the Brotherhood has spread throughout the region and beyond. Largely through its efforts, the role of Islam in politics has now become a central issue that haunts political and social reform in the Middle East. The Arab world's absolute rulers, like Egypt's President Hosni Mubarak, who took office in 1981, have long justified their authoritarian ways by claiming to provide the last bulwark against the tsunami of radical Islamist rule. Their secular opponents label that nonsense, claiming that the Muslim Brotherhood and its offshoots would just be a few parties among many if civil society and political rights were truly unfettered. They consider the broad appeal of political Islam an aberration caused by the lack of any vital political life.

Given that absence over many decades, however, the Muslim parties with their effective organizations built sub rosa through mosques and various religious social groups are the only viable opposition. The hanging question is whether they can be truly democratic or will support free elections only until they achieve power, then implement an Islamic dictatorship. Iran's Shiite Muslim mullahs, for example, eventually quashed all the allies who helped them to overthrow the shah in 1979. The experiment in marrying Islam with democracy has not really been tested in the world of Sunni Muslim Arab states. Hamas, a Muslim Brotherhood offshoot, did win the 2006 elections in the Gaza strip, but it is an imperfect test case given Israel's overarching control there. The junta in Algeria aborted the 1992 election when it seemed the Islamists would dominate, sparking a civil war that has left more than 150,000 dead. That murderous chaos, along with the bloodshed in Iraq in tandem with elections, convinced many in the Arab world that hastening toward voting is a mistake; building civil society first is the better alternative.

Ultimately, the dilemma about how to give the Islamist parties a role has to be resolved for real reform to proceed. Islam is a cultural reference point for many citizens who want it reflected in their political system. Most ordinary Egyptians, and indeed many Arabs, survey their daily life through the prism of their faith. There cannot be true democracy in any Arab country without reaching some kind of accommodation between religion and politics. America's separation between church and state is the product of the particular moment that the U.S. constitution was devised. It is not a scenario that can be casually replicated elsewhere.

░ ░ ░

For Mohamed, the lawyer, the Muslim Brotherhood was excessively accommodating toward the ruling regime. "I joined the Gamaa because they believe in change by violence, by force," he said. The Gamaa would create a country where all the laws governing social and economic behavior would come directly from Islam, and where evil Western habits like bank interest and alcohol would be abolished. "I am from upper Egypt, so I like the strong, confrontational nature of the Gamaa. That is what attracted me, not like the northern Muslim Brotherhood which avoids confrontation at all costs. They are just a bunch of peasants from the north which is why they are weak and tamed. The government never could control the Gamaa, but the Brothers are like domesticated chickens. They do nothing and are always afraid."

Mohamed told me that he began believing in change through violence around age 14, when his parents packed him and his younger brother off to collective noon prayers on Fridays, shooing them out of the house. His parents were clueless that the mosque, with its seemingly wholesome activities like the soccer league organized for teenagers in Qena, a city in upper Egypt, actually provided a smokescreen to attract new Gamaa members. Mohamed showed sufficient zeal in asking questions that he was inducted after just five months. Among other lessons he absorbed at the mosque was how to organize and recruit. The local cell in his undergraduate law department swelled to forty-one members from just two after he joined. "I was totally obsessed by the idea of confronting the regime and using violence as a means of establishing the Islamic State, the greatest mission," he said. "We were very young. We thought we were very powerful and it would take us just a few years to finish off the government, to control the entire country."

The government eventually decimated the Gamaa, killing, jailing, or forcing its members to flee into exile until the group had no active presence in Egypt. Mohamed confessed he avoided the dragnet only because an uncle in the security services tipped him off; he fled just hours before police raided his home to arrest him. His law school recruits were detained during the sweep of 1992–1993 and he told me that he never saw any of them ever again. He remained on the lam for years, living on trains and working all kinds of odd jobs—painting, construction, shop cleaning, washing cars. He never went to class, the cops would surely get wind of it to arrest him, but he always made sure to register and to sit for the finals. He was detained just once, after praying in a mosque that the Gamaa controlled near the city of Minya. But he said he acted crazed, demanding to see the interior minister and other officials, just as his Gamaa instructors had told him. The security police released him. "I think God was with me," he explained. Food was always a problem except during the holy month of Ramadan, when the urban rich throughout Egypt set up sidewalk tents to distribute hearty evening meals for the indigent to break the daily fast. Small acts of solidarity helped sustain him. At one such tent, a beggar told Mohamed that on the last day of Ramadan they habitually gave everyone twenty Egyptian pounds, about $4. So he showed up to collect the princely sum, enough to survive on for a couple weeks.

Mohamed always treated me like a friend, but he had little use for the United States. He felt that President Mubarak and many of his fellow Arab despots had stayed in power over the years because of the economic and political support provided by Washington. In fact, he was typical in his conviction that Washington had a hand in every decision the Egyptian government made—including gunning down his Gamaa colleagues on the streets. "Egypt is ruled from your country, from the White House," he told me in a matter-of-fact manner, as if everyone accepted this at face value. He also scoffed at the idea that the United States somehow represented an ideal of human rights and freedom for the rest of the world. "America does not care about human rights here or the regime's violations because the regime is simply a tool to implement American policy—Why would America care about human rights?" Whenever the Egyptian government did something like prevent voters from getting to the polls because it feared that a candidate affiliated with the Muslim Brotherhood might win, the United States did not speak up about free elections, he said. It might do that in countries it considered an enemy, like Iran, he told me, but never with an ally like Egypt.

I asked why the bulk of the Gamaa leaders, jailed in Egypt since they carried out the assassination of President Anwar Sadat in

1981, had announced from their cells around 2002 that the violent campaign, which left hundreds of police officers and activists dead, was a mistake. "It was a concession for nothing in return," Mohamed said, frowning, appalled at what he saw as capitulation. "It has totally destroyed the Gamaa and finished it off. It lost its credibility on the Egyptian street. I do not understand it. . . . Why? I ask them. Why? It's disappointing, nothing has changed. Why are the Gamaa leaders changing their teaching that they have been feeding us? . . . They taught us what it means to be under the rule of someone who does not rule by God's book, the strong evidence for changing such an incorrect situation by our own hands. What about those who died in operations against the government? Did they die in vain? Their blood went in vain? Those people fought for God, how could you say they were mistaken?" Again he suspected a U.S. or European hand in somehow coercing his former leaders to recant.

By the time I met him, he was working as a lawyer. He did not want to live as an outlaw and settled on the alternative of defending his fellow radicals in court. The work paid little, he was barely surviving. Already in his early 30s, he despaired of saving enough money to underwrite a wedding and an apartment. (Eventually he married a woman with some money of her own.) After I first started spending entire days with him, my dilemma was always trying to navigate ways to pay for lunch without making it seem like charity. Arabs try to insist on paying for everything for foreigners because they are all considered guests in their countries, and it bruised their pride and turned them sullen when I picked up the check. But he couldn't afford it, and it wasn't really charity since he offered a window into an Egyptian reality that I would otherwise have had difficulty exploring.

I saw Mohamed periodically whenever I was in Cairo. He would balk at meeting me in many of the places I suggested like Café Riche, a downtown restaurant popular with students, its walls hung with pictures of famous writers and its waiters dressed in long, traditional blue robes. He condemned it as an "atheist" hangout because it served beer. If I forced the issue, he would spend the meeting muttering darkly that we were besieged by sin. Wherever we went, he demanded to see the bill. If it was too indulgent—if I spent $20 on, say, a chicken lunch with a few vegetables for two or three of us—he would shake his head and lament that he could live off that for a month. Yet I avoided risking instant gastroenteritis by eating at the street falafel stands that sustained him.

One day he took me on his rounds through various courthouses. He showed me the stacks of paperwork for each client. Many had been in jail for more than a decade, the government ignoring repeated orders from the courts to release them. He rifled through the sheaf of papers and read each order. "Release, release, release, release," he kept ticking them off. In dusty, cramped back offices, with files stacked floor to ceiling and spilling onto the floor, Mohamed dug through giant books and piles of papers to determine if there were any new rulings. I never saw any computerized records. According to Mohamed, some of his clients had been neither charged nor acquitted; they just rotted in jail year after year without reaching a courtroom. At every stop, to get anything done he paid the clerk a small bribe, usually five pounds, about a buck, but still the cost of many bus rides for him. The choreography was almost elegant. Mohamed would make his request and the clerk appeared to think, lifting his tea glass with one hand while sliding open his top desk drawer with another. It was full of similarly grubby wadded bank notes, all in small denominations. Mohamed dropped in his five-pound note and then the clerk would help. "The entire system is corrupt," he groused to me later, although he recognized that only through such petty corruption could the clerk survive. It galled him all the same.

It was by promising that Islam would fix all such daily woes—corruption and poverty and unemployment and the absent rule of law—that the Muslim Brotherhood constantly burnished its appeal. Despite Mohamed's distaste for the organization, he preferred it to all secular groups—supporting anyone who sought to institute Islamic rule in Egypt and beyond.

The sprawling port of Alexandria, Egypt's second-largest city, is one of the many places in the Middle East that made me wish for time travel. I longed to go back to witness the now crumbling mansions and clanging tram lines at the height of their early twentieth-century grandeur. It had once been a cosmopolitan place where the many peoples of the Mediterranean—Greeks, Turks, Italians, Armenians, Jews, and Arabs—mixed with relative ease. I could experience it only vicariously through old guide books and the flowery adjectives of Lawrence Durrell's *Alexandria Quartet*. All that seemed particularly remote on the warm November night when I watched Sobhe Saleh, a Muslim Brother candidate for parliament, climb the few steps onto a makeshift stage to address a sidewalk rally. Some tactics that set the Muslim Brotherhood apart were readily apparent. The organization endorses the public segregation of the sexes. The euphemism in their literature is that "women have the right to protection everywhere including public transportation and the workplace." So this election rally was limited to women, opening with a loud burst of ululation when Saleh first appeared to introduce a Koran recitation by a young girl. Roughly 400 women sat on rickety chairs, their bodies obscured under bulky, dull robes and tightly pinned headscarves whose lower edges fluttered in the evening breeze. Clouds scudded overhead, forcing the full moon to play hide and seek.

Framed by their scarves, the women's faces shone with the eager anticipation that Arabs get when they expect to hear soaring, beautiful oratory, and the candidate did not disappoint. "If Islam was applied, the people would not have been crushed!" yelled Saleh, a lawyer with a clipped helmet of steel-grey hair and wearing a quiet gray suit, white shirt, and dark tie. It was something of a Muslim Brother uniform. He continued in a similar vein for thirty minutes, brandishing the same rhetorical flourish through a long list of issues:

"If Islam was applied, the television would not show us prostitution and people lacking all decency!"

"If Islam was applied, no one would be hungry!"

"If Islam was applied, every citizen would have the right to say his opinion and to correct any ruler who deviated!"

"If Islam was applied, Iraq could not have been invaded, Israel could not occupy Jerusalem, and aggression could not have been used to humiliate Muslims everywhere!"

The message proved effective in that campaign season in 2005, with the Muslim Brothers, although officially banned, shattering expectations by capturing 20 percent of the 444 seats in the People's Assembly. It was almost double the number its most enthusiastic supporters had predicted and the result of just the first of three rounds in the staggered election. The Brotherhood would have won even more if the government had not used the full brunt of its security forces in later rounds to block supporters from reaching the polls.

⬚   ⬚   ⬚

Hassan al-Banna, the elementary school Arabic teacher who founded the Society of Muslim Brothers in Egypt in 1928, first articulated the dream of resurrecting the golden age of Muslim empire. His three main ideas were that Sunni Islam contains the only blueprint needed for politics as well as faith, that returning to religion will cure all social ills, and that Islam will eternally face enemies trying to thwart its resurgence. "It is the nature of Islam to dominate, not to be dominated, to impose its law on all nations and to extend its power to the entire planet," he wrote. Pretty much every Muslim political group established since has pursued a similar vision. "All fundamentalist groups have one goal: setting up an Islamic state, an Islamic state with no borders," Mohamed Salah, a journalist who specializes in Egypt's Islamic movements, told me.

For decades, religion has occupied a kind of awkward twilight in Egypt's sluggish political life, grudgingly accepted but technically illegal. Banned for over fifty years, Muslim Brothers run as independents, with members and campaign workers jailed on charges of belonging to an illegal organization even as their candidates triumph. Support for the Brotherhood is too wide to suppress it entirely, yet the ruling National Democratic Party rightfully fears being supplanted if the Brotherhood could organize legally. Its murky status actually serves both sides. The government can point to Brotherhood activity as evidence that democracy is alive in Egypt, while the Ikhwan can blame any failures on suppression rather than testing its theories in the political marketplace. Avoiding a wholesale challenge to the government helped it endure, but has led to the widespread sense among outsiders that the organization's guiding principle has become self-preservation. The deadlock perpetuates Egypt's political stagnation.

The Brotherhood has outlasted British colonialism, then the monarchy, and then President Gamal Abdel Nasser. The group presents itself as the benign future of Islamic politics—working within the system until voters inevitably conclude that Islamic law holds the prescription for all ills plaguing modern Egypt, not to mention the entire Muslim world. In the words of its often analyzed slogan, reviled by critics as meaningless and celebrated by supporters as a universal truth: "Islam is the solution."

Salah, the journalist, believes that the Brothers are content to bide their time. "They are not in a hurry," he said. "They believe they can achieve their goal in 50 or 60 years when the whole society becomes Brothers and they will end up running the country. But the Muslim Brothers are haunted by their history."

Banna, the founder, organized a paramilitary "Special Apparatus" in 1940, ostensibly to train volunteers to fight in Palestine. Many did, but members were also linked to a series of political assassinations including that of an Egyptian prime minister. Banna himself was shot dead by government gunmen in a revenge attack in 1949, just as the organization reached its peak with 500,000 members. A failed attempt to assassinate Nasser in Alexandria in 1954 led to the Muslim Brothers being banned as a political organization based on religion, with its leaders executed and members interned. Up to 20,000 members languished in jail until President Sadat came to power in the early 1970s. The torture and abject conditions of their internment under Nasser inspired a new brand of Islamic militancy articulated by one imprisoned leader, Sayyid Qutb.

Qutb's 1964 manifesto "Milestones," a screed including the idea that unjust rulers could be considered infidels and hence eliminated, galvanized succeeding generations of Islamic radicals, including Osama bin Laden.

While Nasser busily razed the organization, he also attempted to co-opt its conservative message, gradually widening the presence of religion in everyday life to the extent that now it seems as though every Egyptian juice stand sports some Koranic verse. Trying to become more Islamic than the Islamists has also become a hallmark of all Middle Eastern governments seeking to dilute the appeal of religious opponents. Nasser introduced an all-Koran radio station and religious instruction in the schools, creating classroom segregation for the first time between Muslims and the Coptic Christian minority. President Sadat went further, changing the constitution to read that Islamic law, or Shariah, is the most important inspiration for Egypt's laws. By 1971 Sadat had released thousands of Muslim Brothers, using them as a counterweight to opponents fighting his opening Egypt to Western markets and influence. Ultimately, Islamic militants gunned him down for making peace with Israel.

The Muslim Brotherhood supports violence in the Arab-Israeli conflict, calling it a legitimate means for the Palestinians to throw off the Israeli occupation of Arab lands. They have been ardent supporters of Iraqi attacks on Americans there for the same reason. At the entrance to the Alexandria clubhouse of the Doctors' Syndicate, an organization controlled by the Brotherhood, I found a small kiosk belonging to an Islamic bookseller. Glancing through the offerings for children, I opened a pop-up history of the Palestinian fight against Israeli occupation. The figures include an Israeli soldier being stabbed to death, blood squirting across his uniform. When I asked the Brotherhood members I met whether this was an appropriate lesson for children, the inevitable answer was that Israeli soldiers did far worse. One of the most discouraging aspects I found covering the Arab-Israeli conflict is that the majority on both sides are so willfully blind to the suffering of the other. I often think that one of the most important roles the United States could play would be speaking out more forcefully against any violence committed by either side, to leave no shred of doubt that bloodshed only begets more.

※   ※   ※

I spent another warm afternoon in July 2008 in Alexandria, this time at the waterfront club belonging to the Lawyers' Syndicate, talking with Saleh over a lunch of "kofteh," ground meat cooked around skewers. In the nearly three years since he had won his parliament seat, he had lost some of his hair and gained a paunch. He was uncharacteristically late, but the get-things-done attitude that sets Brotherhood members apart from most Egyptians was immediately apparent. He led me to the club's empty banquet room, where dozens of round tables were covered with imitation red satin tablecloths, all stained and scattered with bits of food. When Saleh objected to the room being such a mess, a veiled waitress protested that the wreckage was left from a wedding only the previous evening. "Yesterday was yesterday!" Saleh yelled, and summoned the club manager to rebuke him. The room soon filled with staff clearing the tables and a waiter pushing a whirring vacuum cleaner.

I wanted to know what he thought about the uproar after the political platform of the Muslim Brotherhood, known for its secretive ways, had leaked into the Egyptian press. Along with an ambiguous position toward the peace treaty with Israel, the most contentious planks were one that proposed specifying that the president be a Muslim male, and a second suggesting that a senior council of religious scholars be created to vet all laws for their consistency with Islam. Leftist Egyptians, not to mention the government, were downright gleeful that the Brotherhood had finally given them such a fat target to prove that the Ikhwan were not quite as democratically benign as they liked to pretend. Members tried to quiet the hue and cry by labeling the leaked document merely a working draft.

Although only a Muslim man will likely serve as president, the current constitution limits the post to Egyptian citizens. Barring everyone but Muslim men was considered a slap in the face to Egypt's 10 percent Coptic Christian minority and a signal of the second-class status Islamic political groups accord to women. None serve in the Brotherhood's hierarchy. Other aspects of the way the Brotherhood ran its own affairs also gave people pause. Although the bylaws state that the General Guide running the organization should be elected every six years, all seven since 1928 have held the position for life. Saleh tried to waive the controversy away. Limiting the presidency to Muslim men was just a reflection of reality, he said, and as religious activists on the defensive often do, he dredged up a comparison with the West. Would I ever ask the pope if he could be succeeded by a woman, Saleh wanted to know, elbowing the friend sitting next to him and winking like he had just scored a major point. In terms of the outcry over establishing a Saudi-style council of religious scholars to hold sway over all laws, Saleh and other Brotherhood members noted that it was unlikely that any such body would be needed because the supreme court already undertook similar vetting.

Nothing got Saleh quite as exercised as the question of Egypt's relations with Israel. He told me that it was galling for Israel to demand that Egypt and Jordan respect their peace treaties, while it continued to flaunt all the agreements and United Nations resolutions mandating self-determination for the Palestinians. His color rose and he started to shout whenever he let rip on the subject: "Israel is an aggressor nation, Israel is killing our brothers, occupying our sacred places, degrading our people, threatening our homeland, treating us with arrogance, flouting international law. It possesses nuclear weapons, it occupies our mosque and our qibla. [The Arabic word means both prayer niche and the direction Muslims turn in prayer. Muslims first prayed toward Jerusalem before the Angel Gabriel is said to have instructed Mohamed to switch the direction toward Mecca.] The problem has to be solved first. Israel has to recognize the rights of the Palestinian people, their rights to the holy sites."

He suggested that if the Muslim Brothers controlled Egypt they would put the peace treaty to a referendum and if the voters rejected it, let the chips fall where they may. Among other issues, he objected to the fact that Israel stirred up the entire world accusing Iran of developing nuclear weapons that don't yet exist, while it developed nuclear warheads and refused to join the nonproliferation treaty.

I tried three or four times to get him to answer the question point-blank whether he thought Egypt could end up at war with Israel again, but he dodged and weaved, hinting that it was possible but refusing to state it outright. If voters reject the treaty in a referendum, he told me, then "Israel has to pay the price. We are not a nation that has no value. They are the ones who always create problems and impasses. There is no war now, but the environment is like a war. Peace is not an obligation on Egypt alone." How to deal with Israel remains a controversial issue even among the Ikhwan themselves. Hard-line members told me that Israel had no place in the region, while moderates stressed that the Brotherhood would respect all of Egypt's international agreements. Saleh seemed to be trying to straddle both positions.

It is just this kind of murky position about how the Brotherhood will achieve its ideals both internationally and domestically that provokes lingering unease. The Brotherhood says that it would not force women to wear the veil, but contends that most women would wear it spontaneously. It would not ban alcohol, but would not want it available to Muslims. It would not enforce Islamic law, but insists most people would recognize its superiority.

Egypt's ruling National Democratic Party paints all Muslim groups as violent extremists. The standard government line is that they "all came from the same womb," i.e., the Muslim Brotherhood, which it accuses of at best surreptitiously encouraging carnage carried out by radical fringe groups. The Brotherhood denies any connection with the likes of Islamic Jihad or Gamaa Al-Islamiyya, arguing that it decided to reject bloodshed decades ago and if members of such organization were once Muslim Brothers, they left because their support for violence was unacceptable. Any shadowy aura the Brotherhood maintains, its leaders say, stems from years of persecution. Members are forced to be secretive because they never know when they lay their heads on the pillow at night whether they will wake up in the same room the next morning.

Saleh has been imprisoned twice, including six months in 2003 for leading street demonstrations against the American invasion of Iraq. Supporters often approach him now after Friday prayers, which he usually attends in his home district, to ask him why the Ikhwan do not encourage government opponents to take to the streets, to try to force the government to change through the sheer force of numbers. Saleh's constituency, called Raml, runs from the seafront apartment houses of the very rich to impoverished agricultural villages just outside Alexandria. Its population of almost 2 million is roughly 40 percent of Alexandria, and he pegged the unemployed at some 250,000.

Saleh cautions against demonstrations. Nonviolent, gradual steps might take longer, but they are ultimately more effective, he argued: "Forming public opinion is more important than leading the society." He continued in that vein for some time, laying out the Brotherhood philosophy that time is its ally as more and more people inevitably rediscover their faith. "I am not looking to use the anger of the people to change the government, but I am seeking to contain the anger of the people within a strategy based on educating them, based on thought, seeking serious change from the base to the top gradually. From reform of the individual to the family to the society and then to the government and public policy, not the other way around."

Political opponents across the region suspect that all Muslim parties will support the idea of elections until they win—the concept of one man, one vote, one time. In other words, once they are a majority they will legislate that laws are made by God, not man, so elections contradict the faith. "They think giving the majority the right to legislate is *haram*, forbidden, because law was written by God and those trying to legislate for themselves are atheists," Rifaat Saeed, an aging warhorse of Egyptian politics who heads the liberal Tagammu Party, told me. "They think there are just two parties in the world, the Party of God and the Party of the Devil. If they are the Party of God, everyone else is the Party of the Devil." Once they achieve power, anyone who opposes them will be tarred as an instrument of the Devil, he said. The head of the Muslim Brotherhood returned the favor by describing Saeed as "corrupt and secular," the latter being the more damning sin in his eyes.

Egypt's authoritarian government has habitually warned critics at home and abroad that it is the finger in the dike holding back the raging sea of radical Islam. At each election cycle, government supporters sound the alarm that the feared day is at hand. "The Mullahs Are Coming!" screamed one headline in the government-controlled *Gomhouriyah* newspaper in 2005, using the title reserved for Iran's tyrannical clergy. Adel Hamouda, a leftist intellectual and the editor of the new independent daily *Al-Fajr*, positively frothed at the very idea of a Muslim Brother parliamentary bloc. "No matter what they claim, their plan to control, which they have been hatching for years, can be summed up in one sentence: Stoop to conquer," he wrote in a screed illustrated with a doctored picture of the head of the Muslim Brothers wearing a Nazi uniform. "They once relied upon secrecy, underground organizations and a militia until they decided to ride the wave of democracy to reach power. Once they do, they will embrace dictatorship, fascism, Nazism; they will say that they are God's deputies, God's in-laws, God's friends, God's

spokesmen and whoever opposes them, differs with them or becomes their enemy will become the enemy of God. They are like
scorpions. No matter how much a scorpion becomes civilized,
prayers, fasts and talks about freedom and democracy, a scorpion
can never change its inherited aggressive nature."

Saleh argued that such fears are groundless: "The logic of violence is of no use because ultimately it does more harm than
good." It was more important to persuade the public to change
over time than to produce immediate results, which he claimed is
how the Ikwhan, despite being banned for decades, became the
only viable alternative to the government. Eventually, when the
people are convinced, cracks will appear in the regime itself reflecting popular discontent and then the whole edifice will crash.
That wait, in a nutshell, is why political analysts across the region
believe that if a reform movement ever coalesces, the Muslim
Brothers won't march at the forefront of it in any country despite
their widespread role at the moment as the primary opposition
faction.

⌐   ⌐   ⌐

In many ways Saleh's path from childhood in a Nile River delta village to representing one of the biggest cities on the Mediterranean
in parliament reflects the modern trajectory of the Muslim Brotherhood. Sent to Alexandria for high school, he was 13 when the
Arabs lost the 1967 war against Israel and he joined the mobs of
youths coursing through the streets to reject President Nasser's offer to resign in the face of the disaster. The adolescent Saleh worshipped the president, memorizing lines from Nasser's famous
oratory, which had given Arabs their first sense of dignity in a post-
colonial world. Indeed, Saleh's own speeches echoed Nasser's defiant tone, using some of the same much-loved phrasing in simple
yet classical Arabic. "Leave peacefully with your own will, before
you are forced to leave; go and never come back!" Saleh said in one
speech, referring to the ruling party, using virtually the same lines

that Nasser hurled at Western colonial powers about taking their hats and canes as they exited.

The most lasting shock for Saleh was the lie broadcast repeatedly on Egyptian state radio in 1967 that the Arabs were decimating the Israeli military. His disillusion was cemented in 1971, a year after Nasser died, when he read *The Return of Consciousness* by renowned writer Tewfik al-Hakim, which depicted Nasser as a sorcerer who created a grand illusion. "I thought we would never kneel, but I woke up to a bitter truth, that Israel occupied one-fifth of our land, that Al-Aqsa Mosque in Jerusalem was lost," said Saleh in describing his transition from Arab nationalist to Muslim Brother. "I felt like all my dignity was gone, I was miserable, I felt pain, rejection, bitterness. I was confused, shocked, reeling, looking for a solution and for something other than Abdel Nasser."

He remembered a night years earlier, in 1965, when five neighbors in his native village had been arrested, part of a national sweep against thousands of suspected Muslim Brothers. Saleh, by now in law school at the University of Alexandria, unearthed the transcripts of their trials and began hearing tales of horrible torture from the Brothers trickling out of jail. That too helped shatter the Nasser myth. The arrested men he knew as devout, sincere, and hard-working, he told me. At that point he joined the organization, deciding that only a return to Islam would rescue the Arabs from their plight.

The Middle East's Islamic resurgence has thriven off the identity crisis that the 1967 rout by Israel spawned across the Arab world. That defeat sounded the tocsin for the demise of Arab nationalism. Islamist theology gradually filled the void. It was a watershed, but the idea of Islamism as a form of government suffers an uneasy co-existence with the idea of modernization. Some Arabs anxiously anticipate that Islamist government would just mean substituting one form of despotism for another, a sense not allayed by Saleh's strict prescriptions for social behavior. I found all kinds of people beginning to recognize that if they needed to subscribe to just one "-ism," it had to be "pluralism." They are ready to embrace that as the next stage.

But not everyone. Saleh is an archetype of the most fervent Brotherhood members forged by that 1967 defeat. The Brotherhood message, combining spiritual salvation with an Islamic political renaissance, exactly captures the middle-class mood, the desire to reestablish a sense of dignity and pride. It is not just a question of politics, but cuts across the chaos that seems to swamp all aspects of life. Professionals like doctors, engineers, lawyers, pharmacists, and junior officials fill the ranks of its membership, and their struggle to maintain a middle-class life ensures the Brotherhood a wide following. Religion is the one factor that provides a sense of homogeneity, something people can respect. Ask members and supporters what they want, and they will invariably tell you that they seek an Egypt (or a Syria, or Palestine or Jordan) free of government corruption, economic monopolies, and Western decadence such as advertising featuring scantily dressed women. I also think their philosophy teaches forbearance. Without the idea that all Muslim countries will eventually come around to God, I expect these societies might have exploded into wider violence long ago.

॰॰॰   ॰॰॰   ॰॰॰

Saleh's positions, echoing the platform of the larger organization, are typically populist. Before one campaign speech of his a series of jingles boomed out of the loudspeakers, one both castigating America for pushing privatization and rebuking the Egyptian security services for using their bullets against the people instead of the Israeli army:

> Our country is in trouble, our regime is slaughtering us.
> I am calling upon the small workers who are robbed by the big middlemen, they will be destroyed by American money. Privatization was a disaster for Egypt.
> I am calling upon the security and the soldiers, why are your hands holding bullets against your brother?

> Save your arms for the army of the Jews, save your
> children from the army of the Jews. We are all children
> of Egypt.

The nationalistic, jingoistic message seemed mostly about fear to me. But to Egyptians feeling under assault by outside forces, it struck a chord. Saleh recommended all manner of Islamic prescriptions for everyday life in Egypt. On tourism, he wanted foreigner visitors segregated to specially designated areas in all resorts so the faithful will not be exposed to debauchery, such as wearing shorts. (Forget about topless Russians!) "Alcohol is *haram* in Islam, indecent nakedness is *haram* in Islam," he said, using the Arabic word that combines the sense of both the sinful and the forbidden. "I don't want to restrict tourism, but there have to be rules." In the summer of 2008, his hero of the moment was the owner of the Grand Hyatt, one of Cairo's most visible hotels dominating the banks of the Nile. The man had announced that he was terminating alcohol sales in the bars, that it would be available only from room service. The government reacted by moving to lift one of the hotel's five stars, taking it out of the luxury category—an action that the Muslim Brotherhood was fighting. "Is consuming liquor a basic right guaranteed by the Egyptian constitution?" Saleh thundered at me.

Saleh liked the idea of a special police force to enforce public morality, although with perhaps less sweeping powers than Saudi Arabia's religious police. He thought anyone who cursed religion on the streets should be arrested (mostly an infraction by battling taxi drivers) as well as spouses caught kissing (not a frequent occurrence).

"In Islam, a man doesn't have the right to kiss his wife in public, unless he was away and just returned, so the law needn't be applied in the airports or train stations," said Saleh, who has three daughters, a son, and at least three grandchildren.

Some of his positions sounded simplistic and rather utopian. There will be no theft in an Islamic state, Saleh avowed, because no one will know want. "Our goal is to establish an Islamic Caliphate," he said, comparing it to a coalition akin to the United States or the European Union: "The leader doesn't have to be religious, but he cannot oppose religion." Egypt should reject any American aid that came with strings attached, Saleh said, and particularly objected to any interference in the content of Egyptian textbooks on cultural issues. U.S. input on technical subjects like physics or chemistry would be acceptable to him.

Some of his campaign lines brought guffaws from the faithful. He avowed that before the Muslims Brothers sit in parliament seats formerly occupied by the ruling party, the furniture will be scrubbed seven times, once with sand—the religious formula for purifying objects fouled by exposure to something Muslims abhor as ritually unclean like dogs. When he got going in a campaign speech about the ruling party, fire and brimstone didn't seem hot enough to describe it: "You will be gone. You will be eradicated. You will go to hell! Down with the National Party. Down with the criminals. Down with thuggery! Down with fraudulent elections! Down with the lies. Down with murdering the people. Down with embezzling the wealth of the people. Down with the thieves!"

The audience, electrified, started chanting "Thieves! Thieves! Thieves!"

Aside from imitating Nasser, Saleh's speeches echoed with Koranic allusions and classic poetry. At one point in the same attack on the ruling party he said, "Pray that whoever tries to rig the election, his hand will be paralyzed!" This was drawn from a Koranic verse that says whoever would harm the believers, their hands will be paralyzed. His emotional vitriol made other candidates and campaign aides onstage so visibly nervous that they felt obliged to interject that he meant only bad members of the ruling party, not the entire lot.

Supporters, asked why they would vote for the Brotherhood, inevitably focused on the abysmal living conditions in their neighborhoods despite years of government promises to fix unpaved streets, overflowing sewage systems, undrinkable water, utter lack of garbage collection, and the like. Saleh and most Muslim Brothers are often the very members of the community who organize neighborhood efforts to treat those nagging ills. In his Raml neighborhood, for example, he helped create a street-cleaning brigade that collected the garbage and paid a minimal wage to the unemployed youths doing the work. He sponsored orphans and helped establish a kind of local health insurance where poorer families paid only 50 percent of their medical costs, richer benefactors covering the difference. During Ramadan, his charitable organization distributed free bags of rice, lentils, oil, dates, and apricot juice.

Not all of the faithful are enamored of the Muslim Brothers, of course; some hardcore types find them too secular—since only God can create laws and the clergy alone can interpret them. "All of this is nonsense," said a heavily bearded shopkeeper in his early 20s whom I met near one rally. He sold religious tapes and other Islamic paraphernalia. "They do nothing. They don't change anything. They just serve to make the whole regime legitimate. Anyone who chases power is not a Muslim; you cannot have a religious party and a political party at the same time. . . . The parliament system contradicts Sharia; the election is a sin; the government is going to hell."

As he surveyed candidates crowding the outdoor stage, the shopkeeper froze when he noticed that all the campaign banners and the stage itself were decorated with pictures of a palm tree, the symbol that the Muslim Brothers were using on the ballot for illiterate voters. "What is that?! An idol?" he said, recoiling in horror at the idea. The campaign songs made it even worse, no matter that they were denouncing America and Israel. "What is this music? If they were Muslims you wouldn't hear this music; no drums, no nothing. Those drums are the instruments of the devil." The tape seller wanted Shariah implemented without question, and supported the notion that a good Muslim leader supports only fellow Muslims and shuns everybody else, a notion that is uniquely strong among the Wahhabi sect in Saudi Arabia. The religious tapes he sold included a heavy selection of sermons by senior Saudi clerics. The man was appalled that the head of the Egyptian Muslim Brothers had appeared on television at that time to express his condolences after Pope John Paul II died. "What are we sorry for? Muslims should not extend their condolences to non-Muslims." He said change had to come from above, from religious scholars who rule, and that the doctors, lawyers, and engineers who make up the core of Brotherhood leaders had no business trying to interpret the way a government should subscribe to Islamic law. "Any political party is going to have to make concessions, and there can be no concessions in religion," he concluded.

One notable difference between the Muslim Brotherhood and other Islamist organizations like Al-Qaeda and Islamic Jihad, is that it started as a political organization. Banna founded the Brotherhood among his peers in a café, not a mosque. He did not dabble in Koranic interpretation. Subsequent groups have been more narrowly inspired by religion—their idea of political change boils down to forcing everyone to accept their version of Islam. They take the Islamic understanding of the oneness of God and kind of extend it all down the line—one God, one leader, one party, and so on, as if multiple parties were some kind of innovation that would wreck the idyllic unity of the society. Indeed, when the Muslim Brotherhood's political platform leaked to the press, even opponents gave the organization high marks for endorsing the idea of an open political process, civil society, and an independent judiciary. The platform said Egypt should be ruled by a democratic system of government with a parliament and a constitution. But naturally there was the usual caveat that made it seem as though the group might be crossing its fingers behind its back. The platform said that any government had to exist within the confines of Islam. It was unclear what that meant.

When I went to see Ibrahim Issa, the combative, impish editor of *Al-Doustour* weekly, he told me that the Brotherhood served as a useful foil for Egypt's authoritarian regime. The Brotherhood was the government's main bogeyman, he explained. "It's like you say to children 'The Ikhwan are coming, the Ikhwan are coming to get you.' It does that so we accept political despotism." The editor found a certain irony in the government predicting dire consequences from the Muslim Brothers gaining more political clout.

"The government keeps saying the Brothers will destroy the country, as if the ruling party hasn't destroyed it already," said Issa, a youthful, husky man with black curly hair and a ready laugh. Issa was constantly being hauled into court and accused of slandering the government on the pages of his newspaper, but one thing I especially liked and admired about him was that he never tempered his humorous, barbed remarks one iota, even when he knew they might help to land him in jail. When he ran out of appeals in late 2008 and was finally sentenced to two months in prison, President Mubarak pardoned him. Typically, while expressing gratitude for the pardon, Issa castigated the government for all the restrictions on the press that led to the court case in the first place.

When Egyptians voted for the Brotherhood, it was because they wanted to plant "a dagger in the back of the regime," Issa told me. What is unclear is what chunk of their support can be attributed to a protest vote and how much comes from true believers, but the group had no tangible impact on reform between their parliamentary election victories in 2005 and 2008, he noted. "Their influence in actually legislating was zero," he said. "They did not succeed in changing a word, never mind an article or a law." If they had any influence, he said, it was a negative factor in egging on ruling party members who went on the attack against art or other social matters regarding moral turpitude, like raising questions about the appearance of Dina, a renowned belly dancer, at a high school graduation party.

While I was living in Egypt, parliament members from the Brotherhood attacked any attempt at economic cooperation with Israel, including a deal to sell it natural gas; suggested prisoners be granted monthly conjugal visits to cut down on homosexuality; introduced a law that would mandate lashing for drunkenness; and vociferously attacked the Ministry of Culture for sponsoring a series of novels containing explicit sex and "lewd" language.

"The Arab world has not contributed anything in terms of modern achievements, so it's easy to resort to religion to preserve our identity and to pretend that we have something different," said

Hala Mustapha, an expert on democracy issues at the Al-Ahram Center for Political and Strategic Studies. "But with the Muslim Brothers or any theocratic movement we risk losing the last freedoms we have when it comes to any innovative work in literature, novels, women, and education."

(It was probably too much to expect any kind of change to emerge from the People's Assembly anyway. It was generally a sleepy place seen as a printing machine for any legislation that the president demanded. Egyptians are apathetic about the place. In fact, political apathy, although common throughout the world, is rampant in the Middle East because people sense that their participation will have so little effect. It is one of the challenges in trying to bring political change because so few people feel motivated to try—elections in Egypt brought out only about one-quarter of the eligible voters.)

On a deeper level, the conservatives who control the Ikhwan and set its political agenda are just more comfortable appealing to their supporters through social issues rather than facing the unknown consequences of going out on a limb for reform. "The Ikhwan is not the group that will create reform, they will only begin to agitate after it happens," Issa predicted, summing up the standstill that characterized politics in Egypt. "At the moment, those with the ideas don't have the ability, and those with the ability don't have the desire." No one figure has emerged around whom reformers could coalesce, he said, and given all the laws restricting political debate, it was unlikely one could. He predicted that an energized reform movement would have to be led either by activist judges or by something that emerged from the mushrooming amount of political protest online. Political parties just lack sufficient dynamism.

Muslim Brotherhood activists arrived relatively late in the Egyptian blogosphere compared to their liberal peers, starting only around 2006. But their voices have provided an unusual window into the workings of the party, not least by indicating that the Ikhwan are not quite the monolith that everyone feared. In fact, the extensive debate among Brotherhood members online about the platform prompted party elders to demand that it stop, accusing the bloggers of giving both the ruling party and the press the means to blacken the organization's reputation and to try to exploit differences.

I met Abdelmonem Mahmoud and Magid Saad, two of the most-read Muslim Brotherhood bloggers, on a visit to Cairo in 2008. Both told me that they were drawn to creating their online diaries because they felt the mainstream media boycotted younger Brotherhood voices, and both wanted to fight the stereotype that all Ikhwan were rigid religious puritans. "Blogging at least shows that there is a generation out there who wants change," said Mahmoud, a 29-year-old lawyer. He was criticized within his organization for daring to write in support of a secular (shudder) blogger who attacked the government online. The second blogger I met, Saad, born in 1978 and working as a real-estate manager, wrote a posting entitled "Teach Yourself Rebellion and How to Hurl Stones" about the need for activism in Egypt. "We need to rebel against all stagnant situations—hurling stones moves stagnant water—not surrender to the inherited molds," he told me over a glass of mango juice in the garden of a Cairo hotel. Blogging is a way to show that the Ikhwan do not fit into molds, he said. Both men used their blogs to discuss movies and music, not typical activities for devout Muslims, and Mahmoud said he thought Brotherhood teaching had become more puritanical than religious texts suggest is necessary. Saad detailed his own personal turmoil at being rejected by the family of a potential fiancée because his Brotherhood activities meant he had a police record.

Both men discussed through their blogs their ideas for changing the Brotherhood slogan, "Islam Is the Solution," as too vague. Mahmoud wanted "Together for Reform," while Saad suggested "Reform and Freedom." The old slogan represents "the status quo, whereas what is required is another slogan that attracts people," he said. Airing those thoughts also attracted rebuke from the conservative leadership. Saleh, the Brotherhood parliament deputy, supported the bloggers as a good means to circumvent the limits on freedom of expression in Egypt, although he told me that he doubted the blogosphere will mobilize members.

There is no question that people have become more daring in challenging the government and that the Internet spurs such efforts. When a van driver was sodomized with a broomstick in a local police station, the cell phone video of the torture circulated so quickly that the government was forced to respond. The two guilty officers received three-year jail sentences in late 2007. This kind of exposure was 100 times more effective than scores of human rights reports, activists told me. Young liberal activists have been particularly deft in using online communities like Facebook, which has an estimated 2 million members in Egypt, to drum up support for reform. The most telling example was a nationwide strike on April 6, 2008, called for by a group of young activists via a Facebook group. It attracted tens of thousands of members who then spread the message nationwide. Egyptian friends told me later that the strike was more successful than anyone could have dreamed, at least in Cairo, where the normally chaotic, clogged downtown streets were almost empty. The informal alliance between student activists and factory workers panicked the regime, since it presented a serious challenge if it cemented into a national movement. The government threatened to punish anyone who didn't come to work that day to little avail. Basically any sign of effective opposition, no matter how small, alarms the government. Ayman Nour, a not entirely sympathetic member of parliament who had once been a government supporter, ended up in jail for five years on charges of forging paperwork in his protracted fight to win approval for a new party, Al-Ghad. But his real crime was having the temerity to win more than 7 percent of the vote in the 2005 presidential campaign, coming in a distant second to Mubarak. His treatment effectively intimidated others who might consider a similar effort.

U.S. attempts to free Nour were not particularly coherent. Direct appeals from President Bush and Secretary Rice, though infrequent, made the government and the security services dig in their heels, decrying the attempt by foreigners to interfere in Egypt's internal affairs. Indirect statements about not seeking revenge on political opponents would have been a better, and more discreet, means to keep the pressure on. Even Brotherhood bloggers liked the idea of Washington voicing support for free speech on the Web and other political freedoms, feeling the Egyptian government would not change without such pressure. Evidently success by the Muslim Brothers, whether in Egypt or elsewhere, puts the American government in a bit of a bind. The Brothers are not inherently anti-American, but their vociferous criticism of U.S. policy in the Middle East helps propel their popularity because so many Arabs feel the same way. The Bush administration declared that it would not interact with the group for various reasons, but simultaneously said it sought democratic evolution in the Arab world. Pushing democracy while simultaneously boycotting the main opposition faction seems like planting one leg on each side of a widening chasm. After Hamas won the Gaza elections, Bush administration officials ended up expressing consternation at the outcome while saying they supported the democratic process. It was an easily misunderstood response, and was duly perceived as the Americans supporting democracy only when their allies win.

Gamal al-Banna, the youngest brother of the Brotherhood's founder, was still a prolific writer and thinker at age 85, when I last spoke to him in 2005. He had become a tireless defender of the most moderate interpretation of Islam, often reviled by official clergy and even the government when it sought to prove its Islamic credentials. He also maintained an uneasy relationship with the leadership of the Brotherhood, his contemporaries, because he spoke out against some of the more radical positions they adopted when he thought they strayed from the path his brother intended. Gamal liked to point out that his brother founded the organization when Egypt had a more robust parliamentary system, and accepted that the Muslim Brotherhood had to work under that system. "He did not push for a theocracy, but a democratic government which applied the lessons from the Koran about good governance, consultation, and no dictatorship," he told me. "It was a call for spiritual and moral guidance." Gamal basically dismissed the religious idea that the era of Prophet Mohamed provided a viable model for a modern government. "Their spirit is not the spirit of the age, they want to live as the Prophet lived," Banna told me, practically invisible in a dark apartment filled with some 16,000 books in a no longer grand Cairo neighborhood. "The real test of the Brothers is to let them enter politics. They will be in a different situation when they confront the necessities of ruling and there are only two solutions. They will have to compromise or fail."

⌐⌐⌐

I share Banna's misgivings about any experiment when it comes to religious parties—maybe there is just something inherently American and Western about believing in the separation of religion and the state. I am not suggesting that religious parties should be banned, nor should they be brandished as a threat, providing the excuse for despotic rulers to hang on to power forever as if religious despotism is somehow worse than their own. Instead, the reform needed is to level the playing field so that all parties and organizations can compete equally. Most governments in the region have stalled for decades on opening up their societies, hiding behind the excuse that they were at war to liberate Palestine. President Nasser started it all, of course, as with so much bad governance that plagues the region. He said no voice can rise higher than the liberation battle. But decades later, Arab regimes have neither liberated Palestine nor implemented reform. Now the excuse du jour is that opening the political process would allow religious despots to hijack the region, as has happened in Gaza. If the Muslim Brotherhood parties enjoy popular support, that can be partly attributed to the fact that the general population wants clean government and effective services, which they think they will get from politicians guided by religious principles. But if the entire political process was more vibrant, more people would participate, which would dilute the influence of any one group. The former Jordanian deputy prime minister, Marwan Muasher—among my favorite senior Arab officials, not least because he would answer questions by cell phone text message when he was locked behind closed doors during interminable Arab summit meetings—studied in some detail the means of opening up the political process in Jordan. That reform agenda was stillborn, endorsed by King Abdullah but not implemented. The proposals, outlined in his book *The Arab Center*, included reserving a number of seats in parliament for nonreligious parties, say 10 percent, which would nourish the growth of new parties. He also suggested that religious parties be allowed to participate openly, but must be held to a commitment to respect diversity and not bear arms. Hizbollah has been able to assert its predominance in Lebanon likely beyond its actual level of support because the Party of God fields a militia, for example. Building viable parties is obviously a gradual process. But the main point is that moving from no political life to full-blown democracy by making elections the first step seems to be a recipe for disaster in societies where civic life has been strangled. Muasher's argument is that the law can be used for a time to foster the kind of pluralism absent after decades when all political activity was suspect.

There are times when Egyptians run out of patience, when their sense of humor that helps them cope with their difficult lives evaporates and they erupt into an orgy of rioting. It happened once in the mid-1980s, when the lowest rung of soldiers, angry about their low pay, rampaged through the tourist district out by the Pyramids, burning hotels. Sometimes I think some cataclysmic event will provoke widespread riots and topple the ruling party. But no matter how it unfolds, two thoughts often temper my ideas about reform in Egypt.

First, my friend Ateyyat al-Abnoudy, a documentary filmmaker, cautioned me against thinking that reform will ever transform the country into something other than what its long history dictates. Throughout thousands of years, Egypt has been under the control of a strong central government, and to expect anything radically different is to try to fool history, she argued. Although Egypt had a brief flirtation with parliamentary democracy before the 1952 revolution, with more than twenty active parties under the auspices of British colonial influence, the system did not last. President Nasser and his fellow officers replaced it with a military dictatorship, which has been the model not just for Egypt but for much of the Arab world ever since. If President Mubarak tweaked the system at all during his more than quarter-century in power, it was to remove any senior military officer who gained sufficient public stature to make Egyptians consider the guy presidential material. The question is whether the system of anointing one commander to serve as president will continue once Mubarak is gone, or some kind of open election replaces it. No matter who you talk to about reform in Egypt, everyone basically concedes that change, if it comes, will come only after Mubarak. Having run the country since 1981, he seems to have convinced himself that he alone among 70 million Egyptians is capable of ruling. (A cab driver speculated that he stayed alive and hence in office for so long because he squeezed old mummies in the Egyptian museum into juice and drank it daily.) If thousands of years of history are any guide, the system will likely always center on one strong figure.

Second, whenever I start thinking about Egypt, I always remind myself of a brief description of the country from the book *Personal Narrative of a Pilgrimage to Al Madinah and Mecca* by Richard F. Burton, the storied nineteenth-century British explorer. In one of his initial diary entries, written as he was making his way from Alexandria to Cairo in 1853, he found Egypt caught in a kind of twilight. "The land of the Pharaohs is becoming civilized, and unpleasantly so: Nothing can be more uncomfortable than its present middle state, between barbarism and the reverse." That description, too often, still holds true.

CHAPTER 13

ARRESTED DEVELOPMENT

"The beating heart of Arabism."

I FACED A BIT OF A QUANDARY whenever the police started to cart off my photographer in the midst of some churning story. More often than not, intervening only served to get me arrested too— but at least the photographer had an ally along. Naturally, being arrested put a rather significant damper on reporting the story. But the other choice was really only a question of timing. Before stepping forward I would try to call some senior official first, hoping the photographer would not be whisked away instantly. Then someone knew we were in custody and could hopefully gain our release.

One such incident erupted in downtown Damascus at the so-called parliament—an ornate structure inspired by classical Islamic architecture—where I was covering the first independent street protest in living memory. In March 2004, a small band of rashly brave demonstrators gathered to demand an end to the draconian emergency laws in place since 1963. (Traditionally in Syria demonstrations are a government monopoly, with participants required to return the signs and banners afterwards so they could be used again.) The protest had barely started when the voice of Mohamed el-Dakhakhny, my Egyptian photographer, sailed over the crowd: "Neil, Neil! Help! They are arresting me! They are beating me and trying to take my cameras!" I turned to see a policeman hitting his legs with a small truncheon as he was hustled into the rear of a station wagon. As a foreigner in the Arab world—at least the Arab world outside Iraq—I still had a certain insurance that things would turn out fine. It was more annoying than scary. But in this case, I knew I had to act especially fast because Dakhakhny was an Arab, and risked being treated far worse than any Western journalist.

As I darted through the throng toward the police car, I suddenly recalled the fate of Nick Ludington, my first Mideast bureau chief when I worked for The Associated Press. Ludington had been reporting from Damascus in 1974 when a car bomb exploded. A Beirut newspaper, rather than risk antagonizing the regime by having its own reporter write the story, played up the instability next door by printing Ludington's story under a banner headline: "The Associated Press Reports: Bomb in Damascus!" Ludington was arrested and it took several days to figure out who held him—given the dozen overlapping security agencies, each with its own jails, the search required more than a few phone calls. Fortunately for him, an American senator visiting with a U.S. delegation intervened with then-President Hafez Assad to get him released.

Remembering Ludington's ordeal, I headed into a far alley to telephone Buthaina Shaaban, the lone Syrian official open enough to always take my calls. The alley was empty as I entered, but I had barely put the phone to my ear before I was encircled. My cell phone was yanked away along with the two notebooks tucked into the back of my pants. I should have realized that with about 400 alleged demonstrators on the street, maybe 25 of them real opposition figures and the rest plainclothes secret police agents, the idea of making a discrete phone call was laughable. As a uniformed policeman shoved my head down to push me into the back seat of a squad car, an authentic opposition member swerved out of the mob momentarily and attempted to warn him off: "You know that is the correspondent who interviewed his Excellency the president a few months ago," he hissed. (This was true!)

"Yah? Well the president told me to arrest him!" the cop retorted, pushing me farther into the back seat and then climbing in on top of me. It was about a ten-minute ride to the precinct, where three officers marched me into the building, one on each side and a third pushing from the back. As we entered, another policeman swung open the cage-like iron door leading downstairs to the cells and I groaned inwardly, "Oh no, here we go." Ludington had described his days in prison. He was thrown in among a bunch of Palestinian activists jailed incommunicado for years. (Syria, like most Arab states, prefers its Palestinians servile.) He expected to be freed at some point, however, so Ludington allowed them to write messages to their families in ink on the red silk lining of his brown tweed jacket. When he was sprung after a few days, he turned the jacket over to a Palestinian official. The families were overjoyed; they had long since given up on the disappeared men as dead. As the jail door loomed, I doubted I was going to be able to provide any such service—I wasn't wearing anything lined with red silk or silk of any kind, for that matter. Fortunately the cops veered away from the dungeon and led me up a short flight of stairs to the office of the colonel in charge.

After a few minutes sitting there in silence, the door opened and Dakhakhny was marched in. Relief washed over his face when he saw me and he began berating his captors, complaining that they had bruised his legs. "Mohamed!" I said sharply in English. "I was arrested too, so why don't you wait until we can explain what we were doing." Surprised, he stopped talking. After a while, the colonel turned to us to ask a few questions. We answered honestly without mentioning the word "opposition" and after he left the room for a bit, he came back and ordered tea for everyone. Tea was a good sign. Tea meant we were his guests. The cells no longer loomed. Dakhakhny knew it too, and rather more optimistic or perhaps reckless than me, he turned on the officer sitting next to him and said in Arabic, "You know, it's backwards to arrest foreign journalists. It's going to ruin your reputation on human rights, on democracy, it's really bad for your image. You must not. . . . "

"Mohamed!" I barked this time, wanting to jump up and wring his neck to choke off whatever words might come next. "Stop! We're not outta here yet, we've only gotten to the tea stage. Nobody has said we can leave." It took another twenty minutes before that happened. I got my cell phone back. The officer promised to re-trieve my notebooks—a week's worth of reporting—but I never saw them again. Still, it was always a relief when something poten-tially nasty turned into a short diversion.

Syrian activists had expected a different reality with the ascen-sion of Bashar al-Assad to the presidency, but they proved sadly mistaken. In Syria and in every country where a young leader suc-ceeded his father—including Jordan, Bahrain, and Morocco—the generational switch ushered in high hopes among many locals and the foreigners paying attention that the new ruler would prove more enlightened. There was no solid foundation for this. I think part of it was that people desperate for signs of change were willing to grasp at any straw, including the notion that being exposed to Western democratic ways while studying abroad would somehow translate into the young leaders wanting to implement democracy at home.

President Assad had sent expectations for a different Syria into cartwheels with his inaugural speech in July 2000, when he talked about the need for new ideas, for transparency, for constructive criticism and democracy. Sure, his delivery was beyond wooden— pedantic even. But it certainly sounded like a prescription for change, for loosening the choke hold of Baath Party rule. "Society will not develop, improve or prosper if it were to depend only on one sect or one party or one group; rather, it has to depend on the work of all citizens in the entire society," he said. He called for a "brave dialogue . . . in which we reveal our points of weakness and talk about customs, traditions and concepts which have become a true impediment in the way of any progress."

When he got to the part about democratic thinking, the young president said, "This thinking is based on the principle of accepting the opinion of the other and this is certainly a two-way street." He went on to endorse the rule of law as the best guarantee for freedom.

Beyond the speech, Bashar's biography reinforced expectations that a young man, born in 1965, well-educated and raised with some exposure to the larger world, would be different from his suspicious peasant father. Hafez al-Assad had joined the military to claw his way out of rural poverty and in many ways ran the country like a village chieftain on a grand scale. The new president spoke English! He had studied medicine in England for nine months. He married an attractive young woman of Syrian origin who had worked in an American bank. By becoming chairman of the Syrian Computer Society, he had brought the Internet to Syria at a time when fax machines were not freely available. How could modernization not occur?

"Everyone was waiting for the change when the father died and the son came to power," Usama Mohamed, a dissident filmmaker with a stocky build and long curly hair, told me over Arabic coffee in the Rawda Café. The café served as a kind of unofficial downtown Damascus headquarters for disaffected Syrian intellectuals. A veil of smoke from dozens of hookah pipes hovered over the small, square white marble tables and rattan chairs, filling the room with the slightly sticky smell of apple-infused tobacco. (I loathed the stuff.) A gurgling fountain in the café's tented back courtyard along with dice and backgammon pieces being slapped on wooden boards merged into an arrhythmic background clatter to many of the conversations I had about change in Syria; a disjointed sound track for a disjointed effort.

Around the country, Bashar's inaugural speech inspired a burst of evening discussion forums, where students, intellectuals, and activists met to debate Syria's future and to sharply criticize its past. When I first pitched up in Damascus as the *Times* correspondent in the winter of 2001, people were clambering for seats at events that on the surface seemed a tad dry—like the planning minister addressing the Syrian Society for Economic Science on the subject of fiscal reform. It was not the speech but the debate afterward that packed the auditorium and inspired another 100 people to stand for three hours. The audience listened intently, leaning forward as critics repeatedly flayed the government as a clunky, corrupt pack of scheming fossils. "We have no transparency, no exact monetary figures, no accountability!" Riad Seif, a burly, chain-smoking parliament member with unruly salt-and-pepper hair bellowed into the microphone to cheers from the crowd. "We don't have any development. We don't have dialogue. We don't have strong institutions. We have no anti-corruption campaign."

That giddy sense that everything was up for debate did not last, sadly. Going over the inaugural speech again after the Syrian government reverted to its characteristic oppression, I spied the grand caveat that almost everyone glossed over at the time, so convinced that a new generation meant a new way of thinking. In talking about the challenges ahead, the young president said, "These tasks are very easy because the great leader, Hafez al-Assad, has prepared for us a firm ground, solid basis and a great heritage of values and principles which he defended and adhered to till he parted with us and moved to the afterlife. The political strategy which he put and supervised both its implementation and development proved a great success until this very day."

Indeed Bashar has followed that blueprint with increasing zeal. In July 2000, for example, he ran unopposed in a referendum on who should succeed his father, winning more than 97 percent of the vote. In 2007, on the next such referendum, an empty exercise by which the regime pretends to prove its "democratic credentials," the government said he won a mandate for another seven-year term with 97.62 percent. On my first trip, I had asked a senior Syrian official what he thought of the son, and in his effusive, exaggerated praise, he likely came closer to the mark than I could have guessed at the time. "It seems that every minute he spent with his father was an hour," the man told me.

The "Damascus Spring" quickly chilled into the "Damascus Winter." Forums were ordered to apply for permits with a list of speakers, guests, and the topic of discussion to be presented to the police beforehand, effectively shuttering them. The Syrians most outspoken about the need for change, like Seif, all disappeared into jail. A few saw it coming. Not everyone had been seduced by the idea that a younger generation with a little exposure to the West would somehow automatically be different. When I asked one prescient American ambassador with long experience in the Arab world whether Bashar had any democratic leanings, he told me with a cynicism that Syrians soon adopted, "He's an ophthalmologist. While in the West, Bashar learned a lot about eye diseases and not much else."

I found fewer activists willing to talk every time I went back. I called the grandfather of all Syrian dissidents, Riad al-Turk, a man who spent decades in Syrian prison for criticizing the government, including all the years from 1980 to 1998. I asked him about the mistaken idea that generational change was a synonym for political reform. "There was an illusion among people that the young sons would do something new," he said, speaking not just about Syria but the entire region. "The important thing is for the policy to be young, regardless of the age of the president. These young leaders inherit a regime and Bashar is a the son of this regime," he said, adding, "He got the position by the will of his father and the will of the men around him." The rubber-stamp parliament even altered the constitution, dropping the minimum age of the president from 40 to 34, which conveniently happened to be Bashar's exact age. When such criticism of Bashar appeared in the *Times*, Ms. Shaaban, a presidential advisor, chided me for quoting such an old warhorse. "Riad Turk, is that the best you could do?" she mocked.

I got the chance to ask the young president why all his most prominent critics were in jail when I interviewed him at the end of

2003. His answers to these kinds of questions over the years have remained doggedly similar, although he has since launched sharper attacks against imprisoned dissidents as traitors in thrall to foreign powers. Bashar was particularly elusive when he first came to power, so after much lobbying I was thrilled to land his first lengthy, wide-ranging interview with a Western correspondent based in the region. The interview was evidently for the paper and not for me—granted only on condition that Bill Keller, the executive editor of the Times, come to Damascus from New York for it. Among the many reasons that the Arabs suffer terrible public relations in the West is that their leaders consider talking to the foreign correspondents based in the region as beneath their dignity—thus wasting an enormously easy route to circulating their opinions. The prestige of having someone fly in from the States flatters their vanity, which they value far more than effectively arguing the Arab position.

Our meeting took place in a small sandstone villa perched off by itself in a copse of trees on Mount Kassioun, overlooking Damascus. The president's private office is decorated with a couple black-leather couches and equestrian art inherited from the older brother whose death propelled him into the presidency. When we got around to domestic politics, he objected to my calling the jailed men his most prominent critics, saying, "If you go down to the street now, you will probably see more prominent speakers than them. People in the street criticize everything. If we are putting in prison anyone who criticizes us, I don't think our prisons would be enough. Everybody criticizes in Syria. As I told you a little while ago, anything that would harm our security or national identity is against our law and that will be punished." He also said that such criticism weakened the country. The truth, as several dissidents had pointed out to me before they were imprisoned, was that airing all the musty problems under the Baath could only serve to improve and strengthen Syria.

Asking the president about the pace of reform, I pointed out that the lively discussions I had once witnessed in Damascus were all silenced. He responded by saying I should go visit the forum founded by Jamal al-Atassi, and there were "many others" whose addresses he would provide if needed. There weren't any. I had looked hard. I didn't know whether he was ill-informed or trying to snow me. The Atassi forum had been around for years, tolerated because its founder had once been an ally of Hafez al-Assad, but eventually the government extinguished it too, after a participant read out a letter about political change from the exiled leader of the banned Muslim Brotherhood. Joining it remains such a heinous crime that Article 49 of the Syrian constitution mandates the death penalty for membership.

Ultimately, Bashar polished the answer to the dissident question by saying that Syria was a multiethnic, multicultural society with strict laws barring any kind of discussion that might ignite strife. In his interview with the *Times* he said, "The people who commit mistakes about the issues I have just mentioned go to jail. I didn't issue this law. It is a very old law in Syria. It has been since the independence. So it is not an issue of democracy. It is an issue of the security of the country."

He repeated the same idea more forcefully when speaking with Al-Jazeera satellite television in Paris in 2008. The interviewer politely but sharply questioned the claim that all the jailed dissidents were somehow traitors, pointing out that many had argued publicly that any political change had to be effected by Syrians themselves. The president called the issue of reform, including the arrests, a domestic matter in which no other country should interfere. He said dissidents who approached any foreign power for support transformed the issue into something subversive and illegal. "We have laws in Syria which are strict," he said, shaking his finger like a stern schoolteacher. "You can't talk about sectarianism; you can't talk about anything that threatens national unity, any nationalist or other issues; you can't deal with a foreign body that directly works against your country. These issues are crystal clear in the Syrian law, a strict law, yes, to preserve national unity and we apply the law strictly in practice. As for holding dialogue, we talk with everybody without exception." The Jazeera interviewer didn't buy it, suggesting that Syrians should be allowed to express their opinions. "The issue has nothing to do with opinion, it is a matter of law," the president retorted sharply. It is clear why discussing sectarianism is banned, of course. Bashar belongs to an Alawite minority that wrested power from the Sunnis who once considered them fit only to be servants. Strict Sunnis even consider them heretics.

However, in some ways I found Syria more relaxed than in previous decades, if nowhere near the kind of open society that fueled dissident dreams. As a foreign correspondent, I was much freer to wander around without a government minder, something impossible when I first started reporting there in the late 1980s. A minder shadowed me on one of my first trips to Qunaitra, a city on the edge of the Golan Heights lost to Israel in the 1967 war but returned under the 1974 cease-fire terms. Syria kept it in ruins as its monument to Israeli perfidy, busing in tourists from around the region to visit the bullet-pocked hospital and various dynamited relics. My visit came at one of those moments when Syrian-Israeli peace talks appeared imminent, so I asked a waiter what solution he thought possible over the embattled Golan.

From the restaurant abutting the barbed wire of the cease-fire line, I could look up to see the very top of the mountain where I had gone skiing on the Israeli side. It struck me once more how the region was ridiculously small. Before the era of wars and tight borders and visas, it was relatively easy to travel in a single day by taxi from Damascus to Beirut to Jerusalem to Amman and back to Damascus again. No longer. Now the quarrels over territory stirred bitter hatreds inversely proportional to the short distances involved. But the waiter surprised me. I was pretty sure he responded, "There will be concessions from the Israeli side and concessions from our side and then we will make peace." I was startled by the use of the word "tanazulat" or concessions, because it was not a concept most Arabs and particularly Syrians had embraced publicly in the early 1990s. I thought perhaps I had misunderstood, so I called my Ministry of Information minder over and asked him to translate the sentence. He listened to the waiter intently and then turned to me and said, "He said Israel must return all of the Golan Heights to its rightful owners, the Syrians." That was the government position, the Holy Grail of Syrian foreign policy. Fortunately I had recorded the waiter, so when I got back to Damascus I confirmed that my original understanding was indeed correct. It was just one man, but his more flexible attitude was an affirmation that Syria's despotic government used its unflinching position over the return of the Golan as much to justify its own repression as anything else. Syrians were tired of the conflict. Keeping the country in a protracted state of war, in name if not in practice, gave the government a convenient excuse to maintain its repressive ways.

When asked about repression in Syria, Bashar often pointed out that he has released hundreds of prisoners jailed for opposing the government in the 1980s, while those recently imprisoned are in the "tens." But dissidents note a key strategic shift. Under Hafez al-Assad, security agents jailed all opponents in broad, sweeping drag-nets. Arrests under his son are more selective, targeting the most influential leaders whose extended incarceration decapitated any budding opposition. "The arrests are qualitative, not quantitative, not like in the past," Omar Amiralay, a dissident documentary film-maker, told me in the summer of 2008. "It works. It intimidates everybody else. Years of oppression have destroyed any basis for the opposition."

Amiralay's colleague, Usama Mohamed, had said that soon after Bashar's inauguration, critics recognized the yawning gap between the government's understanding of reform and their own. "The regime said yes, we talked about the rights of the other, but not like that. You have the right to express your opinion, but on the condition that you repeat my opinion," he told me, smiling bitterly. Real change would have required a thorough examination of what went wrong in the past, of how Hafez al-Assad created a dictatorship. In Bashar's early years as president, Syrian dissidents preferred not to focus too closely on how the new president got the job and re-tained hard-line stalwarts from his father's regime. But they came to realize that the son could not stomach a wholesale critique of everything his father had done during thirty years in power; he would not be the heir who tarnished the family legacy. Bashar habitually blamed the slow crawl of reform on the lack of well-trained cadres needed to implement change.

Given how strongly the regime is entrenched, real change requires a complete shift in tactics, Mohamed believed. But I found his work, particularly his two most famous movies, symptomatic of the too subtle, overly cerebral attempts at pushing reform. The films were government-funded, and the script had to be approved in advance, part of the uneasy dance that the regime carried out with its mostly intellectual critics. They despise the government, yet they live off it. Mohamed's dark comedy, *Stars in Broad Daylight* (1988), examined the corrosive violence inside one family, with the actor playing its tyrannical patriarch resembling the late president so much that the metaphor was not lost on anybody. The dialogue was packed with understated digs at the regime too. In public, for example, Syrians will not refer to any member of the ruling Alawite minority by the sect's name, lest someone from the secret police be eavesdropping. In fact, Alawites are so pervasive in the secret police that many Syrians stopped by an officer will try to speak Arabic in the rural Alawite accent in hopes of gaining sympathy. The standard euphemism in public for an Alawite is "German." In *Stars*, one character mentions questions raised surrounding the nationality of a proposed minister returning from living abroad. "Why, is he German?" another character asks. It was a huge laugh line given the Alawite dominance of government positions. Naturally the film was banned in Syria, although widely available on illicit videos and then DVDs.

Dissidents like Mohamed recognized that all attempts to change the regime were mere pinpricks, while an entire cultural shift was required. "It is not enough just to insult the regime every time, to call it a dictatorship and to sign petitions," he told me after screening a couple of his films. "The real work is to create a new culture, a culture of freedom of expression. If we had this, Hafez Assad could not have stayed for forty years. We thought Bashar could change something, but he was just one person. The culture was not there."

Mohamed and others like him believe this shift can succeed because democratic life existed once, before military regimes set in like a viral rash and filled the jails with political prisoners. Most Syrian dissidents got around to telling me that circa 1954 Syria had an elected president, numerous parties, and a substantial parliament. Democracy is hardly the current priority for most citizens, though. In Syria, as in much of the Arab world, most people worry about poverty and unemployment, and when they talk about reform, they usually mean curbing rampant corruption. Bribery underpins every single commercial transaction requiring permits, from opening a restaurant to using a delivery van. By some estimates those bribes add 20 percent to the cost of doing business in Syria. As a correspondent, I viewed corruption as a local story, cases rarely rising to the level requiring coverage. Hence one point that probably does not come across strongly enough to outsiders is the reason that reformers lack popular resonance. Their issues of political freedom and transparency seem rather abstract to ordinary people who just want a little job security and to avoid having to bribe their way through every petty government transaction.

I was as guilty as most foreign correspondents in getting caught on the treadmill of interviewing dissidents, diplomats, and government officials while neglecting encounters with ordinary citizens. Time was always a factor, plus many Arabs tend to be suspicious of outsiders and would give me pallid, rote answers about the wonders of their country that I could never use. But occasionally I would find a little window into the society that reminded me how important it was to get off that treadmill as often as possible. One night on my occasional rounds through downtown Damascus cafés, I happened to share a table with a Baath Party official, a 42-year-old engineer from the provinces wearing a somber coat and tie. We fell into a conversation about domestic ripples in Syria from Iraq. With no prompting he told me that the Syrian Baath party had become an empty shell, and that everyone was working so hard just to put food on the table that they could not worry about much else. "The most important thing here is corruption, we want to put an end to this," he confided. "The party is fragile because many of its members only joined for personal reasons; the fragility comes from this corruption." In his local community, he said, a schoolteacher was fired because he refused to accept bribes from students, nor would he pay his superiors to maintain his position. "When those in authority see a good man trying to make improvements, they crush him," the junior official told me.

I met Omar Amiralay in 2004, just as he was completing a documentary film called *A Flood in Baath Country*. It featured a remote Syrian village called Al-Mashi on the shores of Lake Assad. His stark portrait of the daily routine in a village schoolhouse, where the headmaster also ran the local branch of the Baath Party, brought home the crushing effect of the country's despotic system. In one scene, freshly scrubbed pupils stood three to a desk in pressed khaki uniforms, singing in praise of their country's president and the ruling party. "We the Vanguards of fire and light, salute our leader, Bashar, let all the world hear us," they sang, the words blurring as each child strained to exhibit the most zeal. "We are the voice of the proletariat," they went on. "In sacrifice, we scarcely eat." They did it all by rote, without any conviction or sign of emotion. The headmaster allowed that the uniforms were inspired by a visit Hafez Assad took to North Korea.

Saddam's fall inspired Amiralay to poke his camera into the schoolhouse to illustrate the grim process of an authoritarian state programming young minds. "When you see one of the two Baath parties broken, collapsing, you can only hope that it will be the turn of the Syrian Baath next," Amiralay told me. "The myth of having to live under despots for eternity collapsed." Needless to say, his documentary was officially banned and the Syrian government tried to prevent its screening at Arab film festivals.

In 1970, Amiralay had returned to Syria after graduate studies in Paris. Swept up in the pan-Arab nationalism spouted by Syrian leaders and enthralled with the economic development spurred by the Baath Party, his first documentary was a sixteen-minute, Soviet-style tribute to the Euphrates River dam, which created Lake Assad. Filmed in black and white, it combined shots of striving workers and heavy machinery. Years later, Amiralay said he felt the need to atone, to expose the stifling effect of government propaganda. "The big discovery for us from the war was the overall fragility of the system in Iraq, so I wanted to find the same fragility in the rule of the Syrian Baath," Amiralay said. At that time he thought the fall of Saddam had changed something inside people. "I think the image, the sense of terror, has evaporated," he said in his French-accented English.

But the pendulum swung in the opposite direction when the Syrian people backed their government again, at least for a time, prompted by dramatic events across the western border in Lebanon.

On an unseasonably mild day in Beirut in August 2004, a small group of former Prime Minister Rafik Hariri's closest political allies could tell from his flushed face and subdued manner that something awful had transpired in Damascus, where he had been summoned to an audience with Bashar.

The four men, all Lebanese parliament members, recalled waiting for him at the Beirut mansion of the Druze leader Walid Jumblatt, in the so-called garden, basically a carport paved with concrete bricks, plus one struggling orange tree in a faux terra cotta tub. Hariri—wearing an expensive blue suit and a white shirt, his tie loosened—lumbered over mutely and flung himself onto one of a dozen white plastic chairs.

He sat like that for a moment, his head lolling back and his arms dangling over the edges. Then he leaned forward and described how the Syrian leader had curtly ordered him to amend Lebanon's constitution to give President Émile Lahoud, the man Syria used to block Hariri's every move, another three years in office. Hariri quoted Bashar as threatening to break Lebanon over his head if he did not obey.

"He was like a boxer still reeling from a direct punch," recalled Patrick B. Renaud, the Beirut ambassador for the European Union, who also saw Hariri soon after he returned from Damascus. "He was shocked by the harshness of the message he received from the Syrian president."

The Syrians viewed Hariri, a 60-year-old real-estate tycoon who had run Lebanon for the better part of twelve years, as ominous for two important reasons. He was a Sunni Muslim leader widely admired by his sect in both Lebanon and Syria. Any hint of Sunni resurgence unsettles the Alawite minority. And he had friends in many foreign capitals, particularly Washington, whereas Syria had none.

Damascus had grown used to acting with impunity in Lebanon. But by 2004, the Lebanese were expecting something different from President Assad, not least because the United States had signaled by invading Iraq that totalitarian business-as-usual was unacceptable. The young Syrian leader seemed to have gotten the message, telling a Kuwaiti newspaper that Damascus would not interfere in the Lebanese election. Within months, however, Hariri was ordered to the Syrian presidential palace. Bashar advertised the fact that the meeting was remarkably short—fifteen minutes, when most presidential encounters dragged on for hours—to make it clear that Syria was issuing an order. The Lebanese leader responded by quietly building opposition to Syria at home and abroad, but remained gloomy over his open humiliation in a culture that places paramount value on maintaining dignity. "Hariri said that we are all just gnats to them, he kept repeating that until his death," recalled a senior aide.

On February 14, 2005, a lethal bomb so massive that it rocked all of Beirut struck Hariri's motorcade, killing him and seventeen other people. "The goal of killing him was killing the political movement that could succeed in controlling Lebanon, particularly since it looked like the Syrians would have to leave," Bassem Sebah, an MP from Hariri's bloc, told me. "I think they killed him because they did not want a new political era in Lebanon."

Bashar's regime denied any involvement. But the assassination aroused massive street protests against the Syrians that, combined with Western pressure, compelled the withdrawal of their forces from Lebanon. In Damascus, many dissidents now trace the withering of the opposition movement to this defeat.

In July 2008, I walked through the midday heat to meet Amiralay, the documentary maker, for lunch. I left the intensely quiet, shaded courtyard of Beit Al-Mamlouka, a sixteenth-century Damascus house reborn as a delightful boutique hotel, and slipped into the jostling crowds negotiating the mazy alleyways of the old quarter. I was headed around the corner to Elisar, another Ottoman-era house whose conversion into a restaurant helped spark the transformation of the area from a collapsing slum. I walked surrounded by the sharp smell of thyme pizzas and roasting coffee. I inhaled deeply. The aroma of the bazaar is the aroma of my childhood, always floating me back to my earliest memories of meandering through other, similar alleyways, tugging at the hand of my father or mother. I was eager to talk to Amiralay, but I also wanted to linger, to wander lost from one alleyway to the next for a few hours, stopping occasionally to drink mint tea while bartering for a rug or a wooden chest that caught my eye. I know a key factor that endlessly draws me back to the region is that sense of escaping to a gentler world, another dimension almost, where time unspools at a far slower rate.

At the restaurant, the first thing we ordered was cool, refreshing lemonade turned bright green by a heavy infusion of fresh mint. A white canvas shade high overhead blocked the harsh midday sun, while the courtyard's fountain burbled in the background. Amiralay had always been as ebullient as that fountain in our previous meetings, but this time he seemed depressed, his usually carefully groomed, thinning grey hair askew. He kept talking about the loss of hope.

"Politics in our country is a risky affair," he said. "You basically have two alternatives. You can go to jail, or you can avoid politics." If the younger generation around the world was less engaged politically, it was doubly true in Syria, he said; the new generation was too pragmatic and too materialistic to chase lost causes. I asked him about his prediction in 2004 that the demise of the Baath next door in Iraq might weaken it fatally in Syria. He gave a rueful little laugh. "It has collapsed, but only because Bashar has completely sidelined the party. It didn't take American intervention to deliver the death blow. The dictatorship, however, is still very much alive."

It was a gross misjudgment to think that changing reality through an invasion next door might bring salvation, he said, although he still believed outside pressure holds an important role. Amiralay pointed out that Arab regimes don't really care how they treat their people; they rarely worry that poverty and underdevelopment will somehow threaten their rule. But when outside forces point out the misery of the citizenry, it embarrasses the government and raises questions about the legitimacy of their rule.

In Syria, the population rallied around the government after it was forced to withdraw from Lebanon, with the Arab media, heavily dominated by hostile Lebanese and Saudis, yapping at its heels. The dream of "Greater Syria," of a kind of pan-Arab ideal, died and in mourning Syrians became more nationalistic, Amiralay told me. Syria originally dispatched its soldiers into Lebanon as an Arab peacekeeping force toward the beginning of the 1975–1990 civil war. As their deployment lengthened, it gradually took on the aura of regaining a lost piece of that "Greater Syria" which, the regime maintained, had been wrongfully wrested away by colonial plots. There were other chunks missing on every point of the compass. The eastern plains stretching to the Iraqi city of Mosul were now part of Iraq; the once major northern city of Antioch was Turkish; and of course to the south, Palestine had become Israel.

It always struck me as a more geographic conceit than a political one because for hundreds of years, certainly throughout the Ottoman Empire, the region's major cities had each presided over separate provinces. But the Syrian government succeeded in selling the idea of stolen grandeur to its people, which was among the reasons it treated Lebanon like a vassal state.

"Unconsciously, Syrians were convinced when the army entered Lebanon that they had started to recuperate their lost western areas," Amiralay told me. "When ordinary Syrian people saw the army thrown out of Lebanon, they sensed that history was repeating itself, that they had been living in an illusion, a big lie that Syria is the beating heart of the Arabs. They had to deal with the idea from now on that Syria as it exists today is probably all that it is going to be. That is hard to accept."

"The beating heart of Arabism" was a slogan coined in the Hafez era as a kind of national motto. Where it once seemed to adorn every other banner, I now saw it far less often. But the concept lingered. Amiralay noticed a subtle shift in the way Syrians began to refer to themselves. Previously, whenever they were asked where they were from or who they were, members of his generation (he was born in 1944) would always say "Arab." They had to be coaxed into saying "Syrian." It annoyed them. Now, he said, they pronounced their nationality first but stumbled over it a little, as if still getting used to the idea. "Nationalism replaced the need for change," he said. "Democracy is not a priority, that is my bitter conclusion."

The need to find the answer why has inspired his newest film project, a study of how tribal solidarity and clannishness trump the need for a more open society. "When it is a question of your tribe, it becomes the most important thing," he explained in trying to sum up the way the region worked. It's true that tribes have long survived on a kind of consensus forged by the elders, a custom enshrined in Islam, he said, but it still falls short of full-blown democracy. A secular man, Amiralay surprised me by quoting the famous Koranic verse, carved onto the walls of courthouses and toothless parliaments throughout the region, "Wa amruhum shura binahum" or roughly that the affairs of men are a matter for consultation among them. It is one of the strongest arguments rooted in religion that democracy advocates can wield that enjoys real resonance in the culture. Amiralay noted that the tribal tradition of consensus stands at odds with the way democracy is practiced virtually everywhere else in the world: "There is an antagonism between these two concepts of democracy, between democracy of the people and democracy of the tribe." As our lengthy lunch wound down in the late afternoon, the shade overhead now pulled back to expose a sky no longer white with heat, he began exploring aloud some of the rough ideas for his quest. The Arabic word for clannishness, he noted, stems from the same root as the word for zealotry.

Another Syrian friend pointed out the difficulty of trying to make any change when all the tools to promote change are illegal, another common Arab difficulty. To some extent change had been anticipated as a natural fallout from the advent of the Internet and satellite television—with all the information they brought, the lies the regimes told to stay in power would crumble. The problem with this scenario is that Syrians and indeed most Arabs lacked the means to actually use that information. After decades of Baathist purges, any structured opposition has been destroyed. The fear is such that some professional Syrians, worried that their offices were bugged, would sometimes silently mouth sensitive words to me. To take another example, it's against the law for more than five people to gather without a government permit. Syrians joke that every wedding is in fact illicit, but the larger point is that they have no way to organize. "You can't mobilize because everything is illegal," my friend told me. "You can listen, read, and watch, but there is no means to agitate."

One of the great ironies of Bashar being officially hailed among the founders of the Internet in Syria is that his government has worked harder than most Arab regimes to curb its use. That just increases the resentment among educated Syrians that the Internet should be billed as a "gift" from the first family, rather than something freely adopted as in most of the world. Almost all significant mainstream sites are blocked including Yahoo,

Facebook, Wikipedia, and YouTube. The government always comes up with some anemic excuse. When it blocked Facebook, for example, it said it wanted to prevent Israelis from penetrating Syrian society during a time of warfare. The real reason, young Syrians told me, is that there were scores of pages set up demanding freedom for jailed dissidents.

The government has treated harshly anyone with the temerity to use the Internet to criticize the regime. In March 2008, a blogger named Osama Eduard Moussa made fun of the lack of services accorded to northeastern Syria, where Kurds and other minorities are concentrated, contrasting it with the luxury and advanced technology available to the country's elite (read: Alawites). He wrote about what he called the "Three New No's" followed by the regime: No cooking gas. No heating oil. No electricity. This was a mocking echo of a famous slogan rejecting Israel that emerged from a pan-Arab summit in 1968: No peace. No negotiation. No recognition. His blog disappeared for the nine days that the security police held him in the northern city of Hassakah. Afterward he posted a note saying that he was not going to update it anymore and dropped from sight.

"I guess they beat him," said Mohamed Alabdallah, the strapping son of the Syrian dissident Ali Alabdallah. A law student with thick black hair, he was wearing black wire-rim glasses, a brown T-shirt, and jeans when I met him one night in 2008 in a Beirut café. Mohamed had fled Damascus for Beirut after his father and his brother Omar were jailed. Omar, born in 1985 and younger by two years, had been among a group of seven University of Damascus students who created an online discussion forum to push for greater freedom of expression. Among other highlights it published jokes and cartoons about the Syrian regime. One cartoon depicted a classroom where students were learning "How to talk to a Baath Party official." At each desk a student was licking a naked butt. A photo caption reading "Their arsenal" showed Israeli fighter planes lined up in a neat row. The photo underneath it labeled "Our arsenal" showed Syrian government limousines in a similar line. Another cartoon skewered the many business deals awarded to Rami Makhlouf, the president's first cousin, who has been sanctioned by the United States. The drawing imagined the yellow pages in a future telephone book with every single business under the Makhlouf name: Pizza Makhlouf, Makhlouf Travel, Hotel Makhlouf, etc. (When I met the president, I had asked him about the criticism surrounding his cousin's myriad business dealings, and Bashar denied that his family got any special privileges.)

When Mohamed first stumbled across the website and showed it to Omar, his younger brother laughed and never once let on that he had helped to create it. All the students involved were sentenced to five to seven years by a secret Damascus court in 2007. The meager details about the case, indeed the only thing linking the sentences to the website, came from one student arrested with the others and later released, Mohamed told me. In Syria, meetings are impossible, telephone calls are monitored, and even lists of websites visited by anyone who frequents an Internet café are reported to the government. Despite the limitations, young Syrians still gamble that the government can't monitor everything on the Web. "The Internet is the last space left for activists," Mohamed told me. "It gives us a space to do something, but we cannot achieve much with it." Most Syrians don't use the Internet and probably have never heard of the dissidents sent to jail, he added.

⊡　　⊡　　⊡

Anwar al-Bunni, a slight, middle-aged human rights lawyer with receding black hair, used to hold court in a cramped Damascus office over a corner grocery store. The ceiling was so low that I had to hunch down to walk from the door to his desk. A stream of visitors—other activists, aggrieved Kurds, all manner of clients who had fallen afoul of the government—generated a haze of cigarette smoke that made the already airless room feel even more claustrophobic. But I wouldn't notice after a few minutes, caught up in the constant buzz of activity.

Whenever I arrived, Bunni would disappear into a small kitchen where he produced tiny cups of sharp, syrupy Arabic coffee in a small brass pot held over a gas burner. The first time I sat in front of his desk, he explained to me that Syria lacked an opposition in the usual sense. The term conjured up an organized effort, whereas the opposition in Syria consisted of an unruly collection of government critics who fought as much amongst each other as against the juggernaut of the ruling Baath Party. "The opposition has no real power and no real program," he told me. "There is no connection between all the various branches." They might better be described as a bunch of dissidents, he said, whose main activity sometimes seemed to consist of gathering at the Rawda Café downtown and complaining how they got no respect from the government they opposed. Since Syrian dissidents had no platform to address the public—no access to television, radio, or the newspapers—they spent their time petitioning the very government they wanted to change. Opposition members should address the society more and the government less, many dissidents agreed, but somehow they never quite figured out how. "We have to push them to allow the society to breath, to make it more alive," Bunni said. That was the first step.

It felt strange, almost like space travel, to be in Damascus after the fall of Baghdad, where every sign trumpeting Baath Party rule had been defaced. All manner of signs and banners heralding various Baath Party organizations still crowded the streets of Damascus. These in turn were dwarfed in number and size by innumerable billboards depicting the late President Hafez al-Assad, Bashar, and his older brother Basil. Basil, a handsome man with a trim beard usually shown in hip aviator sunglasses, had been groomed as the heir until he died when he flipped his Mercedes while making a high-speed dash for the airport in 1994. The trio was less present than Saddam, who once seemed to stare down from every wall in Iraq. But they were hard to miss. Syrians quietly referred to the three as the father, the son, and the holy ghost.

Bunni told me that he thought the most important goal of all dissidents was not to confront the regime directly but to make politics and civil society vibrant, to create new parties and especially an effective human rights organization. Eventually reform would become organic that way. "The people who made the system have no desire to reform it; they don't let anyone with real ideas and a clear goal work," he said. Our initial discussion coincided with the first anniversary of the American invasion of neighboring Iraq, so I asked how that had affected his work. It had inspired groups like the Kurds to press harder for minority rights, he said, but overall it was making life more difficult for government critics. Whenever dissidents spoke out about issues like the right to form political parties or a free press, the government accused them of aiding the Americans in trying to foment the kind of bloody chaos that plagued neighboring Iraq.

Taking on so many high-profile cases came with certain consequences. Right before I met Bunni he had responded to two summons by different security agencies that had arrived at his office within hours of each other. He had signed the small paper chits brought by special messenger, acknowledging that he would show up to both Military Intelligence and State Security as requested. He kept telling me how he was sure Syria was changing because even the cops were acting differently. "Friendly" was how he described the visit to State Security, merely an hour-long conversation about contacts between his Human Rights Association in Syria and similar foreign groups.

His visit to Military Intelligence was different, more old school. On day one, he sat alone in a room for the entire day. On day two, he sat in the waiting room of a colonel, but no one spoke to him and he got nothing to drink. On day three, the colonel summoned him into his office. "He told me that I speak too harshly against the government, that they could put me in jail anytime if I continued or could even resort to 'other means,'" Bunni said, grinning and habitually sucking on the cigarette held in whichever hand was not cradling his mobile phone. "The officer kept telling me that the country is changing, that reforms are on the way and that I had to wait." Syria was under constant attack from outside, he was told, so did he really want to help its enemies?

I had heard the same arguments used almost universally across the Arab world. Any criticism, anything other than absolute allegiance to the system and its ruler, was unacceptable. The idea that unquestioning obedience to the system is the mark of a good citizen—taught from the earliest years in school and sometimes rooted in examples drawn from Islamic texts—counts among the significant obstacles to reform. The fact that governments cannot tolerate questions is really a mark of their fragility.

Previously, Bunni noted optimistically, he would have been taken directly to jail for publicly demanding real political parties, a free press, fair trials, or other civil liberties. The arresting officers would also have likely knocked him around, not treated him with a certain offhand civility. He held a front-row seat on the range of abuses not just from his work, but his family. Some of his siblings had been Communist Party activists and, counted together, had served about sixty years behind bars—two of his brothers for seventeen years each. At one time three brothers and a sister were incarcerated simultaneously. That made him all the more determined to avoid jail. He was also an outspoken critic of the common practice of torturing prisoners.

Yet Bunni was typical of most Syrian dissidents I encountered in that he was not interested in sudden regime change. "If the regime left today, there would be no one to run this country," he said. "There has been no political life for forty years," he added, noting that the chaos in Iraq was largely the result of a similar void.

As the opposition grew bolder he became less temperate in his remarks. In early 2006 he started predicting wildly—and mistakenly—that by the end of the summer the country would have a new president. The Lawyers' Syndicate of Damascus sought to disbar Bunni for helping to defend prominent dissidents. The Internet and satellite television were among his best allies, he said, because suddenly there were points of view available that had not existed previously. Before, when the government labeled someone a "traitor" the accused had no effective means to respond. Now the issue was discussed on Arab satellite television, people went online to defend him, and articles about him even in publications like the *New York Times* were suddenly accessible to Syrian readers, albeit a small, elite audience. But he admitted to me, after some prodding, that when one security service or another summoned him, and he sat alone for hour after hour in those interrogation rooms, the fear crept back. "I think maybe some in the regime want to return to those days, they are not comfortable that people speak out," he said, adding, "I think they know the game is finished, at least I hope it is finished."

He was wrong. It wasn't finished.

In May 2006, Bunni was among the organizers of a petition signed by 500 intellectuals and others called the Beirut-Damascus declaration, which basically demanded that the government deal with Lebanon like a good, normal neighbor. He was arrested, accused of being in contact with foreign governments and of "disseminating false information likely to undermine the morale of the nation in wartime." In 2007, a Damascus criminal court sentenced him to five years. Ironically, in late 2008 President Assad announced that Syria and Lebanon would exchange ambassadors.

When I went to visit his wife, Raghida Issa, in their modest apartment on a quiet Damascus street in 2008, she admitted that she was completely fed up with her husband's eternal optimism. "When he was arrested, he said, 'Don't worry my love, the most they will give me is six months in jail," she said, shaking her head. "Then when he was sentenced to five years, he said, "Don't worry my love, I will be out in six months maximum." It had already been more than two years. Issa was expecting he would have to serve the full five years if not more, plus she was fired from the government job she had held for twenty-seven years.

Issa, a handsome woman with dark hair, wearing a black V-neck T-shirt over a black and white flowered skirt, shook her head again and told me a story that she thought perfectly illustrated the width of her husband's stubborn streak. In 1982, Bunni was a recent college graduate living in Hama, where the government began rooting out supporters of the Muslim Brotherhood. The old Muslim quarter was their stronghold and the army eventually turned the entire district into a parking lot. Bunni, a Christian, resided in an adjacent neighborhood, but security agents nabbed him because he sported a beard—often the trademark of a devout Muslim male. Even as they were beating him, he refused to tell them whether he was a Christian or a Muslim. His wife quoted him as saying to them, "I have lived here for twenty years and nobody has ever asked me that question so I won't answer." Finally a neighbor emerged from his house and vouched that Bunni was a Christian. The officers let him go, but first set his beard alight.

In the spring of 2006, Issa had sensed that the government was getting into a similarly intolerant frame of mind and asked her husband to tone it down. He was arrested a week later. "He felt the world would not be silent about all the wrongdoings of this government," she said. "I think he is wrong, I don't think they care at all about what they consider these backward Arab countries." She blamed European states for getting him into the predicament in the first place. They had set him up as the director of a center for human rights training, she said, and assured him that they had received a commitment from the Syrian government it would be allowed to work. Instead, all the Syrians invited to the open reception got mysterious telephone calls the night before telling them not to go, and the center was shuttered the day after it opened. With the exception of a human rights award from the government of Ireland, she felt the European states had done little to win his release beyond occasional statements. Government agents questioned her for hours after she went to Dublin to accept the award, accusing her of colluding in an Israeli plot to embarrass them. She argued back, noting that it was a respectable award that had been presented by Ireland's president. "They told me, 'Yes, but you know the Jews control everything in the world.'"

One of Bunni's brothers, Akram, is back in jail, among the twelve dissidents arrested for leading a group called the Damascus Declaration for Democratic National Change. In December 2007, two years after the release of that petition calling for greater democracy, some 160 members of various political stripes came together to elect a national leadership council. Those elected have been imprisoned ever since, including the president, Dr. Fida al-Hourani, a gynecologist and the daughter of a famous Syrian politician from the 1950s. Dr. Hourani's husband, a Palestinian physician, was deported to Jordan so he cannot visit her in jail. Although there have been occasional protests from human rights groups abroad about the Syrian activists, dissidents are discouraged by the lack of attention.

They note that the activists, all sentenced in October 2008 to thirty months in prison, were pushing for a moderate, secular form of government, something the West professes to want in the Arab world, and not a single one endorsed the idea of a foreign invasion or other outside intervention for regime change. "They believe deeply in democracy," said Mohamed Ali Atassi, a young Syrian dissident whose ability to come and go in Syria has reached the tenuous point where he spends most of his time in exile. "What is shocking about this story is that there is very little attention or effort given to them in the West; they don't take them seriously. But they are real dissidents. They are willing to pay the price and they are paying the price. Look what Anwar Bunni did all those years when he was defending people!"

When it comes to their interaction with the West, dismayed Syrian activists mentioned two or three issues that made them uneasy. First, they believe that Western governments use human rights as a strategic issue rather than as a principle. When they want to put Syria on the defensive, they raise human rights issues. Then the moment when another commercial goal or political strategy comes along, like trying to woo the Assad government away from its close alliance with Tehran, human rights issues evaporate. That undermines the standing of the activists in the eyes of their oppressors as expendable. A couple of Syrian dissidents told me that when the

Syrian government complained to European ambassadors about the nascent human rights training center that they had recruited Bunni to run, they responded by saying they would find another director if he was the problem. That signaled that nobody would raise a ruckus if he was jailed, the dissidents said. Inconsistent pressure was almost worse than no pressure. If Western governments adopted a policy of trying to free Syrian activists, they should follow it through, not just mention someone jailed occasionally, dissidents said. As Amiralay told me, "I am not really sure how sincere the West is when they talk about human rights in Syria. Sometimes you get the impression that if they win two or three new oil contracts, they will forget all about it."

Second, Syrian opposition figures feel that somehow they are always viewed as not quite democratic enough, that they are judged on their commitment to Western methods rather than what should be the yardstick, namely universal principles of human rights. Atassi pointed out the irony of this to me when I sat with him in a seaside Beirut café on a muggy night in July 2008. The sun slowly turned into a glowing red disc that sank into the Mediterranean as we talked and sipped coffee under a scattering of trees.

Atassi, scion of a prominent political family, has been in opposition almost literally his entire life. He downplays his own history, but he was not yet 3 years old when his father, the president of Syria, was arrested in 1970 and spent the next twenty-two years in jail, released just before his death in 1983. Atassi had long volunteered as my quiet, self-effacing guide who explained the activities of the Syrian opposition with earnest sincerity. He was the man I always went to first to gauge its mood, and on that summer night I found him thoroughly discouraged.

I asked him some of the questions I get from audiences in the United States—Do Arabs really support democracy, or is there any hope for women's rights in the Middle East? He was appalled by the idea that Western governments or independent organizations want to impose their own values on the region. "To bring an American agenda or a European agenda and say you need 30 percent women in parliament, or in the opposition parties—that is a mistake," he said with exasperation. "Don't come with your agenda, let it develop on its own." Plus, even when Syrian activists showed a commitment to such principles, it didn't seem to help win sustained support for them in the West, he noted. For him, the fate of the National Council is a perfect example. The 160 activists from different political persuasions came together to hold an election for their leadership and even elected a woman, *a woman!*, as the president, he pointed out. The accusations against them include trying to undermine the government, inciting sectarian violence, and spreading lies. They all denied the charges, saying they were trying to bring democratic change under Syrian law. Yet the West has voiced only muted concern over their plight. Atassi worried that the lukewarm response is rooted in the idea that Arab dissidents don't deserve support because they don't automatically hold up Western democracies as their model. "Let the people struggle inside to define the nature of their own political system," he said. Putting the emphasis on human rights rather than on Western models would make it harder for repressive regimes to paint dissidents as stooges of the Western powers that come to their defense. "To put people in jail for what they say, that is against human rights everywhere in the world," he said. "But to say the system has to be like this or that, no. To create any kind of pressure regarding democratization and the nature of the political system from outside is stupid."

Ultimately, activists try to carry on even in the absence of outside support. Despite all he has been through, Issa said her husband has not altered his opinion that change is inevitable. "Anwar still thinks the government will change sooner or later," she said. "They can't keep on like this. He's optimistic that the whole world is changing."

But a growing despair was more common among the Syrians I encountered on my last visit. One of my oldest friends explained it to me. "Before, I always felt change was on the horizon," he said over an outdoor dinner on a warm summer night. "Maybe it would take two or three or even ten years, but it was out there someplace. Now, that hope is gone, which has a strong psychological impact.

Before you would want to meet people and talk because you had hope. Now, I don't want to go meet people or attend conferences or on some days even get out of bed in the morning. All that is left for you is to accept the minimum. You enjoy the fact that you can go to a coffee shop without being killed like you might be in Baghdad. You can't accept dreams anymore, you have to accept reality."

Watching his young son grow up and begin to go to school under such a deadening system, my friend wondered aloud if he should emigrate to give the boy the chance for a better life, a free life. I didn't know what to tell him. I understood the impulse, but I wondered what will happen to the region if all the smart men and women committed to a secular, pluralistic future decide to pull up stakes. The entire Middle East will be even more deeply held hostage by fanatics on all sides. The last page in my notes from that dinner contains my friend's Arabic scrawl, a proverb he quoted me that I had never heard before. He used it to sum up the mood of resignation: "Just line your head up with the other heads and call out for the executioner."

As I drove south out of Damascus toward the Jordan border early the next morning, looking out over a timeless landscape of farmers harvesting their tomato and citrus crops by hand, I felt depressed. I could not help but think that all the Syrians with whom I enjoyed spending time deserved better lives. The tyranny of the Assad regime casts a pall over what should be a delightful country, like pollution eating away some fine edifice. Despite its oppressive air, I always looked forward to my visits there. Syrians are generally charming, their food delicious, it's cheap, and best of all, the place oozes history. I could spend hours roaming the stunning bazaar quarters of Damascus and Aleppo, and the country divulges endlessly intriguing ruins left by one conquering army after the next.

In the main square of the Damascus bazaar, Roman arches from the temple of Jupiter frame the entrance to the Omayyad mosque—which started life as a cathedral. The glorious Roman city of Palmyra stands in solitary splendor out in the desert toward Iraq. One fantastic crusader redoubt, Krac des Chevaliers, sits astride its hill like a kid's fantasy of everything a castle should be, from the moat to the crenellations topping its robust towers. The Hittite statues of men and animals in the Aleppo museum never failed to make me smile with their exaggerated large white eyes.

Syrians are justly proud of all this, of their history, culture, and language. It was the one country where people habitually made an effort to speak Arabic with me, patiently correcting my mangled grammar. After an extended period of reporting there I always left with the sense that maybe I could master the language after all. Or maybe that conviction stemmed from hearing the same slogans shouted repeatedly. Around 1993, while reporting a story about the Palestine Liberation Organization rift between Yasser Arafat and the more radical factions over the latest peace accord with Israel, one sentence was bellowed at me without fail in every shabby, dim office I visited, and I remember it to this day: "Mustaqbal Arafat alaa mazbala at-taariki!" or "Arafat's future is on the garbage dump of history!"

Syria was the first country where I took friends who wanted to visit the Arab world. Each time I abandoned my reporting and went wandering with them, I habitually found delightful relics of past civilizations that I had never seen before. I knew the ruins were all left by outsiders who tarried briefly in the larger scheme of things. The dissidents within Syria had a much harder task, I realized, because they were not invading from outside, but trying to replace the local power from within while lacking any real leverage to bring about change. The Bush administration had boasted that it would create a domino effect in the region with its invasion in Iraq. It had, but the dominoes had all fallen in the wrong direction, toward more oppression, with the general population accepting it because they feared the possible bloody consequences of experimenting with pluralism.

CHAPTER 14

EPILOGUE

Let us part without any kisses, so I can live in hope of seeing you again.

—Mohamed Abdel Wahab

MY LAST DAY BASED IN the Middle East as a *Times* correspondent dawned foul, with a chilly rain lashing Beirut and icing the roads up into the mountains. Despite the low clouds that turned even the Mediterranean a sullen gray, I was determined to make the trek up to Fadel, a traditional restaurant tucked in among the pine trees on a ridge above a village called Bikfaya. In all my years reporting from Lebanon, I had managed to eat there just once, forcing the occasion by writing a story for the *Times* dining section that required sampling Fadel's silky house arak and stunning array of mezze dishes.

It was, I knew, utterly ridiculous to turn my wish for a last hurrah into a lunch expedition. I had just spent five years crisscrossing the region from Tehran to Marrakesh, engrossed in all manner of compelling tales, and what was I set upon for my final perfect moment? A long, boozy afternoon spent eating hummus in a Lebanese institution that epitomized everything the country had been before its civil war. At one point in my early 20s, I had occasionally imagined life as a Mideast correspondent involving an endless chain of such afternoons. It never came to pass, needless to say. As often as not I skipped lunch, not wanting to pause in my reporting. But tucked into some corner of my brain, an afternoon in a superb restaurant like Fadel harkened back to a simpler era in the region. I knew that time was gone, but it still somehow represented part of the allure.

Once focused on lunch at Fadel, I would be damned if the weather was going to prevent it. Naturally everyone I called, once they glanced out the window, refused to go. I could not even guilt them into it by reminding them it was my last day. "It will give you a reason to come back" was the standard flimsy excuse. I watched the time tick away, and kept calling the restaurant to make sure they were still serving. The kitchen shut officially at 3 P.M., which meant I had to be out of Beirut a little before 1:30 given the condition of the roads. Finally I tracked down Ghaith Abdul-Ahad, a talented Iraqi architecture student who, during the course of the invasion, had become a reporter and translator in Baghdad for the Times. We had worked and lived together practically day and night for the entire two months that I was there in the summer of 2003. He was an absolute boon companion—bright, quiet, unassuming, and witty, who had developed incredible street smarts by staying on the lam in Saddam's Iraq to avoid the draft. He also looked like everyone's idea of a fundamentalist terrorist with his heavy black beard. After he left the Times, Ghaith became a highly accomplished photographer and reporter in his own right. Given his looks and demeanor, he became particularly adept at befriending Islamist insurgents, leaving them a bit stunned when he confessed that he was actually a Christian.

I could never be sure that Ghaith would keep an appointment, but I knew I could rely on his sense of adventure and his appetite. In Beirut, he volunteered instantly to make the dash up icy, foggy mountain roads for lunch. I had been to Fadel just once, so I picked the wrong mountain to ascend. As I roared through the hairpin turns trying to make up for lost time, I kept glancing at my watch, willing the hands to slow down so we could make it. We arrived at about 2:50 and I am not sure they were overjoyed to see us. To compensate we ordered nearly everything on the mezze menu— bitter olives, dewy goat's cheese, radishes, tabouleh, raw minced lamb, zucchini with cinnamon, potatoes in coriander, mashed egg- plant with garlic, and chicken livers in pomegranate juice, to name just a few. The feast held our rapt attention for a couple hours. There was no point in looking out the window, anyway, as the Feb- ruary sun faded. The swirling mist was so thick that we could barely make out the nearest pine tree, much less the Mediterranean far, far below. As I was paying the check, Ghaith pointed out the Ab- del Wahab song that began playing. Mohamed Abdel Wahab was a legendary Egyptian crooner, something of an Arab Bing Crosby. The chorus of the song that day was, "Let us part without any kisses, so I can live in hope of seeing you again."

It was a fine note to go out on, and as I listened to the song I asked myself whether I was leaving the region with any hope. A year earlier, the answer would have been decidedly negative. I had seen and written about too much death and destruction—the gory attacks, the beheadings and bombings—so much terrorism with no apparent aim other than wreaking the maximum amount of de- struction on hapless civilians. Maybe the violence did represent the real Middle East, I thought then, and the rest was just inconsequent background noise. But the year spent tracking down many of the people on these pages altered that perspective; they gave me the sense that there are all manner of smart, energetic, dedicated ac- tivists out there working to transform the region. They may not have reached a critical mass, and they face terrible odds in con- fronting the brutal machinery that keeps so many dictators in power, yet they are determined to make a difference. Some outside support would undoubtedly buttress their efforts significantly, but they were not sitting around wringing their hands, awaiting help.

There seems to be a question mark hanging over the Middle East as to whether its peoples really want democracy, whether they value the idea of living in a free society. (At least I get asked all the time if Arabs aspire to it.) The unstated, underlying presumption is that they are somehow predisposed to endure life under an endless line of despots—either through culture, religion, education, temperament, genetics, tradition, or some combination of them all. When I get asked that question, the men and women I wrote about on these pages parade through my mind. All of them would certainly prefer to live in open societies; to enjoy freedom of expression; freedom from fear of their governments and their wicked secret police; freedom from the vagaries of an unpredictable justice system; freedom to assemble and to form the kind of civic organizations they want; and yes, freedom to choose their own leaders. Sometimes in the larger societies to which they belong, there might be questions of priority. Political freedom may be stuck in line behind the desire to live a life without hunger, to attain some manner of security.

I think the full array of their aspirations sometimes gets lost behind all the static about democratic issues pumped out by the governments in the Middle East, not to mention by the clerics on the official dole. It is the powerful who developed the argument that Western freedoms are a cultural phenomenon foreign to Arab and Islamic values. That mantra is the simplest means to try to brainwash people that living under a dictatorship was somehow ordained by God. Given the general suspicion that the West has targeted Islam, though, the idea does resonate. Naturally that raises doubts in the West that Arabs or Persians welcome any outside interference in gaining them greater freedom. But I think the question of priorities looms far larger than the issue of desire.

What I found in the Arab world and Iran is that the building blocks of a free society remain somewhat abstract in the face of more difficult, tangible problems like poverty, unemployment, corruption, and the lack of opportunity. I remember one moment in particular when that was brought home to me. During Egypt's

2005 parliamentary elections, I spent a night in one of Cairo's sewage-filled slums trailing Muntasir Zayat, a candidate with an Islamist bent who was perhaps most famous as the former jail cell mate of Ayman al-Zawahiri, now the number-two man in Al-Qaeda. Zayat had renounced violence, but the streets around his office were riddled with secret police dispatched by a government that did not entirely trust him. Any visit to him immediately provoked a phone call from the Egyptian secret police demanding to know why I had gone. During his candidacy, Zayat's stump speech was a fairly focused diatribe against the United States, how its evil agenda was bent on picking off Muslim countries one-by-one until there would be none left. An American congressman even suggested bombing the holy city of Mecca, right?! At café after café, when Zayat asked for questions, I leaned forward, wondering if this was the moment when some impoverished Egyptian would finally say he thought the freedom offered by the United States was a menace. Had not countless American politicians, or at least those of a conservative bent, blamed the 9/11 attacks on devout Muslims who "hate freedom"? This alleged constituency was the very group that Zayat was courting. So how many reacted to Zayat's dark image of the doom the Americans were planning to visit on the region? Exactly none. In fact, in the course of an entire evening, when I heard him deliver his stump speech at least four times, not a single person even mentioned it. What did they ask about? They wanted to know how he was going to provide more jobs. They wanted to know what he proposed to do about the lack of a fire station or an ambulance based in their neighborhood, which had sprung out of farm fields practically overnight. "We want a representative who fights for the interests of the poor!" yelled out a man trying to sell falafel off a cart near one café, to murmurs of agreement all around. Nobody wanted to know about the war on Islam, they wanted to know how Zayat planned to improve their immediate lives. (He didn't get the chance. He lost.) There is no question that hopelessness and despair can breed radicalism. But it is far from an automatic response.

For me, that campaign night highlighted the possible importance of one avenue that the United States has neglected in its attempts to sway public opinion in its favor. Washington dedicates minuscule foreign aid to development, to helping people with the kind of health care, education, and improved prospects that inform their daily dreams. The yardstick of real generosity formulated by the United Nations is 70 cents for every $100 generated by any wealthy economy, a standard met by just a few northern European countries. The U.S. gives nearly $22 billion, far more in actual dollars than anyone else, but that represents around 18 cents out of every $100. Of course, part of the problem is that aid is generally channeled through host governments, whose goals don't always coincide with those of the United States, or can taint those organizations helped directly. Advocates in several countries have come up with a possible solution for this—creating a nonprofit umbrella organization outside the government that would dole out the money to groups helping civil society flourish. Easier said than done, but worth considering.

On the larger subject of democracy, whenever someone asks me whether Arabs are really interested in it, I think first of two people. The first is Sameer al-Qudah, the Jordanian poet I wrote about in Chapter 8, who made me laugh when I put the question to him: "Why is it that in the States or in Japan or in India or Brazil they have democracy, they have the right to change whoever is in power, to change their governments, and only people here cannot hope to have the same kind of life? It's as if you came to Jordan and you saw that there were no cars here, that all the people were using donkeys to get around. Would you believe that people don't want to use cars? If anybody told you that, you would have to know right away that the government prevented people from using cars."

The second man was an English-speaking engineer, Ashraf Omar, whom I met on the fringe of the all-women political rally held by Sobhe Saleh, the Muslim Brotherhood candidate for parliament in Alexandria, Egypt. Omar had brought his daughter, a 9-year-old girl with shoulder-length hair tied up with a pink ribbon. Since the rally was segregated by sex, he had to stand with her on the side-walk opposite from where the women were sitting. He had brought the girl, he said, because he wanted her to appreciate the importance of political freedom at an early age.

"For twenty-five years we have heard a lot from Mr. Mubarak and his colleagues about how they are going to change Egypt, but in reality nothing has changed," Omar told me, his hands resting lightly on his daughter's shoulders as she leaned into his legs. "We want some kind of change, something new. Many young people see nothing but a dark future for themselves." Though he supported the conservative social agenda of the Brotherhood, he disliked the idea of simply replacing the ruling party with an equally inflexible Islamic version. "In all our previous experience with government, what we had was far removed from democracy. We want a system in the future where all the people can state their own opinions, where they can change the government when they want to. If we build a good system in the future, we won't repeat the system we have now. If the system is strong, the people can change the government."

Now these were just two men, both living incidentally beneath regimes whose leaders are close allies of Washington, and it is impossible to extrapolate their opinion across an Arab world population roughly the same size as that of the United States.

But the sad fact of the matter is that of the two diametrically opposed visions of the future for the Mideast—the egalitarian versus the violent—it is the violent who monopolize the limelight. A small minority manages to derail the forces of civilization again and again. So the goal should be preventing them from controlling the agenda, of holding them back so the dreams of men like Qudah and Omar can emerge.

God knows I had encountered the extremists in numerous forms. Having traveled to Iran around twenty times, I came away repeatedly with the sense that the Iranians are an amazingly energetic, cosmopolitan people, yearning to be part of the world. Yet a small group of mullahs and their allied politicians seem determined to cement their shah-like grip on power forever, using the Shiite faith to pretend they have a mandate from God and in the process alienating the bulk of the population. On the Sunni side of the coin, intolerant groups like Hamas manage to latch onto the popular imagination. First of all they provide services—day care and schools and clinics—but they also paint a vision of a different tomorrow. They promise to restore a sense of dignity and honor that disappeared through centuries of colonialism and then the bitter battlefield defeats and daily humiliations at the hands of the Israeli occupation. The Jews, too, have their extremists. The settler movement spawned the man who assassinated Prime Minister Yitzhak Rabin, a warrior who had finally reached his own accommodation with the idea that peace was a necessity. Rabin embodied the sense of security Israelis needed to convince them that freeing the Palestinians from occupation would strengthen their country in the long run.

Perhaps no place marks the extent to which extremists feed on each other more than the area around Hebron in the West Bank. When I was living in Jerusalem, I drove out to the Jewish settlement of Qiryat Arba late one night to watch Orthodox women in their long skirts and berets at target practice. The pistol range was in the basement of the community center, with the women blasting away at the picture of an Arab who came whirring at them on an electronic clothes line. On my way home, some Palestinian teenagers, seeing my yellow Israeli license plate and taking me for a settler, heaved such a giant boulder at me that it bent my car door right out of its frame. I gunned the engine and roared away, the broken door banging rapidly at my side almost in cadence with my heart.

But it was another day in Hebron when I harvested perhaps the starkest example of how the two sides mirror each other in claiming a divine mandate to justify their closed-minded, deadening approach to their fight over land. The rolling hills looked grey and sodden beneath a cold, driving rain, the weather reflecting the dark mood in the wake of yet another round of clashes. I had forgotten to bring a pencil that day, so I filled page after page in my notebook with a fountain pen. By the time I got home, the notebook had absorbed too much rain, my writing bleeding across the pages. I could not distinguish any of the names, nor could I tell from the individual sentences which side was speaking because each described the other in such vile terms. It was a notebook overflowing with disembodied hatred. Those kinds of days tended to overwhelm me with dark pessimism.

So which is the real Middle East? All that bloodshed, or the people struggling to improve their lot, to increase their space to breathe? It is both, and the latter are certainly the majority, yet extremists color our entire impression of the region. U.S. policy is too often shaped by the desire to tamp down that violence as fast as possible, rather than fostering the kind of deep-seated, long-term changes that would kill its roots.

To its final hour, the Bush administration seemed convinced that robust military action was the solution to the region's problems, no matter how heavy the civilian toll. Its support for the fierce Israeli incursion into Gaza at the beginning of 2009, in the hope of undermining if not toppling Hamas, underscored its belief in expedient answers rather than something durable. Again and again, that kind of violence only served to bolster support for Hamas or Hizbollah in Lebanon as the kind of "resistance" organization that would somehow answer the brutal punishment that the Palestinian or Lebanese civilians endured. I am convinced that the only way to win over Hamas is to dismantle the conditions that created it, the occupation itself, rather than aiming for a short-term, violent answer. It strengthens the hardliners. Violence just begets more. Israeli officials protested that their withdrawal from Gaza was met with rocket fire from Hamas which they had to silence. Perhaps they convinced themselves that they should be thanked for "withdrawing." But they only pulled back as far as Gaza's perimeter. Palestinians certainly suffered no illusions about who still controlled their destiny. Real peace will come with real compromise. I was in Gaza on July 1, 1994, the day the Palestinian leadership returned from exile. Were residents most excited by the fact that Yasir Arafat was back after twenty-seven years? Hardly. The huge crowd that had gathered took one look as a kind of reassurance that he had actually returned and then wandered off, not even bothering to listen to his speech. The real excitement that day was generated by the sense that they would not have to answer to Israeli soldiers, and that proved a shattering illusion. Rather than encouraging Israel to crush Hamas as the answer to the problem, the United States should have been asking its ally how it envisioned peace in twenty years, not in the next twenty days or weeks or months. Hamas only came into existence in 1987. If Washington had asked that kind of question then, perhaps Israel would not have needed to bomb parts of Gaza to flinders twenty-two years later.

I think one key reason that the United States has faced such a string of failures in the Middle East since the 1979 revolution in Iran is that its policies were too often based on expediency. If Arab dictators and despots did the right thing, they were our friends, no matter how long they stayed in power or how they treated their own people. Among other key issues, they had to pursue normalized relations with Israel; they had to host American military forces and, in recent years, support the war on terrorism; they were supposed to at least try to cooperate on oil issues, and just generally make appreciative noises about the United States. Basically none of those coincided with the sentiments of the general public, but Washington was always on the side of the rulers.

After 9/11 Washington briefly reversed course, announcing that democracy was the key to alleviating the frustrations that the extremists exploited so successfully to recruit their foot soldiers. That change, which did not last, was suspect to most Arabs from the outset because unfortunately the concept that the United States stands up for the little guy had expired. Greater democracy is a long, hard slog, and in the short term might produce countries that are more hostile toward the United States. But in the long run they will be more stable, and that more distant horizon deserves more attention.

The months when I embarked on my search for agents of change was a brief moment of high optimism among reformers in the

Arab world, a time when the U.S. put Arab leaders on notice that business as usual was no longer acceptable. Speaking at the American University in Cairo, Condoleezza Rice, the U.S. secretary of state, explained in June 2005 that Washington had come to understand that the threat from extremism was rooted in years of repression. "For 60 years, my country, the United States, pursued stability at the expense of democracy in this region here in the Middle East, and we achieved neither," Rice said. "Now we are taking a different course. We are supporting the democratic aspirations of all people." That meant, she said, that the U.S. would support the right to free speech, the right to associate, the right to freedom of religion, the right to educate sons and daughters, and "freedom from the midnight knock of the secret police."

Everybody should probably have been suspicious immediately because the next thing she did was cite the king and queen of Jordan as model reformers, and clearly about half the liberties she listed are absent under their rule. But just the fact that she said it inspired reformers to work harder, and forced even allies like Egypt and Saudi Arabia to start making more public noises about change. Unfortunately, as with so much U.S. policy in the Middle East, the follow-up was anemic and consistency nonexistent. As soon as Hamas won the elections in Gaza, Washington stopped talking about democracy. It was as though they had briefly learned a foreign language and then forgotten all the vocabulary. Hamas won because it gave people hope that there was a life free of both occupation and endlessly grasping officials. Palestinians wanted relief from the Israeli control over their daily lives and relief from the corruption and mismanagement of the occupied territories under the heirs of Yasir Arafat, the past master of mismanagement and corruption. By not pushing through a solution to the Arab-Israel conflict, the United States has handed fundamentalist parties a yawning opening they would otherwise lack. The Islamists emphasize restoring Arab rights as the central plank of their platform, allowing them to seize the initiative. Palestinian self-determination is a legitimate grievance that the United States has allowed to infect all manner of other issues by not applying itself to its key role as the designated mediator, the only mediator with the means to knock a few recalcitrant heads together if it so chose. It is not good enough to stand up repeatedly and say that there should be a Palestinian state and then do so little to realize the goal.

There was a time when the United States would have identified any occupation as a moral wrong, when it supported self-determination as a basic principle, and no one could have stolen the lead from Americans on that. But those days are gone. So 2005 was perhaps a high point of American support for reform and change, and it has been downhill ever since. On a swing through the region in 2008, I found the mood decidedly pessimistic, not least because Washington had gone back to its old policy of supporting whatever dictators endorsed its short-term goals and forgetting all about the long term. Despite all the talk, tangible reform was hard to find.

My long years in the Middle East convinced me that there are two key flaws in the way Washington conducts itself there. First, rather than trying to convert the Arabs to American values, to the way we do things, the stress should be put on human values. Too often American officials sound like they wish everyone would become more American, projecting the United States' image onto places where it is an awkward fit. The smarter and more effective means to induce change would be to listen to what people at the grass roots are trying to achieve that might coincide with our values, and adapt accordingly. The second major problem is that American foreign policy has become an extension of domestic policy. Washington tries to solve problems overseas in a way where the benefit to the politician at home matters more than what happens to the people who live with the actual consequences. It would be naïve to expect this to change, but it is a factor in the perception that American initiatives lack sincerity.

When you combine the not listening and the domestic agenda, it means that nobody believes that what the United States proposes is for their good, and anyone who agrees with the Americans instantly becomes suspect, labeled a stooge. The post-9/11 emphasis on introducing democracy is a glaring example of a policy that failed to inspire much hope because it was not presented in such a way that your average Egyptian, Palestinian, Syrian, or Saudi ever believed it was being done for them. In contrast, the inspiration provided by the mere sense that the United States is listening can be astonishing. In 2007, the State Department put two Arabic-speaking bloggers to work, allowing them to troll through the blogosphere to dispute some of the more outrageous claims there directed against the United States government. When my Saudi friend Adel Toraifi, an academic who specializes in extremist movements, went fishing around to find out what kind of effect they were having, one reaction in particular struck him. He noticed just how elated many chat room denizens were to have someone in the United States government listening to them, giving a tiny indication that somehow their opinion mattered. It was not something that ever happened to them at home, as more than one of them wrote.

▫ ▫ ▫

Ultimately, I think my time in the Middle East led me to three main conclusions about the way the U.S. could really be effective in bringing about change there.

The first would be the need to address the concerns of the people in their own countries at their level, the most basic concerns that all parents have about things like their children's education. Frustration over limited educational opportunities certainly creates an opening for the American government, to take just one example. The prime moment was lost post-9/11 by a confrontational approach, with Washington demanding immediate changes in the curriculum, saying the religious content helped breed foot soldiers for Al-Qaeda. Those demands brewed all manner of resentment. The entire approach smacked of Christianity attacking Islam, of the entire Crusades resurrected.

The smarter way to go about it would be for the American government to find ways to raise the kind of questions that parents ask in Saudi Arabia or Egypt or Syria. Why are the Arabs, who once kept science alive, now so weak at it? Why are the enlightened days of Haroun al-Rashid left in the medieval dust? How come the wealthy Gulf countries have failed to produce any Arab Microsofts, any Arab Apple Computers, any real modern innovation of any sort? Western governments, reformers say, should question why curriculums are so weak, why Arab societies contribute virtually nothing to the world's scientific or technological advancements. It's the kind of question that people who want change in the Middle East ask all the time, and if whatever administration in Washington raised the question in that way, it would be an effective yet indirect endorsement of the reformers. It would put those regimes on the defensive, push the need to explain themselves, explain their failures, without seeming to directly confront or disparage their beliefs and values. Instead, Washington focuses on its immediate regional policy goals. Sure, it helps to have Egypt police Gaza or involve the Saudis in calming Iraq's Sunnis. But again those are short-term goals. Criticizing those governments might create tensions that turn Cairo or Riyadh away from Washington, making it harder to get what the United States wants. Conversely, more open societies might oppose Washington because what it pursues so often counters popular opinion. But a stronger civil society is needed to make those countries run better in the long run. There might be a rocky transition period, but a culture of openness will provide fewer opportunities for extremism to flourish.

Secondly, I think Washington should be more vocal in supporting change, no matter how weak its proponents are and whether or not their goals mirror American policy. Agitators need American support, not directly, not as an endorsement, but it just helps them immeasurably when the American government signals that it is watching. The U.S. government also has a terrible knack for seizing on agents of change who have dubious reputations at home—past links with corruption or a history of serving the governments they now attack. When I say that all agents of change deserve American support, I mean the ones with stellar reputations in their own countries, and not just any opportunist who gains American support because he mouths the right platitudes. In this, the large communities from many of these countries who live in the United States should play a role. I am always struck by how smart Iranians who live in the U.S. are about developments in their country—what I hear from them always gives a far more coherent picture of what is happening there than pronouncements from the American administration.

In addition, in all my trips around the region, the extraordinary people I profiled would tell me that the United States should not have been pushing democratic elections so hard. It automatically gave democracy a bad name because the U.S. is so disliked, and most countries were just not ready. Mentally, people had spent so many decades under repression that the political process is more or less dead everywhere. The only groups who were prepared and would thus win were the religious fundamentalists. Not every society is a latent democracy just waiting to come out of the closet. I don't think there is anything wrong with striving to enhance civil society rather than making democratic elections the goal. Some might call that a contradiction, or a sly assault on the rosy election prospects of the Islamists, but just creating more breathing room is a worthwhile goal. I think when the United States pushes "democracy" people tend to hear that as Washington force-feeding people our form of government, despite official U.S. pronouncements that every country needs to develop its own blueprint. So rather than democracy as the mantra, endorsing civil society makes for a stronger argument. It is a way of telling other people that they should shape their own freedom, that they will get support in making the bricks but the structure will be theirs alone. What many activists dearly want is for the U.S. to push on civil rights issues—the right for the activists to speak out freely in their own countries, to print their own newspapers, to form their own organizations, to agitate without fear of arrest or being beaten and jailed. The idea is for Americans, either as a government or through human rights and other organizations, to speak out to improve the systems and to defend individuals trying to change those systems when they are arrested or otherwise abused. And certainly not to invade. Washington should not lose any opportunity to be seen as a friend of the little guy, and not just the friend of the princes or whatever the rulers are called.

Finally, the U.S. government needs to be more vocal in condemning all forms of repression, and in particular the damaging role of the secret police in daily life. Compare the way Washington spoke out against tyranny in the old Soviet bloc with that in the Arab world, whose police agencies are all the stepchildren of the Communist agencies.

Washington needs to speak out about not just who is repressed but who is doing the repressing. Virtually all governments in the Middle East are propped up by vast intelligence agencies and, using the war against terrorism as cover, governments in countries like Morocco and Egypt and Jordan have deployed their security agencies to silence critics. There have been reports in recent years that Washington shipped suspects to those intelligence agencies to outsource torture, and thus an unfortunate link has been made between Washington and the most hated institutions in all these countries known universally by the Arabic term "mukhabarat." Washington rarely speaks out against this scourge, especially against our allies. The secret police always claim to provide security, but real stability and security should be rooted in stronger political systems.

I note that one key reason the U.S. has avoided pushing too hard for real reform in the region is out of fear that radical Islam will win at the polls, a dicey proposition. But in my experience the bulk of the Arabs do not want to change the despotic regimes they have now for despotic regimes based on religion. They just desperately want less corruption and better government services, and they think the religious parties are the only group strong enough to get it for them. It's a gamble, but it certainly appears to be a better proposition than what they live under now.

The kinds of policies listed above would require a certain change in American attitudes, of going back to a time when the U.S. was known for defending the little guy, when the guiding principle of American foreign policy was doing the right thing.

Perhaps the best, simplest summary of that ideal can be lifted from a speech that Robert F. Kennedy delivered in South Africa in 1966, at a time when the fight against the apartheid regime there was just beginning to garner international attention. "We must recognize the full human equality of all of our people—before God, before the law, and in the councils of government," Kennedy said. "We must do this, not because it is economically advantageous—although it is; not because the laws of God command it—although they do; not because people in other lands wish it so. We must do it for the single and fundamental reason that it is the right thing to do." If the country stuck to that as its unwavering guideline, it would never have to worry about fixing an image problem.

The United States seems to have lost sight of these noble ideals in its dealings with the Arab world, that we should be pushing for equality for everyone there because it is the right thing to do. Surely part of the reason we have given up is that everything that dominates our perceptions of the region seems so evil. The United States and its myriad nongovernmental organizations would do well to seek out more of the people of the type I met. They all wanted to replace the despotic regimes they suffer under with freer, more open governments, with a real civil society, but also one they develop on their own, at their own pace.

It's not easy, basing foreign policy on doing the right thing, on trying to walk in the shoes of the people on the ground there toiling to take the smallest steps in an effort that might transform the region at some distant point in the future. It is not sweeping or glamorous. It requires a certain subtlety and a certain cultural fluency in that the statements must try to echo the concerns of local activists, to support them without seeming to endorse them as individuals, and to avoid preaching. But it ensures that change can grow and prosper from within, that it will have roots.

They might also become our natural friends and allies. I don't want to leave the impression that I am some starry-eyed, giddy optimist trying to hum "We Are the World." In terms of basic American interests, making the United States a more empathetic figure on the world stage will serve to increase our own security. Coddling dictators and their secret police agencies has not gotten us far enough on that scale. I am not pretending that working through principles instead will make the process any easier, will automatically defeat extremists. But in the long run, I think doing the right thing will also mean doing well.

A young Saudi woman published a surprise best seller in late 2005, published it in Beirut of course because it was such a frank description of the quiet desperation of young women's lives that it was banned in the kingdom. The book is called *Girls of Riyadh*, and it is written as a long series of postings in an email chat room. At one point the narrator laments being vilified on the Internet for describing some of the many ways women are treated as second-class citizens, one miserable aspect of life in the Saudi kingdom. Toward the end of the book she muses about being an agent of change.

> Instead of revolting against me they would be better off revolting against terrifying ideas and sick traditions, instead of revolting against me who is just trying to write about them. Everybody is rebuking my bold writings and they are blaming me for talking about taboos that our society is not used to discussing, especially by a young girl like me. But maybe everything has a start. Who ever imagined that Martin Luther King could liberate the blacks in America from discrimination and start the protest movement from his simple church? . . . Who knows, maybe I am now facing troubles just like Martin Luther King faced, he was even arrested at the beginning of the struggle. He sacrificed himself and now he is one of the biggest heroes of the century after he was treated like a criminal.

If a talented young woman in Riyadh, all on her own, can look up to Martin Luther King Jr. as her hero, imagine the kind of change the U.S. government could foment if it used powerful, universal icons like his "I have a dream" message to speak out in support of agents of change everywhere. Americans should let other people know that they believe in other dreams, that they will support people trying to do the right thing.

It's almost a cliché that the U.S. has dominated the global economy because of its technology and its seemingly endless ability to foment innovation. That is true, and happily some of that technology provides important political tools. Just look at how inventions like Facebook are spawning political groups in Egypt, groups that succeed at overcoming government laws that ban organizing and the right of assembly. But technology is likely not an edge that can be maintained forever. Having spent so many years of my life in countries where people live under terrible repression, starting with Libya, I would argue that there is an even more powerful export that has been uniquely American for decades. It is an export that no other country has been able to duplicate, and cheap knock-offs just don't exist. That export is hope. Even in the midst of the most vociferous anti-American demonstrations, with blood-curdling cries of "Death to America!," it is inevitable that somebody would stop to ask me the best route to obtain a visa. That was the hope speaking. The United States cannot take them all, but it can nurture the hope that change is coming. Extremists thrive in its absence. Introduce hope, and those fires will start to fade, providing the opening needed for the kinds of men and women like those on these pages to step forward.

ACKNOWLEDGMENTS

TRYING TO GIVE DUE THANKS to the legions who have helped me to navigate the Middle East, starting from my first time there at age three, is impossible. Even if I endeavored to name just those aiding my recent ventures, I am bound to overlook many. So let me start by expressing my undying appreciation for the countless people—from close friends to absolute strangers—who have been so patient with my questions, so willing to meet my incessant requests, and so generous with their boundless hospitality. I would especially include all those who undertake the important and often risky work of tracking human rights violations and similar ills across the region.

There is one small group of energetic reporters to whom I am enormously indebted—without them my task of covering some twenty-two countries from Iran to Morocco for the New York Times would have been practically impossible. Abeer Allam, my main associate throughout much of my tenure as Cairo bureau chief, is foremost among them. Through her intelligence, humor, and hard work, she widened my understanding of the region immeasurably. The others are Mona el-Naggar in Egypt, Nazila Fathi in Iran, Leena Saidi in Lebanon, George Baghdadi in Syria, Suha Ma'ayeh in Jordan, Khaled al-Hammadi in Yemen, and Souad Mekhennet in

Morocco. This group includes Mohamed "el-Liwa" el-Dakhakhny, my Alexandrian photographer.

A few others kept life on an even keel while I concentrated on the news. Cairo can be a charming city, but like any Third World megalopolis it is prone to ordinary disasters. Electric circuit boxes erupt in flames. Toilets implode. Computers die and phone lines commit suicide. But Gamal Moheieldin, the legendary office manager for the *Times* in Cairo for fifty-three years until he retired in 2006, always managed to restore order, twenty-four hours a day, seven days a week. Hussein Alameh in Beirut and Hasan "Abu Karrar" Juad in Baghdad also extracted me repeatedly from technological or other meltdowns.

Outside my professional life, a few people in each country lifted my spirits regularly. Life can prove lonely in an endless round of hotel rooms, and these friends rescued me countless times no matter what time of day or night I would suddenly call—offering me dinner or a unique weekend in some enchanted place like Fayoum or Wadi Rum. This list includes Ateyyat el-Abnoudy, Aziz Abu Hamad, Mohamed Ajlouni, Aysar Akrawi, Faiza Ambah, Rula Amin, Ragui Assaad, Rula Atalla, Mohamed Atiyeh, Fatima al-Bacha, Hatoon al-Fassi, Zena Hamadi, Ibrahim Hamidi, Sulaiman al-Hattlan, Sarah Gauch, Fadi Ghandour, Mai Guindi, Hisham Kassem, Karima Khalil, Jamal Khashoggi, Goli Mahmoudi, Hassan Mroue, Khalil Nasrallah, Mary Nazzal-Batayneh, the late Nuha al-Radhi and her family, Max Rodenbeck, Rana Sabbagh, Zeinab Osseiran Saidi, Norbert Schiller and Majeed al-Shatti.

I am often asked what the *New York Times* orders me to write, and met with a certain skepticism when I respond "Almost nothing." One of the great blessings of working for such a unique institution is that its editors basically push you out the door saying "Go do great work." The entire enterprise is a collective effort and again, too many people helped along the way for me to name them individually. But I am particularly appreciative that Foreign Editor Susan Chira, in tandem with her deputy, Ethan Bronner, let me wander at will during my last year as Mideast correspondent. The entire Foreign Desk deserves endless gratitude for polishing the results.

The process of turning those wanderings into a book was helped enormously by the charmed folks at The MacDowell Colony, who provided the cottage where scattered thoughts were transformed into a book outline. Likewise, the little cabin on the Middle Fork of the Salmon River offered by Alex Kuczynski and Charles Stevenson along with their hospitable crew fueled a much-needed burst of intensive work.

Writers cannot progress very far without someone reading over their shoulder and I was very fortunate in my advisors, namely Donna Abu-Nasr, Peter Waldman, Nan Richardson, and, on policy matters, Professor Gregory Gause of the University of Vermont, an old Arabic school classmate. Others who provided important help and counsel include Mark Bailey, Ethan Canin, Frances Dinkelspiel, Jim Wilson, and the entire title party gang.

Of course no one influenced this book more than my editor Clive Priddle, whom I cannot thank enough for his uncanny ability and patience in separating the wheat from the chaff. I also appreciate the support from my agent, David Halpern, every step of the way.

But I owe the greatest debt to Kerry Kennedy, who reviewed each chapter as I finished it and spurred me on to the next. She supplied boundless encouragement, the (very) occasional bowl of pesto-glazed mussels, and basically all that was needed whenever my motivation wavered to keep me on the path to finish this endeavor. I am forever grateful that she found time for that amidst raising three lovely daughters and her otherwise hectic schedule. Every writer should be inspired by such a muse.

New York City
January 2009

Select Bibliography

Alireza, Marianne. *At the Drop of a Veil: The True Story of a California Girl's Years in an Arabian Harem*. Boston: Houghton Mifflin, 1971.

Alsanea, Rajaa. *Girls of Riyadh*. New York: Penguin, 2008.

Armstrong, Karen. *Islam: A Short History*. New York: Modern Library, 2000.

Asali, K. J, ed. *Jerusalem in History*. New York: Olive Branch Press, 1990.

Burgot, Francois. *Face to Face with Political Islam*. London: I. B. Taurus, 2003.

Burton, Richard F. *Personal Narrative of a Pilgrimage to Al-Madinah & Mecca*, vol. I and II. New York: Dover, 1964.

_____, trans. *The Book of the Thousand Nights and a Night*. New York: The Heritage Press, 1934.

Clapp, Nicholas. *Sheba: Through the Desert in Search of the Legendary Queen*. New York: Houghton Mifflin, 2001.

Danielson, Virginia. *The Voice of Egypt: Umm Kulthum, Arabic Song and Egyptian Society in the Twentieth Century*. Chicago: University of Chicago Press, 1998.

Gabrieli, Francesco. *Arab Historians of the Crusades*. Berkeley: University of California Press, 1984.

Al-Hamad, Turki. *Adama*. St. Paul: Ruminator Books, 2003.

_____. *Shumaisi*. London: Saqi Books, 2005.

Harris, Walter. *Morocco That Was.* London: Eland, 2002.

Hitti, Philip K. *History of the Arabs.* New York: Palgrave Macmillan, 2002.

Horwitz, Tony. *Baghdad Without a Map.* New York: Penguin, 1991.

Hourani, Albert. *A History of the Arab Peoples.* London: Faber and Faber, 1991.

Kepel, Gilles. *The War for Muslim Minds.* Cambridge: Harvard University Press, 2004.

El-Kikhia, Mansour O. *Libya's Qaddafi: The Politics of Contradiction.* Gainesville: University Press of Florida, 1997.

Lapidus, Ira M. *A History of Islamic Societies.* Cambridge: Cambridge University Press, 1989.

Lewis, Bernard. *The Assassins: A Radical Sect in Islam.* New York: Basic Books, 2003.

Maalouf, Amin. *The Crusades Through Arab Eyes.* London: Al-Saqi Books, 1984.

Macintosh-Smith, Tim. *Travels with a Tangerine.* New York: Random House, 2004.

———. *Yemen: Travels in Dictionary Land.* London: Picador, 1999.

Marzouki, Ahmed. *Tazmamart: Cellule 10.* Casablanca: Tarik, 2000.

Muasher, Marwan. *The Arab Center: The Promise of Moderation.* New Haven: Yale University Press, 2008.

Munif, Abdelrahman. *Cities of Salt.* New York: Random House, 1987.

———. *The Trench.* New York: Vintage, 1993.

Nakash, Yitzhak. *The Shi'is of Iraq.* Princeton: Princeton University Press, 1994.

Qadhafi, Muammar. *Commentary on The Green Book,* vol. I–III. Tripoli: World Center for Research and Studies of the Green Book, 1990.

Rodenbeck, Max. *Cairo: The City Victorious.* New York: Knopf, 1999.

Runciman, Steven. *A History of the Crusades.* London: Penguin, 1978.

Saad-Ghorayeb. *Hizbu'llah: Politics & Religion.* London: Pluto Press, 2002.

Al-Shaykh, Hannan. *Only in London*. London: Bloomsbury Publishing, 2002.

Theroux, Peter. *Sandstorms: Days and Nights in Arabia*. New York: W. W. Norton, 1990.

Thesiger, Wilfred. *Arabian Sands*. London: Penguin, 1980

_____. *The Marsh Arabs*. London: Penguin, 1980.

INDEX